The Essential Lippmann

The ESSENTIAL LIPPMANN

A Political Philosophy for Liberal Democracy

EDITED BY

CLINTON ROSSITER

&

JAMES LARE

Harvard University Press
Cambridge, Massachusetts
1982

Printed in the United States of America

This Harvard University Press paperback is published by arrangement with Random House, Inc.

Library of Congress Catalog Card Number: 81-85311

ISBN 0-674-26775-3

Acknowledgments

The selections in this volume have been drawn from the following sources:

1. BOOKS:
   - *A Preface to Politics* (New York and London: Mitchell Kennerley, 1913).
   - *Drift and Mastery* (New York: Henry Holt, 1914). Paperback edition by Spectrum Books, Prentice-Hall, Inc., 1961.
   - *The Stakes of Diplomacy* (New York: Henry Holt, 1915).
   - *Liberty and the News* (New York: The Macmillan Company, 1920).
   - *Public Opinion* (New York: The Macmillan Company, 1922). Paperback edition by Macmillan, 1960.
   - *The Phantom Public* (New York: Harcourt, Brace and Company, 1925).
   - *A Preface to Morals* (New York: The Macmillan Company, 1929). Paperback edition by Beacon Press, 1960.
   - *The Method of Freedom* (New York: The Macmillan Company, 1934).
   - *The New Imperative* (New York: The Macmillan Company, 1935).
   - *The Good Society* (Boston: Little, Brown and Company, 1937). Paperback edition by Grosset's Universal Library, Grosset and Dunlap, n. d.
   - *Essays in the Public Philosophy* (Boston: Little, Brown and Company, 1955). Paperback edition by Mentor Books, New American Library, 1956.

2. PAMPHLETS:
A Tribute to Theodore Roosevelt (1935)
Class Dinner Speech for the Thirtieth Reunion of the Harvard Class of 1910 (1940).

3. EDITORIALS:
The World (New York), 1921-1931.

4. COLUMNS:
Today and Tomorrow, *The New York Herald Tribune*, 1931-1962.

5. ARTICLES:
From *The American Magazine, The American Scholar, The Annals of the American Academy of Political and Social Science, The Atlantic Monthly, The Commonweal, Forum and Century, Harper's Magazine, The Harvard Monthly, Life, Look, Metropolitan, The New Republic, The Saturday Evening Post, Social Forces, Vanity Fair, Vital Speeches of the Day, Woman's Home Companion,* and *The Yale Review.*

The editors acknowledge gratefully the generous assistance of Robert O. Anthony, Adviser to the Walter Lippmann Collection in the Yale University Library, who has labored faithfully for more than three decades to gather materials by and about Lippmann; Howard B. Gotlieb, Archivist of Yale University, who put the Lippmann Collection at our disposal; and Walter Lippmann himself, who blessed this project without in the least attempting to direct it.

Contents

Introduction, 1963

This treasury of the writings of Walter Lippmann is a witness to our conviction that he is perhaps the most important American political thinker of the twentieth century. The strength of this conviction can be measured in our title, which recommended itself to us on three counts.

In the first place, we look upon Lippmann as one of the few truly "essential" men of private station in the past fifty years. In our opinion, he deserves to be ranked with such as John Dewey, Thorstein Veblen, Frank Lloyd Wright, Charles A. Beard, H. L. Mencken, Eugene O'Neill, Robert Frost, Lewis Mumford, Roscoe Pound, and Reinhold Niebuhr as a major contributor to the American way of life and thought. The dialogue among men who are informed, large-minded, and reasonable is the life-blood of democracy, and in most of the great political and moral dialogues of modern America, Walter Lippmann has been a leading participant. In his own style, at his own pace, and largely on his own terms, he has spoken out on the issues of the age—and spoken with an authority that persuades presidents, premiers, foreign ministers, and perhaps even cardinals and commissars to pause and listen. Holding no public office, adhering to no party, representing no organized interest, claiming no disciples, and thus exercising no strictly political power, he has nevertheless been a person of immense influence in clarifying the values and shaping the policies of two generations of Americans. In all this he has been, as Niebuhr has written, "one of the great educators preparing a young and powerful nation to assume responsibilities commensurate with its power and to exercise them without too much self-righteousness."

Second, one aspect of the writings of this essential man is really more "essential" than any other, and we have therefore chosen to concentrate upon it in this volume. This is not a treasury of the whole Lippmann. Those who look through it for his most celebrated performances as journalist, prophet, diplomatic historian, and leader of dialogues are certain to be disappointed. It is, rather, a presentation of Lippmann the political thinker, the man who speaks in general terms about ethical and social problems that have been with us in the West from the beginning and will be with us to the end, and thus who speaks not only to the living but also to generations unborn.

We do not mean to divide this indivisible man into two or more only distantly related selves. To the contrary, having moved with careful steps through millions of his words, we are more alert than most persons in his vast audience to the close and necessary connection between, say, the Lippmann who sat in moral judgment on the moral judgments of John Foster Dulles and the Lippmann who has tried to interpret the dictates of the universal moral order. We agree with him when he says that he has "lived two lives"—a life of philosophy that provides the "context" of his day-to-day observations on men and events, a life of journalism that provides the "laboratory" in which to "test the philosophy and keep it from becoming too abstract"—yet we go further to insist that the philosopher never sleeps, even at the end of a long day of give-and-take with Khrushchev, and that he is the most "essential" of all possible Lippmanns. More than incidentally, if we read Walter Lippmann correctly, he will be content to be remembered in years to come as having been first of all a political thinker.

Finally, we have called this volume *The Essential Lippmann* because it contains the essence of his contributions to American political thought. We have labored hard to separate the wheat of contemplation from the chaff of interpretation in the great harvest of his writings, and we have sifted and resifted the wheat in an effort to present only the purest samples of his political principles. We hope that the gist of his message to posterity can be found in the pages of this book.

Although we have profited intellectually in the course of our labors, and thus stand in no need of consolation, we are bound to report that the problem of compressing the philosophical Lippmann into one volume of over two hundred thousand words was not easily solved. While this may seem like a lot of words, it is only a fraction of the total yield of a man who, by our rough count, has offered more than ten million words of opinion and advice to the American public. For the enlightenment of those who think of Lippmann primarily as the producer of a thirty-year wonder called *Today and Tomorrow*, we would note that, while it is indeed a wonder, it represents something less than one-half of his work. His four thousand columns add up to perhaps four million words; his ten books of political philosophy, dozen books of comment on men and events, scores of contributions to *The New Republic*, two thousand or more editorials in *The World*, and nearly three hundred articles in nearly fifty magazines add up to even more words than that. This vast output of a half-century is a monument to his creative genius; it is also testimony to the easily forgotten truth that his audience has been the largest and most insatiable ever to pay the homage of thoughtful attention to a serious-minded American writer.

It is remarkable how many of all these words are still worth reading in the Baconian sense, how many invite us to chew, swallow, and digest them with care and imagination. Although there is much that is dated (and that was intended to be dated) in his writings, much also has a timeless quality. This book appears on the fiftieth anniversary of the publication of *A Preface to Politics*, and whole passages of that book are as fresh and meaningful in the third year of John F. Kennedy as they were in the first year of Woodrow Wilson. Lippmann the political thinker has returned again and again to his major themes, yet he almost always restates them in the form of subtle variations. Our chief problem as editors has been, therefore, to do in one volume what we would like to have done in five—and could have done, thanks to the self-replenishing creativity of our author, in ten or twelve. If we have done nothing else, we hope that we have encouraged others to go digging in the rich lodes of his work. *Lippmann on Diplomacy*, *Lippmann on Journalism*, and *Lippmann in Praise and Scorn of Famous Men* are three titles that would promise good reading to large audiences. We are distressed by the thought that we could give only a few pages to each of these enduring interests of Walter Lippmann, comforted by the hope that this may be only the first of several treasuries of his wisdom.

It might be useful to set down the rules we followed in choosing the materials for this book and in threading them together.

The first was to remember that every page of the editors would mean one less page of Lippmann. We have therefore kept this introduction as short as possible, stifled our eager impulse to sprinkle explanatory and transitional remarks through the text, and relied on titles and subtitles to give the correct emphasis to each category of Lippmann's thought. We trust that no one will begrudge us the pages allotted to the index of men and ideas.

The second was to draw upon the writings of Lippmann wherever they have appeared. All other things being equal—that is to say, there being nothing to choose between two or more pieces on the same subject—we preferred columns and articles to passages from books, passages from books out of print to passages from books in print. Some of Lippmann's best work as political thinker has been buried too long in the files of the *New York Herald Tribune*, and we are especially pleased to have exhumed such notable pieces as "The American Idea," "Reflections on Gandhi," and "The Coronation of a Queen." We are no less pleased to have made it possible for Lippmann the annoyed undergraduate, the admirer of Theodore Roosevelt, and the orator of the Thirtieth Reunion of the Harvard Class of 1910 to be heard by tens of thousands instead of a few hundred Americans. At the same time, we have not been deterred from drawing, as the need arose, upon the five of his books that have been reissued in paperback editions. *The Essential Lippmann* would have lost something of its essence if we had not made room for the musings on the political tasks of liberalism in *The Good Society*, on the limits of popular understanding in *Public Opinion*, and on the tradition of civility in *The Public Philosophy*.

The third rule was to draw upon his writings whenever they have appeared. Again, all things being equal, we preferred the column of 1962 to the column of 1932, the book of 1955 to the book of 1914, for Lippmann is almost unique among American writers in the way he has grown in wisdom, eloquence, and even freshness of outlook with the passing of the years. Since we are primarily concerned with his political thought, we have been a good deal less impressed than some of his critics by the ease with which he is said to have changed his mind from one decade or one Administration or even one year to the next. Whatever bouts of self-contradiction he may have indulged in as a leader of public dialogues—and surely a man who has been at it for fifty years is entitled to change his mind at least as often as that other fifty-year veteran, Thomas Jefferson—he has displayed a remarkable consistency of principle and purpose as political philosopher. A liberal democrat of critical bent and temperate counsel in the days of Wilson and Harding, he is still a liberal democrat of critical bent and temperate counsel in the days of Eisenhower and Kennedy. A role for the state that goes well beyond indulgent policing and falls well short of officious planning, a Constitutional balance that produces alert and prudent Executive leadership, a Constitutional process that sobers yet rarely frustrates the decisions of the majority, a pattern of education and communication that gives priority to the voices of reason, a pattern of values that displays both unity and diversity—these are only a few of the major convictions to which he has remained faithful in all his philosophical writings. While Lippmann has been disappointed from time to time in his search for reliable normative answers to the staggering questions of giant democracy, he has never abandoned the search nor even been turned aside from it. His answers to these questions have been more numerous, far-ranging, and internally consistent than those of any other American political thinker.

Our last rule, which gave us more than one painful moment, was to let the order of this book develop naturally out of Lippmann's writings rather than to impose an order of our own. There is a compelling logic in the eleven chapters into which these selections have been grouped, and the logic is the author's rather than the editors'. Nor have we tried to squeeze some kind of answer out of Lippmann to every question with which political philosophers are supposed to deal. Like Locke, Hobbes, Machiavelli, Rousseau, and Mill, like Jefferson, Madison, Hamilton, Adams, and Calhoun, he has centered his attention upon the ethical and political implications of the great issues of his own age. One must therefore let him speak, as one lets even Plato speak, about the many things that have seemed most important to him, and let him be silent, as one lets even Marx be silent, about some things to which he probably should have paid more heed. In any case, Lippmann's best thoughts on such subjects as the role of religion or the uses of federalism are to be found in passages devoted primarily to some of his other and larger concerns as political philosopher.

We ought to explain why we have come, in the course of our labors, to the judgment that Walter Lippmann is perhaps the most important American political thinker of the twentieth century, and that he may be honored for his achievement by the men of centuries to come.

The stature of a political thinker, like the stature of a political doer, arises from the interaction of challenge and response. If he is to be judged important, the challenge to his creative powers must have been important, which means that a good part of his destiny as tutor to posterity lies beyond his control. Like Rousseau he can foresee the existence of such a challenge while it is still impending, or like Hobbes, clarify its meaning for the fuzzy-minded men of his own generation, but he cannot, even if he is a Marx, create it out of whole cloth. Yet, while the man must wait upon the event to give him an opportunity to be a memorable political thinker, his response to the challenge of the event will in the end determine his stature. Scores of wise old heads agreed with Hobbes that the real problem of the middle years of the seventeenth century in England was the securing of peace and order, yet he alone was capable of making a response that still persuades us to think hard about the nature and needs of men as social animals and the extent to which they must submit to the dictates of authority.

The challenge to American political thought in this century has been one of the most demanding ever made. It is a challenge, quite simply, to the logic of what Lippmann likes to call "liberal democracy." The question has been put, by events as well as by men, whether liberal democracy—the open society that functions through Constitutional processes—is or can ever again be a viable way of life. Once upon a time, when we lived under the spell of Thomas Jefferson, John Locke, John Stuart Mill, and Adam Smith (and lived more happily and hopefully than all but a few fortunate men have ever lived), liberal democracy owned the future outright. It was working in America, it was moving from strength to strength in Western Europe, and sooner or later, in history's good time, it would become the standard pattern of politics and society all over the world. Although the critics of democracy were legion, most of them could be identified as men who had never been democrats in the first place. Among democrats themselves there were precious few doubts about the excellence and indestructibility of democracy.

In the past fifty years all that has changed, and liberal democracy has lost most of the patina of legitimacy which coats the ideas and institutions of a way of life favored by the fortunes of history. The democracies of the West are menaced from without by the armed dogmatism of the totalitarian states and the willful impatience of the newly emerging nations. They are weakened from within by the rise and "revolt" of the masses, by the unforeseen or simply undigested advances of science and technology, by the dislocations of industrialism, and by the creation of a social situation in which the dependence of men upon one another and thus their capacity to do damage to one another have increased enormously. The most shattering blow of all to the morale of men of good will and keen perception is the recognition that some of the rosiest promises of the great prophets of liberal democracy now appear to have been idle boasts. Not only is the world quite unsafe for democracy; in every country of the world in which democracy continues to govern life and politics, it seems a good deal less confident, clear-headed, fruitful, and respectful of liberty than our fathers had assumed that it would be or become.

The political thinkers of the West, especially those of the United States, have responded to this challenge in several ways. Some have found it so incomprehensible that they pretend it does not exist and simply go on quoting Jefferson and Mill; others have found it so shattering that they have surrendered to despair and now predict the end of democracy; still others have found it so unmanageable that they refuse even to talk about values and have beaten a retreat from the broad field of political philosophy to some narrow defile of political "science." A few of our best minds, however, have not been content with platitudes or jeremiads or statistics. They have looked the crisis of liberal democracy full in the face, and are perhaps as stunned by it as Ortega or Michels or Mosca; yet, refusing to despair, they have set themselves the fateful task of refurbishing the best values of the American political tradition, suggesting other values to fill the yawning gaps in the tradition, and in general toughening our dominant Jeffersonian faith for the prodigious tasks that lie ahead. Like Winston Churchill they can say half-seriously that democracy is "the worst form of government except all others that have ever been tried," yet also like him they have a commitment to democracy that leaves them no choice but to serve it as faithfully and imaginatively as they can. If one had to pin a label on this entirely unofficial and formless group, which includes such men of intellect and purpose as Crane Brinton, Eric Fromm, Harold Lasswell, David Riesman, Peter Drucker, Hans Morgenthau, Daniel Boorstin, Herbert Agar, and Reinhold Niebuhr, one might call them "the critical, cautionary, and yet committed democrats." They tread a fine line between hope and despair for all men, and especially for those who want to be democrats, yet they can take heart from the thought that Madison, Adams, Hamilton, and Lincoln also trod this line—and with benevolent consequences for their posterity.

The commanding figure in this group is Walter Lippmann. Only Niebuhr is a match for him in the keenness of his perception of the discontents of liberal democracy in the modern world; no one is a match for him in the prudence of his prescriptions for curing them—or, as he might put it, for learning to live with them. From first to last, from his strictures on popular prejudices in *A Preface to Politics* to his most recent observations on the limits of private initiative, he has been a stern, penetrating, candid critic of the congenital weaknesses of the open society and its popular institutions. If he had written nothing in his life except *Public Opinion,* he would be quoted and studied for generations to come as the first American political thinker to draw out the political implications of instant, incessant, and mass-consumed communications. Yet the insights of this remarkable book make up only the first of a sizable number of points in his bill of indictment of the abuses of liberal democracy, and our descendants who devote thought to the age-old yet always fresh agenda of political theory will also quote and study *A Preface to Morals, The Method of Freedom, The Good Society, The Public Philosophy,* and scores of his columns and articles. Although new particulars may be added as the years pass and our genius for mocking the hopes of Jefferson continues to have free play, the hard core of the case of the liberal democrat against liberal democracy has now been stated once and for all. This, of course, is why Lippmann is presently an important political thinker and potentially a memorable one: he has probed the diseases of modern democracy not as an announced or secret enemy, and thus not with the relish of the Marxist, the Fascist, the Bitter-Ender, or the New Machiavellian, but as an open and unwavering friend, and thus with a proper blend of sorrow and hope. We in the West have heard more than we want or need to hear about our follies and derangements and impossible aspirations from those who hate us and wish us only ill; we have only begun to listen attentively to the criticisms and injunctions of those who, like Lippmann, wish us only well.

Yet even the severe honesty of Lippmann's probe of the discontents of liberal democracy does not account for his real and potential stature as political thinker. It is not so much the fact that he has revealed many weaknesses in our way of life that makes him essential to us in America and may make him famous to our descendants, but that he has also rehearsed its strengths, restated its promises, and, above all, sought relentlessly to find philosophical and even institutional remedies for the most enfeebling weaknesses. His attempts to delimit the role of public opinion in a constitutional democracy or to revive the concept of a higher law in an age of positivism or to celebrate leadership in an age of populism are already beginning to win him the kind of respectful attention in anthologies of American political thought that has hitherto been reserved for such memorable performances as Madison's analysis of the group basis of politics or Calhoun's elaboration of the doctrine of the concurrent majority.

If Lippmann had been content as political thinker merely to criticize, he would himself have been criticized a good deal less. It is not his diagnosis of our ills that has laid him open to charges of inconsistency, inadequacy, imprudence, and romanticism, but his prognosis for alleviating them. It is not the statement of the problem of runaway pluralism and positivism in his early books that has earned him his scars, such as they are, but the search for a solution to this problem in all his books, which has ended, to the dismay of many of his strongest admirers, in the revival of the ancient doctrine of the higher law—this time in the guise of "the Western traditions of civility" or "the public philosophy."

We do not, incidentally, feel this dismay quite as keenly as do, for example, Arthur Schlesinger, Jr., Morton White, and Archibald MacLeish, all of whom have had occasion to doubt the logic and viability of Lippmann's version of the higher law. Although as students of Hume and Bentham we are aware of the vulnerability of what might now be described as the neo-Lockeian position, we are more impressed by the tenacity of Lippmann's search for the enduring ideals of Western civilization than by his failure—in which, after all, he is associated with the likes of

Locke and Jefferson—to demonstrate their existence to men determined not to believe in their existence in the first place. Lippmann may be wrong in pressing "the public philosophy" upon the more dogmatic positivists and pragmatists, but he is right in insisting that the last redoubt of democracy is the belief in "principles of right behavior in the good society" upon which all men who are "sincerely and lucidly rational" can agree. If he has not persuaded all such men in our society of the sources, content, and sanctions of these principles, he has at least forced them to consider the practical consequences of the abandonment of this belief.

Whatever else it may have done to and for his reputation as political thinker, the debate over "the public philosophy" has reminded all those who have read him carefully that he is defender as well as critic of liberal democracy. We hope that the selections in this book will prove this point to even the most hostile of his detractors. Walter Lippmann has been for more than fifty years a liberal democrat in whom hope has never yet surrendered to doubt or fear. He has wrestled more intelligently than any political thinker of his time with both the old tensions of liberal democracy—liberty and authority, populism and constitutionalism, the rule of the majority and the rights of the minority—and the new—individualism and collectivism, the private sector and the public sector, "drift" and "mastery"—and he has not wrestled any less tenaciously because he knows that the victory will be a narrow one and will offer sour fruits along with the sweet. It is, indeed, the unresolved tension in his own mind between tough-minded liberalism and warm-hearted conservatism that makes him one of the most appealing of modern American thinkers.

No final judgment can be made about Lippmann's full stature as a political thinker in the years to come, for much depends upon the fate of liberal democracy. If it should fall at last before the assaults of license, fear, and ignorance, his words of warning will be found "inscribed on its ruins." If it should repel these assaults and prove itself equal to the political tasks of the America to come, at least some of his words of advice will have become reality. In the one instance he will be studied grudgingly as the most interesting of the old breed, in the other studied admiringly as the most insightful of the new. In either instance, he has a future that other political thinkers may well envy.

We trust that no one who reads and ponders the selections

that follow can have any doubt which fate Walter Lippmann would choose for liberal democracy. This book, which is his and not ours, is a declaration of faith and hope in the future of freedom.

James Lare
Clinton Rossiter

I

The Dilemma of Liberal Democracy

1 · *Should the Majority Rule?*

"The American Idea," Today and Tomorrow, *February 22, 1954, a shortened version of an address delivered at the unveiling of the statue of George Washington in the Washington Cathedral on February 3, 1947.*

In the oration which Henry Lee delivered in the House of Representatives a few days after Washington's death, he spoke the words that have become so celebrated. Washington, he said, was "everywhere present . . . himself a host, he assuaged our sufferings, limited our privations, and upheld our tottering Republic. . . . First in war, first in peace, first in the hearts of his countrymen, he was second to none in the humble and endearing scenes of private life." Yet in the veneration which has always been given to Washington, must we not add that he has in these later days become separated somehow from the inner life of his countrymen?

The cause of it is not in the legend of his immaculate perfection. Nor is it in any want of flesh and blood in the man himself. The cause is much deeper and it cannot be removed by proving that he was less perfect than his legend, or by popularizing anecdotes of his life and aspects of his character which provide what is called human interest.

The truth of the matter, I believe, is that we are separated not from the man but from his ideas. There is an opposition between what he believed to be the conditions and the first principles of free government and what has come increasingly to be the working belief of the great masses of the people who, in their impact on public affairs, invoke the ideals of democracy.

This opposition appeared while Washington was still alive, and it has been accentuated during the past hundred and fifty years. In our time it has reached its climax and its crisis. If then we wish to understand Washington, and to appreciate the universal importance of his example, what is it that we must do? We must, I believe, refuse to identify the cause of freedom, justice and good government with the rule of the majority.

There lies the root of the matter. Washington believed that the people should rule. But he did not believe that *because* the people ruled, there would be freedom, justice, and good government. He did not believe that the sovereign people, any more than the royal sovereigns whom they succeeded, could be trusted with absolute power.

He did not deceive himself. As a young man, he had served the royal governor, Dinwiddie. Later on, as Commander-in-Chief, he had served the Continental Congress. He had no illusion that the mere transfer of power from a king to the people would insure free, just, and good government.

He knew, on the contrary, that the new popular sovereign, like its royal predecessors, was subject, as he once said to Edmund Randolph, to "the various passions" which are "the concomitants of fallibility." He did not believe in what has become the prevailing ideology of democracy—that whatever the mass of the people happen to think they want must be accepted as the right. "I am sure," he once wrote to John Jay, "that the mass of citizens in these United States *mean well,* and I firmly believe that they will always *act well,* whenever they can obtain a right understanding of matters: but . . . it is not easy to accomplish this, especially as is the case invariably when the inventors and abettors of pernicious measures are infinitely more industrious in disseminating their poison than the well-disposed part of the community to furnish the antidote."

Thus Washington did not look upon the rise of popular government as the triumphant culmination of the struggle for freedom and justice. He knew that there was no guarantee that the rule of the people would not in its turn be despotic, arbitrary, corrupt, unjust, and unwise. The people, too, had to be restrained. They, too, had to be held to account. They, too, had to be taught. They, too, had to be raised above their habitual conduct. Because their power, when passionately aroused, was overwhelming, it could be fearfully abused.

Though he was an ardent supporter of the new Constitution, he did not believe that any mechanical device, such as the system of checks and balances, would in itself insure freedom and good government. Least of all did he believe that bad government could be cured by weak government. He had learned from his own hard experience that popular government tends to be weak, and that local and private interests may so divide its authority and may so paralyze its decisions that the time may come when there seems to be no remedy for anarchy except the surrender of freedom to a despot. He knew that in the last analysis there was nothing which could save a nation from this choice between anarchy and tyranny except the restraint imposed by the virtue of its citizens and the wisdom of those leaders whom they are sufficiently enlightened to follow.

This conception of popular government has become obscured by another, which, though it uses many of the same terms and proposes the same ideal ends, is its profound opposite. There the will of a majority of the people is held to be sovereign and supreme. That majority is bound by no laws because it makes the laws. It is itself the final judge, from whom there is no appeal, of what is right and what is wrong. This doctrine has led logically and in practice to the totalitarian state—to that modern form of despotism which does not rest upon hereditary titles or military conquest but springs directly from the mass of the people. For if all power is in the people, if there is no higher law than their will, and if by counting their votes, their will may be ascertained—then the people may entrust all their power to anyone, and the power of the pretender and the usurper is then legitimate. It is not to be challenged since it came originally from the sovereign people.

This is the supreme political heresy of our time. It masquerades as democracy. Though it is widely current among us, here at home at least it is not uncontested. But elsewhere, in many countries, it has led to a fantastic and tragic paradox. We have seen a majority of the people vote away their own right to continue to live by majority rule; we have seen the declared enemies of human freedom allowed to exploit free institutions until they had captured the power to destroy them. We have seen the right of a nation to be independent interpreted to mean that it was independent of all the laws of God and of man.

We, who have seen these things happen, are perhaps prepared, as we could not have been before, to appreciate the significance of the original American idea: that the sovereignty of the people is never absolute, that the people are under the law, and that the people may make no law which does not conform to that higher law which has been gradually revealed to the awakening conscience of mankind. In this, the American doctrine, the will of the people does not, then, determine its own standard of what is right and what is wrong. It is itself accountable to standards superior to its own opinions and its own will. Here the moral order does not stem from the will of the people. The people, like all other rulers, are within the moral order, and they are subject to it.

This American doctrine is also the ancient and central doctrine of civilized mankind. Washington himself lived by and worked in that tradition, and by his achievements and his example he did more than any other to establish it in this new land. We are greatly blessed that such a man was the Father of this country.

"Why Should the Majority Rule?" Harpers Magazine *CLII* (*1926*), *399. The trial of John Scopes for teaching the principle of evolution in violation of a Tennessee law evoked this important statement on the doctrine of majority rule. William Jennings Bryan, in the last act of his long career, served as counsel for the State of Tennessee.*

Mr. Bryan was as true to his political as he was to his religious faith. He had always believed in the sanctity of the text of the Bible. He had always believed that a majority of the people should rule. Here in Tennessee was a majority which believed in the sanctity of the text. To lead this majority was the logical climax of his career, and he died fighting for a cause in which the two great dogmas of his life were both at stake.

Given his two premises, I do not see how it is possible to escape his conclusions. If every word of the first chapter of Genesis is directly inspired by an omniscient and omnipotent God, then there is no honest way of accepting what scientists teach about the origin of man. And if the doctrine of majority rule is based on the eternal and inherent rights of man, then it is the only true basis of government, and there can be no fair objections to the moral basis of a law made by a fundamentalist majority in Tennessee. It is no answer to Mr. Bryan to say that the law is absurd, obscurantist, and reactionary. It follows from his premises, and it can be attacked radically only by attacking his premises.

This first premise: that the text of the Bible was written, as John Donne put it, by the Secretaries of the Holy Ghost, I shall not attempt to discuss here. There exists a vast literature of criticism. I am interested in his second premise: that the majority is of right sovereign in all things. And here the position is quite different. There is a literature of dissent and of satire and denunciation. But there exists no carefully worked-out higher criticism of a dogma which, in theory at least, constitutes the fundamental principle of nearly every government in the Western world. On the contrary, the main effort of political thinkers during the last few generations has been devoted to vindicating the rights of masses of men against the vested rights of clerics and kings and nobles and men of property. There has been a running counterattack from those who distrusted the people, or had some interest in opposing their enfranchisement, but I do not know of any serious attempt to reach a clear understanding of where and when the majority principle applies.

Mr. Bryan applied it absolutely at Dayton, and thereby did a service to democratic thinking. For he reduced to absurdity a dogma which had been held carelessly but almost universally, and thus demonstrated that it was time to reconsider the premises of the democratic faith. Those who believed in democracy have always assumed that the majority should rule. They have assumed that, even if the majority is not wise, it is on the road to wisdom, and that with sufficient education the people would learn how to rule. But in Tennessee the people used their power to prevent their own children from learning, not merely the doctrine of evolution, but the spirit and method by which learning is possible. They had used their right to rule in order to weaken the agency which they had set up in order that they might learn how to rule. They had founded popular government on the faith in popular education, and then they had used the prerogatives of democracy to destroy the hopes of democracy.

After this demonstration in Tennessee it was no longer possible to doubt that the dogma of majority rule contains within it some sort of deep and destructive confusion.

In exploring this dogma it will be best to begin at the very beginning with the primitive intuition from which the whole democratic view of life is derived. It is a feeling of ultimate equality and fellowship with all other creatures.

There is no worldly sense in this feeling, for it is reasoned from the heart: "There you are, sir, and there is your neighbor. You are better born than he, you are richer, you are stronger, you are handsomer, nay, you are better, wiser, kinder, more likable; you have given more to your fellowman and taken less than he. By any and every test of intelligence, of virtue, of usefulness, you are demonstrably a better man than he, and yet—absurd as it sounds—these differences do not matter, for the last part of him is untouchable and incomparable and unique and universal." Either you feel this or you do not; when you do not feel it, the superiorities that the world acknowledges seem like mountainous waves at sea; when you do feel it, they are slight and impermanent ripples upon a vast ocean. Men were possessed by this feeling long before they had imagined the possibility of democratic government. They spoke of it in many ways, but the essential quality of feeling is the same from Buddha to St. Francis to Whitman.

There is no way of proving the doctrine that all souls are precious in the eyes of God, or, as Dean Inge recently put it, that "the personality of every man and woman is sacred and inviolable." The doctrine proceeds from a mystical intuition. There is felt to be a spiritual reality behind and independent of the visible character and behavior of a man. We have no scientific evidence that this reality exists, and in the nature of things we can have none. But we know each of us, in a way too certain for doubting, that after all the weighing and comparing and judging of us is done, there is something left over which is the heart of the matter. Hence our conviction when we ourselves are judged that mercy is more just than justice. When we know the facts as we can know only the facts about ourselves, there is something too coarse in all the concepts of the intelligence and something too rough in all the standards of morality. The judgments of men fall upon behavior. They may be necessary judgments, but we do not believe they are final. There is something else, which is inadmissible, perhaps, as evidence in this world, which would weigh mightily before divine justice.

Each of us knows that of himself, and some attribute the same reserved value to others. Some natures with a genius for sympathy extend it to everyone they know and can imagine; others can barely project it to their wives and children. But even though few really have this sympathy with all men, there is enough of it abroad, reinforced perhaps with each man's dread of his fate in the unknown, to establish the doctrine rather generally. So we execute the murderer, but out of respect for an inviolable part of him we allow him the consolation of a priest and we bury him respectfully when he is dead. For we believe that, however terrible was his conduct, there is in him, nevertheless, though no human mind can detect it, a final quality which makes him part of our own destiny in the universe.

I can think of no inherent reason why men should entertain this mystical respect for other men. But it is easy to show how much that we find best in the world would be lost if the sense of equality and fellowship were lost. If we judged and were judged by our visible behavior alone, the inner defenses of civility and friendship and enduring love would be reached. Outward conduct is not good enough to endure a cold and steady analysis. Only an animal affection become habitual and reflected in mystical respect can blind people sufficiently to our faults. They would not like us enough to pardon us if all they had to go on was a strict behaviorist account of our conduct. They must reach deeper, blindly and confidently, to something which they know is likable although they do not know why. Otherwise the inequalities of men would be intolerable. The strong, the clever, the beautiful, the competent, and the good would make life miserable for their neighbors. They would be unbearable with their superiorities, and they would find unbearable the sense of inferiority they implanted in others. There would be no term upon the arrogance of the successful and the envy of the defeated. For without the mystic sense of equality the obvious inequalities would seem unalterable.

These temporal differences are seen in perspective by the doctrine that in the light of eternity there are no differences at all.

It is not possible for most of us, however, to consider anything very clearly or steadily in the light of eternity. The doctrine of ultimate human equality cannot be tested in human experience; it rests on a faith which transcends experience. That is why those who understood the doctrine have always been ascetic; they ignored or renounced worldly goods and worldly standards. These things belonged to Caesar. The mystical democrat did not say that they should not belong to Caesar; he said that they would be of no use to Caesar ultimately, and that, therefore, they were not to be taken seriously now.

But in the reception of this subtle argument the essential reservation was soon obscured. The mystics were preaching equality only to those men who had renounced their carnal appetites; they were welcomed as preachers of equality in this world. Thus the doctrine that I am as good as you in eternity because all the standards of goodness are finite and temporary, was converted into the doctrine that I am as good as you are in this world by this world's standards. The mystics had attained a sense of equality by transcending and renouncing all the standards by which we measure inequality. The populace retained its appetites and its standards and then sought to deny the inequalities which they produced and revealed.

The mystical democrat had said, "Gold and precious stones are of no account"; the literal democrat understood him to say that everybody ought to have gold and precious stones. The mystical democrat had said, "Beauty is only skin deep"; and the literal democrat preened himself and said, "I always suspected I was as handsome as you." Reason, intelligence, learning, wisdom dealt, for the mystic, only with passing events in a temporal world and could help men little to fathom the ultimate meaning of creation; to the literal democrat this incapacity of reason was evidence that one man's notion was intrinsically as good as another's.

Thus the primitive intuition of democracy became the animus of a philosophy which denied that there could be an order of values among men. Any opinion, any taste, any action was intrinsically as good as any other. Each stands on its own bottom and guarantees itself. If I feel strongly about it, it is right; there is no other test. It is right not only as against your opinion, but against my own opinions, about which I no longer feel so strongly. There is no arbitrament by which the relative value of opinions is determined. They are all free, they are all equal, all have the same rights and powers.

Since no value can be placed upon an opinion, there is no way in this philosophy of deciding between opinions except to count them. Thus the mystical sense of equality was translated to mean in practice that two minds are better than one mind and two souls better than one soul. Your true mystic would be horrified at the notion that you can add up souls and that the greater number is superior to the lesser. To him souls are imponderable and incommensurable; that is the only sense in which they are truly equal. And yet in the name of that sense of equality which he attains by denying that the worth of a soul can be measured, the worldly democrats have made the mere counting of souls the final arbiter of all worth. It is a curious misunderstanding; Mr. Bryan brought it into high relief during the Tennessee case. The spiritual doctrine that all men will stand at last equal before the throne of God meant to him that all men are equally good biologists before the ballot box of Tennessee. That kind of democracy is quite evidently a gross materialization of an idea that in essence cannot be materialized. It is a confusing interchange of two worlds that are not interchangeable.

Although the principle of majority rule derives a certain sanctity from the mystical sense of equality, it is really quite unrelated to it. There is nothing in the teachings of Jesus or St. Francis which justifies us in thinking that the opinions of fifty-one per cent of a group are better than the opinions of forty-nine per cent. The mystical doctrine of equality ignores the standards of the world and recognizes each soul as unique; the principle of majority rule is a device for establishing standards of action in this world by the crude and obvious device of adding up voters. Yet owing to a confusion between the two, the mystical doctrine has been brutalized and made absurd, and the principle of majority rule has acquired an unction that protects it from criticism. A mere political expedient, worth using only when it is necessary or demonstrably useful to the conduct of affairs, has been hallowed by an altogether adventitious sanctity due to an association of ideas with a religious hope of salvation.

Once we succeed in disentangling this confusion of ideas, it becomes apparent that the principle of majority rule is wholly alien to what the humane mystic feels. The rule of the majority is the rule of force. For while nobody can seriously maintain that the greatest number must have the greatest wisdom or the greatest virtue, there is no denying that under modern social conditions they are likely to have the most power. I say likely to have, for we are reminded by the recent history of Russia and of Italy that organized and armed minorities can under certain circumstances disfranchise the majority. Nevertheless, it is a good working premise that in the long run the greater force resides in the greater number, and what we call a democratic society might be defined for certain purposes as one in which the majority is always prepared to put down a revolutionary minority.

The apologists of democracy have done their best to dissemble the true nature of majority rule. They have argued that by some mysterious process the opinion to which a majority subscribes is true and righteous. They have even attempted to endow the sovereign majority with the inspiration of an infallible church and of kings by the grace of God. It was a natural mistake. Although they saw clearly enough that the utterances of the church were the decisions of the ruling clergy, and that the divine guidance of the king was exercised by his courtiers, they were not prepared to admit that the new sovereign was a purely temporal ruler. They felt certain they must ascribe to the majority of the voters the same supernatural excellence which had always adhered to the traditional rulers. Throughout the nineteenth century, therefore, the people were flattered and mystified by hearing that deep within a fixed percentage of them there lay the same divine inspiration and the same gifts of revelation which men had attributed previously to the established authorities.

And then just as in the past men had invented a mythical ancestry for their king, tracing his line back to David or Æneas or Zeus himself, so the minnesingers of democracy have invented their own account of the rise of popular government. The classic legend is to be found in the theory of the Social Contract, and few naïve democrats are without traces of belief in this legend. They imaginc that somehow "the people" got together and established nations and governments and institutions. Yet the historic record plainly shows that the progress of democracy has consisted in an increasing participation of an increasing number of people in the management of institutions they neither created nor willed. And the record shows, too, that new numbers were allowed to participate when they were powerful enough to force their way in; they were enfranchised not because "society" sought the benefits of their wisdom, and not because "society" wished them to have power; they were enfranchised because they had power, and giving them the vote was the least disturbing way of letting them exercise their power. For the principle of majority rule is the mildest form in which the force of numbers can be exercised. It is a pacific substitute for civil war in which the opposing armies are counted and the victory is awarded to the larger before any blood is shed.

Except in the sacred tests of democracy and in the incantations of the orators, we hardly take the trouble to pretend that the rule of the majority is not at bottom a rule of force. What other virtue can there be in fifty-one per cent except the brute fact that fifty-one is more than forty-nine? The rule of fifty-one per cent is a convenience, it is for certain matters a satisfactory political device, it is for others the lesser of two evils, and for still others it is acceptable because we do not know any less troublesome method of obtaining a political decision. But it may easily become an absurd tyranny if we regard it worshipfully, as though it were more than a political device. We have lost all sense of its true meaning when we imagine that the opinion of fifty-one per cent is in some high fashion the true opinion of the whole hundred per cent, or indulge in the sophistry that the rule of a majority is based upon the ultimate equality of man.

At Dayton, Mr. Bryan contended that in schools supported by the state the majority of the voters had a right to determine what should be taught. If my analysis is correct, there is no fact from which that right can be derived except the fact that the majority is stronger than the minority. It cannot be argued that the majority in Tennessee represented the whole people of Tennessee; nor that fifty-one Tennesseeans are better than forty-nine Tennesseeans; nor that they were better biologists, or better Christians, or better parents, or better Americans. It cannot be said they are necessarily more in tune with the ultimate judgments of God. All that can be said for them is that there are more of them, and that in a world ruled by force it may be necessary to defer to the force they exercise.

When the majority exercises that force to destroy the public schools, the minority may have to yield for a time to this force but there is no reason why they should accept the result. For the votes of a majority have no intrinsic bearing on the conduct of a school. They are external facts to be taken into consideration like the weather or the hazard of fire. Guidance for a school can come ultimately only from educators, and the question of what shall be taught as biology can be determined only by biologists. The votes of a majority do not settle anything here and they are entitled to no respect whatever. They may be right or they may be wrong; there is nothing in the majority principle which will make them either right or wrong. In the conduct of schools, and especially as to the details of the curriculum, the majority principle is an obvious irrelevance. It is not even a convenient device as it is in the determination, say, of who shall pay the taxes.

But what good is it to deny the competence of the majority when you have admitted that it has the power to enforce its decisions? I enter this denial myself because I prefer clarity to confusion, and the ascriptions of wisdom to fifty-one per cent seems to me a pernicious confusion. But I do it also because I have some hope that the exorcising of the superstition which has become attached to majority rule will weaken its hold upon the popular imagination, and tend therefore to keep it within convenient limits. Mr. Bryan would not have won the logical victory he won at Dayton if educated people had not been caught in a tangle of ideas which made it seem as if the acknowledgment of the absolutism of the majority was necessary to faith in the final value of the human soul. It seems to me that a rigorous untangling of this confusion may help to arm the minority for a more effective resistance in the future.

2 · *How Can the People Rule?*

The Good Society (*1937*), *Chapter 12.*

The American faith in democracy has always been accompanied by efforts to limit the action of the democracy. Distrust of popular rule has by no means been confined to the well-to-do. It has been general and continuous. At one time men fighting for liberty of conscience have defied the enacted will of the people; at another men defending the privileges of business corporations have sought to circumvent it. In our own day, for example, the very same men who have defied the will of the people—when it imposed national prohibition, outlawed revolutionists, censored books and the stage, prohibited the teaching of methods of birth control—are enthusiasts for the national regulation, the more authoritative the better, of all phases of economic activity. The Democratic party, which was the habitual defender of the sovereignty of the separate states, is today the advocate of a centralized nationalism which would have astonished Alexander Hamilton and John Marshall. Most of us are for the people when we think the people are for us, and against them when they are not. The Republicans, having for fifty years after the Civil War countenanced the impairment of state sovereignty under the due-process clause of the Fourteenth Amendment, had by 1936 become the ardent disciples of Thomas Jefferson and James Madison. It is evident that the American people as a whole have never consistently believed that all their interests could be placed unreservedly at the disposal of the people, however refined the representation, however conscientiously the people's will was checked and balanced.

They have not believed whole-heartedly that democracy was safe for the world. This unbelief is, I believe, an intuition that there is something lacking in the theory of democracy, that somewhere the doctrine of popular sovereignty as conceived by its apostles is inconsistent with essential facts of human experience. Popular government has not worked out as promised, and all through the nineteenth century democrats speculated on the reasons for their disappointment.

They had various answers to the riddle: if they were impressed with the evils of demagoguery, they said that in the long run popular education was the remedy and that the supremacy of a static law was the immediate defense. If they were impressed with the evils of plutocracy and of political corruption, they said that the cure for the evils of democracy was more democracy. They have tried all the remedies. They have spent immense sums on education. They have developed a popular press which is by and large the most informative in the world. They have also developed a technic of propaganda which was, until the totalitarian states put their minds to it, the most effective in all history. They have elaborated judicial restraint to a remarkable degree. And they have widened the electoral franchise and greatly facilitated the direct election of their officials.

Though I regard the American passion for education as noble, and the technic of propaganda as pernicious, the superconstitutional law of the judges as untenable, and so-called "pure" democracy as a mistake, I mention these diverse things together at this point in the argument because they are all evidences of the same thing: the intuitive conviction of the people that democracy will not work merely by making it accurately representative.

The propaganda, the pressure groups, the formulation of a law that is higher than the Constitution, and the breaking down of the checks and balances are evidences, it seems to me, of a radical defect in the conception of democracy. Thus the reliance upon education, in the sense of schools, and lectures for adults and popularized knowledge in books and magazines, is, it seems to me, merely begging the question. It is true, of course, that a people thoroughly educated in mind and character would find the answers to their problems. But it is a mere truism. For the question is how a democracy is to become so well educated, and we may be sure, I think, that the necessary education for popular government cannot be obtained in the schools and colleges, from books, newspapers, lectures, and the radio, alone. Popular education is indispensable, and I should be the last to decry it. But it is insufficient.

The kind of self-education which a self-governing people must obtain can be had only through its daily experiences. In other words, a democracy must have a way of life which educates the people for the democratic way of life. The pioneers of democracy, particularly in America, dimly apprehended but never, I think, fully comprehended this truth. They had made the great discovery that henceforth the people would rule, that they have the right to rule, and that the government through which they rule must be made truly representative. But what they did not master was the corollary of their discovery: that *if the people do rule, they must rule in a particular way.* I am not suggesting that they were altogether oblivious of the question; it would perhaps be accurate to say that they took the answer for granted and did not examine it.

For during the formative period of democratic ideas, the assumption was general that any good government would remain consistent with the spirit of the English common law. The early democrats did not, it would seem, expect the people to legislate much or to legislate radically. So they did not recognize the urgency of the problem which arose later when radically new legislation was needed and desired. As a consequence they handed down to us a conception of democracy which is deeply discerning about the importance of truly representative government, but is without guiding principles as to how the people shall legislate.

The lack of these guiding principles has caused the profoundest confusion. For in the absence of a well-defined conception of how a democracy shall govern, the sovereign people simply took to themselves the attributes of the kings whom they had deposed. It was supposed that the powers of the monarchy had passed to the people, that every man, as Senator Huey Long put it, was a king. "All that was necessary," says Duguit, "was to substitute the nation for the king. The king was a person, a subject of right, the holder of sovereign power; like him, the nation will be a person, a subject of right, the holder of sovereign power." Since the theorists of democracy had not come to grips with the problem of how the people can rule, they thought of the people as the inheritors of the kingly power. They did not fully appreciate the radical nature of the revolution in which they were engaged, and so they failed to realize that when the people rule they must rule in a radically different manner than a king.

When the people's representatives have sought to govern as if they had inherited the royal prerogatives, they soon produced the same evils which men had complained about under royal government. Officialdom aggrandized itself and escaped accountability. It became corrupt, arbitrary, exacting, inefficient, parasitical, irresolute, and insensitive. Instead of hereditary rulers, there were political machines self-perpetuated at the expense of the taxpayers; instead of courtiers there were place hunters. For the social order needed adjustment to the progressive economy. The representatives of the people had to legislate. Having no clear conception of how a democracy can legislate appropriately, they drew upon the ideas which they had inherited from the kings. They aggrandized the number and power of public officials.

The effect was to cause confusion and disappointment in democratic societies. Those who saw the need of reform, or hoped to profit by it, knew no way of achieving reform except by inflating the executive and the administrative branches of the government; those whose interests were threatened, as well as those who remembered the experiences of the past, resisted reform by pointing to the perils of a powerful, ubiquitous, and self-perpetuating bureaucracy. Reformers justified the return to an authoritarian state by the fiction that the state now belonged to the people; as a matter of fact, the official state has grown so large that the legislature has only the vaguest idea of what the officials are doing, and is wholly incapable of holding them to account. Conservatives justified their resistance by appealing to the indubitable lessons of history, that the aggrandized state becomes eventually a tyranny tempered only by its incompetence. Reformers made the unanswerable argument that the laws must change in a progressive economy, and the conservatives retorted that the remedy was worse than the disease. The reformers exalted the rights of the state, the conservatives the rights of the individual; the one doctrine became collectivism, which ends in militarized despotism, and the other doctrine became *laissez faire,* which meant at last that no one must do anything.

But this is a false issue. For it is not necessary to choose between social control administered by the aggrandized state and a self-assertive individualism subject to no social control. That supposedly exclusive choice, which causes such furious party antagonism in our society, overlooks entirely one of the oldest, best established, and most successful methods of social control in human experience. It is social control, not by authority from above commanding this man to do this and that man to do that, but social control by a common law which defies the reciprocal rights and duties of persons and invites them to enforce the law by proving their case in a court of law.

This method of social control is, I submit, the appropriate method for a self-governing people to use. The pioneers of liberalism fought successfully to vindicate this method of social control as against the prerogatives of the king. From the early days of the Norman Conquest they stood for the common law as against the commands from the king on high. This method of social control the founders of the American Constitution took for granted, like the air they breathed. So much did they take it for granted that they neglected to define it and fix it in the tradition of democracy. But in the debacle of liberalism during the delusion of *laissez faire,* this method of social control was unappreciated and then forgotten. The reformers forgot it when they multiplied officials instead of revising the rules of the game; the conservatives forgot it when, in effect, they announced that the existing rules were immutable.

Truly conceived, a democracy is not the government of a people by elected representatives exercising the prerogatives of their former lords and masters. It is the government of the people by a common law which defines the reciprocal rights and duties of persons. This common law is defined, applied, and amended by the representatives of the people.

Merely to enfranchise the voters, even to give them a true

representation, will not in itself establish self-government; it may just as well lead, and in most countries has in fact led, to a new form of absolute state, a self-perpetuating oligarchy and an uncontrollable bureaucracy which governs by courting, cajoling, corrupting, and coercing the sovereign but incompetent people. For the people cannot govern by entrusting their representatives with the prerogatives of the king. They can govern only when they understand how a democracy *can* govern itself; when they have realized that it cannot govern by issuing commands; that it can govern only by appointing representatives to adjudicate, enforce, and revise laws which declare the rights, duties, privileges, and immunities of persons, associations, communities, and the officials themselves, each in respect to all the others.

This is the constitution of a free state. Because democratic philosophers in the nineteenth century did not see clearly that the indispensable corollary of representative government is a particular mode of governing, they were perplexed by the supposed conflict between law and liberty, between social control and individual freedom. These conflicts do not exist where social control is achieved by a legal order in which reciprocal rights are enforced and adjusted. Thus in a free society the state does not administer the affairs of men. It administers justice among men who conduct their own affairs.

This definition of popular rule is not an abstraction which I have invented because I think it is desirable. It is, I believe, a deduction from historic experience in the long struggle to disestablish the dominion of men over men. The idea must gradually crystallize in men's minds as they deny that their kings, their lords and masters, and their leaders, are appointed by God to rule over them. For when they no longer think of government as the liege man thinks of his king, the slave of his lord, the servant of his master, then they must think of government as a legal order in which individuals have equal and reciprocal rights and duties.

This change of mind marks the beginning of the manhood, the ending of the childhood of the race. Men do not accept this conception of government easily. For psychologically it calls for a profound change of attitude, and the change is accompanied by all the troubles of adolescence; the individual is too grown-up to be treated as a child, he is too immature to bear the responsibilities of an adult. But those who grow up must grow up. The change is irrevocable. Though here and there whole nations find the burden of self-government intolerable, and relapse for a moment, seeking to live securely once more as children, the manifest destiny of mankind is to become adult and to replace paternal authority with fraternal association.

Public Opinion (1922), *Chapters 6 and 20.*

In the absence of institutions and education by which the environment is so successfully reported that the realities of public life stand out sharply against self-centered opinion, the common interests very largely elude public opinion entirely, and can be managed only by a specialized class whose personal interests reach beyond the locality. This class is irresponsible, for it acts upon information that is not common property, in situations that the public at large does not conceive, and it can be held to account only on the accomplished fact.

The democratic theory by failing to admit that self-centered opinions are not sufficient to procure good government, is involved in perpetual conflict between theory and practice. According to the theory, the full dignity of man requires that his will should be, as Mr. Cole says, expressed "in any and every form of social action." It is supposed that the expression of their will is the consuming passion of men, for they are assumed to possess by instinct the art of government. But as a matter of plain experience, self-determination is only one of the many interests of a human personality. The desire to be the master of one's own destiny is a strong desire, but it has to adjust itself to other equally strong desires, such as the desire for a good life, for peace, for relief from burdens. In the original assumptions of democracy it was held that the expression of each man's will would spontaneously satisfy not only his desire for self-expression, but his desire for a good life, because the instinct to express one's self in a good life was innate.

The emphasis, therefore, has always been on the mechanism for expressing the will. The democratic El Dorado has always been some perfect environment, and some perfect system of voting and representation, where the innate good will and instinctive statesmanship of every man could be translated into action. In limited areas and for brief periods the environment has been so favorable, that is to say, so isolated, and so rich in opportunity, that the theory worked well enough to confirm men in thinking that it was sound for all time and everywhere. Then when the isolation ended, and society became complex, and men had to adjust themselves closely to one another, the democrat spent his time trying to devise more perfect units of voting, in the hope that somehow he would, as Mr. Cole says, "get the mechanism right, and adjust it as far as possible to men's social wills." But while the democratic theorist was busy at this, he was far away from the actual interests of human nature. He was absorbed by one interest: self-government. Mankind was interested in all kinds of other things, in order, in its rights, in prosperity, in sights and sounds and in not being bored. In so far as spontaneous democracy does not satisfy their other interests, it seems to most men most of the time to be an empty thing. Because the art of successful self-government is not instinctive, men do not long desire self-government for its own sake. They desire it for the sake of the results. That is why the impulse to self-government is always strongest as a protest against bad conditions.

The democratic fallacy has been its preoccupation with the origin of government rather than with the processes and results. The democrat has always assumed that if political power could be derived in the right way, it would be beneficent. His whole attention has been on the source of power, since he is hypnotized by the belief that the great thing is to express the will of the people, first because expression is the highest interest of man, and second because the will is instinctively good. But no amount of regulation at the source of a river will completely control its behavior, and while democrats have been absorbed in trying to find a good mechanism for originating social power, that is to say, a good mechanism of voting and representation, they neglected almost every other interest of men. For no matter how power originates, the crucial interest is in how power is exercised. What determines the quality of civilization is the use made of power. And that use cannot be controlled at the source.

If you try to control government wholly at the source, you inevitably make all the vital decisions invisible. For since there is no instinct which automatically makes political decisions that produce a good life, the men who actually exercise power not only fail to express the will of the people, because on most questions no will exists, but they exercise power according to opinions which are hidden from the electorate.

If, then, you root out of the democratic philosophy the whole assumption in all its ramifications that government is instinctive, and that therefore it can be managed by self-centered opinions, what becomes of the democratic faith in the dignity of man? It takes a fresh lease on life by associating itself with the whole personality instead of with a meager aspect of it. For the traditional democrat risked the dignity of man on one very precarious assumption, that he would exhibit that dignity instinctively in wise laws and good government. Voters did not do that, and so the democrat was forever being made to look a little silly by tough-minded men. But if, instead of hanging human dignity on the one assumption about self-government, you insist that man's dignity requires a standard of living, in which his capacities are properly exercised, the whole problem changes. The criteria which you then apply to government are whether it is producing a certain minimum of health, of decent housing, of material necessities, of education, of freedom, of pleasures, of beauty, not simply whether at the sacrifice of all these things, it vibrates to the self-centered opinions that happen to be floating around in men's minds. In the degree to which these criteria can be made exact and objective, political decision, which is inevitably the concern of comparatively few people, is actually brought into relation with the interests of men.

There is no prospect, in any time which we can conceive, that the whole invisible environment will be so clear to all men that they will spontaneously arrive at sound public opinions on the whole business of government. And even if there were a prospect, it is extremely doubtful whether many of us would wish to be bothered, or would take the time to form an opinion on "any and every form of social action" which affects us. The only prospect which is not visionary is that each of us in his own sphere will act more and more on a realistic picture of the invisible world, and that we shall develop more and more men who are expert in keeping these pictures realistic. Outside the rather narrow range of our own possible attention, social control depends upon devising standards of living and methods of audit by which the acts of public officials and industrial directors are measured. We cannot ourselves inspire or guide all these acts, as the mystical democrat has always imagined. But we can steadily increase our real control over these acts by insisting that all of them shall be plainly recorded, and their results objectively measured. I should say, perhaps, that we can progressively hope to insist. For the working out of such standards and of such audits has only begun.

The Dilemma of Liberal Democracy

The Good Society (1937), *Chapter 12.*

One of the hallmarks of genius, someone has said, is the faculty for asking the right questions. The leaders of the American Revolution proved their genius by going straight to the heart of the question to which any modern society must find the answer or perish. For as the progress of the industrial revolution destroys legitimacy, prescription, and habitual obedience to established authority, the fundamental question is how the formless power of the masses shall be organized, represented, and led. In the generation after the Revolutionary War, the American leaders faced this question. It is an even more urgent question today than it was a hundred and fifty years ago.

For in the interval the acids of modernity have dissolved, more thoroughly than the constitutional Fathers could have anticipated, the psychological bonds of the ancestral order. Since their time virtually the whole traditional social organization of Europe has decayed or has been uprooted, and even in the very depths of Asia and Africa the mass of men have begun to assert their power. The question which the American founders raised was how the inchoate mass of the people, as they assert their power, could be organized into a civil society.

So, as in previous ages men had studied the personal history of kings, they studied the biography of the masses. From books and from their own observation they had learned that unless the people are successfully organized in a state, so they can act through officials who represent them under laws to which they have consented, the people's power is mere ineffective, self-destroying violence. Without civil organization the people are at one time a helpless crowd, at another a horde trampling all before them; then they are mobs which destroy each other; then isolated individuals, each man against all the others in a life that is "solitary, poor, nasty, brutish, and short"; until again, in the cycle of their impotent violence, they become a horde led by a master of the crowd.

It has been said that the authors of the Constitution were not democrats, and their warnings against the irrational power of the formless mass are cited as evidence. But to credit this is to misunderstand their genius. They did not identify the power of the masses with democracy. They were able to see that the essential problem is to organize this power of the masses so that it may function as a democracy. That is why they made a lasting contribution to political thought and made so great a mark on the history of mankind. Had they been "democrats" in the sense which their confused critics have in mind, the ensuing turmoil and impotence would have made America, not the land of promise, but a gigantic Macedonia.

The American Founders saw that the problem was no longer what it had been under the Stuart kings against whom theirs ancestors had rebelled: to obtain protection for the common man as against his masters. In their time the common man already had the power of his former masters; the captains and the kings had departed. Their problem was how to organize the indubitable and inalienable power of the mass in order that it might achieve its own best interests. And since it was obvious that no mass of men can as a mass make more than the simplest decisions of yes and no, and is physically incapable of administering its affairs, the practical question was how a government could be made to represent the people.

It was here that the Founders set themselves apart forever from the naïve theorists of democracy. They saw, in Burke's phrase, that the constitution of a state is not a "problem of arithmetic." So they refused to identify the will of the people with the transient plurality of the voters in one constituency. They did not say, for example, that if the whole mass of persons votes once, and if one party has thirty-four per cent of the votes and the other two have thirty-three per cent each, the winner in the contest is the true representative of the people. They thought of "the people" as having many dimensions in space, in time, in weight, in quality. They thought, as Burke did, that a society is "a partnership in all science; a partnership in all art; a partnership in every virtue, and in all perfection," and "as the ends of such a partnership cannot be obtained in many generations," a civil society is "a partnership not only between those who are living, but between those who are living, those who are dead, and those who are to be born." The American Founders sought to represent this many-sided people and they thought of the people's will as an equilibrium of its many elements.

And so in their practical arrangement they sought to make the government as nearly representative as possible of the many facets of the popular will, of the people acting as citizens of local communities, acting as citizens of regions, of states, of the nation, acting with remembrance of the past, acting as they felt at the moment, acting as they would feel after fuller consideration. For they gave no credence to the idea that one periodic count of heads could elicit the real will of a large population.

The Founders sought to approximate a true representation of the people by providing many different ways of counting heads. For the national government, itself a federation of states with complex forms of representation, they provided a House elected for two years from fairly small constituencies of equal size; a Senate in which one-third only was elected every two years from the states—that is, from constituencies of varying size; a President, chosen, as they conceived it, by electors from the separate states, and for a term of four years, which did not correspond with that of any one group of the legislators; a judiciary appointed for life after confirmation by the Senate. Thus no two branches of the government were chosen by the same constituency or for the same term of office.

They provided that for ordinary laws a majority of both Houses and the President must concur, that a two-thirds majority may prevail over the President, that for treaties two-thirds of the Senate must concur with the President. They then provided that all the powers exercised by the legislative and the executive branch were subject to the supreme law of the land, and that their specific acts would be invalid if contrary to the Constitution. They provided that the supreme law of the Constitution could be amended only by a complex vote which would ensure as nearly as possible that the decision had been fully considered, that all men had had a chance to hear the issues debated, and that many more than a mere majority had been convinced.

How different is this conscientious attempt to ascertain the true will of the people from the cynical plebiscites conducted by dictators, where there is no choice, no opportunity to discuss the issues, and where the momentary, manufactured, majority opinion is treated as the will of the nation. Yet what the dictators do cynically, many who think themselves democrats would do naïvely: they would identify the will of the transient majority with the people, and stake everything on its decisions. The logic of their ideal would call for the election of all officials in one universal ballot empowering these officials to do anything they chose as long as they were in office. If the naïve democrats had the full courage of their convictions, they would break down all the complex and differentiated forms of representation and would remove all legal restraint upon the power of the representatives. This is sometimes described as pure democracy. But a little reflection will show that it emasculates the sovereignty of the people; for if the supreme lawmaking power is entrusted to the representatives of a transient majority, they can at any time disfranchise not only the minority but the majority as well, and confirm themselves permanently in the seats of authority. A "pure" democracy, as the American Founders saw so prophetically, is really brute, inchoate democracy, and the certain foundation of absolutism.

No doubt it is true that the mechanical devices of the American political system are defective, and could be improved. Much more pertinently it may be said that all mechanical devices are necessarily inadequate to ensure true representation, and presently we must explore what I believe is the unrecognized corollary of popular rule. But before we come to that we must appreciate fully the deep wisdom of the original Constitution in its demonstration that the will of a people can only be refined and ascertained by a complex system of representation differentiated in time and space. The devices were only the means and have no universal importance: but the end, to which they were the means, has far greater importance today than when the Founders first discerned it.

Its importance will increase. For with literacy general in the whole population, with inventions for communicating instantaneously with the population of the entire earth, a political system that will refine, rather than respond abjectly to, manufactured mass opinion is more than ever indispensable. The Founders of the American Republic realized that the demagogue is not a romantic fellow who appears now and then, but that he appears whenever government is not effectively representative. Demagoguery is the falsification of representative government, the cultivation of the transient and apparent rather than of the considered and real will of the people. James Madison would not have been astonished at Hitler. He had studied carefully the classical demagogues. That is why the Constitutional Convention attempted to set up truly representative government; in order to protect the masses from the hypnosis of the moment, they invented devices for balancing the constituencies and delaying their decisions. They sought to make the people safe for democracy. What they meant to do every civilized people has to do, and if the checks and balances of the American Constitution are now antiquated, others will have to be devised to replace them.

II

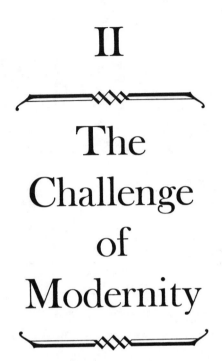

The Challenge of Modernity

1 · *The Decline of the West*

"The Shortage of Education," The Atlantic Monthly, *CXCIII (May 1954), 35, an address delivered at the fifth annual dinner of the National Citizens' Commission for the Public Schools in San Francisco on March 19, 1954.*

What I am going to say is the result of a prolonged exposure to the continuing crisis of our Western society—to the crisis of the democratic governments and of free institutions during the wars and revolutions of the twentieth century. Now it does not come easily to anyone who, like me, has breathed the soft air of the world before the wars that began in 1914—who has known a world that was not divided and frightened and full of hate—it does not come easily to such a man to see clearly and to measure coolly the times we live in. The scale and scope and the complexity of our needs are without any precedent in our experience, and indeed, we may fairly say, in all human experience.

In 1900 men everywhere on earth acknowledged, even

when they resented, the leadership of the Western nations. It was taken for granted that the liberal democracies were showing the way toward the good life in the good society, and few had any doubts of the eventual, but certain, progress of all mankind toward more democracy and a wider freedom.

The only question was when—the question was never whether—the less fortunate and the more backward peoples of the world would have learned to use not only the technology of the West but also the political institutions of the West. All would soon be learning to decide the issues which divided them by free and open and rational discussion; they would soon learn how to conduct free and honest elections, to administer justice. Mankind would come to accept and comprehend the idea that all men are equally under the laws and all men must have the equal protection of the laws.

At the beginning of this century the acknowledged model of a new government, even in Russia, was a liberal democracy in the British or the French or the American style. Think what has happened to the Western world and to its ideas and ideals during the forty years since the World Wars began. The hopes that men then took for granted are no longer taken for granted. The institutions and the way of life which we have inherited, and which we cherish, have lost their paramount, their almost undisputed, hold upon the allegiance and the affections and the hopes of the peoples of the earth. They are no longer universally accepted as being the right way toward the good life on this earth. They are fiercely challenged abroad; they are widely doubted and they are dangerously violated even here at home.

During this half century the power of the Western democratic nations has been declining. Their influence upon the destiny of the great masses of people has been shrinking. We are the heirs of the proudest tradition of government in the history of mankind. Yet we no longer find ourselves talking now—as we did before the First World War—about the progress of liberal democracy among the awakening multitudes. We are talking now about the defense and the survival of liberal democracy in its contracted area.

We are living in an age of disorder and upheaval. Though the United States has grown powerful and rich, we know in our hearts that we have become, at the same time, insecure and anxious. Our people enjoy an abundance of material things, such as no large community of men has ever known. But our people are not happy about their position or confident about their future. For we are not sure whether our responsibilities are not greater than our power and our wisdom.

We have been raised to the first place in the leadership of the Western society at a time when the general civilization of the West has suffered a spectacular decline and is gravely threatened. We, who have become so suddenly the protecting and the leading power of that civilization, are not clear and united among ourselves about where we are going and how we should deal with our unforeseen responsibilities, our unwanted mission, our unexpected duties.

It is an awe-inspiring burden that we find ourselves compelled to bear. We have suddenly acquired responsibilities for which we were not prepared—for which we are not now prepared—for which, I am very much afraid, we are not now preparing ourselves.

We have had, and probably we must expect for a long time to have, dangerous and implacable enemies. But if we are to revive and recover, and are to go forward again, we must not look for the root of the trouble in our adversaries. We must look for it in ourselves. We must rid ourselves of the poison of self-pity. We must have done with the falsehood that all would be well were it not that we are the victims of wicked and designing men.

In 1914, when the decline of the West began, no one had heard of Lenin, Trotsky, Mussolini, Hitler, Stalin, and Mao Tse-tung. We have not fallen from our pre-eminence because we have been attacked. It would be much truer to say, and it is nobler to say it, that we have been attacked because our capacity to cope with our tasks had begun to decline.

We shall never have the spirit to revive and to recover so long as we try to console ourselves by shutting our eyes, and by wringing our hands and beating our breasts and filling the air with complaints that we have been weakened because we were attacked, and that we have been making mistakes because we were betrayed.

We must take the manly view, which is that the failure of the Western democracies during this catastrophic half of the twentieth century is due to the failings of the democratic peoples. They have been attacked and brought down from their pre-eminence because they have lacked the clarity of purpose and the resolution of mind and of heart to cope with the accumulating disasters and disorders. They have lacked the clarity of purpose and the resolution of mind and of heart to prevent the wars that have ruined the West, to prepare for these wars they could not prevent, and, having won them at last after exorbitant sacrifice and at a ruinous cost, to settle those wars and to restore law and order upon the face of the globe.

2 · *A Big World and Little Men*

Drift and Mastery (*1914*), *Chapter 8.*

We are unsettled to the very roots of our being. There isn't a human relation, whether of parent and child, husband and wife, worker and employer, that doesn't move in a strange situation. We are not used to a complicated civilization, we don't know how to behave when personal contact and eternal authority have disappeared. There are no precedents to guide us, no wisdom that wasn't made for a simpler age. We have changed our environment more quickly than we know how to change ourselves.

And so we are literally an eccentric people, our emotional life is disorganized, our passions are out of kilter. Those who call themselves radical float helplessly upon a stream amidst the wreckage of old creeds and abortive new ones, and they are inclined to mistake the motion which carries them for their own will. Those who make no pretensions to much theory are twisted about by fashions, "crazes," at the mercy of milliners and dressmakers, theatrical producers, advertising campaigns, and the premeditated gossip of the newspapers.

We live in great cities without knowing our neighbors, the loyalties of place have broken down, and our associations are stretched over large territories, cemented by very little direct contact. But this impersonal quality is intolerable; people don't like to deal with abstractions. And so you find an overwhelming demand upon the press for human interest stories, for personal details opened to the vast public. Gossip is organized; and we do by telegraph what was done in the village store.

Institutions have developed a thousand inconsistencies. Our schools, churches, courts, governments were not built for the kind of civilization they are expected to serve. In former times you could make some effort to teach people what they needed to know. It was done badly, but at least it could be attempted. Men knew the kind of problems their children would have to face. But today education means a radically different thing. We have to prepare children to meet the unexpected, for their problems will not be the same as their fathers'. To prepare them for the unexpected means to train them in method instead of filling them with facts and rules. They will have to find their own facts and make their own rules, and if schools can't give them that power then schools no longer educate for the modern world.

The churches face a dilemma which is a matter of life and death to them. They come down to us with a tradition that the great things are permanent, and they meet a population that needs above all to understand the meaning and the direction of change. No wonder their influence has declined, no wonder that men fight against the influence they have. Ministers are as bewildered as the rest of us, perhaps a little more so. For they are expected to stand up every week and interpret human life in a way that will vitalize feeling and conduct. And for this work of interpretation they have the simple rules of a village civilization, the injunctions of a pastoral people. Of course they can't interpret life on Sunday so that the interpretation will mean something on Monday. Even supposing that the average minister understood the scientific spirit, had studied sociology, and knew what are the forces which agitate men, even under those circumstances, interpretation would be an almost impossible task. For the least hampered minds, the most imaginative and experienced men, can only stumble through to partial explanations. To ask the clergy to find adequate meaning in this era is to expect each minister to be an inspired thinker. If the churches really could interpret life they would be unable to make room for the congregations; if men felt that they could draw anything like wisdom from them, they would be besieged by bewildered and inquiring people. Think of the lectures people flock to, the political meetings they throng, the dull books they work their way through. It isn't indifference to the great problems that leaves the churches empty; it is the sheer intellectual failure of the churches to meet a sudden change.

The courts have not been able to adjust themselves either. But while people can ignore the churches, they have to fight the courts. They fight blindly without any clear notion as to what they would like the courts to do. They are irritated and constrained by a legal system that was developed in a different civilization, and they find the courts, as Professor Roscoe Pound says, "doing nothing and obstructing everything." They find that whenever a legislature makes an effort to fit law to the new facts of life, a court is there to nullify the work. They find the courts masters of our political system, and yet these masters will not really take the initiative. They have enormous power, but they refuse the responsibility that goes with it. The courts are making law all the time, of course. Now if they made law that met the new situations, there would be no revolt against the judiciary. The American voters are not doctrinaires. They don't care in any academic way whether Congress, the President, or the courts, frame legislation. They form their opinions almost entirely by the results. If the President can legislate better than Congress, as Roosevelt and Wilson could, the people will support the President no matter how many lawyers shout that the rights of Congress are being usurped. If the courts made law that dealt with modern necessities, the people would, I believe, never question their power. It is the bad sociology of judges and their class prejudices that are destroying the prestige of the bench. That bad sociology and those prejudices are in the main due to the fact that judges have not been trained for the modern world, have never learned how to understand its temper.

And of course, when you come to the political structure of our government, you find that it has only the faintest relation to actual conditions. Our political constituencies are to American life what the skeleton of a two-humped camel would be to an elephant. One is not made to fit the other's necessities. Take the City of New York for example. For all practical purposes the metropolitan district extends up into Connecticut and across into New Jersey. By "practical purposes" I mean that as a health problem, a transportation problem, a housing problem, a food problem, a police problem, the city which sprawls across three states ought to be treated as one unit. Or take New England: for any decent solution of its transportation difficulties or for any scientific use of its natural resources its state lines are a nuisance. On the other hand, it mustn't be imagined that the old political units are always too small. Far from it: thus many of the vital functions of New York City are managed by the State Legislature. The political system which comes down to us from a totally different civilization is sometimes too large in its unit—sometimes too small, but in a thousand bewildering ways its does not fit. Every statesman is hampered by conflicts of jurisdiction, by divided responsibility, by the fact that when he tries to use the government for some public purpose, the government is a clumsy instrument.

Liberty and the News (1920), *Chapter 3.*

The real enemy is ignorance, from which all of us, conservative, liberal, and revolutionary, suffer. If our effort is concentrated on our desires—be it our desire to have and to hold what is good, our desire to remake peacefully, or our desire to transform suddenly—we shall divide hopelessly and irretrievably. We must go back of our opinions to the neutral facts for unity and refreshment of spirit. To deny this, it seems to me, is to claim that the mass of men is impervious to education, and to deny that, is to deny the postulate of democracy, and to seek salvation in a dictatorship. There is, I am convinced, nothing but misery and confusion that way. But I am equally convinced that democracy will degenerate into this dictatorship either of the Right or of the Left, if it does not become genuinely self-governing. That means, in terms of public opinion, a resumption of that contact between beliefs and realities which we have been losing steadily since the small-town democracy was absorbed into the Great Society.

The Phantom Public (1925), *Chapter 1.*

The private citizen today has come to feel rather like a deaf spectator in the back row, who ought to keep his mind on the mystery off there, but cannot quite manage to keep awake. He knows he is somehow affected by what is going on. Rules and regulations continually, taxes annually, and wars occasionally remind him that he is being swept along by great drifts of circumstance.

Yet these public affairs are in no convincing way his affairs. They are for the most part invisible. They are managed, if they are managed at all, at distant centers, from behind the scenes, by unnamed powers. As a private person he does not know for certain what is going on, or who is doing it, or where he is being carried. No newspaper reports his environment so that he can grasp it; no school has taught him how to imagine it; his ideals, often, do not fit with it; listening to speeches, uttering opinions, and voting do not, he finds, enable him to govern it. He lives in a world which he cannot see, does not understand, and is unable to direct.

In the cold light of experience he knows that his sovereignty is a fiction. He reigns in theory, but in fact he does not govern. Contemplating himself and his actual accomplishments in public affairs, contrasting the influence he exerts with the influence he is supposed according to democratic theory to exert, he must say of his sovereignty what Bismarck said of Napoleon III: "At a distance it is something, but close to it is nothing at all." When, during an agitation of some sort, say a political campaign, he hears himself and some thirty million others described as the source of all wisdom and power and righteousness, the prime mover and the ultimate goal, the remnants of sanity in him protest. He cannot all the time play Chanticleer, who was so dazzled and delighted because he himself had caused the sun to rise.

For when the private man has lived through the romantic age in politics and is no longer moved by the stale echoes of its hot cries, when he is sober and unimpressed, his own part in public affairs appears to him a pretentious thing, a second-rate, an inconsequential. You cannot move him then with a good straight talk about service and civic duty, nor by waving a flag in his face, nor by sending a boy scout after him to make him vote. He is a man back home from a crusade to make the world something or other it did not become; he has been tantalized too often by the foam of events, has seen the gas go out of it.

Drift and Mastery (*1914*), *Chapter 12.*

Generally we create the bogey by pulling the bedclothes over our heads. A friend of mine couldn't be cured of his socialist phobia until he happened one day to see the most terrible agitator of them all buying a pair of suspenders. For in the seclusion and half-light of class tradition and private superstition, in a whispered and hesitant atmosphere, phantoms thrive. But in direct contact by an unromantic light evil is no longer a bogey but a problem. That is the way to approach evil: by stating it and manhandling it, the fevered gloom subsides, for that gloom does not belong to evil; it it is merely the feeling of a person who is afraid of evil. "Death," said a wise man, "is not feared because it is evil, but it is evil because it is feared."

To overcome the subjective terrors: that is an important aspect of the age-long struggle out of barbarism. Romantic persons like to paint savages as carefree poets living in thoughtless happiness from day to day. Nothing could be further from the facts. The life of a savage is beset by glowering terrors: from birth to death he lives in an animated world; where the sun and the stars, sticks, stones, and rivers are obsessed with his fate. He is busy all the time in a ritual designed to propitiate the abounding jealousies of nature. For his world is magical and capricious, the simplest thing is occult. In that atmosphere there is no possibility of men being able to face their life without heroics and without terror, simply and gladly. They need authority: they need to be taken in charge; they cannot trust themselves.

That is why the exorcising of bogeys is so intimate a part of the effort at self-government. Think of the ordinary businessman's notion of an anarchist, or the anarchist's notion of a businessman; many men's feeling about Theodore Roosevelt, or Bill Haywood, or the Capitalist Class, or the Money Power, or Sex Reform—I use capital letters because these fantasies have become terrific monsters of the imagination. Our life is overwrought with timidities and panics, distorting superstitions and fantastic lures: our souls are misshapen by the plucking of invisible hands.

The regiment of bogeys is waiting for people at birth, where the cruellest unreason clusters about illegitimacy. It attacks the young child who asks how he was born. For answer he is given lies and a sense of shame; for ever afterwards he too lies and is ashamed. And so we begin to build up the sense of sin and the furtiveness of sex. The body becomes the object of a sneaking curiosity, of a tingling and embarrassing interest. We surround the obvious with great wastes of silence, and over the simplest facts we teach the soul to stutter.

What we call purity is not honest and temperate desire, but a divided life in which our "better nature" occasionally wins a bankrupt victory. Children are immured in what their parents fondly picture to be a citadel of innocence. In reality, they are plunged into fantastic brooding or into a haphazard education. Behind innocence there gathers a clotted mass of superstition, of twisted and misdirected impulse; clandestine flirtation, fads, and ragtime fill the unventilated mind.

Then too the whole edifice of class-feeling—what "is done" and what "isn't done," and who are "the best people" and who are the "impossible," and sleepless nights over whether you were correctly dressed, or whether you will be invited to be seen with Mrs. So-and-So. It makes sheep out of those who conform and freaks out of those who rebel. Every fairly intelligent person is aware that the price of respectability is a muffled soul bent on the trivial and the mediocre. The mere fact that the weight of custom is on the accidents of class is a tremendous item in the lives of those who try to live in a human sphere. No one escapes the deformity altogether. Certainly not the modern rebel. His impulse is to break away from the worship of idols to central human values. But the obstruction of class feeling is so great that he becomes a kind of specialist in rebellion. He is so busy asserting that he isn't conventional that the easy, natural humanity he professes to admire is almost the last thing he achieves. Hence the eccentricity and the paradox, the malice and the wantonness of the iconoclast.

The fear of losing one's job, the necessity of being somebody in a crowded and clamorous world, the terror that old age will not be secured, that your children will lack opportunity—there are a thousand terrors which arise out of the unorganized and unstable economic system under which we live. These are not terrors which can be blown away by criticism; they will go only when society is intelligent enough to have made destitution impossible, when it secures opportunity to every child, when it establishes for every human being a minimum of comfort below which he cannot sink. Then a great amount of social hesitancy will disappear. Every issue will not be fought as if life depended upon it, and mankind will have emerged from a fear economy. There are those who cannot conceive of a nation not driven by fear. They seem to feel that enterprise would diminish in a sort of placid contentment. That, it seems to me, is a serious error. The regime of fear produces dreaming and servile races, as in India and China and parts of Ireland. The enterprise that will be fruitful to modern civilization is not the undernourished child of hard necessity, but the high spirits and exuberant well-being of a happy people.

It is a common observation that no man can live well who

fears death. The overcareful person is really dying all his life. He is a miser, and he pays the miser's penalty: he never enjoys his own treasure because he will not spend it. And so when we hear that he who would find his own soul must lose it first, we are not listening to an idle paradox or to some counsel of perfection. Those who hold life lightly are the real masters of it: the lavish givers have the most to give.

But anyone who picks his way through the world as if he were walking on eggs will find it a difficult and unsatisfactory place. Writers and scientists and statesmen who are forever preoccupied with their immediate reputation, always counting the costs, are buying rubbish for a fortune. The thinker who has a mortal fear of being wrong will give all that is valuable in himself to that little ambition. A mistake matters far less than most of us imagine: the world is not brittle, but elastic.

If we could know the inner history of weakness, of what disappoints us in leaders, the timidity of thought, the hesitancy and the drift, we should find in endless cases that the imagination had been blinded and the will scattered by the haunting horror of constructed evils. We falter from childhood amidst shames and fears, we move in closed spaces where stale tradition enervates, we grow hysterical over success and failure, and so by surrounding instinct with terror, we prepare the soul for weakness.

There is a brilliant statement of Freud's that in the Middle Ages people withdrew to a monastery, whereas in modern times they become nervous. He means that formerly men could find refuge from their sense of sin, their bogeys, and their conflicts, in a special environment and a fulfilling religion. But today they are the victims of their weakness. So if confidence is to become adequate for us we must set about expunging that weakness and disciplining a new strength.

A great deal can be done by exorcising bogeys—by refusing to add the terrors of the imagination to the terrors of fact. But there is in addition more positive work to do. We have to build up a disciplined love of the real world. It is no easy task. As yet, we see only in the vaguest way the affirmative direction of democratic culture. For the breakdown of absolutism is more evident than the way to mastery.

Public Opinion (1922), *Chapter 17.*

The outsider, and every one of us is an outsider to all but a few aspects of modern life, has neither time, nor attention, nor interest, nor the equipment for specific judgment. It is on the men inside, working under conditions that are sound, that the daily administrations of society must rest.

The general public outside can arrive at judgments about whether these conditions are sound only on the result after the event, and on the procedure before the event. The broad principles on which the action of public opinion can be continuous are essentially principles of procedure. The outsider can ask experts to tell him whether the relevant facts were duly considered; he cannot in most cases decide for himself what is relevant or what is due consideration. The outsider can perhaps judge whether the groups interested in the decision were properly heard, whether the ballot, if there was one, was honestly taken, and perhaps whether the result was honestly accepted. He can watch the procedure when the news indicates that there is something to watch. He can raise a question as to whether the procedure itself is right, if its normal results conflict with his ideal of a good life. But if he tries in every case to substitute himself for the procedure, to bring in Public Opinion like a providential uncle in the crisis of a play, he will confound his own confusion. He will not follow any train of thought consecutively.

For the practice of appealing to the public on all sorts of intricate matters means almost always a desire to escape criticism from those who know by enlisting a large majority which has had no chance to know. The verdict is made to depend on who has the loudest or the most entrancing voice, the most skilful or the most brazen publicity man, the best access to the most space in the newspapers. For even when the editor is scrupulously fair to "the other side," fairness is not enough. There may be several other sides, unmentioned by any of the organized, financed and active partisans.

The private citizen, beset by partisan appeals for the loan of his Public Opinion, will soon see, perhaps, that these appeals are not a compliment to his intelligence, but an imposition on his good nature and an insult to his sense of evidence. As his civic education takes account of the complexity of his environment, he will concern himself about the equity and the sanity of procedure, and even this he will in most cases expect his elected representative to watch for him. He will refuse himself to accept the burden of these decisions, and will turn down his thumbs in most cases on those who, in their hurry to win, rush from the conference table with the first dope for the reporters.

Only by insisting that problems shall not come up to him until they have passed through a procedure, can the busy citizen of a modern state hope to deal with them in a form that is intelligible. For issues, as they are stated by a partisan, almost always consist of an intricate series of facts, as he has observed them, surrounded by a large fatty mass of stereotyped phrases charged with his emotion. According to the fashion of the day, he will emerge from the conference room insisting that what he wants is some soul-filling idea like Justice, Welfare, Americanism, Socialism. On such issues the citizen outside can sometimes be provoked to fear or admiration, but to judgment never. Before he can do anything with the argument, the fat has to be boiled out of it for him.

That can be done by having the representative inside carry on discussion in the presence of some one, chairman or mediator, who forces the discussion to deal with the analyses supplied by experts. This is the essential organization of any representative body dealing with distant matters. The partisan voices should be there, but the partisans should find themselves confronted with men, not personally involved, who control enough facts and have the dialectical skill to sort out what is real perception from what is stereotype, pattern and elaboration. It is the Socratic dialogue, with all of Socrates' energy for breaking through words to meanings, and something more than that, because the dialectic in modern life must be done by men who have explored the environment as well as the human mind.

"The South and the New Society," Social Forces, *VI* (*1927*), *1*.

The man born into this American society of ours confronts a world which differs radically in its character from that world into which his ancestors were born. Whether he lives in a big city, or in a country district which is closely related to a big city, makes little difference here. The world to which he has to adapt himself, the world in which he has to find his way, the world which he has ultimately to master, is essentially unlike the world into which his grandfather was born. There is a change of scale; there is a change of pace; there is a change in fundamental assumptions which make the intellectual, and the moral, and the spiritual problem of the modern man unique.

Let us examine briefly three major respects in which the environment of the modern man is unique. He lives, first of all, in a world where most of the facts he has to deal with, and where most of the forces that affect him, are unseen. The greater part of his environment is invisible. His great-grandfather, who lived in a village community, could see with his own eyes practically all the people with whom he had to do business. The main affairs of his community were in the hands of men whom he knew. The economic relations of his time were between people whom he knew. He saw with his own eyes the farms, the workshops, the stores, the market places, which affected his livelihood. The modern man's position is totally different. He works and sells his goods to unknown people in a distant market. He buys goods from people living on distant continents. If he is an industrial worker, he sees only a part of the product on which he works. He works for owners whom he has never seen. He is directed by executives, by bankers on whom he has never laid eyes. He votes for politicians about whom he knows only through the newspapers. His knowledge of events comes to him through great impersonal organizations like the press, the moving picture and the radio. On most of the great events of the day his knowledge is not vivid and direct, but second-hand and pale.

And these events which he knows so indirectly are in themselves so extraordinarily complicated that experts who devote their lives to understanding them can master only fragments of their subject. Theoretically each man is a sovereign citizen directing the destinies of this nation, but he has to direct those destinies in regard to questions about which it is, humanly speaking, impossible for him to have adequate knowledge, or normally to have accurate knowledge. Moreover, just because the events with which he has to deal are both invisible and complicated, they are to him very often dull and uninteresting. It is one of the greatest paradoxes of modern democracy that the questions of greatest interest to the mass of mankind are not interesting. To most of mankind the great questions of diplomacy, which ultimately work themselves out in terms of war and peace; the great questions of national economy, which affect the livelihood, the prosperity, the social standing of every person, are so intricate, so technical, and therefore, to most men so dull, that they produce a yawn rather than vivid interest.

The second respect in which the situation of the modern man differs from that of his ancestor is that there exists today no authoritative and organized body of knowledge which it is possible for any living man to absorb. At the climax of the Greek civilization Aristotle could encompass the whole field of human knowledge; at the climax of the great medieval civilization St. Thomas Aquinas could do the same with the knowledge of his day. It is no longer possible to present anyone with a complete and digestible statement of human knowledge. Where once the knowledge of mankind was inclusive and within the range of human power to learn, the knowledge of today is in constant flux, is vaster than anyone's memory, and the essential spirit of it is, that what is believed to be true today may tomorrow prove to be wrong.

In the third place, the situation of the modern man is unique because in regard to the world in which he has daily to act there no longer exists an authoritative body of morals in which he can find rules for the guidance of his conduct. I do not wish to deny that there are still great general principles of morality to which people sincerely adhere. I do wish to point out that in the application of these principles to the concrete situations of today, whether in industry, in politics, or in family life, there is great disagreement, and there is no authoritative interpretation.

"How Liberty Is Lost," Today and Tomorrow,
July 16, 1938.

We live in a time when great masses of civilized men have either voluntarily surrendered their personal liberties or at least have submitted without serious protest or resistance to the destruction of their liberties. It is important that we should understand the causes. This is not too difficult. For while a library of books might profitably be written on the subject, one fundamental aspect of the question at least is clear enough to any one who passes back and forth between the totalitarian and the free nations of Europe.

It is that the peoples who have lost their civil rights had

previously lost or had never obtained the means of economic independence for individuals, families and local communities. It is very clear, I think, that the masses who have fallen under the spell of demagogic dictators and their terroristic bands were recruited from individuals who had no property, no savings, and either no job at all or a job which they could not feel sure of holding. They were in the exact sense of the term proletarians even if they happened to be earning fairly high salaries at the moment. For they had no reserves to fall back upon. They could not afford to lose their jobs. They could not afford, therefore, to speak their minds or to take any risks, to be in any real sense of the word individual citizens. They had to be servile or they starved. Wherever a dictatorship has been set up in Europe, the mass of individuals had already become so insecure that they no longer dared to exercise the legal liberties that the demagogue was attacking.

To have economic independence a man must be in a position to leave one job and go to another; he must have enough savings of some kind to exist for a considerable time without accepting the first job offered. Thus the peasant, for all his poverty and the exploitation which he suffers, is relative to his own needs still the freest man in central Europe. The fact that he can exist by his own labor on his own piece of land gives him an independence which every dictatorial regime, except the Russian perhaps, has been forced to respect.

But the industrial worker who has a choice between working in one factory and not working at all, the white collar intellectuals who compete savagely for the relatively few private positions and for posts in the bureaucracy—these are the people who live too precariously to exercise their liberties or to defend them. They have no savings. They have only their labor to sell, and there are very few buyers of their labor. Therefore, they have only the choice of truckling to the powerful or of perishing heroically but miserably. Men like these, having none of the substance of liberty themselves, have scant respect for any law or any form of civil rights.

The reason why the love of liberty, as we understand it in America, is so strong in France is undoubtedly, it seems to me, that France still is a country where the great mass of the people have their own farms, their own shops, their own little business enterprises and some savings for a rainy day and an emergency. This is the solid foundation of French liberty. The French electorate, except perhaps in a few industrial centers, is not a frightened crowd but a collection of independent families, stubbornly attached to their farms, shops, homes and bank accounts.

They are not easy to terrorize because they have reserves for their independence. They have resistance to mass propaganda because they have so much independence as individuals. And that is why they have such a dread of inflation, which would destroy their individual savings, and such a dislike of monopoly and the concentrating of big business, which would make them the hirelings of a single master.

The more I see of Europe the more deeply convinced do I become that the preservation of freedom in America, or anywhere else, depends upon maintaining and restoring for the great majority of individuals the economic means to remain independent individuals. The greatest evil of the modern world is the reduction of the people to a proletarian level by destroying their savings, by depriving them of private property, by making them the helpless employees of a private monopoly or of government monopoly. At that point they are no longer citizens. They are a mob. For when the people lose this sense of their separate and individual security, they cease to be individuals. They are absorbed into a mass. Their liberties are already lost and they are a frightened crowd ready for a master.

Though the actual measures to be taken are debatable, the objective for a free government is, I think, clear. It should use its authority to enable the independent farmer, the small and moderate sized enterprise, the small saver, to survive. It should use its authority to see that large enterprise is no larger than technology requires, depriving big business of corporate privileges and other forms of legal and economic advantage which make it bigger than on economic grounds it needs to be. A resolute democracy should favor the dispersion of industry rather than its concentration, and it should favor the rise in as many communities as possible of different kinds of enterprise rather than a high degree of specialization on some one product.

For unless the means of independence are widely distributed among the people themselves, no real resistance is possible to the advance of tyranny. The experience of Europe shows clearly that when a nation becomes proletarian, the result is not, as the communists taught, a dictatorship by the proletariat but a dictatorship over the proletariat.

3 · *The Dangers of Big Government*

The Good Society (*1937*), *Chapter 7.*

It is fair to say that the advance of collectivism has not been determined by the image of a collectivist society. The advance has consisted of a series of definite measures, all more or less within the same general category, to be sure. But these measures have come not from a general theory but from a series of efforts to deal with specific grievances and to provide particular benefits.

Such has been the inner principle of the gradual and democratic collectivist movement. It is, I believe, its only possible principle. Because a democracy cannot adopt a plan for collectivism, the practical initiative in each measure of its gradual advance comes not from the energy of a general ideal but from organized interests seeking protection and privileges. In practice gradual collectivism is not an ordered scheme of social reconstruction. It is the polity of pressure groups.

The movement advances by measures adopted from time to time at the instigation of aggrieved or aspiring groups of voters. Through their leaders and lobbyists they persuade, cajole, coerce, and occasionally corrupt the electorate or the parliament; often they conspire with other organized interests to form majorities by coalition. Though exceptions could be cited, it is substantially true that, while the moral and intellectual justification for each measure is derived from the general ideology of collectivism, the initiative comes from organized interests. There has been some legislation for the welfare of the weak and the dependent which may be said to be the work of humane and disinterested men. But these measures do not deeply affect the conduct of business and government. Though they are humanly important, they are peripheral and superficial, and by all thoroughgoing collectivists are recognized as such.

The measures which have profoundly affected the social order because they have meant the shift of important social benefits from one group to another, from one region or occupation to another, from individuals to great corporations or from individuals to the government—all such decisive measures have proceeded from the pressure of interested groups upon the electorate and upon the politicians. The particular measures would not have been adopted when they were adopted but for the organized agitation, the lobbying, and the exercise of influence by these interested groups. Thus no serious historian of politics would imagine that he had accounted for the protective tariff or the system of bounties or subsidies, for the monetary and the banking laws, for the state of the law in regard to corporate privileges and immunities, for the actual status of property rights, for agricultural or for labor policies, until he had gone behind the general claims and the abstract justifications and had identified the specifically interested groups which promoted the specific law.

Such an understanding of the actual history should not be confused with the arbitrary classification of society into a capitalist class and a proletarian class. For while it may serve the purposes of a revolutionary propaganda to say with Marx that the modern state is "nothing more than a committee for the administration of the consolidated affairs of the bourgeois class as a whole," the specific measures taken by modern states are unintelligible on the hypothesis that there is a "bourgeois class" which has "consolidated affairs." Consider, for example, the American tariff as it existed when President Hoover signed the Hawley-Smoot Bill in 1930. It would be admitted by all, I suppose, that with negligible exceptions each item in each schedule originated with at least some of the producers of the article protected by the duty, and that the rate was either a grant of their demands or a compromise between their demands and the objections raised by representatives of some other interest. No one would pretend that this tariff which profoundly affected the whole American economy, not to speak of the economy of the world, was in any sense of the term conceived by "the bourgeois class" as a whole. The very essence of that tariff, and of all its predecessors, was that, far from representing the "consolidated" interests of businessmen as a class, it represented the special interests of some of them.

What "protection," for example, do tariffs on steel, or for that matter on anything else, give to such industries as the railroads, the light, power, telephone, and telegraph companies, the building trades, automobile manufacturers, newspapers, hotels, bakeries, milk producers and distributors, streetcars, buses, ferries, lake and river steamboats, the freight business, or the service industries, such as garages and filling stations? The anatomy of the tariff bill itself contains conclusive proof that certain producer interests, not American producers as a whole, are responsible for the fact that commerce is being regulated in the particular way that the law regulates it. The Marxian assumption that Congress legislated for "the consolidated affairs" of "the bourgeois class" is as misleading as the assumption of the defenders of the tariff that it legislated for the American people as a whole.

Under gradual collectivism, precisely because it is gradual, the measures of state interference are almost invariably promoted by particular groups. Invariably they claim that their particular interest is identical with the national interest. But it is the particular interest which moves them to raise the issue. The Legislature may reject the claim if someone is able to expose its fallacy. But in so far as the Legislature acts, it must listen to some petition. It does not move unless it has been provoked by the claim of some group. For it has no other criterion by means of which it can decide where and when and to what end it should intervene. Suppose, for example, that there were no tariff and that no lobbyist could communicate with any member of Congress, and then that Congress, believing in the abstract principle of national protection, were able to hear only from absolutely disinterested economists—let us say, from a group of men who had acquired complete knowledge of all the available data after a lifetime of study in a Tibetan monastery. Would the law resemble any existing tariff? Could any law be written by men who were equally interested in helping the automobile industry to obtain cheap steel and the steel industry to maintain a fixed and protected price? In helping the house builder or the manufacturer to obtain inexpensive materials and the producers of those materials to obtain a protected price?

The protective tariff does not stand alone. The same principle is no less evident in the collectivist measures designed to assist farmers or workers. The very fact that they are generally proposed on the ground that something must be done to equalize burdens, privileges, and bargaining power is in itself a most significant indication of the real nature of the process. If we examine such measures in detail we shall rarely fail to observe that in fact they are promoted not by "the farmers" or by "labor" as a whole but by particular interests among farmers and workingmen.

The Agricultural Adjustment Act, for example, in its dealings with cotton, paid little attention to the tenant farmers, the sharecroppers, not to speak of the agricultural laborers who were displaced by the curtailment of cotton production. Moreover, the curtailment of cotton production by the method of acreage reduction paid scant attention to the claims of the efficient producer as against those of the less efficient. Moreover, initially the act itself selected seven "basic" commodities which were entitled to benefit payments; by subsequent amendment in response to the pressure of organized interests the number was increased to sixteen. All the other farmers had to contribute to these benefits by paying the processing taxes. Thus a dairyman paid a tax on cotton, wheat, hogs, and corn. But he received no benefit payments. I do not mean to argue that in the critical conditions which prevailed in the year 1933 special legislation of this sort may not have been temporarily in the general interest. My concern is merely to illustrate the underlying principle of gradual collectivism, which is that its specific measures owe their origin to particular interests and that its design follows the pattern of the influences exerted by pressure groups.

The same principle tends to control labor legislation. Anyone who will analyze the laws passed to benefit labor will find that, apart from some few of a humanitarian character, they reflect fairly well the strategic advantages of certain groups of workers. Thus railroad employees are more highly protected by special laws than any other group, and among railroad employees the members of the brotherhoods are more carefully protected than the shopmen or the unskilled workers who maintain the tracks. The social-security laws providing for insurance against unemployment, for example, and the laws to promote collective bargaining give protection to well-established, strategically placed, and highly organized groups. They are quite unable to give the same degree of protection, let us say, to domestic servants, or to casual workers.

It appears to make no difference where collectivism of this sort begins. Whether it begins with tariffs for some manufacturers, special laws for certain groups of workingmen, or bounties for farmers, the one certain thing is that in a democratic society the granting of some privileges must be followed by the granting of more privileges. In fact it might be said that when modern states abandoned the Jeffersonian principle of special privileges to none they became committed to the principle of special privileges for all.

Thus a tariff for one industry will make irresistible the demands of other industries for equal protection. At the end of the process, very nearly reached by the United States in 1930, tariffs became universal and well-nigh exclusive against all products that can be made domestically. But such tariffs only mark the beginning. The agricultural interests will demand protection and bounties in order to achieve "parity." An advanced system of labor legislation always demands the support of an exclusive tariff. Thus under the National Industrial Recovery Act, which sought by federal laws, called codes, to elevate wages and working conditions, it was provided that if "substantial quantities" of any article were imported and might "render ineffective" the "maintenance of any code," such imports could be prohibited.

Now the effect of attempting to give protection to all the interests capable of bringing influence to bear upon the government is to cancel out many of their special advantages. One tariff-protected manufacturer in an economy otherwise committed to free trade will, of course, obtain a substantial advantage. But if the producer from whom he buys his raw materials is also given protection, some of the benefit is canceled, for the costs of production are increased. If, then, bounties and tariffs have to be given to the farmers in order to protect them also, the first lobbyist not only has to contribute to the benefits out of his profits, but he finds that the cost of living has risen for his employees. When they organize to increase their real wages, more of his benefits are canceled.

If the sole effect of this cumulative collectivism were to cancel out the special advantages of the various pressure groups, it might be regarded as a harmless method of letting them enjoy the appearance of special privileges while the community escaped the consequences. If, by making privilege universal, special advantages were neutralized; if, by giving one interest after another a special favor, all the interests came to be on an equal footing, the process might be silly, but it would not be dangerous. The believers in gradual collectivism seem to have some such comforting thought in the backs of their minds.

The notion of equal privileges for every interest has, as it happens, been elaborated into a scheme of social organization. It is known in Italy as the Corporative State. In Russia it is partially embodied in the Soviet system of government. And long before that the idea was adopted by several schools of social reconstruction, among them the guild socialists and syndicalists of many sorts. The theory of these schemes is that government should be "functional" rather than geographical—that is to say, in the state each person should be represented as a worker rather than as a citizen. Many democrats have been attracted by the idea, thinking that the avowed representation of particular interests would be better than the lobbying of pressure groups pretending to be disinterested patriots. They have been tempted to hope that the open avowal of all special interests would neutralize their self-regarding purposes into a realistic but harmonious conception of the general interest.

But the trouble with these schemes is that they sanctify the self-regarding purposes of special interests and do nothing to subdue them. For many particular interests do not in any conceivable combination constitute the general interest; to entrust the government of a nation to such a body would be to turn the sovereign power over to a coalition of its most powerful interests. As a matter of fact, though the semblance of such a political organization exists in Italy, in Russia, and even in Germany, in none of these states is real power entrusted to it. The sovereign power resides in the dictatorship, and in fact only a dictatorship could hope to keep a chamber of special interests from conspiring continually against the national welfare.

There is no reason to think that the self-regarding activities of special groups can be balanced or regulated by organizing more and more of them. In the historical period during which organized interests have been increasingly active and their activities have been treated as more and more reputable, there have been two momentous developments. By organized restrictions of many sorts the production of wealth has been retarded, the method of monopoly being employed to enrich the favored interests. The imprimatur of respectability having been put upon organized privilege, the whole population has become imbued with the idea that as a matter of right everyone is entitled to invoke the law to increase his income.

This is the vicious paradox of the gradual collectivism which has developed in Western society during the past sixty years: it has provoked the *expectation* of universal plenty provided by action of the state while, through almost every action undertaken or tolerated by the state, the production of wealth is *restricted*. By these measures modern states have frustrated the hopes which their policies have aroused. They have put into effect measures of scarcity, and all the while they have taught the people to believe that the effect of the policy would be to give them abundance. To that paradox no small part of the dangerous tension in modern society is due.

The Phantom Public (*1925*), *Chapter 16.*

The democracies are haunted by this dilemma: they are frustrated unless in the laying down of rules there is a large measure of assent; yet they seem unable to find solutions of their greatest problems except through centralized governing by means of extensive rules which necessarily ignore the principle of assent. The problems that vex democracy seem to be unmanageable by democratic methods.

In supreme crises the dilemma is presented absolutely. Possibly a war can be fought for democracy; it cannot be fought democratically. Possibly a sudden revolution may be made to advance democracy; but the revolution itself will be conducted by a dictatorship. Democracy may be defended against its enemies but it will be defended by a committee of safety. The history of the wars and revolutions since 1914 is ample evidence on this point. In the presence of danger, where swift and concerted action is required, the methods of democracy cannot be employed.

That is understandable enough. But how is it that the democratic method should be abandoned so commonly in more leisurely and less catastrophic times? Why in time of peace should people provoke that centralization of power which deprives them of control over the use of that power? Is it not a probable answer to say that in the presence of certain issues, even in time of peace, the dangers have seemed sufficiently menacing to cause people to seek remedies, regardless of method, by the shortest and easiest way at hand?

It could be demonstrated, I think, that the issues which have seemed so overwhelming were of two kinds: those which turned on the national defense or the public safety and those which turned on the power of modern capitalism. Where the relations of a people to armed enemies are in question or where the relations of employee, customer, or farmer to large industry are in question the need for solutions has outweighed all interest in the democratic method.

In the issues engendered by the rise of the national state and the development of large-scale industries are to be found the essentially new problems of the modern world. For the solution of these problems there are few precedents. There is no established body of custom and law. The field of international affairs and the field of industrial relations are the two great centers of anarchy in society. It is a pervasive anarchy. Out of the national state with its terrifying military force, and out of great industry with all its elaborate economic compulsion, the threat against personal security always rises. To offset it somehow, to check it and thwart it, seemed more important than any finical regard for the principle of assent.

"Morale and Discipline," Today and Tomorrow, *December 2, 1952.*

General Eisenhower has shown by the quality of the committee he has just appointed that he is seriously interested in "simplifying the structure of the government." That being so, Mr. Nelson Rockefeller and his two associates, Mr. Flemming and Mr. Milton Eisenhower, could fairly and properly go beyond the problems of organization to a general problem which affects all modern governments. They might recognize the fact that the real problem is not how to "streamline" a new Administration but how to keep an Administration streamlined as it grows older. For it is the inevitable, unavoidable, incurable tendency of all modern governments to expand, and the need to contract and to reduce them is therefore never finished.

Like those who unhappily are made to get fat, the new Administration will have to learn how big is the difference between reducing and staying reduced. Every new Administration starts off on one of those ten-day miracle diets consisting of lettuce and a hard-boiled egg; always in the past it has ended as has the outgoing Truman Administration—especially in the outer world—on a diet of waffles and fudge. For this reason Mr. Rockefeller's committee might consider devices for a continuing review, like being weighed every day, to watch and to warn as the structure of the government, once it has been streamlined, begins again, as it surely will, to swell and to bulge.

The fatty degeneration of government is a serious disease. It is serious not only, or mainly, because it means the waste of so much money. The worst of the disease is that it destroys the effective control of the government, with its vast powers at home and in all parts of the globe. The Truman Administration is a bad case of fatty degeneration. As time went on, the Administration has acquired more and more powers and has spent more and more money but it has had less and less control over the use of that power and of that money.

The re-establishment of effective control over the enormously expanded government is the first and the fundamental task of the new Administration. That loss of control, the condition where departments, bureaus, officials, and missions are out of control and out of hand—this is the crucial trouble. It is the trouble that will have to be corrected. It is the "mess" that will have to be cleared up. It is the condition that will have to be "changed" if the Eisenhower Administration is to make good on its promises to the people.

"Eisenhower's Farewell Warning," Today and Tomorrow, *January 19, 1961.*

President Eisenhower's farewell address will be remembered and quoted in the days to come. Rising above the issues which divide the parties and were the material of the election campaign, he dwelt on a question, never before discussed publicly by any responsible official, which is of profound importance to the nation's future.

The question on which he has been brooding is how in the presence "of an immense military establishment and a large arms industry" the supremacy of the civil power is to be maintained. "In the councils of government," he said, "we must guard against the acquisition of unwarranted influence whether *sought or unsought* by the military-industrial complex." Surely it is impressive that the old soldier should make this warning the main theme of his farewell address. Yet he was in the great tradition. Washington made the theme of his farewell address a warning against allowing the influence of foreign governments to invade our political life. That was then the menace to the civilian power. Now Eisenhower, speaking from his experience and looking ahead, is concerned with a contemporary threat to the supremacy of the civilian power. This is a problem rarely discussed in public, but if it were not a real and serious problem, General Eisenhower would not have devoted to it so much of the emphasis of his last official message to the nation.

He did not mean, of course, that civilian supremacy can or should be upheld by reducing the military power of the military establishment. And as we know, the Kennedy Administration is committed to an increase in the military power of the military establishment. How then can the danger of unwarranted military influence—or to use an old phrase for it, the danger of militarism—be prevented? Only by making civilian influence greater, not by reducing military power.

How is that to be done? Essentially, it can be done by appointing to the civilian posts of decision in the Pentagon, the State Department, and the National Security Council, civilians with some military experience of their own who have had personal experience in public life and possess a trained and educated intelligence. These civilians must work with, they must not defer abjectly to, the professional soldiers. One reason why President Eisenhower has seen the militarist danger grow is that, with the exception of the last one, he never had a Secretary of Defense who was the intellectual equal of the professional soldiers he had to deal with.

Once the civilians have the self-confidence to exercise civilian supremacy, they can and should impose a strict civilian discipline on the statements and speeches issued by the chiefs of staff and by local commanders throughout the world.

The talkativeness of American military men, most of them reading speeches written by professional speech writers who are paid by the government, is an international scandal. Throughout the world it causes us trouble, it causes great loss of respect and confidence. Anyone who travels about the world talking with leaders, be it behind the Iron Curtain or on this side of it, will find himself confronted constantly with the loud talk of some admiral or general. There is not any other military establishment on earth, except perhaps in small disorderly countries, which permits a running commentary on critical affairs by its generals and admirals and the colonels down the line.

The true solution of the problem that President Eisenhower warned the country against is to be found in civilian appointees who are confident and willing to command. When such civilians are in office, it will be possible for the Administration to wean the Congress and portions of the press from their undue reliance upon the military establishment as the true source of the true American policy. For then those who have to deal with our problems will learn by trial and error that the true source of the true policy is among the civilians who make the policy.

4 · *Dictatorship and Democracy*

"Louisiana: Notes on Defense of Free Institutions," Today and Tomorrow, *February 5, 1935.*

The dictatorship of Senator Long presents a question of principle about which there is a dangerous confusion in the minds of many who believe in democracy. The question is whether men must acquiesce in the overthrow of democracy if the dictator can obtain the support of a majority of the voters. I believe there can be only one answer to that question. To answer in the affirmative would be to reduce democracy to an absurdity. It would mean that today's majority had the right to deprive tomorrow's majority of its rights. Who can make such a claim? Who will say that a dictator may use free institutions to destroy free institutions? That a temporary majority may impose its transient will upon all future majorities? That men may use freedom of speech to acquire the power to destroy freedom of speech? That they may use elections to abolish elections? That they may exploit the constitutional guarantees to subvert them?

The idea that a dictatorship may be established by democratic processes is a sophistry. It could be entertained only in an age when men had enjoyed liberty so long that they had forgotten what it means and how it was won.

One can have respect for dictators who overthrow free institutions by force and frankly say they intend to rule by force. But dictators who were elected, and then pretend to rule by popular consent, though they have destroyed the institutions through which the popular will can express itself freely, are practicing an ugly fraud. And those who acquiesce in the tyranny because it was achieved by majority rule are pretending to be convinced when in fact they are cowed.

Free institutions are not the property of any majority. They do not confer upon majorities unlimited powers. The rights of the majority are limited rights. They are limited not only by the constitutional guarantees but by the moral principle implied in those guarantees. That principle is that men may not use the facilities of liberty to impair them. No man may invoke a right in order to destroy it. The right of free speech belongs to those who are willing to preserve it. The right to elect belongs to those who mean to transmit that right to their successors. The rule of the majority is morally justified only if another majority is free to reverse that rule.

To hold any other view than this is to believe that democracy alone, of all forms of government, is prohibited by its own principles from insuring its own preservation. It is high time that free men repudiated so preposterous a doctrine. There is nothing in the principles of democracy which requires a people to surrender democracy or relieves them of the obligation to defend it.

In many countries in the world today there are armed bands of men using the democratic liberties of free assemblage and of free speech to organize for the overthrow of democratic liberties. Is there any doubt that democratic governments have the right to suppress them? If they become strong, that they have the duty to suppress them? That there is no democratic right to destroy democracy and that revolutionists against democracy may be tolerated only if they are so weak as to be negligible?

A free nation can tolerate much, and ordinarily toleration is its best defense. It can tolerate feeble Communist parties and feeble Fascist parties as long as it is certain that they have no hope of success. But once they cease to be debating societies and become formidable organizations for action, they present a challenge which it is suicidal to ignore. They use liberty to assemble force to destroy liberty. When that challenge is actually offered, when it really exists in the judgment of the sober and the well-informed, it is a betrayal of liberty not to defend it with all the power that free men possess.

"Mr. John Strachey's Case and the Law," Today and Tomorrow, *October 13, 1938.*

Not until the rise of communism and then of fascism had any one imagined that civil liberties and the democratic ballot could and would be used to destroy civil liberties and the democratic ballot. Only in the postwar period have we seen the appearence of revolutionary movements which claim all the rights of free men during their march to power and then exterminate all the rights of free men when they have attained power. Only in the last twenty years or so has it been demonstrated how effectively the principles of democracy can be exploited in order to destroy those principles.

In former times democrats have always believed that they could tolerate any agitation, short of open incitement to violence, because by counteragitation and democratic methods they would always have the chance to repair the mischief. But in the postwar era this optimistic assumption has been disproved. It has been demonstrated that after a totalitarian victory, the chance to repair the mischief disappears.

Thus totalitarian revolutionists operating within a democratic regime can lose any number of elections and yet they can always try again. But if the democracy loses one election, it can never try again. That being the case, democrats throughout the world have come to realize in the last ten years that an active and positive defense of democratic institutions is an absolute necessity.

The extent to which the more immediately threatened democracies of Europe have already begun to legislate on the subject is not perhaps fully appreciated here. Thus, for example, all the democratic states of Europe have in recent years enacted laws against private political armies, against political uniforms, and the carrying of symbols which represent semi-military, revolutionary organizations. Laws of this kind were passed in 1933-1934 by Norway, Sweden, Denmark, Finland, The Netherlands, Czechoslovakia, Switzerland, Belgium, and by France and England in 1936. Many of these same nations have laws prohibiting private armies, party militias, bodyguards, and storm troopers. Military training by unauthorized persons is forbidden in Belgium, France, and Great Britain.

Laws have been enacted in Sweden, Norway, Finland, The

Netherlands, and Great Britain making it a criminal offense to conduct propaganda which incites extreme hatred and thus leads to violence, and the right to meet and to parade, when used to provoke trouble, is now regulated in Great Britain.

Many countries have felt compelled to go even further and to restrict freedom of speech and freedom of the press when they are used to defame public authorities and to destroy the dignity of democratic institutions. In the Scandinavian countries specially trained political police have been constituted.

Laws of this kind mark a great departure from the older theories of democracy. But the fact that all the democracies of Europe have felt compelled to turn away from the older tolerance of all agitation is an impressive reminder of the degree to which democracy is on the defensive in the modern world.

Moreover, the problem has by no means been solved by this legislation, and in all probability it is not entirely soluble by repressive laws alone. It is, therefore, a problem which democrats will have to study very carefully. It is a problem which ought to be made the subject of serious study by the most competent people in the land. It should be thoroughly examined in the universities, in the bar associations, in the civic societies, and by legislative commissions. For unless democracy is to commit suicide by consenting to its own destruction, it will have to find some formidable answer to those who come to it saying: "I demand from you in the name of your principles the rights which I shall deny to you later in the name of my principles."

"Two Talks in Rome," Today and Tomorrow, *October 21, 1954.*

Shortly before leaving Rome I had two talks which interested me very much.

One was with an official who is working on the plan for the economic development of Italy. Essentially it is a plan which calls for capital development designed to create productive jobs for the unemployed and the underemployed. The official argued his case with much force and eloquence.

But being an American, I was bound to wonder when he would get around to explaining the American contribution to the plan in the way of credits or grants in aid. He never did get around to that, and finally I asked him whether Italy would be able to execute the plan out of her own resources.

His answer threw much light, I think, on the underlying realities. "If this were a Communist government," he said, "it could carry out the plan without foreign assistance. It would be able to tax. It would be able to compel workers to accept temporarily less pay. It would dare to cut down consumption in all classes. It would form capital by forced savings. It would remove the displaced workers of obsolete industries to other regions. It would impose measures of agricultural improvement. It would be able to do all these things because it would not have to worry about the Chamber of Deputies and about elections and about newspapers and about being put out of office. . . .

"But," he went on to say, "the democratic parties cannot do this even if they wanted to because they are not strong enough as governments to impose so much sacrifice upon the population. So in Italy, which is a free country by a fairly narrow margin, democracy requires subsidies from abroad. It needs them to make up the difference between what can be done by democratic consent and what needs to be done in order to solve economic and social problems."

I had a talk with another man who was much concerned about the revival of fascism. I asked him to spell out his fears in view of the fact that the Neo-Fascists are only a splinter party while the Communists are the most powerful party organization in Italy. "We have decided," he said, "not to surrender the state to the Communists, not to allow them to take power even if circumstances were to give them the legal votes.

"We shall use the whole force of the state to prevent their taking power legally. That in the last resort will be our answer to Communist propaganda. But of course the answer will require actions which will in fact put in charge of our affairs soldiers, policemen, and men who are temporarily akin to the Fascists. So we shall avert the Communist danger but the price may be the loss of our democracy and our liberties."

In reporting these remarks, which reflect one of the crucial issues of the present phase of the cold war, I might say that the danger of fascism is almost certain to be greater or less as the government of the day is weak and ineffectual or is strong and purposeful.

In principle it is clear, it seems to me, that democracies cannot permit totalitarian parties to enjoy civil rights and to win elections and then, having taken over power, to abolish elections and civil rights. If the Italian democratic parties have really decided not to surrender the state, they have in principle taken the right decision.

But the danger of a Fascist reaction lies in the chance that the democratic parties may be too weak and confused to carry out the measures of resistance, that these measures would be carried out furtively, so to speak shamefacedly. With weak democratic government there is a great danger that the democrats would simply be pushed aside, would abdicate their responsibilities, and would leave the dirty work to be done by a minority. If that is so, the great question arises as to whether the basic decision should not now be brought into the open, and publicly declared and its principle openly discussed and vindicated.

The question of principle is whether a free and democratic state has the right to allow institutions to be used by totalitarian parties to destroy freedom and democracy.

5 · *The Totalitarian Counterrevolution*

The Public Philosophy (*1955*), *Chapter 7.*

We are living in a time of massive popular counterrevolution against liberal democracy. It is a reaction to the failure of the West to cope with the miseries and anxieties of the twentieth century. The liberal democracies have been tried and found wanting—found wanting not only in their capacity to govern successfully in this period of wars and upheavals, but also in their ability to defend and maintain the political philosophy that underlies the liberal way of life.

If we go back to the beginnings of the modern democratic movements in the eighteenth century, we can distinguish two diverging lines of development. The one is a way of progress in liberal constitutional democracy. The other is a morbid course of development into totalitarian conditions.

One of the first to realize what was happening was Alexis

de Tocqueville. He foresaw that the "democratic nations are menaced" by a "species of oppression . . . unlike anything that ever before existed in the world." But what is more, he discerned the original difference between the healthy and the morbid development of democracy. . . .

Although the two ways of evolution appear to have the same object—a society with free institutions under popular government—they are radically different and they arrive at radically different ends.

The first way, that of assimilation, presumes the existence of a state which is already constitutional in principle, which is under laws that are no longer arbitrary, though they may be unjust and unequal. Into this constitutional state more and more people are admitted to the governing class and to the voting electorate. The unequal and the unjust laws are revised until eventually all the people have equal opportunities to enter the government and to be represented. Broadly speaking, this has been the working theory of the British movement toward a democratic society at home and also in the Commonwealth and Empire. This, too, was the working theory of the principal authors of the American Constitution, and this was how—though few of them welcomed it—they envisaged the enfranchisement of the whole adult population.

The other way is that of the Jacobin revolution. The people rise to power by overthrowing the ruling class and by liquidating its privileges and prerogatives. This is the doctrine of democratic revolution which was developed by French thinkers in the eighteenth century and was put into practice by the Jacobin party in the French Revolution. In its English incarnation the doctrine became known as Radicalism. In America, though it had its early disciples, notably Tom Paine, not until the era of the Founding Fathers was over, not until the era of Andrew Jackson, did the Jacobin doctrine become the popular political creed of the American democracy. . . .

Of the two rival philosophies, the Jacobin is almost everywhere in the ascendant. It is a ready philosophy for men who, previously excluded from the ruling class, and recently enfranchised, have no part in the business of governing the state, and no personal expectation of being called upon to assume the responsibilities of office. The Jacobin doctrine is an obvious reaction, as de Tocqueville's observation explains, to government by a caste. When there is no opening for the gradualness of reform and for enfranchisement by assimilation, a revolutionary collision is most likely.

The Jacobin doctrine is addressed to the revolutionary collision between the inviolable governing caste and the excluded men claiming the redress of their grievances and their place in the sun. Though it professes to be a political philosophy, the doctrine is not, in fact, a philosophy of government. It is a gospel and also a strategy for revolution. It announces the promise that the crusade which is to overthrow the ruling caste will by the act of revolution create a good society.

The peculiar essence of the dogma is that the revolution itself is the creative act. Toward the revolution as such, because it is the culmination and the climax, all the labor and the sacrifice of the struggle are to be directed. The revolutionary act will remove the causes of evil in human society. Again and again it has been proved how effective is this formula for arousing, sustaining, and organizing men's energies for revolution: to declare that evil in society has been imposed upon the many by the few—by priests, nobles, capitalists, imperialists, liberals, aliens—and that evil will disappear when the many who are pure have removed these few who are evil.

The summons to revolution in the *Communist Manifesto* in 1848 uses the same formula as the Jacobins had used a half century earlier. Marx and Engels were men steeped in the Western revolutionary tradition, and habituated, therefore, to the notion that the act of revolution removes the source of evil and creates the perfect society. The French Revolution had not made this perfect society. For by 1848 there were the capitalist oppressors. Marx and Engels called for the next revolutionary act, announcing that now the Third Estate, the bourgeois capitalists, needed to go the way of the liquidated nobles and clergy.

This is the formula: that when the revolution of the masses is victorious over the few, there will exist the classless society without coercion and violence and with freedom for all. This formula reappears whenever conditions are revolutionary—that is to say, when necessary reforms are being refused. The formula is the strategy of rebellion of those who are unable to obtain the redress of grievances. The rulers are to be attacked. So they are isolated. They are few. So they are not invincible. They bear the total guilt of all the sufferings and grievances of men. To remove them is then to cure all evil. Therefore their overthrow, which is feasible, will be worth every sacrifice. Since the world will be good when the evil few have been overthrown, there is no need for the doubts and the disputes which would arise among the revolutionists if they had to make serious practical decisions on the problems of the post-revolutionary world.

The Public Philosophy (1955), *Chapter 6.*

We can learn something about the kind of incapacity which has brought on disaster for the modern democracies by the nature of the counterrevolutions that have undermined and overthrown so many of them. There are various types of counterrevolutions. The most notable are the Soviet Communist, Italian Fascist, German National Socialist, Spanish Falangist, Portuguese Corporatist, the Titoist, and Peronist. . . . Besides these organized counterrevolutionary movements, professing doctrines of an anti-liberal and undemocratic character, there is, in large areas of the world, a very strong tendency to nullify the democratic system behind the façade of democratic institutions. The countries where elections are free and genuine, where civil liberty is secure, are still powerful. But they embrace a shrinking minority of mankind.

Now in all these counterrevolutionary movements there are two common characteristics. One is the separation of the governing power from the large electorate. In the totalitarian states this is done by not holding free elections; in the great number of non-totalitarian but also non-democratic states, it is done by controlling and rigging the elections.

The other common characteristic of the counterrevolutions is that political power, which is taken away from the electorate, the parties, and the party bosses, is then passed to an elite corps marked off from the mass of the people by special training and by special vows. The totalitarian revolutions generally liquidate the elite of the old regime, and then recruit their own elite of specially trained and specially dedicated and highly disciplined men. Elsewhere, when the liberal democratic system fails, the new rulers are drawn from the older established elites—from the army officers, from the clergy, the higher bureaucracy, and the diplomatic corps, from university professors.

It is significant that in the reaction against the practical failure of the democratic states, we find always that the electoral process is shut down to a minimum or shut off entirely, and that the executive function is taken over—more often than not with popular assent—by men with a special training and a special personal commitment to the business of ruling the state. In the enfeebled democracies the politicians have with rare exceptions been men without sure tenure of office. Many of the most important are novices, improvisers, and amateurs. After a counterrevolution has brought them down, their successors are almost certain to be either the elite of the new revolutionary party, or an elite drawn from predemocratic institutions like the army, the church, and the bureaucracy.

In their different ways—which ideologically may be at opposite ends of the world—the post-democratic rulers are men set apart from the masses of the people. They are not set apart only because they have the power to arrest others and to shoot them. They would not long hold on to that kind of power. They have also an aura of majesty, which causes them to be obeyed. That aura emanates from the popular belief that they have subjected themselves to a code and are under a discipline by which they are dedicated to ends that transcend their personal desires and their own private lives.

The nature of the counterrevolution reflects a radical deficiency in the modern liberal democratic state. This deficiency is . . . the enfeeblement and virtual paralysis of the executive governing functions. The strong medicine of the counterrevolution is needed, on the one hand, to stop the electoral process from encroaching upon and invading the government, and, on the other hand, to invest the government not only with all material power but also with the imponderable force of majesty.

It is possible to govern a state without giving the masses of the people full representation. But it is not possible to go on for long without a government which can and does in fact govern. If, therefore, the people find that they must choose whether they will be represented in an assembly which is incompetent to govern, or whether they will be governed without being represented, there is no doubt at all as to how the issue will be decided. They will choose authority, which promises to be paternal, in preference to freedom, which threatens to be fratricidal. For large communities cannot do without being governed. No ideal of freedom and of democracy will long be allowed to stand in the way of their being governed.

The plight of the modern democracies is serious. They have suffered great disasters in this century and the consequences of these disasters are compounding themselves. The end is not yet clear. The world that is safe for democracy and is safely democratic is shrunken. It is still shrinking. For the disorder which has been incapacitating the democracies in this century is, if anything, becoming more virulent as time goes on.

A continuing practical failure to govern will lead—no one can say in what form and under what banners—to counterrevolutionary measures for the establishment of strong government. The alternative is to withstand and to reverse the descent toward counterrevolution. It is a much harder way. It demands popular assent to radical measures which will restore government strong enough to govern, strong enough to resist the encroachment of the assemblies and of mass opinions, and strong enough to guarantee private liberty against the pressure of the masses.

It would be foolish to attempt to predict whether the crisis of the democratic state will be resolved by such an internal restoration and revival or by counterrevolution. No doubt the danger of counterrevolution is greater in countries where the margins of life are thinner. No doubt the prospects of a restoration and revival are best in countries where the traditions of civility, as the public philosophy of Western society, have deep roots and a long history.

6 · *The Portent of the Moon*

"The Portent of the Moon," Today and Tomorrow, *October 10, 1957.*

The few who are allowed to know about such things, and are able to understand them, are saying that the launching of so big a satellite signifies that the Soviets are much ahead of this country in the development of rocket missiles. Their being so much ahead cannot be the result of some kind of lucky guess in inventing a gadget. It must be that there is a large body of Soviet scientists, engineers, and production men, plus many highly developed subsidiary industries, all successfully directed and co-ordinated, and bountifully financed.

In short, the fact that we have lost the race to launch the satellite means that we are losing the race to produce ballistic missiles. This in turn means that the United States and the Western world may be falling behind in the progress of science and technology.

This is a grim business. It is grim, in my mind at least, not because I think the Soviets have such a lead in the race of armaments that we may soon be at their mercy. Not at all. It is a grim business because a society cannot stand still. If it loses the momentum of its own progress, it will deteriorate and decline, lacking purpose and losing confidence in itself.

The critical question is how we as a people, from the President down, will respond to what is a profound challenge to our cultural values—not to the ideal of the American way of life but to the way in fact we have been living our life. One response could be to think of it all in terms of propaganda, and to look around for some device for doing something spectacular to outmatch what the Russians have done. The other response would be to look inward upon ourselves, and to concern ourselves primarily with our own failings, and to be determined not so much to beat the Russians as to cure ourselves.

The question then might be defined in this way: why is it that in the twelve years that have passed since the end of World War II, the United States which was so far in the lead has been losing its lead to the Russians who at the end of the war were so nearly prostrate? Mr. Khrushchev would say, no doubt, that this is because communism is superior to capitalism. But that answer really begs the question, which is not why the Soviets have moved ahead so fast but why we, who had moved very fast, have not been moving fast enough. For while our society is undoubtedly progressive, it has not in the postwar years been progressive enough.

I do not pretend to know the whole answer to what is for us and for our future so fateful a question. But I venture to think that even now we can discern certain trends that since the World War have appeared in American life and must be taken into account.

We must put first, I think, the enormous prosperity in which, as the politicians have put it to the voters, the private standard of life is paramount as against the public standard of life. By the public standard of life I mean such necessities as defense, education, science, technology, the arts. Our people have been led to believe in the enormous fallacy that the highest purpose of the American social order is to multiply the enjoyment of consumer goods. As a result, our public institutions, particularly those having to do with education and research, have been, as compared with the growth of our population, scandalously starved.

We must put second, I think, a general popular disrespect for, and even suspicion of, brains and originality of thought. In other countries, in Germany and in most of Europe and in Russia, it is an honor, universally recognized, to be a professor. Here it is something to put a man on the defensive, requiring him to show that he is not a highbrow and that he is not subversive.

What McCarthyism did to the inner confidence of American scientists and thinkers has constituted one of the great national tragedies of the postwar era. It is impossible to measure the damage. But the damage that was done was very great. It was done in the kind of thinking where the difference between creation and routine lies in the special courage to follow the truth wherever it leads.

With prosperity acting as a narcotic, with Philistinism and McCarthyism rampant, our public life has been increasingly doped and without purpose. With the President in a kind of partial retirement, there is no standard raised to which the people can repair. Thus we drift with no one to state our purposes and to make policy, into a chronic disaster like Little Rock. We find ourselves then without a chart in very troubled waters.

"Explorer and Sputnik," Today and Tomorrow, *February 4, 1958.*

The American satellite Explorer has made us all feel better, having given tangible proof that the science of rocketry is known in this country and that our experts possess the art of making and guiding rockets. The event has confirmed the testimony of those who have been saying that the Russians have a considerable lead but that we are in the race.

Explorer is, therefore, a good popular antidote to the panicky view that we are in mortal danger. But it does not wash out the main portent of Sputnik—which is not that the Russians launched a satellite first, and that their satellite is very much bigger and heavier than Explorer. The main portent is that, starting at the end of World War II with their country devastated, their technology far more primitive than our own, the Russians have achieved a *rate* of scientific and technological development which is faster than our own. What they did with the Sputnik shows not merely that they have mastered a particular specialty but that they have generated a termendous momentum in the physical sciences and their application.

Though Explorer is in the sky, there is no reason to think that the comparative rate of development is now back in balance, much less that it is in our favor. We are still the bigger and the stronger. But they are still moving forward the faster.

There is, therefore, much for us to do, and as I see it we must move forward simultaneously along three broad paths. The first is that we have to find out how to make the government much better able than it is now to take and to carry out long-range decisions. There is little doubt that American progress in missiles has been retarded by bureaucratic confusion presided over by political appointees who did not understand the issues they were supposed to decide.

Undoubtedly, this requires a reorganization in the Pentagon. But the trouble will not be cured in the Pentagon alone. The White House and the relevant committees of Congress have at least an equal responsibility.

The second path we must take is even broader. It is the transformation of American education which on the average and by and large is declining in quality as the quantity of those to be educated grows larger and larger. Our schools and colleges are overwhelmed by the growth of the population they are supposed to educate, and they are under enormous pressure—for the most part irresistible—to lower their intellectual standards. There is an ominous tendency in American education to teach more and more students less and less of the great disciplines which form an educated man.

It is in this, more than in the ups and downs in the military balance of power, that there lies the deepest danger to our American society. We can most surely defend ourselves against conquest or domination. What we have to worry about is that with the declining level of education, with the vulgarization of the cultural standards in our mass society, we shall become a big but second-rate people, fat, Philistine, and self-indulgent.

The third path on which we must travel is to learn to adjust our minds to the hard facts of life—particularly to the fact that our Western society, of which we are the strongest member, is no longer paramount, is now only an equal, among the great societies of the globe.

Britain and France have had to learn in this generation what Sweden and Spain learned in earlier days—that they are no longer the main centers of power and influence for all mankind. At the end of World War II for a few short years the United States was the paramount center of power and influence in the world. Our conception of our role, as we have formed it in the postwar years, has had as its fundamental premise the paramountcy of the Western society led by the United States. This was a fact. But it was transitory.

The postwar era is ending and the great reality to which we have now to adjust our thinking is that we are an equal but not a paramount power.

"The Country Is Waiting for Another Innovator," Life, *XLVIII (June 20, 1960), 114.*

If, as so many of us think today, we are now without such a general and inspired sense of national purpose, where shall we look for the cause and the remedy?

The cause of the vacancy is, I believe, this: we have reached a point in our internal development and in our relations with the rest of the world where we have fulfilled and outlived most of what we used to regard as the program of our national purposes.

We are rather like a man whose purpose it is to cross the continent, and having started from New York he has gotten to Chicago. Which way shall he go then? There is more than one way to cross the continent, and until he has chosen which way and then has worked out the intermediate stops, he will remain in Chicago, feeling worried and without a sense of direction and of clear purpose.

As I see it, the American people today are like the man who got to Chicago, and needs a new road map to show him the way from there on.

In this century, the sense of national purpose has been a composite wrought under three innovating Presidents, under Theodore Roosevelt, Woodrow Wilson, and Franklin Roosevelt.

They led the country on the road which it has taken for some fifty years—since America emerged as a great power in the world, and since here at home it has become an ever more industrialized and urbanized society.

Time has passed and history has not stood still. The Roosevelt-Wilson-Roosevelt formulae and policies and programs no longer fit the character of the world Americans are now concerned with, the world as it has developed since the Second World War. We are now waiting to be shown the way into the future. We are waiting for another innovator in the line of the two Roosevelts and Wilson.

The innovator for whom the country is waiting will not come with a new revelation of the ultimate ends and commitments of our society. The ultimate ends are fixed. They are lasting and they are not disputed. The nation is dedicated to freedom. It is dedicated to the rights of man and to government with the consent of the governed. The innovation, which is now beginning, will be in the means, in the policies and programs and measures, by which the ultimate ends of our free society can be realized in the world today.

My thesis is that to affirm the ultimate ends—as every public man does in almost every speech—is not a substitute for, is not the equivalent of, declaring our national purpose and of leading the nation. These affirmations are like standing up when "The Star-Spangled Banner" is played, and then doing nothing further about anything. They beg the question, which is not whither the nation should go, but how it should get there.

The remedy, then, will not be found in the restatement of our ideals, however resounding the rhetoric. It will be found in the innovation of the political formulae, the concrete measures, the practical programs, by which our ideals can be realized in the greatly changed world we now live in. I feel sure that innovators will appear with the new generation that is rising to power. For it is not the nation which is old, but only its leaders. . . .

In the fifteen years which have passed since the end of the Second World War, the condition of mankind has changed more rapidly and more deeply than in any other period within the experience of the American people. There has been a swift and radical change in the balance of power in the world. Among the masses of the people in the underdeveloped countries there is in all the continents a mounting revolution. There is a radical change in the technology of war and in the technology of industry. There is in the United States and in the advanced countries a great and threatening agglomeration of peoples in cities. There is a menacing increase in the population of the world. There is a development of the mass media of communication which, because it marks a revolution in popular education and in the presentation of information, and in the very nature of debate and deliberation, is affecting profoundly the assumptions of the older democratic system.

Nobody, it is fair to say, not the most sensitive and knowing among us, is as yet able to realize fully what all these changes mean and to point out specifically and with sufficient clarity how this country should deal with them. But what we do know is that the formulations of national purpose which were made in the first half of this century are now inadequate. In part we have fulfilled them. In part we have outlived them. In part they have become irrelevant because of the unexpected changes in the condition of things. In part they are out of focus. All in all, they do not now mobilize our energies.

Necessity will again be the mother of invention, and in the time to come we shall close the gap which now exists between the new realities and the old formulations of our national purpose. I do not presume to anticipate the innovators for whom we are waiting. But there is already visible, it seems to me, the shape of the land across which the innovators must lead the nation.

Thus for the first time in American experience we are confronted with a rival power which denies the theory and the practice of our society, and has forced upon us a competition for the leadership of the world. This challenge coincides with the radically new fact that the oceans have ceased to be our ramparts and that our land is no longer invulnerable.

As there is no chance that our immensely formidable rival will disarm or disappear, we shall have to live in the same world with him. We shall have to solve problems which did not exist for Wilson and for the two Roosevelts. We shall have to devise ways of protecting our vital interests, which are world-wide, and we shall have to do this without precipitating an insoluble crisis that would generate an inevitable war. This will demand a deep reformulation of our foreign policy, which has hitherto been, and in a great part still is, addressed to a very different world situation. It will demand a re-education of American opinion, not only when it yearns for the lost innocence of our old isolation but also when it plunges into a new globalism which supposes that we are omnipotent, and averts its eyes from the hard reality of the power of the Communist bloc.

We know, of course, that the challenge is a broad one. The competition is in the whole field of national power. It is a competition not only in military power but in all forms of power, the power to produce wealth and the power to use wealth for education, for the advancement of science and for public as well as private ends.

On our success in achieving military security by arms and by an astute diplomacy depend our national existence. Our ability to meet the whole challenge depends upon our success in learning to use our growing wealth for something more than more and more private satisfaction. It depends upon our being able and willing to use it for imponderable and immaterial ends, like science and education and the public amenities.

To use increments of our growing wealth wisely and prudently for public and immaterial ends: that is the goal, so I believe, toward which our national purpose will now be directed. We have to pay for defense, and there can be no serious dispute that we must pay for it. But we have also to be able and willing to pay for the things which cannot be consumed privately, such as the education of children, the development of beautiful cities, and the advancement of knowledge. We have to be able and willing to pay for what is, to put it briefly, civilization itself.

At bottom, we have to do these things because they need to be done, because they have to be done, and because they are supremely worth doing. Even if we were not challenged, we would need to do them for their own sake. We would need to do them even if the Soviet Union and the whole Communist orbit were still where they were fifty years ago.

But now we are in fact challenged, and because of that we must do these civilized things, not only to make a better life for ourselves but in order to mobilize the power to avoid a much worse life. Were there no great rival and challenger, we might dawdle along, we might indulge in a growing private affluence while we suffered a declining national greatness. But for us there is no choice but to respond to the challenge, even though this demands that we change many of our cherished dogmas and harden ourselves to a sterner way of life. For our freedom and our system of democratic government are not likely to survive just because we believe in them and enjoy them. We shall have to prove that with them and through them we can satisfy the needs of our people and be equal to the challenge of the time we live in.

Western freedom will not survive just because it is a noble ideal. In the age we live in it will survive if, and I think only if, we can take freedom down with us into the hurly-burly of the competition and conflict and prove that a free society can make itself the good society.

. . . With all the danger and trouble and worry it causes us, the Soviet challenge may yet prove to have been a blessing in disguise. For without it, what would become of us if we felt that we were invulnerable, if our influence in the world were undisputed, if we had no need to prove that we can rise above a comfortable, tranquil self-satisfaction?

We would, I feel sure, slowly deteriorate and fall apart, having lost our great energies because we did not exercise them, having lost our daring because everything was so warm and so comfortable and so cozy. We would then have entered into the decline which has marked the closing period in the history of so many societies—when they have gotten everything they wanted, when they have come to think that there is no great work to be done, and that the purpose of life is to hold on and stay put. For then the night has come and they doze off and they begin to die.

7 · *The Challenge of Greatness*

"Reflections on Sidonius," Today and Tomorrow, *December 25, 1937.*

To the men of our time who inherit the ideas which have been current in the West during the past three or four centuries, it must always seem an anomaly that civilization should have a frontier, whether on the Rhine, the Vistula, or the Amur. . . .

Unlike any people of the past, we have ceased to think that civilizations have frontiers at which the barbarian must be held back; we had fallen into the habit of thinking that our civilization is destined to be universal and that all the peoples of the globe can and will participate in it.

In the hundred years between the Battle of Waterloo and the Battle of the Marne, the spiritual leaders of the West came to think it self-evident that there would be a steady progress toward a universal civilization. And it is by this criterion that the generation which knew the prewar world judge the condition of the present world; because their hopes were pitched so high, their discouragement has sunk so deep.

Yet if, as events would seem to declare, we must for our generation give up the hope of a steady and predestined advance toward a universal civilization, we can at least remember that it is our hope, perhaps our illusion, that we must revise. To a degree, which it is impossible to estimate, the prewar generations seem to have thought that the docility and unawakened lethargy of the great masses of mankind was the same thing as sympathy with the progress which was so impressive. A generation ago, the vast Russian, Chinese, Indian, and Arab masses, a great majority of mankind, lay quietly within their immemorial customs, and within the Western nations themselves the working classes and the peasantry expected little, and were easily satisfied.

When the progressive minority in Western Europe and America broadcast civilization to all the quarters of the globe, and, by universal education, forced it down through all ranks of society, they little realized that the first effect of this progress must be to startle these masses of men out of their ancient lethargy, to destroy the customs which had held them quiet, to bring them forward not as grateful receivers of blessings provided, but as active, clamorous, contentious men insisting upon their own notions of their own just deserts.

Thus it was the advance of civilization which aroused the masses of mankind from the lethargy and peace of ancient custom, and it is from these awakened masses that there arise all the pressures and tensions throughout the world. They are tremendous. No government can survive that does not respond to them; it is in the heat of this awakening that the fierce passions of our age are generated.

From this condition there is no retreat. For when the sleeper awakes, he cannot be put to sleep again. Nor in the long view could any one wish that he should sleep again. With that great fact the discouraged prewar generation must come to terms, finding, if not personal hope in the immediate prospect, then philosophy to understand it. They must come to see that their hopes were founded on an illusion, the illusion that the great masses of men could enter into civilization quietly, without first going through the immense, the catastrophic, agitation of their own awakening, that a world-wide civilization could come into being without the labor pains of so great a birth.

Perhaps it is this that we must learn, that the destiny which men dreamed of in the prewar world works in a way we had not imagined, that before the masses of men can achieve their destiny, they must pass through, perhaps for many long generations, the terrifying experience of opening their eyes as they emerge from the dark security of the womb of ancient custom.

"Reflection After Armistice Day," Today and Tomorrow, *November 12, 1931.*

The tempo of history is hard to judge correctly, and therefore, at a time like this, men divide, some despairing because their hopes of a better day are not yet fulfilled, some confirmed in their belief that such hopes can never be fulfilled. But if we look into the future with eyes that have seen the past, we dare not make our judgments by the transient events which are recorded on the front pages of daily newspapers. It is a slow and complex business between Germany and France. There is a new epoch in Asia. It is a gigantic task to organize mankind. But let us remember that it required eighty years before a national authority was indisputably established here. Let us remember that Germany, France, and Italy are, as we know them politically, not so old as many men who are still alive. It is false to hope for much quickly and it is false to lose hope quickly. The movement of history always deceives us when we look near-sightedly at any phase of it.

It is the gift of civilized man, the surest mark to distinguish him, that he can at times see through the transient and the complicated to the simple and the certain, and that he can live by that vision, and with it master or endure his lot. It is by this gift that multitudes in our Western world are today sustained through all the disorders and disappointments about them. They know that the processes of history point unmistakably to the necessity of a world-wide organization of man. They know that the inexorable pressure of the machines man has invented, of the liberties he has achieved, of the methods by which he gets his living compel him to forge unity out of the anarchy of separate states. The prophecy is as certain as it was that the American colonies had to unite, that the German principalities had to sink their differences, that the Italian communes could not forever go each its own way.

How long it will take for the prophecy to be fulfilled, no one can say. That is guesswork, and prophecy is not guessing. Prophecy is seeing the necessary amidst confusion and insignificance, and by the light which it furnishes to see more clearly how to act with purpose. The prophecy of a world moving toward political unity is the light which guides all that is best, most vigorous, most truly alive in the work of our time. It gives sense to what we are doing. Nothing else does. Without it, without the conviction that all this negotiating, and planning, and bargaining and debating is a struggle for unity and peace, it would in reality be as pointless and insane as almost daily it appears to be.

"The Rise of the United States," Today and Tomorrow, *September 11, 1945.*

Thanks to those who gave their lives, and to all who have suffered and toiled, the United States has been delivered from its most dangerous enemies and has been raised to a leading place of power and influence throughout the world. Their achievement is clear and unmistakable amidst all the complications and difficulties of the demobilization and the pacification in the wake of so great a war.

Never before have the young men of any American generation had spread out before them such a prospect of a long peace within which there is so much they can do that is useful and fascinating. There never was a better time than this to be an American and to be young, nor a more interesting one in which to be alive. The time to come is peculiarly their own because they have themselves earned it and done so much to make it possible. They are not merely the heirs of stronger and more resolute forefathers but they are, once again, a generation of explorers, discoverers, and pioneers, who can become the founders of good and enduring things. The opportunity can, of course, be stupidly and lazily missed. But if it is used, as it can be, there is no reason to doubt that this cycle of twentieth-century wars is over, and that Americans have at their disposal all that they need in order to take a foremost part in inaugurating an age that mankind will long remember gratefully.

Great works are not for the faint-hearted who doubt themselves. Yet only with that humility which opens men's minds to wisdom, can greatness be understood. We have much that we must learn to understand. When a nation rises as suddenly as we have risen in the world, it needs above all to measure its power in the scheme of things. For it is easier to develop great power than it is to know how to use it well. Wisdom always lags behind power, and for the newcomer, which is what we are, the lag is bound to be greater than in an old established state where the exercise of world power is a matter of long experience and settled habit.

Even more than the Soviet Union, which is now resuming its connection with Russia's past, the United States is the newest world power. We have never been a world power before, and we might say that in relation to the world we are just now at the end of our colonial experience and at the beginning of the time when all great affairs are as a matter of course American affairs. For isolationism, as it has persisted in our day, is in essence the view of the colonial who feels that the great affairs of history are not for the likes of him, and that he must live in a world which is ruled mysteriously from afar by others, who are shrewder if less righteous than he is.

An awareness that the great power we now possess is newly acquired is the best antidote we can carry about with us against our moral and political immaturity. There is no more difficult art than to exercise great power well; all the serious military, diplomatic, and economic decisions we have now to take will depend on how correctly we measure our power, how truly we see its possibilities *within* its limitations. That is what Germany and Japan, which also rose suddenly, did not do; those two mighty empires are in ruins because their leaders and their people misjudged their newly acquired power, and so misused it.

Our own position in the world is fully recognized, and our real interests are such that they need never be hidden. But there are many pitfalls for a nation which is not yet accustomed to the exercise of great power. We can be honest with ourselves, then, and recognize that nothing is so tempting as to overestimate one's own influence and to underestimate one's own responsibilities, to be more interested in the rights than in the duties of a powerful state, and like so many of the newly rich and just arrived to be jealously fearful of losing privileges which, in fact, can in the long run be retained only by using them well. Nothing is easier, too, than to dissipate influence by exerting it for trivial or private ends, or to forget that power is not given once and forever but that it has to be replenished continually by the effort which created it in the first place. The wisdom which may make great powers beneficent can be found only with humility, and also the good manners and courtesy of the soul which alone can make great power acceptable to others.

Great as it is, American power is limited. Within its limits, it will be greater or less depending on the ends for which it is used. It is, for example, altogether beyond the limits of any power we possess to dictate to any one of our allies, even the smallest, how it must organize its social and economic order. We can preserve our own order if we improve so that it produces progressively that greater freedom and plenty which we believe it can produce. By proving the results, not by declaiming generalities and making threats, we can offer an example which others may wish to follow if and as they have the means to do so.

In regard to our military power, including the atomic bomb, we must have no illusions whatsoever. It is sufficient, if properly maintained, to make the United States invulnerable to conquest by any other nation. But no military power we can conceivably muster can keep us secure if we dissolve our alliances, if we provoke or permit the other great states to combine against us. Friendly and reliable neighbors on both sides of our ocean frontiers are indispensable to our security and to our peace of mind. It would be as childish as it is churlish to think that because of the atomic bomb, or the prodigious size of our industry, we can now dismiss the friends with whom we fought the good fight side by side.

Nor must we fall into the trap of imagining that the devastating power we brought to bear upon our enemies can be used to enforce our arguments with our allies. Our influence is great, perhaps leading, but it is not commensurate with the alleged fact that we possess a weapon which could, theoretically, kill several hundred thousand people without notice and at one blow. If we are intelligent, we shall never entertain such a monstrous delusion. We could no more use such a weapon in such a way than we could hire thugs to assassinate foreign statesmen with whom we disagree. But if we allow fools among us to brandish the atomic bomb with the idea that it is a political argument, we shall certainly end by convincing the rest of the world that their own safety and dignity compel them to unite against us.

Our power and influence will endure only if we measure them truly and use them for the ends that we have always avowed and can proclaim with pride. We are the latest great power developed by and committed to the tradition of the West. We are among the bearers of this tradition, and we are numbered now among its proudest defenders. That is the polestar by which we must set our course. At the center of that tradition resides the conviction that man's dignity rises from his ability to reason and thus to choose freely the good in preference to evil. We may claim without offense that this inner principle of the Western tradition is not local, tribal, or national, but universal, and in so far as we are its faithful servants, we shall, in learning how to use our power, win the consent of mankind.

"To Ourselves Be True," Today and Tomorrow, *May 9, 1961.*

We have been forced to ask ourselves recently how a free and open society can compete with a totalitarian state. This is a crucial question. Can our Western society survive and flourish if it remains true to its own faith and principles? Or must it abandon them in order to fight fire with fire?

There are those who believe that in Cuba the attempt to fight fire with fire would have succeeded if only the President had been more ruthless and had had no scruples about using American forces. I think they are wrong. I think that success for the Cuban adventure was impossible. In a free society like ours a policy is bound to fail which deliberately violates our pledges and our principles, our treaties and our laws. It is not possible for a free and open society to organize successfully a spectacular conspiracy.

The United States, like every other government, must employ secret agents. But the United States cannot successfully conduct large secret conspiracies. It is impossible to keep them secret. It is impossible for everybody concerned, beginning with the President himself, to be sufficiently ruthless and unscrupulous. The American conscience is a reality. It will make hesitant and ineffectual, even if it does not prevent, an un-American policy. The ultimate reason why the Cuban affair was incompetent is that it was out of character, like a cow that tried to fly or a fish that tried to walk.

It follows that in the great struggle with communism, we must find our strength by developing and applying our own principles, not in abandoning them. Before anyone tells me that this is sissy, I should like to say why I believe it. Especially after listening carefully and at some lengths to Mr. Khrushchev, I am very certain that we shall have the answer to Mr. Khrushchev if, but only if, we stop being fascinated by the cloak and dagger business and, being true to ourselves, take our own principles seriously.

Mr. K. is a true believer that communism is destined to supplant capitalism as capitalism supplanted feudalism. For him this is an absolute dogma, and he will tell you that while he intends to do what he can to assist the inevitable, knowing that we will do what we can to oppose the inevitable, what he does and what we do will not be decisive. Destiny will be realized no matter what men do.

The dogma of inevitability not only gives him the self-assurance of a man who has no doubts but is a most powerful ingredient of the Communist propaganda. What do we say to him, we who believe in a certain freedom of the human will and in the capacity of men to affect the course of history by their discoveries, their wisdom, and their courage?

We can say that in Mr. K.'s dogma there is an unexamined premise. It is that the capitalist society is static, that it is and always will be what it was when Marx described it a hundred years ago, that—to use Mr. K.'s own lingo—there is no difference between Governor Rockefeller and his grandfather. Because a capitalist society cannot change, in its dealings with the underdeveloped countries it can only dominate and exploit. It cannot emancipate and help. If it could emancipate and help, the inevitability of communism would evaporate.

I venture to argue from this analysis that the reason we are on the defensive in so many places is that for some ten years we have been doing exactly what Mr. K. expects us to do. We have used money and arms in a long losing attempt to stabilize native governments which, in the name of anti-communism, are opposed to all important social change. This has been exactly what Mr. K.'s dogma calls for—that communism should be the only alternative to the status quo with its immemorial poverty and privilege.

We cannot compete with communism in Asia, Africa, or Latin America if we go on doing what we have done so often and so widely—which is to place the weak countries in a dilemma where they must stand still with us and our client rulers, or start moving with the Communists. This dilemma cannot be dissolved unless it is our central and persistent and unswerving policy to offer these unhappy countries a third option, which is economic development and social improvement without the totalitarian discipline of communism.

For the only real alternative to communism is a liberal and progressive society.

III

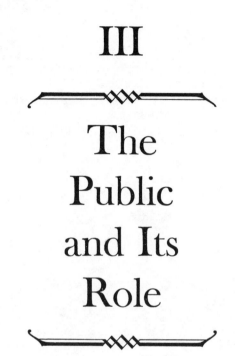

The Public and Its Role

1 · *The Public and The People*

The Public Philosophy (*1955*), *Chapter 3.*

It is necessary at the outset to reduce the ambiguity of the term "the people." For it has two different meanings, which it may be convenient to distinguish typographically. When we speak of popular sovereignty, we must know whether we are talking about The People, as voters, or about *The People,* as a community of the entire living population, with their predecessors and successors.

It is often assumed, but without warrant, that the opinions of The People as voters can be treated as the expression of the interests of *The People* as an historic community. The crucial problem of modern democracy arises from the fact that this assumption is false. The voters cannot be relied upon to represent *The People*. The opinions of voters in elections are not to be accepted unquestioningly as true judgments of the vital interests of the community. . . .

Because of the discrepancy between The People as voters

and *The People* as the corporate nation, the voters have no title to consider themselves the proprietors of the commonwealth and to claim that their interests are identical with the public interest. A prevailing plurality of the voters are not *The People.* The claim that they are is a bogus title invoked to justify the usurpation of the executive power by representative assemblies and the intimidation of public men by demagogic politicians. In fact, demagoguery can be described as the sleight of hand by which a faction of The People as voters are invested with the authority of *The People.* That is why so many crimes are committed in the people's name.

There are eminent political philosophers who reject this analytical distinction. Those who are strongly nominalist in their cast of mind, which modern men tend to be, look upon the abstract concept of a corporate people as mere words and rather like conjuring up spooks. Thus, according to that resolute nominalist, Jeremy Bentham, "the community is a fictitious *body,* composed of the individual persons who are considered as constituting as it were its *members.* The interest of the community then is, what?—The sum of the interests of the several members who compose it."

There is an apparent toughness and empirical matter-of-factness in this statement. But the hard ice is thin. For Bentham has forgotten that "the several members who compose" the community are never identically the same members from one hour to another. If a community were what he says it is, then in theory it should be possible to make a directory of its members, each with his address. But no such list could ever be compiled. While it was being compiled, new members would be being born and old members would be dying. That is why it makes no sense to describe "The People of the United States" who ordained and established the Constitution as the inhabitants of the United States on that particular June 21, 1788, when the Constitution was established and ordained. Between sunrise and sunset of that historic day the persons composing *The People* had changed. In thirty years they had changed greatly; and in a hundred years, entirely.

The people, then, is not only, as Bentham assumed, the aggregate of living persons. The people is also the stream of individuals, the connected generations of changing persons, that Burke was talking about when he invoked the partnership "not only between those who are living" but also with "those who are dead, and those who are to be born." *The People* are a corporation, an entity, that is to say, which lives on while individuals come into it and go out of it.

For this reason Bentham cannot have been right when he said that the interests of the community are no more than the sum of the interests of the several members who happen to compose it at any particular instant of time. He cannot have been right when he said that "the happiness of the individuals, of whom a community is composed, that is their pleasures and their security, is the end and the sole end which the legislator ought to have in view."

For besides the happiness and the security of the individuals of whom a community is at any moment composed, there are also the happiness and the security of the individuals of whom generation after generation it will be composed. If we think of it in terms of individual persons, the corporate body of *The People* is for the most part invisible and inaudible. Indeed, as a whole it is nonexistent, in that so many are dead and so many are not yet born. Yet this corporate being, though so insubstantial to our senses, binds, in Burke's words, a man to his country with "ties which though light as air, are as strong as links of iron." That is why young men die in battle for their country's sake and why old men plant trees they will never sit under.

This invisible, inaudible, and so largely nonexistent community gives rational meaning to the necessary objectives of government. If we deny it, identifying the people with the prevailing pluralities who vote in order to serve, as Bentham has it, "their pleasures and their security," where and what is the nation, and whose duty and business is it to defend the public interest? Bentham leaves us with the state as an arena in which factions contend for their immediate advantage in the struggle for survival and domination. Without the invisible and transcendent community to bind them, why should they care for posterity? And why should posterity care about them, and about their treaties and their contracts, their commitments and their promises? Yet without these engagements to the future, they could not live and work; without these engagements the fabric of society is unraveled and shredded.

The Public Philosophy (*1955*), *Chapter 4.*

We are examining the question of how, and by whom, the interest of an invisible community over a long span of time is represented in the practical work of governing a modern state.

In ordinary circumstances voters cannot be expected to transcend their particular, localized, and self-regarding opinions. As well expect men laboring in the valley to see the land as from a mountain top. In their circumstances, which as private persons they cannot readily surmount, the voters are most likely to suppose that whatever seems obviously good to them must be good for the country, and good in the sight of God.

I am far from implying that the voters are not entitled to the representation of their particular opinions and interests. But their opinions and interests should be taken for what they are and for no more. They are not—as such—propositions in the public interest. Beyond their being, if they are genuine, a true report of what various groups of voters are thinking, they have no intrinsic authority. The Gallup polls are reports of what people are thinking. But that a plurality of the people sampled in the poll think one way has no bearing upon whether it is sound public policy. For their opportunities of judging great issues are in the very nature of things limited, and the statistical sum of their opinions is not the final verdict on an issue. It is, rather, the beginning of the argument. In that argument their opinions need to be confronted by the views of the executive, defending and promoting the public interest. In the accommodation reached between the two views lies practical public policy.

Let us ask ourselves, How is the public interest discerned and judged? From what we have been saying we know that we cannot answer the question by attempting to forecast what the invisible community, with all its unborn constituents, will, would, or might say if and when it ever had a chance to vote. There is no point in toying with any notion of an imaginary plebiscite to discover the public interest. We cannot know what we ourselves will be thinking five years hence, much less what infants now in the cradle will be thinking when they go into the polling booth.

Yet their interests, as we observe them today, are within the public interest. Living adults share, we must believe, the same public interest. For them, however, the public interest is mixed with, and is often at odds with, their private and special interests. Put this way, we can say, I suggest, that the public interest may be presumed to be what men would choose if they saw clearly, thought rationally, acted disinterestedly and benevolently.

2 · *The Phantom Public*

The Phantom Public (1925), *Chapters 6, 10, 14 and 16.*

The accepted theory of popular government . . . rests upon the belief that there is a public which directs the course of events. I hold that this public is a mere phantom. It is an abstraction. The public in respect to a railroad strike may be the farmers whom the railroad serves; the public in respect to an agricultural tariff may include the very railroad men who were on strike. The public is not, as I see it, a fixed body of individuals. It is merely those persons who are interested in an affair and can affect it only by supporting or opposing the actors.

Since these random publics cannot be expected to deal with the merits of a controversy, they can give their support with reasonable assurance that it will do good only if there are easily recognizable and yet pertinent signs which they can follow. Are there such signs? Can they be discovered? Can they be formulated so they might be learned and used?

The signs must be of such a character that they can be recognized without any substantial insight into the substance of a problem. Yet they must be relevant to the solution of the problem. They must be signs which will tell the members of a public where they can best align themselves so as to promote the solution. In short, they must be guides to reasonable action for the use of uninformed people.

The environment is complex. Man's political capacity is simple. Can a bridge be built between them? The question has haunted political science ever since Aristotle first formulated it in the great seventh book of his *Politics*. He answered it by saying that the community must be kept simple and small enough to suit the faculties of its citizens. We who live in the Great Society are unable to follow his advice. The orthodox democrats answered Aristotle's question by assuming that a limitless political capacity resides in public opinion. A century of experience compels us to deny this assumption. For us, then, the old question is unanswered; we can neither reject the Great Society as Aristotle did, nor exaggerate the political capacity of the citizen as the democrats did. We are forced to ask whether it is possible for men to find a way of acting effectively upon highly complex affairs by very simple means. . . .

The membership of the public is not fixed. It changes with the issue; the actors in one affair are the spectators of another, and men are continually passing back and forth between the field where they are executives and the field where they are members of a public. The distinction between the two is not . . . an absolute one; there is a twilight zone where it is hard to say whether a man is acting executively on his opinions or merely acting to influence the opinion of someone else who is acting executively. There is often a mixture of the two types of behavior. And it is this mixture, as well as the lack of a clear line of distinction in all cases, which permits a very large confusion in affairs between a public and a private attitude toward them. The public point of view on a question is muddied by the presence in the public of spurious members, persons who are really acting to bend the rule in their favor while pretending or imagining that they are moved only by the common public need that there shall be an acceptable rule.

At the outset it is important, therefore, to detect and to discount the self-interested group. In saying this I do not mean to cast even the slightest reflection on a union of men to promote their self-interest. It would be futile to do so, because we may take it as certain that men will act to benefit themselves whenever they think they conveniently can. A political theory based on the expectation of self-denial and sacrifice by the run of men in any community would not be worth considering. Nor is it at all evident that the work of the world could be done unless men followed their private interest and contributed to affairs that direct inner knowledge which they thus obtain. Moreover, the adjustments are likely to be much more real if they are made from fully conscious and thoroughly explored special points of view.

Thus the genius of any illuminating public discussion is

not to obscure and censor private interest but to help it to sail and to make it sail under its own colors. The true public, in my definition of that term, has to purge itself of the self-interested groups who become confused with it. It must purge itself not because private interests are bad but because private interests cannot successfully be adjusted to each other if any one of them acquires a counterfeit strength. If the true public, concerned only in the fact of adjustment, becomes mobilized behind a private interest seeking to prevail, the adjustment is false; it does not represent the real balance of forces in the affair and the solution will break down. It will break down because the true public will not stay mobilized very long for anything, and when it demobilizes, the private interest which was falsely exalted will find its privileges unmanageable. It will be like a man placed on Jack Dempsey's chest by six policemen, and then left there after the policemen have gone home to dinner. It will be like France placed by the Allies upon a prostrate Germany and then left there after the Allies have departed from Europe.

The separation of the public from the self-interested group will not be assisted by the self-interested group. We may be sure that any body of farmers, businessmen, trade unionists will always call themselves the public if they can. How then is their self-interest to be detected? No ordinary bystander is equipped to analyze the propaganda by which a private interest seeks to associate itself with the disinterested public. It is a perplexing matter, perhaps the most perplexing in popular government, and the bystander's only recourse is to insist upon debate. He will not be able, we may assume, to judge the merits of the arguments. But if he does insist upon full freedom of discussion, the advocates are very likely to expose one another. Open debate may lead to no conclusion and throw no light whatever on the problem or its answer, but it will tend to betray the partisan and the advocate. And if it has identified them for the true public, debate will have served its main purpose. . . .

A false ideal of democracy can lead only to disillusionment and to meddlesome tyranny. If democracy cannot direct affairs, then a philosophy which expects it to direct them will encourage the people to attempt the impossible; they will fail, but that will interfere outrageously with the productive liberties of the individual. The public must be put in its place, so that it may exercise its own powers, but no less and perhaps even more, so that each of us may live free of the trampling and the roar of a bewildered herd.

The source of that bewilderment lies, I think, in the attempt to ascribe organic unity and purpose to society. We have been taught to think of society as a body, with a mind, a soul, and a purpose, not as a collection of men, women, and children whose minds, souls, and purposes are variously related. Instead of being allowed to think realistically of a complex of social *relations*, we have had foisted upon us by various great propagative movements the notion of a mythical entity, called Society, the Nation, the Community. . . .

I have conceived public opinion to be, not the voice of God, nor the voice of society, but the voice of the interested spectators of action. I have, therefore, supposed that the opinions of the spectators must be essentially different from those of the actors, and that the kind of action they were capable of taking was essentially different too. It has seemed to me that the public had a function and must have methods of its own in controversies, qualitatively different from those of the executive men; that it was a dangerous confusion to believe that private purposes were a mere emanation of some common purpose.

This conception of society seems to me truer and more workable than that which endows public opinion with pantheistic powers. It does not assume that men in action have universal purposes; they are denied the fraudulent support of the fiction that they are the agents of a common purpose. They are regarded as the agents of special purposes, without pretense and without embarrassment. They must live in a world with men who have other special purposes. The adjustments which must be made are society, and the best society is the one in which men have purposes which they can realize with the least frustration. When men take a position in respect to the purposes of others they are acting as a public. And the end of their acting in this role is to promote the conditions under which special purposes can be composed.

It is a theory which puts its trust chiefly in the individuals directly concerned. They initiate, they administer, they settle. It would subject them to the least possible interference from ignorant and meddlesome outsiders, for in this theory the public intervenes only when there is a crisis of maladjustment, and then not to deal with the substance of the problem but to neutralize the arbitrary force which prevents adjustment. It is a theory which economizes the attention of men as members of the public, and asks them to do as little as possible in matters where they can do nothing very well. It confines the effort of men, when they are a public, to a part they might fulfill, to a part which corresponds to their own greatest interest in any social disturbance; that is, to an intervention which may help to allay the disturbance, and thus allow them to return to their own affairs.

For it is the pursuit of their special affairs that they are most interested in. It is by the private labors of individuals that life is enhanced. I set no great store on what can be done by public opinion and the action of masses.

3 · *The Limits of Public Opinion*

Public Opinion (1922), *Chapter 1.*

There is an island in the ocean where in 1914 a few Englishmen, Frenchmen, and Germans lived. No cable reaches that island, and the British mail steamer comes but once in sixty days. In September it had not yet come, and the islanders were still talking about the latest newspaper which told about the approaching trial of Madame Caillaux for the shooting of Gaston Calmette. It was, therefore, with more than usual eagerness that the whole colony assembled at the quay on a day in mid-September to hear from the captain what the verdict had been. They learned that for over six weeks now those of them who were English and those of them who were French had been fighting in behalf of the sanctity of treaties against those of them who were Germans. For six strange weeks they had acted as if they were friends, when in fact they were enemies.

But their plight was not so different from that of most of the population of Europe. They had been mistaken for six weeks, on the Continent the interval may have been only six days or six hours. There was an interval. There was a moment when the picture of Europe on which men were conducting their business as usual, did not in any way correspond to the Europe which was about to make a jumble of their lives. There was a time for each man when he was still adjusted to an environment that no longer existed. All over the world as late as July 25th men were making goods that they would not be able to ship, buying goods they would not be able to import, careers were being planned, enterprises contemplated, hopes and expectations entertained, all in the belief that the world as known was the world as it was. Men were writing books describing that world. They trusted the picture in their heads. And then over four years later, on a Thursday morning, came the news of an armistice, and people gave vent to their unutterable relief that the slaughter was over. Yet in the five days before the real armistice came, though the end of the war had been celebrated, several thousand young men died on the battlefields.

Looking back we can see how indirectly we know the environment in which nevertheless we live. We can see that the news of it comes to us now fast, now slowly; but that whatever we believe to be a true picture, we treat as if it were the environment itself. It is harder to remember that about the beliefs upon which we are now acting, but in respect to other peoples and other ages we flatter ourselves that it is easy to see when they were in deadly earnest about ludicrous pictures of the world. We insist, because of our superior hindsight, that the world as they needed to know it, and the world as they did know it, were often two quite contradictory things. We can see, too, that while they governed and fought, traded and reformed in the world as they imagined it to be, they produced results, or failed to produce any, in the world as it was. They started for the Indies and found America. They diagnosed evil and hanged old women. They thought they could grow rich by always selling and never buying. A caliph, obeying what he conceived to be the Will of Allah, burned the library at Alexandria. . . .

The only feeling that anyone can have about an event he does not experience is the feeling aroused by his mental image of that event. . . .

It is the insertion between man and his environment of a pseudo-environment. To that pseudo-environment his behavior is a response. But because it *is* behavior, the consequences, if they are acts, operate not in the pseudo-environment where the behavior is stimulated, but in the real environment where action eventuates. If the behavior is not a practical act, but what we call roughly thought and emotion, it may be a long time before there is any noticeable break in the texture of the fictitious world. But when the stimulus of the pseudo-fact results in action on things or other people, contradiction soon develops. Then comes the sensation of butting one's head against a stone wall, of learning by experience, and witnessing Herbert Spencer's tragedy of the murder of a Beautiful Theory by a Gang of Brutal Facts, the discomfort, in short, of a maladjustment. For certainly, at the level of social life, what is called the adjustment of man to his environment takes place through the medium of fictions.

By fictions I do not mean lies. I mean a representation of the environment which is in lesser or greater degree made by man himself. The range of fiction extends all the way from complete hallucination to the scientists' perfectly self-conscious use of a schematic model, or his decision that for his particular problem accuracy beyond a certain number of decimal places is not important. A work of fiction may have almost any degree of fidelity, and so long as the degree of fidelity can be taken into account, fiction is not misleading. In fact, human culture is very largely the selection, the rearrangement, the tracing of patterns upon, and the stylizing, of what William James called "the random irradiations and resettlements of our ideas." The alternative to the use of fictions is direct exposure to the ebb and flow of sensation. That is not a real alternative, for however refreshing it is to see at times with a perfectly innocent eye, innocence itself is not wisdom, though a source and corrective of wisdom.

For the real environment is altogether too big, too complex, and too fleeting for direct acquaintance. We are not equipped to deal with so much subtlety, so much variety, so many permutations and combinations. And although we have to act in that environment, we have to reconstruct it on a simpler model before we can manage with it. To traverse the world men must have maps of the world. Their persistent difficulty is to secure maps on which their own need, or someone else's need, has not sketched in the coast of Bohemia. . . .

I should like to think only about the world-wide spectacle of men acting upon their environment, moved by stimuli from their pseudo-environments. For when full allowance has been made for deliberate fraud, political science has still to account for such facts as two nations attacking one another, each convinced that it is acting in self-defense, or two classes at war, each certain that it speaks for the common interest. They live, we are likely to say, in different worlds. More accurately, they live in the same world, but they think and feel in different ones.

It is to these special worlds, it is to these private or group, or class, or provincial, or occupational, or national, or sectarian artifacts, that the political adjustment of mankind in the Great Society takes place. Their variety and complication are impossible to describe. Yet these fictions determine a very great part of men's political behavior. We must think of perhaps fifty sovereign parliaments consisting of at least a hundred legislative bodies. With them belong at least fifty hierarchies of provincial and municipal assemblies, which with their executive, administrative, and legislative organs, constitute formal authority on earth. But that does not begin to reveal the complexity of political life. For in each of these innumerable centers of authority there are parties, and these parties are themselves hierarchies with their roots in classes, sections, cliques, and clans; and within these are the individual politicians, each the personal center of a web of connection and memory and fear and hope.

Somehow or other, for reasons often necessarily obscure, as the result of domination or compromise or a logroll, there emerge from these political bodies commands, which set armies in motion or make peace, conscript life, tax, exile, imprison, protect property or confiscate it, encourage one kind of enterprise and discourage another, facilitate immigration or obstruct it, improve communication or censor it, establish schools, build navies, proclaim "policies," and "destiny," raise economic barriers, make property or unmake it, bring one people under the rule of another, or favor one class as against another. For each of these decisions some view of the facts is taken to be conclusive, some view of the circumstances is accepted as the basis of inference and as the stimulus of feeling. What view of the facts, and why that one?

And yet even this does not begin to exhaust the real complexity. The formal political structure exists in a social environment, where there are innumerable large and small corporations and institutions, voluntary and semi-voluntary associations, national, provincial, urban and neighborhood groupings, which often as not make the decision that the political body registers. On what are these decisions based?

The Public Philosophy (*1955*), *Chapter 2.*

The movement of opinion is slower than the movement of events. Because of that, the cycle of subjective sentiments on war and peace is usually out of gear with the cycle of objective developments. Just because they are mass opinions there is an inertia in them. It takes much longer to change many minds than to change a few. It takes time to inform and to persuade and to arouse large scattered varied multitudes of persons. So before the multitude have caught up with the old events there are likely to be new ones coming up over the horizon with which the government should be preparing to deal. But the majority will be more aware of what they have just caught up with near at hand than with what is still distant and in the future. For these reasons the propensity to say No to a change of course sets up a compulsion to make mistakes. The opinion deals with a situation which no longer exists.

When the world wars came, the people of the liberal democracies could not be aroused to the exertions and the sacrifices of the struggle until they had been frightened by the opening disasters, had been incited to passionate hatred, and had become intoxicated with unlimited hope. To overcome this inertia the enemy had to be portrayed as evil incarnate, as absolute and congenital wickedness. The people wanted to be told that when this particular enemy had been forced to unconditional surrender, they would re-enter the golden age. This unique war would end all wars. This last war would make the world safe for democracy. This crusade would make the whole world a democracy.

As a result of this impassioned nonsense public opinion became so envenomed that the people would not countenance a workable peace; they were against any public man who showed "any tenderness for the Hun," or was inclined to listen to the "Hun food snivel."

"Everybody's Business and Nobody's," Today and Tomorrow, *April 10, 1941.*

In an interview which she gave to the newspapers a few days ago Mrs. Roosevelt said that among several industrial disputes she had personally studied only two or three sufficiently to form a definite opinion about the issues. She hoped that the general public would likewise suspend judgment until they had studied the issues in each case, and in order that everyone might be sufficiently informed, she suggested that local committees of private citizens be formed to report on the facts where there is a serious dispute.

This sounds democratic and open-minded and reasonable. Yet with great respect for Mrs. Roosevelt's sincerity and good will it must be said, I submit, that her plausible comment comes out of a dangerously unworkable, though widely accepted, philosophy of government. There is the assumption that Mrs. Roosevelt, in the course of her very busy days, has in fact been able to study two or three large industrial disputes, get to the bottom of them, and reach a sound judgment. There is the assumption that the rest of the adult population can, will, and should attempt to have definite opinions not only on Mrs. Roosevelt's two or three cases, but on any number of other intricate controversies as well. There is the assumption that the mass of these opinions constitutes a verdict by "public opinion" which in a democracy is final and controlling.

The notion that public opinion can and will decide all issues is in appearance very democratic. In practice it undermines and destroys democratic government. For when everyone is supposed to have a judgment about everything, nobody in fact is going to know much about anything. If Mrs. Roosevelt, for example, knows the facts and has weighed the merits in two or three of these recent industrial disputes, she has a capacity for rapid investigation and quick analysis which not many of us possess. It took the mediation board, with all the experts of the federal and state governments helping them, twenty hours of hard work to get to the bottom of the Allis-Chalmers affair; how many private citizens in this country can give twenty minutes to Allis-Chalmers, and another twenty minutes to Ford, and another twenty to coal, and so on and so on?

The only effect of inviting everybody to judge every public question is to confuse everybody about everything. It is not in fact possible for all the people to know all about all things, and the pretense that they can and that they do is a bad illusion. It is in the exact sense of the word not democracy but demagogy. It rests on the idea that everyone has the time to study everything, and that is not true—on the idea that everyone is competent to judge everything, and that is not true.

The general public can judge whether employers and employees are co-operating or are quarreling and it can demand that they find ways of co-operating. It can judge whether Secretary Perkins and the National Labor Relations Board and the Mediation Board are or are not achieving uninterrupted production. If they are not, the general public can insist that the President and Congress do something effective about it. But the general public cannot be the judge and the jury in each case. Nor can it decide just what specific measures the President and the Congress ought to adopt. The general public consists of men and women who read the newspapers and listen to the radio for a little time each day in the midst of busy lives. They can no more hope to have final opinions on every disputed question than they can have opinions on what to do about pneumonia. All they can do about pneumonia is to get the best doctor they can find, and then call in another doctor if the first one does not seem to be satisfactory.

But worse still, this notion that everybody is to decide everything destroys the sense of responsibility in public men and deprives public opinion of responsible leadership. Effective government cannot be conducted by legislators and officials who, when a question is presented, ask themselves first and last, not what is the truth and which is the right and the necessary course but "what does the Gallup poll say?" and "what does the fan mail say?" and "how do the editors and commentators line up?"

It is not deference to democracy for public men to evade their responsibilities and ask the mass of the people to do the work that public men are supposed to do. Once they refuse to lead opinion and prefer to be led by public opinion, they make impossible the formation of a sound public opinion. For obviously the President and the Administration officials and the congressmen in touch with them have the means for informing themselves on the realities of the labor situation and of the defense program and of the war that no one else, not even the most conscientious newspaper reporters, can possess. If with their responsibilities and their means of knowing what is what, they sit around waiting for the Gallup poll and the fan mail, they will get a Gallup poll and a fan mail from a people that have not been able to know what men must know in order to judge wisely. They will have failed to give to the people the leadership which democracy must have—that is, to face their responsibility and to decide questions by consulting other responsible men and then to explain their decision, leaving to the people to judge whether the decision is reasonable and the results good.

It is possible to run the affairs of a village by a town meeting. But the methods of the town meeting will not regulate the affairs of a great republic which embraces a continent, which is defending a hemisphere, and is involved in one of the great crises of history. What is a virtue in a town meeting—to let everyone decide everything—becomes in the conduct of a great government the vice of irresponsibility, indecision, demagogy, and moral timidity. Mrs. Roosevelt cannot weigh and judge every industrial dispute and the rest of us certainly cannot. All we can do is to uphold the hands of, and then hold responsible for the results, those entrusted with the task of maintaining industrial peace.

The same principle applies to most of the difficult questions that now confront us. We have, for example, the problem of the blockade and the feeding of various countries in Europe and northern Africa, and the country today is full of argumentative committees and sincere men and women who think they know enough to know what should be done. I do not know why they think they know enough. For having studied most of the information which is publicly available and talked with a great many more people who have some first-hand knowledge of the facts, all I know is that I do not know enough to have an opinion. All I know is that this infinitely complicated question will have to be decided by Mr. Churchill and the British government and by Mr. Roosevelt and the really informed officials of the American government, and whether their decisions are wise or unwise, it is certain that I do not know enough to decide it for them.

The same principle applies to the question of delivering the goods to the Allies under the lease-lend program. The decision as to how that can best be done is one that must be made by the President in consultation with his advisers and with other responsible public men. How is the outside public to know what "convoying" involves and whether it is the best system of protecting cargoes when, as a matter of fact, there is a respectable body of expert opinion which thinks there is a better system of protecting cargoes? The question is not one which can be solved for the President by public debate. For the public cannot possibly foresee the consequences of doing or not doing certain things.

It is the President's responsibility, of which he cannot divest himself, to judge as wisely as he can what in the end is likely to be the right course, to make that judgment on the best advice he can obtain, to explain his decision and then trust that the people will support a conscientious, carefully considered decision.

"The Nixon Affair," Today and Tomorrow, *September 25, 1952.*

Watching the Nixons, as the senator was fighting for his political life, was a disturbing experience. For this thing in which I found myself participating was, with all the magnification of modern electronics, simply mob law.

The charges against Senator Nixon were so serious that for five days General Eisenhower reserved his own judgment on whether to clear him or to condemn him. Why? Because the evidence, the law, and the moral principles at issue are none of them simple or obvious. They have to do with matters that are not within the field of ordinary political discussion—as for example the wisdom or unwisdom of this or that policy. They have to do with matters which can be decided only by some sort of judicial process. How, then, can a television audience be asked, or allowed, to judge the matter before General Eisenhower finished his inquiry and reached his decision?

Though this is an election campaign, and though the people are no doubt the final court of appeals, the Nixon affair is most emphatically one where the first judgment cannot be made by the public. The appeal to the people should have come after, not before, the case had been judged by General Eisenhower.

What the television audience should have been given was not Senator Nixon's personal defense. That should have been made first before General Eisenhower. What the television audience should have been given was General Eisenhower's decision, backed up by a full and objective account of the facts and of the points of law and of morals which are involved.

The case is a hard one, and the burden of decision on General Eisenhower has been heavy. But for that very reason he should have made it clear from the outset that he would decide it, that he would not ask the public to decide it for him, and that in deciding it, he would use a procedure appropriate to so serious and difficult a decision.

Public Opinion (*1922*), *Chapter 14.*

On all but a very few matters for short stretches in our lives, the utmost independence that we can exercise is to multiply the authorities to whom we give a friendly hearing. As congenital amateurs our quest for truth consists in stirring up the experts, and forcing them to answer any heresy that has the accent of conviction. In such a debate we can often judge who has won the dialectical victory, but we are virtually defenseless against a false premise that none of the debaters has challenged, or a neglected aspect that none of them has brought into the argument. . . .

The people on whom we depend for contact with the outer world are those who seem to be running it. They may be running only a very small part of the world. The nurse feeds the child, bathes it, and puts it to bed. That does not constitute the nurse an authority on physics, zoölogy, and the Higher Criticism. Mr. Smith runs, or at least hires, the man who runs the factory. That does not make him an authority on the Constitution of the United States, nor on the effects of the Fordney tariff. Mr. Smoot runs the Republican Party in the State of Utah. That in itself does not prove he is the best man to consult about taxation. But the nurse may nevertheless determine for a while what zoölogy the child shall learn, Mr. Smith will have much to say on what the Constitution shall mean to his wife, his secretary, and perhaps even to his parson, and who shall define the limits of Senator Smoot's authority?

The priest, the lord of the manor, the captains and the kings, the party leaders, the merchant, the boss, however these men are chosen, whether by birth, inheritance, conquest, or election, they and their organized following administer human affairs. They are the officers, and although the same man may be field marshal at home, second lieutenant at the office, and scrub private in politics, although in many institutions the hierarchy of rank is vague or concealed, yet in every institution that requires the co-operation of many persons, some such hierarchy exists. In American politics we call it a machine, or "the organization."

There are a number of important distinctions between the members of the machine and the rank and file. The leaders, the steering committee and the inner circle, are in direct contact with their environment. They may, to be sure, have a very limited notion of what they ought to define as the environment, but they are not dealing almost wholly with abstractions. There are particular men they hope to see elected, particular balance sheets they wish to see improved, concrete objectives that must be attained. I do not mean that they escape the human propensity to stereotyped vision. Their stereotypes often make them absurd routineers. But whatever their limitations, the chiefs are in actual contact with some crucial part of that larger environment. They decide. They give orders. They bargain. And something definite, perhaps not at all what they imagined, actually happens. . . .

Distance alone lends enchantment to the view that masses of human beings ever co-operate in any complex affair without a central machine managed by a very few people. "No one," says Bryce, "can have had some years' experience of the conduct of affairs in a legislature or an administration without observing how extremely small is the number of persons by whom the world is governed." He is referring, of course, to affairs of state. To be sure, if you consider all the affairs of mankind the number of people who govern is considerable, but if you take any particular institution, be it a legislature, a party, a trade union, a nationalist movement, a factory, or a club, the number of those who govern is a very small percentage of those who are theoretically supposed to govern.

Landslides can turn one machine out and put another in; revolutions sometimes abolish a particular machine altogether. The democratic revolution set up two alternating machines, each of which in the course of a few years reaps the advantage from the mistakes of the other. But nowhere does the machine disappear. Nowhere is the idyllic theory of democracy realized. Certainly not in trades unions, nor in socialist parties, nor in communist governments. There is an inner circle, surrounded by concentric circles which fade out gradually into the disinterested or uninterested rank and file.

Democrats have never come to terms with this commonplace of group life. They have invariably regarded it as perverse. For there are two visions of democracy: one presupposes the self-sufficient individual; the other an Oversoul regulating everything. Of the two the Oversoul has some advantage because it does at least recognize that the mass makes decisions that are not spontaneously born in the breast of every member. But the Oversoul as presiding genius in corporate behavior is a superfluous mystery if we fix our attention upon the machine. The machine is a quite prosaic reality. It consists of human beings who wear clothes and live in houses, who can be named and described. They perform all the duties usually assigned to the Oversoul.

The reason for the machine is not the perversity of human nature. It is that out of the private notions of any group no common idea emerges by itself. For the number of ways is limited in which a multitude of people can act directly upon a situation beyond their reach. Some of them can migrate, in one form or another; they can strike or boycott; they can applaud or hiss. They can by these means occasionally resist what they do not like, or coerce those who obstruct what they desire. But by mass action nothing can be constructed, devised, negotiated, or administered. A public as such, without an organized hierarchy around which it can gather, may refuse to buy if the prices are too high, or refuse to work if wages are too low. A trade union can by mass action in a strike break an opposition so that the union officials can negotiate an agreement. It may win, for example, the *right* to joint control. But it cannot exercise the right except through an organization. A nation can clamor for war, but when it goes to war it must put itself under orders from a general staff.

The limit of direct action is for all practical purposes the power to say yes or no on an issue presented to the mass. For only in the very simplest cases does an issue present itself in the same form spontaneously and approximately at the same time to all the members of a public. There are unorganized strikes and boycotts, not merely industrial ones, where the grievance is so plain that virtually without leadership the same reaction takes place in many people. But even in these rudimentary cases there are persons who know what they want to do more quickly than the rest, and who become impromptu ringleaders. Where they do not appear, a crowd will mill about aimlessly beset by all its private aims, or stand by fatalistically, as did a crowd of fifty persons the other day, and watch a man commit suicide.

For what we make out of most of the impressions that come to us from the invisible world is a kind of pantomime played out in revery. The number of times is small that we consciously decide anything about events beyond our sight, and each man's opinion of what he could accomplish if he tried, is slight. There is rarely a practical issue, and therefore no great habit of decision. This would be more evident were it not that most information when it reaches us carries with it an aura of suggestion as to how we ought to feel about the news. That suggestion we need, and if we do not find it in the news we turn to the editorials or to a trusted adviser. The revery, if we feel ourselves implicated, is uncomfortable until we know where we stand, that is, until the facts have been formulated so that we can feel yes or no in regard to them.

When a number of people all say yes, they may have all kinds of reasons for saying it. They generally do. For the pictures in their minds are, as we have already noted, varied in subtle and intimate ways. But this subtlety remains within their minds; it becomes represented publicly by a number of symbolic phrases which carry the individual emotion after evacuating most of the intention. The hierarchy, or if it is a contest, then the two hierarchies, associate the symbols with a definite action, a vote of yes or no, an attitude pro or con. Then Smith who was against the League and Jones who was against Article X, and Brown who was against Mr. Wilson and all his works, each for his own reason, all in the name of more or less the same symbolic phrase, register a vote *against* the Democrats by voting for the Republicans. A common will has been expressed.

A concrete choice had to be presented, the choice had to be connected, by the transfer of interest through the symbols, with individual opinion. The professional politicians learned this long before the democratic philosophers. And so they organized the caucus, the nominating convention, and the steering committee as the means of formulating a definite choice. Everyone who wishes to accomplish anything that requires the co-operation of a large number of people follows their example. Sometimes it is done rather brutally as when the Peace Conference reduced itself to the Council of Ten, and the Council of Ten to the Big Three or Four; and wrote a treaty which the minor allies, their own constituents, and the enemy were permitted to take or leave. More consultation than that is generally possible and desirable. But the essential fact remains that a small number of heads present a choice to a large group.

4 · *The Task of the Public*

The Phantom Public (*1925*), *Chapters 4, 5 and 13.*

Renunciation is a luxury in which all men cannot indulge. They will somehow seek to control the behavior of others, if not by positive law then at least by persuasion. When men are in that posture toward events they are a public, as I am here defining the term; their opinions as to how others ought to behave are public opinions. The more clearly it is understood what the public can do and what it cannot, the more effectively it will do what lies within its power to do well and the less it will interfere with the liberties of men.

The role of public opinion is determined by the fact that its relation to a problem is external. The opinion affects an opinion, but does not itself control the executive act. A public opinion is expressed by a vote, a demonstration of praise or blame, a following or a boycotting. But these manifestations are in themselves nothing. They count only if they influence the course of affairs. They influence it, however, only if they influence an actor in the affair. And it is, I believe, precisely in this secondary, indirect relationship between public opinion and public affairs that we have the clue to the limits and the possibilities of public opinion.

It may be objected at once that an election which turns one set of men out of office and installs another is an expression of public opinion which is neither secondary nor indirect. But what in fact is an election? We call it an expression of the popular will. But is it? We go into a polling booth and mark a cross on a piece of paper for one of two, or perhaps three or four names. Have we expressed our thoughts on the public policy of the United States? Presumably we have a number of thoughts on this and that with many buts and ifs and ors. Surely the cross on a piece of paper does not express them. It would take us hours to express our thoughts, and calling a vote the expression of our mind is an empty fiction.

A vote is a promise of support. It is a way of saying: I am lined up with these men, on this side. I enlist with them. I will follow. I will buy. I will boycott. I will strike. I applaud. I jeer. The force I can exert is placed here, not there.

The public does not select the candidate, write the platform, outline the policy any more than it builds the automobile or acts the play. It aligns itself for or against somebody who has offered himself, has made a promise, has produced a play, is selling an automobile. The action of a group as a group is the mobilization of the force it possesses. . . .

While an election is in essence sublimated warfare, we must take care not to miss the importance of the sublimation. There have been pedantic theorists who wished to disqualify all who could not bear arms, and woman suffrage has been deplored as a falsification of the value of an election in uncovering the alignment of martial force in the community. One can safely ignore such theorizing. For while the institution of an election is in its historical origins an alignment of the physical force, it has come to be an alignment of all kinds of force. It remains an alignment, though in advanced democracies it has lost most of its primitive association with military combat. It has not lost it in the South where the Negro population is disfranchised by force, and not permitted to make its weight felt in an election. It has not lost it in the unstable Latin American republics where every election is in some measure still an armed revolution. In fact, the United States has officially recognized this truth by proclaiming that the substitution of election for revolution in Central America is the test of political progress.

I do not wish to labor the argument any further than may be necessary to establish the theory that what the public does is not to express its opinions but to align itself for or against a proposal. If that theory is accepted, we must abandon the notion that democratic government can be the direct expression of the will of the people. We must abandon the notion that the people govern. Instead we must adopt the theory that, by their occasional mobilizations as a majority, people support or oppose the individuals who actually govern. We must say that the popular will does not direct continuously but that it intervenes occasionally. . . .

In estimating the burden which a public can carry, a sound political theory must insist upon the largest factor of safety. It must understate the possibilities of public action.

The action of a public, we had concluded, is principally confined to an occasional intervention in affairs by means of an alignment of the force which a dominant section of that public can wield. We must assume, then, that the members of a public will not possess an insider's knowledge of events or share his point of view. They cannot, therefore, construe intent, or appraise the exact circumstances, enter intimately into the minds of the actors or into the details of the argument. They can watch only for coarse signs indicating where their sympathies ought to turn.

We must assume that the members of a public will not anticipate a problem much before its crisis has become obvious, nor stay with the problem long after its crisis is past. They will not know the antecedent events, will not have seen the issue as it developed, will not have thought out or willed a program, and will not be able to predict the consequences of acting on that program. We must assume as a theoretically fixed premise of popular government that normally men as members of a public will not be well informed, continuously interested, nonpartisan, creative, or executive. We must assume that a public is inexpert in its curiosity, intermittent, that it discerns only gross distinctions, is slow to be aroused and quickly diverted; that, since it acts by aligning itself, it personalizes whatever it considers, and is interested only when events have been melodramatized as a conflict.

The public will arrive in the middle of the third act and will leave before the last curtain, having stayed just long enough perhaps to decide who is the hero and who the villain of the piece. Yet usually that judgment will necessarily be made apart from the intrinsic merits, on the basis of a sample of behavior, an aspect of a situation, by very rough external evidence.

We cannot, then, think of public opinion as a conserving or creating force directing society to clearly conceived ends, making deliberately toward socialism or away from it, toward nationalism, an empire, a league of nations or any other doctrinal goal. For men do not agree as to their aims, and it is precisely the lack of agreement which creates the problems that excite public attention. It is idle, then, to argue that though men evidently have conflicting purposes, mankind has some all-embracing purpose of which you or I happen to be the authorized spokesman. We merely should have moved in a circle were we to conclude that the public is in some deep way a messianic force.

The work of the world goes on continually without conscious direction from public opinion. At certain junctures problems arise. It is only with the crises of some of these problems that public opinion is concerned. And its object in dealing with a crisis is to help allay that crisis.

I think this conclusion is unescapable. For though we may prefer to believe that the aim of popular action should be to do justice or promote the true, the beautiful, and the good, the belief will not maintain itself in the face of plain experience. The public does not know in most crises what specifically is the truth or the justice of the case, and men are not agreed on what is beautiful and good. Nor does the public rouse itself normally at the existence of evil. It is aroused at evil made manifest by the interruption of a habitual process of life. And finally, a problem ceases to occupy attention not when justice, as we happen to define it, has been done but when a workable adjustment that overcomes the crisis has been made. If all this were not the necessary manner of public opinion, if it had seriously to crusade for justice in every issue it touches, the public would have to be dealing with all situations all the time. That is impossible. It is also undesirable. For did justice, truth, goodness, and beauty depend on the spasmodic and crude interventions of public opinion, there would be little hope for them in this world.

Thus we strip public opinion of any implied duty to deal with the substance of a problem, to make technical decisions, to attempt justice or impose a moral precept. And instead we say that the ideal of public opinion is to align men during the crisis of a problem in such a way as to favor the action of those individuals who may be able to compose the crisis. The power to discern those individuals is the end of the effort to educate public opinion. The aim of research designed to facilitate public action is the discovery of clear signs by which these individuals may be discerned.

The signs are relevant when they reveal by coarse, simple, and objective tests which side in a controversy upholds a workable social rule, or which is attacking an unworkable rule, or which proposes a promising new rule. By following such signs the public might know where to align itself. In such an alignment it does not, let us remember, pass judgment on the intrinsic merits. It merely places its force at the disposal of the side which, according to objective signs, seems to be standing for human adjustments according to a clear rule of behavior and against the side which appears to stand for settlement in accordance with its own unaccountable will.

Public opinion, in this theory, is a reserve of force brought into action during a crisis in public affairs. Though it is itself an irrational force, under favorable institutions, sound leadership, and decent training, the power of public opinion might be placed at the disposal of those who stood for workable law as against brute assertion. In this theory, public opinion does not make the law. But by canceling lawless power it may establish the condition under which law can be made. It does not reason, investigate, invent, persuade, bargain, or settle. But, by holding the aggressive party in check, it may liberate intelligence. Public opinion in its highest ideal will defend those who are prepared to act on their reason against the interrupting force of those who merely assert their will.

The action of public opinion at its best would not, let it be noted, be a continual crusade on behalf of reason. When power, however absolute and unaccountable, reigns without provoking a crisis, public opinion does not challenge it. Somebody must challenge arbitrary power first. The public can only come to his assistance.

That, I think, is the utmost that public opinion can effectively do. With the substance of the problem it can do nothing usually but meddle ignorantly or tyrannically. It has no need to meddle with it. Men in their active relation to affairs have to deal with the substance, but in that indirect relationship when they can act only through uttering praise or blame, making black crosses on white paper, they have done enough, they have done all they can do if they help to make it possible for the reason of other men to assert itself.

For when public opinion attempts to govern directly it is either a failure or a tyranny. It is not able to master the problem intellectually, nor to deal with it except by wholesale impact. The theory of democracy has not recognized this truth because it has identified the functioning of government with the will of the people. This is a fiction. The intricate business of framing laws and of administering them through several hundred thousand public officials is in no sense the act of the voters nor a translation of their will.

But although the acts of government are not a translation of public opinion, the principal function of government is to do specifically, in greater detail, and more continually what public opinion does crudely, by wholesale, and spasmodically. It enforces some of the working rules of society. It interprets them. It detects and punishes certain kinds of aggression. It presides over the framing of new rules. It has organized force which is used to counteract irregular force.

It is also subject to the same corruption as public opinion. For when government attempts to impose the will of its officials, instead of intervening so as to steady adjustments by consent among the parties directly interested, it becomes heavy-handed, stupid, imperious, even predatory. For the public official, though he is better placed to understand the problem than a reader of newspapers, and though he is much better able to act, is still fundamentally external to the real problems in which he intervenes. Being external, his point of view is indirect, and so his action is most appropriate when it is confined to rendering indirect assistance to those who are directly responsible.

Therefore, instead of describing government as an expression of the people's will, it would seem better to say that government consists of a body of officials, some elected, some appointed, who handle professionally, and in the first instance, problems which come to public opinion spasmodically and on appeal. Where the parties directly responsible do not work out an adjustment, public officials intervene. When the officials fail, public opinion is brought to bear on the issue.

This, then, is the ideal of public action which our inquiry suggests. Those who happen in any question to constitute the public should attempt only to create an equilibrium in which settlements can be reached directly and by consent. The burden of carrying on the work of the world, of inventing, creating, executing, of attempting justice, formulating laws and moral codes, of dealing with the technic and the substance, lies not upon public opinion and not upon government but on those who are responsibly concerned as agents in the affair. Where problems arise, the ideal is a settlement by the particular interests involved. They alone know what the trouble really is. No decision by public officials or by commuters reading headlines in the train can usually, and in the long run, be so good as settlement by consent among the parties at interest. No moral code, no political theory can usually and in the long run be imposed from the heights of public opinion, which will fit a case so well as direct agreement reached where arbitrary power has been disarmed.

It is the function of public opinion to check the use of force in a crisis, so that men, driven to make terms, may live and let live. . . .

The principles underlying the public's role in governing are these:

1. Executive action is not for the public. The public acts only by aligning itself as the partisan of someone in a position to act executively.

2. The intrinsic merits of a question are not for the public. The public intervenes from the outside upon the work of the insiders.

3. The anticipation, the analysis, and the solution of a question are not for the public. The public's judgment rests on a small sample of the facts at issue.

4. The specific, technical, intimate criteria required in the handling of a question are not for the public. The public's criteria are generalized for many problems; they turn essentially on procedure and the overt, external forms of behavior.

5. What is left for the public is a judgment as to whether the actors in the controversy are following a settled rule of behavior or their own arbitrary desires. This judgment must be made by sampling an external aspect of the behavior of the insiders.

6. In order that this sampling shall be pertinent, it is necessary to discover criteria, suitable to the nature of public opinion, which can be relied upon to distinguish between reasonable and arbitrary behavior.

7. For the purposes of social action, reasonable behavior is conduct which follows a settled course whether in making a rule, in enforcing it, or in amending it.

It is the task of the political scientist to devise the methods of sampling and to define the criteria of judgment. It is the task of civic education in a democracy to train the public in the use of these methods. It is the task of those who build institutions to take them into account.

These principles differ radically from those on which democratic reformers have proceeded. At the root of the effort to educate a people for self-government there has, I believe, always been the assumption that the voter should aim to approximate as nearly as he can the knowledge and the point of view of the responsible man. He did not, of course, in the mass, ever approximate it very nearly. But he was supposed to. It was believed that if only he could be taught more facts, if only he would take more interest, if only he would read more and better newspapers, if only he would listen to more lectures and read more reports, he would gradually be trained to direct public affairs. The whole assumption is false. It rests upon a false conception of public opinion and a false conception of the way the public acts. No sound scheme of civic education can come of it. No progress can be made toward this unattainable ideal.

This democratic conception is false because it fails to note the radical difference between the experience of the insider and the outsider; it is fundamentally askew because it asks the outsider to deal as successfully with the substance of a question as the insider. He cannot do it. No scheme of education can equip him in advance for all the problems of mankind; no device of publicity, no machinery of enlightenment can endow him during a crisis with the antecedent detailed and technical knowledge which is required for executive action.

The democratic ideal has never defined the function of the public. It has treated the public as an immature, shadowy executive of all things. The confusion is deep-seated in a mystical notion of society. "The people" were regarded as a person; their wills as a will; their ideas as a mind; their mass as an organism with an organic unity of which the individual was a cell. Thus the voter identified himself with the officials. He tried to think that their thoughts were his thoughts, that their deeds were his deeds, and even that in some mysterious way they were a part of him. All this confusion of identities led naturally to the theory that everybody was doing everything. It prevented democracy from arriving at a clear idea of its own limits and attainable ends. It obscured for the purposes of government and social education the separation of function and the specialization in training which have gradually been established in most human activities.

Democracy, therefore, has never developed an education for the public. It has merely given it a smattering of the kind of knowledge which the responsible man requires. It has, in fact, aimed not at making good citizens but at making a mass of amateur executives. It has not taught the child how to act as a member of the public. It has merely given him a hasty, incomplete taste of what he might have to know if he meddled in everything. The result is a bewildered public and a mass of insufficiently trained officials. The responsible men have obtained their training not from the courses in "civics" but in the law schools and law offices and in business. The public at large, which includes everybody outside the field of his own responsible knowledge, has had no coherent political training of any kind. Our civic education does not even begin to tell the voter how he can reduce the maze of public affairs to some intelligible form.

Critics have not been lacking, of course, who pointed out what a hash democracy was making of its pretensions to government. These critics have seen that the important decisions were taken by individuals, and that public opinion was uninformed, irrelevant, and meddlesome. They have usually concluded that there was a congenital difference between the masterful few and the ignorant many. They are the victims of a superficial analysis of the evils they see so clearly. The fundamental difference which matters is that between insiders and outsiders. Their relations to a problem are radically different. Only the insider can make decisions, not because he is inherently a better man but because he is so placed that he can understand and can act. The outsider is necessarily ignorant, usually irrelevant and often meddlesome, because he is trying to navigate the ship from dry land. That is why excellent automobile manufacturers, literary critics, and scientists often talk such nonsense about politics. Their congenital excellence, if it exists, reveals itself only in their own activity. The aristocratic theorists work from the fallacy of supposing that a sufficiently excellent square peg will also fit a round hole. In short, like the democratic theorists, they miss the essence of the matter, which is, that competence exists only in relation to function; that men are not good, but good for something; that men cannot be educated, but only educated for something.

Education for citizenship, for membership in the public, ought, therefore, to be distinct from education for public office. Citizenship involves a radically different relation to affairs, requires different intellectual habits and different methods of action. The force of public opinion is partisan, spasmodic, simple-minded, and external. It needs for its direction a new intellectual method which shall provide it with its own usable canons of judgment.

5 · *Government in the People*

A Preface to Morals (1929), *Chapter 13.*

It has been the cause of considerable wonder to many persons that the most complex modern communities, where the old loyalties are most completely dissolved, where authority has so little prestige, where moral codes are held in such small esteem, should nevertheless have proved to be far more impervious to the strain of war and revolution than the older and simpler types of civilization. It has been Russia, China, Poland, Italy, Spain, rather than England, Germany, Belgium, and the United States which have been most disorderly in the postwar period. The contrary might have been expected. It might well have been anticipated that the highly organized, delicately poised social mechanisms would disintegrate the most easily.

Yet it is now evident why modern civilization is so durable. Its strength lies in its sensitiveness. The effect of bad decisions is so quickly felt, the consequences are so inescapably serious, that corrective action is almost immediately set in motion. A simple society like Russia can let its railroads go gradually to rack and ruin, but a complex society like London or New York is instantly disorganized if the railroads do not run on schedule. So many persons are at once affected in so many vitally important ways that remedies have to be found immediately. This does not mean that modern states are governed as wisely as they should be, or that they do not neglect much that they cannot really afford to neglect. They blunder along badly enough in all conscience. There is nevertheless a minimum of order and of necessary services which they have to provide for themselves. They have to keep going. They cannot afford the luxury of prolonged disorder or of a general paralysis. Their own necessities are dependent on such fragile structures, and everyone is so much affected, that when a modern state is in trouble it can draw upon incomparable reserves of public spirit.

"I made ninety-one local committees in ninety-one local communities to look after the Mississippi flood," Mr. Hoover once explained, "that's what I principally did. . . . You say: 'A couple of thousand refugees are coming. They've got to have accommodations. Huts. Water mains. Sewers. Streets. Dining halls. Meals. Doctors. Everything.' . . . So you go away and they go ahead and just simply do it. Of all those ninety-one committees there was just one that fell down." Mr. Hard, who reports these remarks, goes on to make Mr. Hoover say that: "No other Main Street in the world could have done what the American Main Street did in the Mississippi flood; and Europe may jeer as it pleases at our mass production and our mass organization and our mass education. The safety of the United States is its multitudinous mass leadership." Allowing for the fact that these remarks appeared in a campaign biography at a time when Mr. Hoover's friends were rather concerned about demonstrating the intensity of his patriotism, there is nevertheless substantial truth in them. I am inclined to believe that "multitudinous mass leadership" will be found wherever industrial society is firmly established, that is to say, wherever a people has lived with the machine process long enough to acquire the aptitudes that it calls for. This capacity to organize, to administer affairs, to deal realistically with necessity can hardly be due to some congenital superiority in the American people. They are, after all, only transplanted Europeans. That their aptitudes may be somewhat more highly developed is not, however, inconceivable; the new civilization may have developed more freely in a land where it did not have to contend with the institutions of a military, feudal, and clerical society.

The essential point is that as the machine technology makes social relations complex, it dissolves the habits of obedience and dependence; it disintegrates the centralization of power and of leadership; it diffuses the experience of responsible decision throughout the population, compelling each man to acquire the habit of making judgments instead of looking for orders, of adjusting his will to the wills of others instead of trusting to custom and organic loyalties. The real law under which modern society is administered is neither the accumulated precedents of tradition nor a set of commands originating on high which are imposed like orders in an army upon the rank and file below. The real law in the modern state is the multitude of little decisions made daily by millions of men.

Because this is so, the character of government is changing

radically. This change is obscured for us in our theorizing by the fact that our political ideas derive from a different kind of social experience. We think of governing as the act of a person; for the actual king we have tried to substitute a corporate king, which we call the nation, the people, the majority, public opinion, or the general will. But none of these entities has the attributes of a king, and the failure of political thinking to lay the ghosts of monarchy leads to endless misunderstanding. The crucial difference between modern politics and that to which mankind has been accustomed is that the power to act and to compel obedience is almost never sufficiently centralized nowadays to be exercised by one will. The power is distributed and qualified so that power is exerted not by command but by interaction.

The prime business of government, therefore, is not to direct the affairs of the community but to harmonize the direction which the community gives to its affairs. The Congress of the United States, for example, does not consult the conscience and its God and then decree a tariff law. It enacts the kind of tariff which at the moment represents the most stable compromise among the interests which have made themselves heard. The law may be outrageously unfair. But if it is, that is because those whose interests are neglected did not at that time have the power to make themselves felt. If the law favors manufacturers rather than farmers, it is because the manufacturers at that time have greater weight in the social equilibrium than the farmers. That may sound hard. But it is doubtful whether a modern legislature can make laws effective if those laws are not the formal expression of what the persons actually affected can and wish to do.

The amount of law is relatively small which a modern legislature can successfully impose. The reason for this is that unless the enforcement of the law is taken in hand by the citizenry, the officials as such are quite helpless. It is possible to enforce the law of contracts, because the injured party will sue; it is possible to enforce the law against burglary, because almost everybody will report a burglary to the police. But it is not possible to enforce the old-fashioned speed laws on the highways because the police are too few and far between, the pedestrians are uninterested, and motorists like to speed. There is here a very fundamental principle of modern lawmaking: insofar as a law depends upon the initiative of officials in detecting violations and in prosecuting, that law will almost certainly be difficult to enforce. If a considerable part of the population is hostile to the law, and if the majority has only a platonic belief in it, the law will surely break down. For what gives law reality is not that it is commanded by the sovereign but that it brings the organized force of the state to the aid of those citizens who believe in the law.

What the government really does is not to rule men but to add overwhelming force to men when they rule their affairs. The passage of a law is, in effect, a promise that the police, the courts, and the officials will defend and enforce certain rights when citizens choose to exercise them. For all practical purposes this is just as true when what was once a private wrong to be redressed by private action in law courts on proof of specific injury has been made by statute a public wrong which is preventable and punishable by administrative action. When the citizens are no longer interested in preventing or punishing specific instances of what the statute declares is a public wrong, the statute becomes a dead letter. The principle is most obviously true in the case of a sumptuary law like prohibition. The reason prohibition is unenforceable in the great cities is that the citizens will not report the names and addresses of their bootleggers to the prohibition officials. But the principle is no less true in less obvious cases, as, for example, in tariffs or laws to regulate railroads. Thus it is difficult to enforce the tariff law on jewels, for they are easily smuggled. In so far as the law is enforced it is because jewelers find it profitable to maintain an organization which detects smuggling. Because they know the ins and outs of the trade, and have men in all the jewelry markets of the world who have an interest in catching smugglers, it is possible for the United States Government to make a fair showing in administering the law. The government cannot from hour to hour inspect all the transactions of its people, and any law which rests on the premise that government can do this is a foolish law. The railroad laws are enforced because shippers are vigilant. The criminal laws depend upon how earnestly citizens object to certain kinds of crime. In fact, it may be said that laws which make certain kinds of conduct illicit are effective in so far as the breach of these laws arouses the citizenry to call in the police and to take the trouble to help the police. It is not enough that the mass of the population should be law-abiding. A minority can stultify the law if the population as a whole is not also law-enforcing.

This is the real sense in which it can be said that power in the modern state resides not in the government but in the people. As that phrase is usually employed it alleges that "the people," as articulated by elected officials, can govern by command as the monarch or tribal chieftain once governed. In this sense government by the people is a delusion. What we have among advanced communities is something that might perhaps be described as government in the people. The naïvely democratic theory was that out of the mass of the voters there arose a cloud of wills which ascended to heaven, condensed into a thunderbolt, and then smote the people. It was supposed that the opinion of masses of persons somehow became the opinion of a corporate person called The People, and that this corporate person then directed human affairs like a monarch. But that is not what happens. Government is in the people and stays there. Government is their multitudinous decisions in concrete situations, and what officials do is to assist and facilitate this process of governing. Effective laws may be said to register an understanding among those concerned by which the law-abiding know what to expect and what is expected of them; they are insured with all the force that the state commands against the disruption of this understanding by the recalcitrant minority. In the modern state a law which does not register the inward assent of most of those who are affected will have very little force as against the breakers of that law. For it is only by that inward assent that power becomes mobilized to enforce the law.

6 · *Masters of Their Fate*

"Masters of Their Fate," Today and Tomorrow, *August 11, 1933.*

If you talk with the men who are directing the movement for recovery you will be given all sorts of theories to explain what they are doing. You will not find, I think, that they are working according to a comprehensive and definite plan. You will not find that there exists a clearly formulated policy embracing and co-ordinating the many different matters with which the government is concerned. Much is said about the New Deal. But there is no dogmatic creed, enunciated from on high, which everyone believes in who has responsibility in Washington.

Not only in the details of administration; but in the decisions of policy as well, circumstance and personality, individual force and eccentricity, factionalism and favoritism, accident and improvisation, rather than logic and theory and formulae, are usually the deciding elements. To some temperaments a close view of the conduct of affairs will, therefore, be discouraging. Looking for a sense of definite direction and clear purpose, they will find only arguments and practical expedience; they will see not a revolution and a reconstruction but a very active and energetic example of muddling through. To other temperaments the character of this movement will be neither astonishing nor discouraging. They will recall that the method of muddling through is the classic method of the English-speaking peoples, and that using this method these peoples have succeeded, as no other peoples have, in riding out the storms of history and remaining free.

Clear doctrine and rigid purposes that apply to a whole nation have to be paid for; their price is the suppression of individuality and the regimentation of opinion. A community of free men, who proceed by argument to leadership and consent, necessarily work out their policies as they go along. Events rather than theories, experience rather than doctrine, supply the reasons by which men are brought into line. They do not advance in a straight line, but forward and backward and sideways, and most of the time they look as if they did not know what they were doing or where they were going. Sometimes they do not know. But our political traditions teach us that it is better to move irregularly but with the minds of the people participating and convinced, than to impose grandiose logical patterns of conduct upon them, and compel them to obey.

As we look back over the spectacular history of the past six months, nothing, it seems to me, is so impressive or so deeply reassuring as the evidence we have had that there are indeed great reserves of political wisdom in a nation habituated to self-government. The knowledge to do this or that particular thing may be lacking. We cannot be certain, for example, that we have chosen the best of all possible monetary policies. We do not know as yet how to adjust our internal measures to the outer world. We cannot see very far ahead as to how the agricultural control will work or what will be the consequences of N.R.A.

But what we do know is that in the spring we overcame the paralysis of government in Washington, and were able to achieve unity of action. We do know that we were able to sweep aside the obstructions of organized minorities and the influences of private powers. We do know that we have seen new energies, new faces, young men, enterprising and hopeful minds in the responsible posts. We do know that the national spirit has been revived, that frightened calculation is giving way to confidence and even to magnanimity. Men no longer feel, as they did some months ago, that our society is doomed and that they are impotent, that they are caught in a current of forces which carries them irresistibly along.

Thus, although the statistics do not show that we have recovered prosperity, though millions are still without the decencies of life, we have recovered our courage, our self-respect, our faith in the power of mind and will to determine our fate. While this lasts there can be no doubt as to the outcome. We shall not be destroyed by mistakes. We shall not be saved by bright ideas. We can be destroyed only by demoralization; we can be saved only by our own resolution. As long as the spirit of the nation is as coherent and as temperate, as confident and as magnanimous as it is today, there is no danger. Decisions can be made, and if they are wrong they can be reversed. Plans can be adopted, and when they don't work they can be changed.

For recovery is not a fitting together of cogs in a broken-down machine; it is a renascence in the energy and character of a people. For whatever the right or the wrong of this or that, in a nation as among individuals, when their spirit is strong they are invincible to circumstance and masters of their fate.

"The New Congress," Today and Tomorrow,
December 8, 1931.

The extent to which government by elected officials has been discredited is impressive. In one country after another the politicians have temporized with the crisis solely because they were trying to please their constituents. And in one country after another these men have found themselves overwhelmed by the people they were trying to please. The men whom the people have turned to have been the men who offered them the bitter medicine, who have promised to tax them, to reduce their benefits, to cut and economize and deflate. The reason is plain. When people feel safe and at ease they like to be jollied and told that all is well. But when they are frightened and realize that things are really wrong, they despise the easy optimists and like men who are resolute in applying stern remedies.

The ordinary politician has a very low estimate of human nature. In his daily life he comes into contact chiefly with persons who want to get something or to avoid something. Beyond this circle of seekers after privileges, individuals and organized minorities, he is aware of a large unorganized, indifferent mass of citizens who ask nothing in particular and rarely complain. The politician comes after a while to think that the art of politics is to satisfy the seekers after favors and to mollify the inchoate mass with noble sentiments and patriotic phrases. In easy times the politician is probably about right. Certainly he gets himself elected regularly by these methods.

But in really hard times the rules of the game are altered. The inchoate mass begins to stir. It becomes potent, and when it strikes, . . . it strikes with incredible emphasis. Those are the rare occasions when a national will emerges from the scattered, specialized, or indifferent blocs of voters who ordinarily elect the politicians. Those are for good or evil the great occasions in a nation's history.

An occasion of this sort is probably forming itself here and now. For ten years the American people have been sunk first in the political lethargy of war-weariness and then in the stupor of the great inflation. They are coming out of it. There has been more thought and more feeling about public affairs in the last year than in the ten which preceded it. There is, too, a new generation at the threshold of authority, the generation which survived the war and the postwar era, and they have no emotional commitments to that past. They are tired of the old dull calculating faces. They are tired of stuffed shirts. They are tired of the fawning and the flattery, of the evasiveness and the straddling, of the soft and the fat and the timorous, of the shoddy optimists, the ignobly self-indulgent, the greedy and the parvenu who battened upon the distortion of values which the inflation produced.

"Reflections on the Public's Nerves," Today and Tomorrow, *January 1, 1932.*

At the turn of the year the best sign is the falling off in the demand for rosy promises. There will be, I suppose, here and there, the usual predictions by gentlemen who would be as much ashamed not to issue an optimistic statement for January 1st as to appear in public without a necktie. But the people have decided that the professional optimists are funny, and have even made a hobby of collecting the more hideously optimistic remarks of recent years.

This dour cynicism is nature's purge for the high-powered buncomb in which the nation was saturated during the great inflation. It would be a great mistake to deplore it and to suppose that it is the cause of that general nervousness which has produced the present crisis of confidence. The prevailing nervousness is the result, not of what the people at large have suffered, but of their disappointments. The very great majority of us are still in a material sense far better supplied than any people in all history. The nervousness comes from the fact that we have lost so much of what we imagined we had that we do not at the moment see an end to our losses. We are magnifying our losses because we had inflated our gains. The memory of those phantom profits haunts us and has established in our minds a wholly false measure of what we have the right to expect; it has been the false standard of what is normal that has, during the disappointments of this year, exaggerated out of all proportion our real losses and our real perils. It is requiring the acids of a strong cynicism to wash clean the accumulated follies of the boom.

There is no reason to suppose that people have lost the capacity for confidence because they have lost confidence in their illusions. It is no real test of the popular mood to ply the people with the old optimism and ascertain that they respond pessimistically. Man's capacity to hope and his ability to endure have never been dependent upon quick and easy returns. The politicians and speculators of the blessed New Era thought so, and, since they are still more or less in command, they continue to think that the way to please and to reassure the people is to pat them gently and feed them pap. These commanders are wrong. They do not understand the human animal. They have seen how the people liked the inflation, how they took to the soft living which went with it, and they have forgotten that these people are of the same race that in the long and terrible record of history has again and again faced battle, and disease, flood, earthquake, and disaster.

They have forgotten the immensely mysterious character of man, how, with his laziness, his selfishness, his cowardice, he has also a power to endure, and at times a willingness to die for distant and abstract ideas. They have forgotten that in the carnal nature of man there are chords of fortitude and heroism which, when they are struck, vibrate with an unaccountable energy. How else explain the great periods of history that punctuate the drab and flat routine of existence, except by the fact that when they must, men can rise so far above themselves that they hardly know themselves?

It is not necessary to talk softly to the people and to pamper them as if they were invalids. One has only to look back and see how the real leaders of men have talked to their people in a time of crisis to see how false it is to offer men mere optimism and reassurance. The officer talking to his men does not tell them the enemy's guns aren't loaded, and that all is pretty nearly well. The captain of the ship in a great sea does not send messages denying that the gale is blowing. The true morale of men in a crisis is their determination to seize the thing that menaces them, and look at it, and face it out, and to do what is needed and complain not at all, and be done with it. There is no reason to suppose that this people, or the other peoples involved with it today, have lost the capacity for occasional greatness.

IV

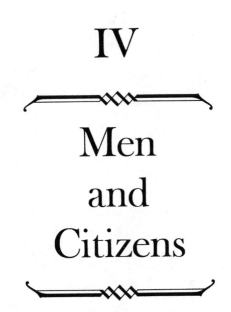

Men and Citizens

1 · *The Importance of Man*

"In the Shadow of the Moon," The World, *January 24, 1925.*

No human power can direct the shadow of the moon as it falls upon the earth today. Yet human foresight can predict within a fraction of a mile and within a second of time where that shadow will fall. Once all men would have tried by magic and sacrifice to alter the inexorable course of the shadow. Today they are going outdoors to enjoy the spectacle and to understand it more accurately. In the record of that change of attitude toward the universe in which it lives lies the story of the emancipation of the human mind.

A free mind is an understanding mind, a mind that has found its place, judged its power, and made its peace with the natural order of which it is a part. The mind that is not free can be impressed only by a rupture of the order of nature or by some miracle which flatters its lust of omnipotence. So men have bitterly resisted the knowledge which has gradually forced them into a cosmic perspective. They would like still, many of them, to think themselves unique among living creatures, on a unique planet, lords of time and space and destiny. They do not surrender easily their ancestral conceit. They still think and frantically stoke up the conviction that their little piece of ground is the earth, their earth the universe, and the meaning of it all confined to them and their clan. They pay the universe the poor compliment of insisting that they know it all and are the end of all its labors.

Let them look into the heavens this morning and then in humility seek to realize who and where they are, individual members of a little branch of a race that is only part of the life of this planet, a planet not very large turning around a fair-sized sun in one middling solar system in an unfathomed ocean of space and time. Rather small creatures, if you think of it that way, but capable of one surpassing dignity: they can become aware of themselves, they can make for themselves pictures of their universe, they can find delight and serenity in the thought of them and charity in that for creatures like themselves.

To see the world in the aspect of as much of eternity as a limited mind can grasp is to give order and grace to the ambitions and desires of a day. To do that fellow down, to outshine him, to ride a little faster and be noticed a little more, to profit a little here and win a bit there—what are all these things tomorrow? Nothing, unless in some measure they have helped to brighten the spirit so that for a brief moment it may reflect the natural order of the universe.

"The Forgotten Foundation," Today and Tomorrow, *December 17, 1938.*

In every nation there is the danger, for example, in France as respects Alsace, Savoy, Corsica, Tunis—in Brazil as respects certain of her provinces—that the principle of nationality will be exploited to dismember the existing nations. This is what was done to the Czechoslovak Republic. It will probably be done to Poland. If we are wise and vigilant, we shall make up our minds that it is not going to be done on this side of the Atlantic.

In insisting that it shall not be done, we shall be affirming a principle which has its roots in the deepest conviction of Western civilization. Mr. Eden said recently, as have many others, that what separates us from the totalitarian regimes is our belief that man does not belong to the state. This is true. But if we are to be clear about what that really means, we must say also what it is that man does belong to.

There are, perhaps, many different ways of saying it. But there is no better way of saying it than to say it as the authors of our liberties were accustomed to say it. They said that man belonged to his Creator, and that since he was, therefore, an immortal soul, he possessed inalienable rights as a person which no power on earth had the right to violate. This was what the founders of the American nation meant when they said that all men were created equal, and not, as foolish people suppose, that all men were created equally capable of writing the plays of Shakespeare or of running a hundred yards in ten seconds flat.

And because they believed that each man is a soul and not a thing, they inevitably believed that no government could be absolute or totalitarian. On that conviction they established constitutional government; that is, government which is under and not above the law. And because they believed that men had in them an eternal essence, they felt in honor bound to respect it, to practice the courtesy of the spirit, and even in war to be chivalrous and in victory magnanimous.

The decay of decency in the modern age, the rebellion against law and good faith, the treatment of human beings as things, as the mere instruments of power and ambition, is without a doubt the consequence of the decay of the belief in man as something more than an animal animated by highly conditioned reflexes and chemical reactions. For, unless man is something more than that, he has no rights that anyone is bound to respect, and there are no limitations upon his conduct which he is bound to obey.

This is the forgotten foundation of democracy in the only sense in which democracy is truly valid and of liberty in the only sense in which it can hope to endure. The liberties we talk about defending today were established by men who took their conception of man from the great central religious tradition of Western civilization, and the liberties we inherit can almost certainly not survive the abandonment of that tradition. And so perhaps the ordeal through which mankind is passing may be necessary. For it may be the only way in which modern men can recover the faith by which free and civilized people must live.

"The Bill of Rights," Today and Tomorrow, *December 14, 1939.*

Friday of this week is the anniversary of the ratification of the first ten amendments to the Constitution. They are known as the Bill of Rights. Though in form these amendments are a part of the Constitution, and therefore in theory subject to repeal or amendment by the ordinary procedure, in fact the American tradition holds that the Bill of Rights rests upon self-evident, inalienable, eternal, and universal principles which no government, and no majority of people, may violate.

The rest of the Constitution is a framework of government designed to establish a federal union operated by representative democracy; it is also the outline of a policy for the ordering of affairs. This constitutional system comes from the people, that is to say, from majorities among the people, and in the course of history is subject to change by other majorities. But the Bill of Rights does not come from the people and is not subject to change by majorities. It comes from the nature of things. It declares the inalienable rights of man not only against all government but also against the people collectively.

It establishes rights which no majority may abrogate, and as Jefferson put it in his first inaugural, "to violate would be oppression." Those words are pregnant, for in the philosophy of the American Founders oppression was illegal even if it was done under the forms of law, and such men as Jefferson and Franklin were fond of saying that "rebellion to tyrants is obedience to God."

That was not a rhetorical phrase. They really believed that the rights of man came from his Creator and that they are derived from the laws of the universe itself. In defending these rights against all earthly powers, against kings or tyrants or popular majorities, they held that they were practicing obedience to God. In their view the framework of government and the form of the social order were the things of Caesar; but the rights of man were not Caesar's but the things of God.

This belief is outlawed in the lands where liberty has been crushed and the ideas themselves are scornfully rejected as vapors from a dying social order. But even here, where the usages of freedom still persist, the multitude of men is no longer very sure why they believe in freedom. In the course of the nineteenth century it ceased to be intellectually respectable to affirm that any principle is self-evident, inalienable, eternal, and universal. And thus there was cut away the ultimate ground on which liberty can alone be defended as against the argument from expediency and the prestige of power and success.

So on this anniversary it is useful to remember where our liberties originate, from what source come their irrepressible and enduring energies. For we shall need to rediscover what we had become too sophisticated to believe.

The sophists among modern historians like to tell us that our liberties come from the self-serving action of the barons who extracted the Magna Carta from King John, and from successive classes of landowners, merchants, and working men. The explanation is inadequate. If the struggle for liberty is no more than the struggle of a special class at a special moment, then how does one explain the fact that millions have enlisted who had no special interest, or, if they had, were destined to die before they could enjoy it?

These struggles are at once too general and too passionate to be explained on the ground of calculated self-interest. Men respond to the cause of liberty who can never hope to enjoy its fruits. So it must be that the tree of liberty has its root in some deep and abiding need of man. The founders of our liberties knew this. They knew that the need to be free, once awakened in man, is as imperative a passion, and almost as universal a passion, as hunger and love.

In safety and comfort men who enjoy liberty may forget this. They may think that the language of liberty is rhetorical. In the security of their own liberties they will often be unable to comprehend how ordinary men like themselves can be so impractical as to leave their homes, their families, their careers, to go out to dwell in mud and darkness, and to be cold and bored and dirty, and to be exposed to death and mutilation rather than live without the conviction that they are free.

It seems so silly, so incomprehensible to comfortable, sensible people. It is often equally difficult for those who are well fed, never having missed their regular meals, to comprehend how they themselves would feel and behave if they were starving. They find it hard to imagine how men feel when they are starved for liberty.

What then is this passion, apparently so abstract that many today think it is an invention of the propagandists—this passion which has moved ordinary selfish, sensual men like ourselves, the Greeks who stood at Thermopylae and the Frenchmen who stand on the Maginot Line, the British who guard the infested seas, and the Finns who stand in the Karelian Isthmus —that has moved them to such deeds of bravery and self-sacrifice?

That is what needs to be explained when we read our own Bill of Rights and marvel at the succession of brave men who paid with their blood for those rights, when we wonder if we, who are their heirs, are made of the same stuff.

The root of the passion which has moved such men is in some measure present in all men; it is the will to live, not as a thing and not as an animal, but as an inviolable, self-respecting and respected, human person. This is the indestructible cause of man's desire to be free. Man is so constituted that he has this passion. Because he is endowed with the faculty of reason, he is suffocated and strangled and literally done to death if he is compelled for too long and too completely to submit to unreason, and irrational arbitrariness, and sheer brute circumstance. So far as we know, man alone is this kind of being. This is how his nature differs radically from that of other animals, even from the ants and the bees who also live in highly organized communities. For they do their collective and servile labors without having to be coerced by an OGPU or a Gestapo. But man has to be coerced. Man has to be oppressed. Why? Because his passion to live as a human person is so indestructible that his oppressors can never for a moment relax their vigilance.

This energy of the soul has been awakened—and awakened has become insistent, and insistent it is irresistible—by means of a progressive revelation which began in the Mediterranean world. On this revelation of man our civilization is founded. This revelation is the central belief of the enduring religion; it is the argument of the perennial philosophy; it is the beginning and the end of the developing science; it is the subject matter of the expressive arts; and it is the major premise of the laws and institutions of the civilized world.

Without a comprehension of this truth about the nature of man, nothing that we value is comprehensible.

Thus no one can explain the Bill of Rights to someone who does not believe that the soul is rational and, that, therefore, the human person is inviolable. If he has not grasped this truth, if he has not had this revelation, if he does not know the idea which these words express, how will you convince him that his religion shall not be prescribed by public officials, or that he has the right to speak and to listen, or that the powers not delegated to the government are reserved to the people?

How will you affirm that freedom is better than tyranny if you are not able to affirm that it is the destiny of man's nature that he should be free? No one can prove the value of liberty by drawing up a balance sheet of profits and losses. If men do not understand that the origin of their liberties is in the nature of man, they will not really understand their liberties, nor learn to value their liberties until they have let them be destroyed. And so, though they live in freedom, they will squander their inheritance, having forgotten how it was earned and accumulated.

2 · *The Varieties of Human Nature*

Public Opinion (1922), *Chapter 9.*

At the core of every moral code there is a picture of human nature, a map of the universe, and a version of history. To human nature (of the sort conceived), in a universe (of the kind imagined), after a history (so understood), the rules of the code apply. So far as the facts of personality, of the environment and of memory are different, by so far the rules of the code are difficult to apply with success. Now every moral code has to conceive human psychology, the material world, and tradition some way or other. But in the codes that are under the influence of science, the conception is known to be an hypothesis, whereas in the codes that come unexamined from the past or bubble up from the caverns of the mind, the conception is not taken as an hypothesis demanding proof or contradiction, but as a fiction accepted without question. In the one case, man is humble about his beliefs, because he knows they are tentative and incomplete; in the other he is dogmatic, because his belief is a completed myth. The moralist who submits to the scientific discipline knows that though he does not know everything, he is in the way of knowing something; the dogmatist, using a myth, believes himself to share part of the insight of omniscience, though he lacks the criteria by which to tell truth from error. For the distinguishing mark of a myth is that truth and error, fact and fable, report and fantasy, are all on the same plane of credibility.

The myth is, then, not necessarily false. It might happen to be wholly true. It may happen to be partly true. If it has affected human conduct a long time, it is almost certain to contain much that is profoundly and importantly true. What a myth never contains is the critical power to separate its truths from its errors. For that power comes only by realizing that no human opinion, whatever its supposed origin, is too exalted for the test of evidence, that every opinion is only somebody's opinion. And if you ask why the test of evidence is preferable to any other, there is no answer unless you are willing to use the test in order to test it.

The statement is, I think, susceptible of overwhelming proof, that moral codes assume a particular view of the facts. Under the term moral codes I include all kinds: personal, family, economic, professional, legal, patriotic, international. At the center of each there is a pattern of stereotypes about psychology, sociology, and history. The same view of human nature, institutions or tradition rarely persists through all our codes. Compare, for example, the economic and the patriotic codes. There is a war supposed to affect all alike. Two men are partners in business. One enlists, the other takes a war contract. The soldier sacrifices everything, perhaps even his life. He is paid a dollar a day, and no one says, no one believes, that you could make a better soldier out of him by any form of economic incentive. That motive disappears out of his human nature. The contractor sacrifices very little, is paid a handsome profit over costs, and few say or believe that he would produce the munitions if there were no economic incentive. That may be unfair to him. The point is that the accepted patriotic code assumes one kind of human nature, the commercial code another. And the codes are probably founded on true expectations to this extent, that when a man adopts a certain code he tends to exhibit the kind of human nature which the code demands.

That is one reason why it is so dangerous to generalize about human nature. A loving father can be a sour boss, an earnest municipal reformer, and a rapacious jingo abroad. His family life, his business career, his politics, and his foreign policy rest on totally different versions of what others are like and of how he should act. These versions differ by codes in the same person, the codes differ somewhat among persons in the same social set, differ widely as between social sets, and between two nations, or two colors, may differ to the point where there is no common assumption whatever. That is why people professing the same stock of religious beliefs can go to war. The element of their belief which determines conduct is that view of the facts which they assume.

A Preface to Politics (*1913*), *Chapter 4*.

We make our picture of man, knowing that, though it is crude and unjust, we have to work with it. If we are wise we shall become experimental toward life; then every mistake will contribute toward knowledge. Let the exploration of human need and desire become a deliberate purpose of statecraft, and there is no present measure of its possibilities.

In this work there are many guides. A vague common tradition is in the air about us—it expresses itself in journalism, in cheap novels, in the uncritical theater. Every merchant has his stock of assumptions about the mental habits of his customers and competitors; the prostitute hers; the newspaperman his; P. T. Barnum had a few; the vaudeville stage has a number. We test these notions by their results, and even "practical people" find that there is more variety in human nature than they had supposed.

We forge gradually our greatest instrument for understanding the world—introspection. We discover that humanity may resemble us very considerably—that the best way of knowing the inwardness of our neighbors is to know ourselves. For after all, the only experience we really understand is our own. And that, in the least of us, is so rich that no one has yet exhausted its possibilities. It has been said that every genuine character an artist produces is one of the characters he might have been. By re-creating our own suppressed possibilities we multiply the number of lives that we can really know. That as I understand it is the psychology of the Golden Rule. For note that Jesus did not set up some external fetich; he did not say, make your neighbor righteous, or chaste, or respectable. He said do as you would be done by. Assume that you and he are alike, and you can found morals on humanity.

But experience has enlarged our knowledge of differences. We realize now that our neighbor is not always like ourselves. Knowing how unjust other people's inferences are when they concern us, we have begun to guess that ours may be unjust to them. Any uniformity of conduct becomes at once an impossible ideal, and the willingness to live and let live assumes high place among the virtues. A puzzled wisdom remarks that "it takes all sorts of people to make a world," and half-protestingly men accept Bernard Shaw's amendment, "Do not do unto others as you would that they should do unto you. Their tastes may not be the same."

We learn perhaps that there is no contradiction in speaking of "human nature" while admitting that men are unique. For all deepening of our knowledge gives a greater sense of common likeness and individual variation. It is folly to ignore either insight. But it is done constantly, with no end of confusion as a result. Some men have got themselves into a state where the only view that interests them is the common humanity of us all. Their world is not populated by men and women, but by a Unity that is Permanent. You might as well refuse to see any differences between steam, water, and ice because they have common elements. And I have seen some of these people trying to skate on steam. Their brothers, blind in the other eye, go about the world so sure that each person is entirely unique, that society becomes like a row of packing cases, each painted on the inside, and each containing one ego and its own.

Public Opinion (*1922*), *Chapter 1.*

Before we involve ourselves in the jungle of obscurities about the innate differences of men, we shall do well to fix our attention upon the extraordinary differences in what men know of the world. I do not doubt that there are important biological differences. Since man is an animal it would be strange if there were not. But as rational beings it is worse than shallow to generalize at all about comparative behavior until there is a measurable similarity between the environments to which behavior is a response.

The pragmatic value of this idea is that it introduces a much needed refinement into the ancient controversy about nature and nurture, innate quality and environment. For the pseudo-environment is a hybrid compounded of "human nature" and "conditions." To my mind it shows the uselessness of pontificating about what man is and always will be from what we observe man to be doing, or about what are the necessary conditions of society. For we do not know how men would behave in response to the facts of the Great Society. All that we really know is how they behave in response to what can fairly be called a most inadequate picture of the Great Society. No conclusion about man or the Great Society can honestly be made on evidence like that.

This, then, will be the clue to our inquiry. We shall assume that what each man does is based not on direct and certain knowledge, but on pictures made by himself or given to him. If his atlas tells him that the world is flat he will not sail near what he believes to be the edge of our planet for fear of falling off. If his maps include a fountain of eternal youth, a Ponce de Leon will go in quest of it. If someone digs up yellow dirt that looks like gold, he will for a time act exactly as if he had found gold. The way in which the world is imagined determines at any particular moment what men will do. It does not determine what they will achieve. It determines their effort, their feelings, their hopes, not their accomplishments and results.

"The Pair of Winged Horses and the Charioteer," Today and Tomorrow, *November 15, 1938.*

If thoughtful men have differed about the psychological springs of malevolence, there has been no difference of opinion among the great teachers of the Western world that there is in human nature a disposition to evil, that government is not government which cannot restrain it, and that religion is satanic that does not seek incessantly to overcome it. Long ago Plato fixed the image of man's moral problem as that of a charioteer who drives a pair of winged horses: "one of them is noble and of noble breed, the other is ignoble and of ignoble breed." And living as he did in an age of disaster and disorder, Plato added that "the driving of them of necessity gives a great deal of trouble to the charioteer."

He perhaps had seen what we have seen, the use of civil authority to arouse the disposition to kill, to maim, to plunder, rather than to subdue and control these lusts. For he too lived in an age of revolution, and this is the very essence of revolution. For whatever the outward and temporary appearances of order and even of splendor, the certain sign that a people is in the grip of revolution is that government and what passes for the official religion surrender to, cultivate, and then use for their own purposes the slumbering barbarian in man's nature.

For it is only a revolutionary government that can, and by its own inexorable logic must, organize the primitive lusts of mankind into methodical violence. Left to themselves, the resentments and hatreds of men are fitful, soon sated and quickly regretted. But revolutionary governments cannot maintain themselves for long if they permit the normal instincts for decency to reassert themselves. For revolutionary dictatorships are so entirely abnormal, are so alien to the lasting interests and ideals of all civilized men, that they can prolong their existence only by an ever-growing intensification of violence.

Public Opinion (*1922*), *Chapter 12.*

There is no one self always at work. And therefore it is of great importance in the formation of any public opinion, what self is engaged. The Japanese ask the right to settle in California. Clearly it makes a whole lot of difference whether you conceive the demand as a desire to grow fruit or to marry the white man's daughter. If two nations are disputing a piece of territory, it matters greatly whether the people regard the negotiations as a real estate deal, an attempt to humiliate them, or, in the excited and provocative language which usually enclouds these arguments, as a rape. For the self which takes charge of the instincts when we are thinking about lemons or distant acres is very different from the self which appears when we are thinking even potentially as the outraged head of a family. In one case the private feeling which enters into the opinion is tepid, in the other, red hot. And so while it is so true as to be mere tautology that "self-interest" determines opinion, the statement is not illuminating, until we know which self out of many selects and directs the interest so conceived.

Religious teaching and popular wisdom have always distinguished several personalities in each human being. They have been called the Higher and Lower, the Spiritual and the Material, the Divine and the Carnal; and although we may not wholly accept this classification, we cannot fail to observe that distinctions exist. Instead of two antithetic selves, a modern man would probably note a good many not so sharply separated. He would say that the distinction drawn by theologians was arbitrary and external, because many different selves were grouped together as higher provided they fitted into the theologian's categories, but he would recognize nevertheless that here was an authentic clue to the variety of human nature.

We have learned to note many selves, and to be a little less ready to issue judgment upon them. We understand that we see the same body, but often a different man, depending on whether he is dealing with a social equal, a social inferior, or a social superior; on whether he is making love to a woman he is eligible to marry, or to one whom he is not; on whether he is courting a woman, or whether he considers himself her proprietor; on whether he is dealing with his children, his partners, his most trusted subordinates, the boss who can make him or break him; on whether he is struggling for the necessities of life, or successful; on whether he is dealing with a friendly alien, or a despised one; on whether he is in great danger, or in perfect security; on whether he is alone in Paris or among his family in Peoria.

People differ widely, of course, in the consistency of their characters, so widely that they may cover the whole gamut of differences between a split soul like Dr. Jekyll's and an utterly single-minded Brand, Parsifal, or Don Quixote. If the selves are too unrelated, we distrust the man; if they are too inflexibly on one track we find him arid, stubborn, or eccentric. In the repertory of characters, meager for the isolated and the self-sufficient, highly varied for the adaptable, there is a whole range of selves, from that one at the top which we should wish God to see, to those at the bottom that we ourselves do not dare to see. There may be octaves for the family: father, Jehovah, tyrant—husband, proprietor, male—lover, lecher; for the occupation: employer, master, exploiter—competitor, intriguer, enemy—subordinate, courtier, snob. Some never come out into public view. Others are called out only by exceptional circumstances. But the characters take their form from a man's conception of the situation in which he finds himself. If the environment to which he is sensitive happens to be the smart set, he will imitate the character he conceives to be appropriate. That character will tend to act as modulator of his bearing, his speech, his choice of subjects, his preferences. Much of the comedy of life lies here, in the way people imagine their characters for situations that are strange to them: the professor among promoters, the deacon at a poker game, the cockney in the country, the paste diamond among real diamonds.

The Public Philosophy (*1955*), *Chapter* 8.

There are those who would say, using the words of philosophers to prove it, that it is the characteristic illusion of the tender-minded that they believe in philosophy. Those who can, do; those who cannot, teach and theorize. And being theorists by profession, they exaggerate the efficacy of ideas, which are mere airy nothings without mass or energy, the mere shadows of the existential world of substance and of force, of habits and desires, of machines and armies.

Yet the illusion, if it were one, is inordinately tenacious. It is impossible to remove it from the common sense in which we live and have our being. In the familiar daylight world we cannot act as if ideas had no consequences. The whole vast labor and passion of public life would be nonsense if we did not believe that it makes a difference what is done by parties, newspapers, books, broadcasts, schools, and churches. All their effort would be irrelevant, indeed nonsense, like an argument about what Nebuchadnezzar should be served for tomorrow morning's breakfast.

The most thoroughgoing skeptic is unable, in practice, to make a clean sweep—to say that since ideas have no consequences there is no such thing as a good idea or a bad one, a true idea or a false one. For there is no escaping the indubitable fact of experience that we are often mistaken, and that it makes a difference to have been wrong.

The chemistry of our bodies is never mistaken. The reaction of one chemical element to another chemical element is always correct, is never misled by misinformation, by untruth, and by illusion. The doctor can be mistaken about the chemistry of his patient, having failed to detect a substance which falsifies his diagnosis. But it is only the doctor who can be wrong; the chemical process cannot be.

Why do men make mistakes? Because an important part of human behavior is reaction to the pictures in their heads. Human behavior takes place in relation to a pseudo-environment—a representation, which is not quite the same for any two individuals, of what they suppose to be—not what *is*—the reality of things. This man-made, this cultural environment, which has its being in the minds of men, is interposed between man as a biological organism and the external reality. It is in this realm that ideas are efficacious. They are efficacious because men react to their ideas and images, to their pictures and notions of the world, treating these pictures as if they were the reality.

The airy nothings in the realm of essence are efficacious in the existential world when a man, believing it to be true or good, treats the idea as if it were the reality. In this way faith in an idea can quite literally remove a mountain. To be sure, no man's idea can remove a mountain on the moon. But if the American people took it into their heads that life would not be worth living until Pike's Peak was in the suburbs of Chicago, they could move Pike's Peak. They could do it if they and their descendants were sufficiently devoted to the idea for a long enough time.

Nothing would happen to Pike's Peak if the idea of removing it were merely proclaimed and celebrated. The idea would have to become, like the idea of winning a war, the object and the focus of the nation's energies. Then the idea would operate in the minds of men who voted, who planned, who would engineer the undertaking, who would raise the money, would recruit the labor, would procure the equipment, and—shall we say—would suppress the mounting resistance of the objectors to the project.

Because ideas have the power to organize human behavior, their efficacy can be radical. They are indeed radical when, as the image of what a man should be, they govern the formation of his character and so imprint a lasting organization on his behavior. Because the images of man are the designs of the molds in which characters are formed, they are of critical concern. What is the image of the good king, the good courtier, the good subject—of the good master and of the good slave—of the good citizen, the good soldier, the good politician, the good boss, the good workingman? The images matter very much. The ones which prevail will govern education. The ideas of what men should be like become efficacious in the existential world because, as they are imposed by the family, the school, and the community, they cause men to "acquire the kind of character which makes them *want* to act in the way they *have* to act as members of the society or of a special class within it." They learn "to *desire* what, objectively, it is necessary for them to do," and "*outer force* is . . . replaced by" the "*inner compulsion*" of their own characters.

That there are limits to education in this sense, we cannot doubt. But we do not know where they are. There is, that is to say, no clear and certain boundary between character which is acquired and those more or less uneducable traits of human nature, evolved during the long ages and transmitted by inheritance. We are quite unable to predict with any certainty or precision how far the individual pupil is educable—or rather how far he is still educable by the time a particular educator gets hold of him, and after he has already acquired a character of sorts in his infancy.

Yet, however crude and clumsy our knowledge of the process, there is no doubt that a character is acquired by experience and education. Within limits that we have not measured, human nature is malleable. Can we doubt it when we remember that when Shakespeare was alive there were no Americans, that when Virgil was alive there were no Englishmen, and that when Homer was alive there were no Romans? Quite certainly, men have acquired the ways of thinking, feeling, and acting which we recognize as their ethnic, national, class, and occupational characteristics. Comparatively speaking, these characteristics are, moreover, recently acquired. Even within the brief span of historical time characters have been acquired and have been lost and have been replaced by other characters. This is what gives to man's history, despite his common humanity, its infinite variety.

Because human nature is, as Hocking puts it, "the most plastic part of the living world, the most adaptable, the most educable," it is also the most mal-adaptable and mis-educable. The cultural heritage which contains the whole structure and fabric of the good life is acquired. It may be rejected. It may be acquired badly. It may not be acquired at all. For we are not born with it. If it is not transmitted from one generation to the next, it may be lost, indeed forgotten through a dark age, until somewhere and somehow men rediscover it, and, exploring the world again, re-create it anew.

The acquired culture is not transmitted in our genes, and so the issue is always in doubt. The good life in the good society, though attainable, is never attained and possessed once and for all. So what has been attained will again be lost if the wisdom of the good life in a good society is not transmitted.

3 · *The Moral Responsibility of Man*

"The Captains of Their Souls," Today and Tomorrow, *July 31, 1943.*

For an answer to the deepest questions of policy which face us in dealing with our enemies, and also with our friends, we must return for guidance to the first and last things of our spiritual heritage. Let us not shrink from the moral effort. For this is the hour of decision. It is the most fateful moment of our lives, and only if we believe truly can we hope to think clearly and then to act effectively.

The fundamental question, which faces us everywhere, and in many forms, has to do with the nature of man, and most precisely it is whether adult men and women are to be regarded as having that freedom of the will which makes them personally responsible for their conduct. The supreme heresy of our enemies is that they have carried ruthlessly to the logical conclusion the denial of man's personal responsibility, and therefore of his human dignity. . . .

Our response to this heresy usually takes the form of asserting the rights of men and of nations against the arbitrary tyrants and their adherents. But this is only the negative and partial aspect of the truth. For men are not really free when they are released from bondage. They are only freed men. They are not free men until they are the captains of their souls and know that they themselves have the power and the duty to choose between good and evil.

The distinction is crucial. If we bear it in mind we shall not make the moral error of saying to the Italians or the Germans or to anyone else: you were all the innocent victims of the tyrants whom you obeyed. That is a pernicious sentimentality which denies man's moral responsibility. Nor shall we say to them: because you obeyed these tyrants, you and your children are one and all congenitally and forever cursed. That is the damnable heresy of our enemies which denies the inviolability of the human soul, or in the ancient language of faith, the fatherhood of God. Nor shall we say: leave it to us and we shall give you back liberty. That is the moral blindness and the intellectual error of not knowing that freedom is personal responsibility. Nor shall we say: surrender, and we shall stuff freedom down your throats at the point of the bayonet. That is a doctrinaire self-righteousness which makes freedom meaningless and odious.

The true view is the ancient view that men are responsible for their acts of commission and of omission, and that therefore the adult Germans and Italians are accountable for the acts of their governments. This is the rule of justice which comes first in the restoration of order. Far from being inhuman, it is a recognition of the humanity of our enemies. For no one who uses words exactly speaks of justice except among adult human beings who are in possession of their faculties. We treat animals, children, the insane, with kindness. But justice we invoke only among responsible men.

The rule of justice, which is primary, is then tempered with mercy, which stems at last from the knowledge that we too are sinners and must therefore give to others what we must ask for ourselves.

Finally, mercy becomes illuminated with grace, which in the dealing of men with other men in the world means that there is in each man an indestructible essence by which he can by repentance and reparation redeem himself. Thus, in the golden words which the Salvation Army has so often offered to the stricken: a man may be down, but he is never out.

These considerations are not remote from practical policy. They are the very considerations to which we must hold firmly if we are not to become lost in a maze of sophistry and improvised casuistry. It is an awful responsibility that we hold in our hands, the overwhelming force which now we wield, and we must not be unworthy of it. We must not descend to the notion that any catch-as-catch-can opinion about how to exercise such power is realistic and humane and that to remember and to examine the issues for which men are dying is inconvenient and too much trouble.

The constant knowledge must be with us that our power, like all power, is good only within the moral order. Therefore, when we send forth our men to kill or be killed, let us not in moral inertia and laziness of spirit refuse the effort of making sure that their battles are not meaningless and their sacrifices are not vain.

"The Drouth: On Self-Reliance in This Age,"
Today and Tomorrow, *June 5, 1934.*

While no one will grudge relief in the emergency, the question is bound to be raised in many minds as to how far the government can and should go in assuming the burdens caused by natural and by man-made calamities. The traditional view is, of course, that farmers must take the weather as it comes; relying not at all upon government devices, they become the self-reliant independent stock from which the nation renews its vitality. In this view a paternalistic policy for the farmer is undesirable, not so much because it costs money, but because it softens him as an individual.

There are few persons who would not feel that while there is something in this view, it is infected with a kind of moral blindness. Is the modern American farmer the same kind of farmer around whom there has grown the ideal of complete self-reliance? The traditional view is an ancient one based upon the experience of farmers working their own land for their own needs and for a neighboring community. But the wheat farmer in the Dakotas and Kansas and Nebraska does not live that kind of life. He produces for a world market and he supplies his own needs out of a world market. He is no longer even approximately self-sufficient. Can he then be expected to be wholly self-reliant?

In earlier days if his crop was bad, he suffered and accepted his lot. But today if his crop is bad, his competitor in another region makes a big profit. In earlier days, because he supplied his principal needs at home or in the neighborhood, his standard of life was relatively independent of the consequences of political and economic policies. Today his real income fluctuates spectacularly due to causes which he cannot control by his own prudence, thrift, or industry.

These are the underlying reasons why we now recognize that to protect the farmer against great natural calamities or economic convulsions is a social duty. If he is to be self-reliant, he must be more or less self-sufficient; in so far as he is not, he must either be led back to self-sufficiency or insured against those forces of nature and of society which self-reliance alone cannot deal with.

The difficult aspect of the matter is to know where to draw the line and then to have the political courage to draw it. The farmer, being only human, will expect more protection than society can afford or than he is really entitled to have. But the rule which ought to govern in these affairs is reasonably clear, however hard it may be to apply it in many particular cases. Taking into consideration its resources in the light of its obligations to other groups in the nation, society ought to attempt to insure men against those risks which a reasonably prudent man cannot be expected to avert or to deal with singlehanded. . . .

If the virtues and values of individualism and self-reliance are to be preserved, we must not put upon the individual person burdens that are greater than he can by self-reliance carry. This is the surest way to kill individualism: by making it intolerable. In the misery of the past few years the individual burden has been greater than individuals could carry. That is why the very word "individualism," though it is the name of a noble conception of life, has suddenly fallen into such disrepute. To restore men's faith in it, and all that it means in the preservation of liberty and of the free growth of the human spirit, individualism has to be made safe for reasonably prudent men.

For that reason it can be said that those who are laboring to distribute justly the social risks of our immensely complicated society are the true defenders of individual liberty against the diseases of paternalism and the dangers of tyranny.

---

4 · *The Making of the Citizen*

The Phantom Public (1925), *Chapter 2.*

I have tried to imagine how the perfect citizen could be produced. Some say he will have to be born of the conjunction of the right germ plasms, and, in the pages of books written by

Madison Grant, Lothrop Stoddard, and other revivalists, I have seen prescriptions as to just who ought to marry whom to produce a great citizenry. Not being a biologist I keep an open but hopeful mind on this point, tempered, however, with the knowledge that certainty about how to breed ability in human beings is on the whole in inverse proportion to the writer's scientific reputation.

It is then to education that logically one turns next, for education has furnished the thesis of the last chapter of every optimistic book on democracy written for one hundred and fifty years. Even Robert Michels, stern and unbending anti-sentimentalist that he is, says in his "final considerations" that "it is the great task of social education to raise the intellectual level of the masses, so that they may be enabled, within the limits of what is possible, to counteract the oligarchical tendencies" of all collective action.

So I have been reading some of the new standard textbooks used to teach citizenship in schools and colleges. After reading them I do not see how anyone can escape the conclusion that man must have the appetite of an encyclopedist and infinite time ahead of him. To be sure, he no longer is expected to remember the exact salary of the county clerk and the length of the coroner's term. In the new civics he studies the problems of government, and not the structural detail. He is told, in one textbook of five hundred concise, contentious pages, which I have been reading, about city problems, state problems, national problems, international problems, trust problems, labor problems, transportation problems, banking problems, rural problems, agricultural problems, and so on *ad infinitum*. In the eleven pages devoted to problems of the city there are described twelve sub-problems.

But nowhere in this well-meant book is the sovereign citizen of the future given a hint as to how, while he is earning a living, rearing children, and enjoying his life, he is to keep himself informed about the progress of this swarming confusion of problems. He is exhorted to conserve the natural resources of the country because they are limited in quantity. He is advised to watch public expenditures because the taxpayers cannot pay out indefinitely increasing amounts. But he, the voter, the citizen, the sovereign, is apparently expected to yield an unlimited quantity of public spirit, interest, curiosity, and effort. The author of the textbook, touching on everything, as he thinks, from city sewers to Indian opium, misses a decisive fact: the citizen gives but a little of his time to public affairs, has but a casual interest in facts and but a poor appetite for theory.

It never occurs to this preceptor of civic duty to provide the student with a rule by which he can know whether on Thursday it is his duty to consider subways in Brooklyn or the Manchurian Railway, nor how, if he determines on Thursday to express his sovereign will on the subway question, he is to repair those gaps in his knowledge of that question which are due to his having been preoccupied the day before in expressing his sovereign will about rural credits in Montana and the rights of Britain in the Sudan. Yet he cannot know all about everything all the time, and while he is watching one thing a thousand others undergo great changes. Unless he can discover some rational ground for fixing his attention where it will do the most good, and in a way that suits his inherently amateurish equipment, he will be as bewildered as a puppy trying to lick three bones at once.

I do not wish to say that it does the student no good to be taken on a sightseeing tour of the problems of the world. It may teach him that the world is complicated. . . . He may learn humility, but most certainly his acquaintance with what a high-minded author thought were American problems in 1925 will not equip him to master American problems ten years later. Unless out of the study of transient issues he acquires an intellectual attitude, no education has occurred.

That is why the usual appeal to education as the remedy for the incompetence of democracy is so barren. It is, in effect, a proposal that schoolteachers shall by some magic of their own fit men to govern after the makers of laws and the preachers of civic ideals have had a free hand in writing the specifications. The reformers do not ask what men can be taught. They say they should be taught whatever may be necessary to fit them to govern the modern world.

The usual appeal to education can bring only disappointment. For the problems of the modern world appear and change faster than any set of teachers can grasp them, much faster than they can convey their substance to a population of children. If the schools attempt to teach children how to solve the problems of the day, they are bound always to be in arrears. The most they can conceivably attempt is the teaching of a pattern of thought and feeling which will enable the citizen to approach a new problem in some useful fashion. But that pattern cannot be invented by the pedagogue. It is the political theorist's business to trace out that pattern. In that task he must not assume that the mass has political genius, but that men, even if they had genius, would give only a little time and attention to public affairs.

The moralist, I am afraid, will agree all too readily with the idea that social education must deal primarily not with the elements and solutions of particular phases of transient problems but with the principles that constitute an attitude toward all problems. I warn him off. It will require more than a good conscience to govern modern society, for conscience is no guide in situations where the essence of the difficulty is to find a guide for the conscience.

When I am tempted to think that men can be fitted out to deal with the modern world simply by teaching morals, manners, and patriotism, I try to remember the fable of the pensive professor walking in the woods at twilight. He stumbled into a tree. This experience compelled him to act. Being a man of honor and breeding, he raised his hat, bowed deeply to the tree, and exclaimed with sincere regret: "Excuse me, sir, I thought you were a tree."

Is it fair, I ask, as a matter of morality, to chide him for his conduct? If he had encountered a tree, can anyone deny his right to collide with it? If he had stumbled into a man, was his apology not sufficient? Here was a moral code in perfect working order, and the only questionable aspect of his conduct turned not on the goodness of his heart or the firmness of his principles but on a point of fact. You may retort that he had a moral obligation to know the difference between a man and a tree. Perhaps so. But suppose that instead of walking in the woods he had been casting a ballot; suppose that instead of a tree he had encountered the Fordney-McCumber tariff. How much more obligation to know the truth would you have imposed on him then? After all, this walker in the woods at twilight with his mind on other things was facing, as all of us think we are, the facts he imagined were there, and was doing his duty as he had learned it.

In some degree the whole animate world seems to share the inexpertness of the thoughtful professor. Pavlov showed by his experiments on dogs that an animal with a false stomach can experience all the pleasures of eating, and the number of mice and monkeys known to have been deceived in laboratories is surpassed only by the hopeful citizens of a democracy. Man's reflexes are, as the psychologists say, conditioned. And, therefore, he responds quite readily to a glass egg, a decoy duck, a stuffed shirt, or a political platform. No moral code, as such, will enable him to know whether he is exercising his moral faculties on a real and an important event. For effective virtue, as Socrates pointed out long ago, is knowledge; and a code of the right and the wrong must wait upon a perception of the true and the false.

But even the successful practice of a moral code would not emancipate democracy. There are too many moral codes. In our immediate lives, within the boundaries of our own society, there may be commonly accepted standards. But a political theorist who asks that a local standard be universally applied is merely begging one of the questions he ought to be trying to solve. For, while possibly it may be an aim of political organization to arrive at a common standard of judgment, one of the conditions which engenders politics and makes political organization necessary is the conflict of standards. . . .

If then eugenics cannot produce the ideal democratic citizen, omnicompetent and sovereign, because biology knows neither how to breed political excellence nor what that excellence is; if education cannot equip the citizen, because the schoolteacher cannot anticipate the issues of the future; if morality cannot direct him, first, because right or wrong in specific cases depends upon the perception of true or false, and, second, on the assumption that there is a universal moral code, which, in fact, does not exist, where else shall we look for the method of making the competent citizen? Democratic theorists in the nineteenth century had several other prescriptions which still influence the thinking of many hopeful persons.

One school based their reforms on the aphorism that the cure for the evils of democracy is more democracy. It was assumed that the popular will was wise and good if only you could get at it. They proposed extensions of the suffrage, and as much voting as possible by means of the initiative, referendum, and recall, direct election of senators, direct primaries, an elected judiciary, and the like. They begged the question, for it has never been proved that there exists the kind of public opinion which they presupposed. Since the Bryan campaign of 1896 this school of thought has made great conquests in most of the states, and has profoundly influenced the federal government. The eligible vote has trebled since 1896; the direct action of the voter has been enormously extended. Yet that same period has seen a decline in the percentage of the popular vote cast at presidential elections from 80.75 per cent in 1896 to 52.36 per cent in 1920. Apparently there is a fallacy in the first assumption of this school that "the whole people" desires to participate actively in government. Nor is there any evidence to show that the persons who do participate are in any real sense directing the course of affairs. The party machines have survived every attack. And why should they not? If the voter cannot grasp the details of the problems of the day because he has not the time, the interest, or the knowledge, he will not have a better public opinion because he is asked to express his opinion more often. He will simply be more bewildered, more bored, and more ready to follow along.

Another school, calling themselves revolutionary, have ascribed the disenchantment of democracy to the capitalistic system. They have argued that property is power, and that until there is as wide a distribution of economic power as there is of the right to vote the suffrage cannot be more effective. No serious student, I think, would dispute that socialist premise which asserts that the weight of influence on society exercised by an individual is more nearly related to the character of his property than to his abstract legal citizenship. But the socialist conclusion that economic power can be distributed by concentrating the ownership of great utilities in the state, the conclusion that the pervasion of industrial life by voting and referenda will yield competent popular decisions, seems to me again to beg the question. For what reason is there to think that subjecting so many more affairs to the method of the vote will reveal hitherto undiscovered wisdom and technical competence and reservoirs of public interest in men? The socialist scheme has at its root the mystical fallacy of democracy, that the people, all of them, are competent; at its top it suffers from the homeopathic fallacy that adding new tasks to a burden the people will not and cannot carry now will make the burden of citizenship easily borne. The socialist theory presupposes an unceasing, untiring round of civic duties, an enormous complication of the political interests that are already much too complicated.

These various remedies, eugenic, educational, ethical, populist, and socialist, all assume that either the voters are inherently competent to direct the course of affairs or that they are making progress toward such an ideal. I think it is a false ideal. I do not mean an undesirable ideal. I mean an unattainable ideal, bad only in the sense that it is bad for a fat man to try to be a ballet dancer. An ideal should express the true possibilities of its subject. When it does not it perverts the true possibilities. The ideal of the omnicompetent, sovereign citizen is, in my opinion, such a false ideal. It is unattainable. The pursuit of it is misleading. The failure to achieve it has produced the current disenchantment.

The individual man does not have opinions on all public affairs. He does not know how to direct public affairs. He does not know what is happening, why it is happening, what ought to happen. I cannot imagine how he could know, and there is not the least reason for thinking, as mystical democrats have thought, that the compounding of individual ignorances in masses of people can produce a continuous directing force in public affairs.

A Preface to Morals (*1929*), *Chapter 9*.

The critical phase of human experience is the passage from childhood to maturity; the critical question is whether childish habits and expectations are to persist or to be transformed. We grow older. But it is by no means certain that we shall grow up. The human character is a complicated thing, and its elements do not necessarily march in step. It is possible to be a sage in some things and a child in others, to be at once precocious and retarded, to be shrewd and foolish, serene and irritable. For some parts of our personalities may well be more mature than others; not infrequently we participate in the enterprises of an adult with the mood and manners of a child.

The successful passage into maturity depends, therefore, on a breaking-up and reconstruction of those habits which were appropriate only to our earliest experience.

In a certain larger sense this is the essence of education. For unless a man has acquired the character of an adult, he is a lost soul no matter how good his technical equipment. The world unhappily contains many such lost souls. They are often in high places, men trained to manipulate the machinery of civilization, but utterly incapable of handling their own purposes in any civilized fashion. For their purposes are merely the relics of an infancy when their wishes were law, and they knew neither necessity nor change.

When a childish disposition is carried over into an adult environment the result is a radically false valuation of that environment. The symptoms are fairly evident. They may appear as a disposition to feel that everything which happens to a man has an intentional relation to himself; life becomes a kind of conspiracy to make him happy or to make him miserable. In either case it is thought to be deeply concerned with his destiny. The childish pattern appears also as a deep sense that life owes him something, that somehow it is the duty of the universe to look after him, and to listen sharply when he speaks to it. The notion that the universe is full of purposes utterly unknown to him, utterly indifferent to him, is as outrageous to one who is imperfectly matured as would be the conduct of a mother who forgot to give a hungry child its lunch. The childish pattern appears also as a disposition to believe that he may reach out for anything in sight and take it, and that having gotten it nobody must ever under any circumstances take it away. Death and decay are, therefore, almost an insult, a kind of mischief in the nature of things, which ought not to be there, and would not be there, if everything only behaved as good little boys believe it should. There is indeed authority for the belief that we are all being punished for the naughtiness of our first grandmother; that work and trouble and death would not really be there to plague us but for her unhappy transgression; that by rights we ought to live in paradise and have everything we want forever and ever.

Here, too, is the source of that common complaint of the world-weary that they are tired of their pleasures. They have what they yearned for; yet having it they are depressed at finding that they do not care. Their inability to enjoy what they can have is the obverse of the desire to possess the unattainable: both are due to carrying over the expectations of youth into adult life. They find themselves in a world unlike the world of their youth; they themselves are no longer youths. But they retain the criteria of youth, and with them measure the world and their own deserts.

Here, too, is the origin of the apparent paradox that as men grow older they grow wiser but sadder. It is not a paradox at all if we remember that this wisdom which makes them sadder is, after all, an incomplete wisdom. They have grown wiser as to the character of the world, wiser too about their own powers, but they remain naïve as to what they may expect of the world and themselves. The expectations which they formed in their youth persist as deeply ingrained habits to worry them in their maturity. They are only partially matured; they have become only partially wise. They have acquired skill and information, but the parts of them which are adult are embedded in other parts of their natures which are childish. For men do not necessarily mature altogether and in unison; they learn to do this and that more easily than they learn what to like and what to reject. Intelligence is often more completely educated than desire; our outward behavior has an appearance of being grown up which our inner vanities and hopes, our dim but powerful cravings, often belie. In a word, we learn the arts and the sciences long before we learn philosophy.

If we ask ourselves what is this wisdom which experience forces upon us, the answer must be that we discover the world is not constituted as we had supposed it to be. It is not that we learn more about its physical elements, or its geography, or the variety of its inhabitants, or the ways in which human society is governed. Knowledge of this sort can be taught to a child without in any fundamental way disturbing his childishness. In fact, all of us are aware that we once knew a great many things which we have since forgotten. The essential discovery of maturity has little if anything to do with information about the names, the locations, and the sequences of facts; it is the acquiring of a different sense of life, a different kind of intuition about the nature of things.

A boy can take you into the open at night and show you the stars; he might tell you no end of things about them, conceivably all that an astronomer could teach. But until and unless he feels the vast indifference of the universe to his own fate, and has placed himself in the perspective of cold and illimitable space, he has not looked maturely at the heavens. Until he has felt this, and unless he can endure this, he remains a child, and in his childishness he will resent the heavens when they are not accommodating. He will demand sunshine when he wishes to play, and rain when the ground is dry, and he will look upon storms as anger directed at him, and the thunder as a personal threat.

The discovery that our wishes have little or no authority in the world brings with it experience of the necessity that is in the nature of things. The lesson of this experience is one from which we shrink and to which few ever wholly accommodate themselves. The world of the child is a kind of enchanted island. The labor that went into procuring his food, his clothes, his toys, is wholly invisible at first. His earliest expectations are, therefore, that somehow the Lord will provide. Only gradually does the truth come home to him how much effort it costs to satisfy his wants. It takes even longer for him to understand that not only does he not get what he wants by asking for it but he cannot be sure to get what he wants by working for it. It is not easy to accept the knowledge that desire, that prayer, that effort can be and often are frustrated, that in the nature of things there is much fumbling, trial and error, deadlock and defeat.

Public Opinion (1922), *Chapter 17.*

On many subjects of great public importance, and in varying degree among different people for more personal matters, the threads of memory and emotion are in a snarl. The same word will connote any number of different ideas; emotions are displaced from the images to which they belong to names which resemble the names of these images. In the uncriticized parts of the mind there is a vast amount of association by mere clang, contact, and succession. There are stray emotional attachments, there are words that were names and are masks. In dreams, reveries, and panic, we uncover some of the disorder, enough to see how the naïve mind is composed, and how it behaves when not disciplined by wakeful effort and external resistance. We see that there is no more natural order than in a dusty old attic. There is often the same incongruity between fact, idea, and emotion as there might be in an opera house, if all the wardrobes were dumped in a heap and all the scores mixed up, so that Madame Butterfly in a Valkyr's dress waited lyrically for the return of Faust. "At Christmastide," says an editorial, "old memories soften the heart. Holy teachings are remembered afresh as thoughts run back to childhood. The world does not seem so bad when seen through the mist of half-happy, half-sad recollections of loved ones now with God. No heart is untouched by the mysterious influence. . . . The country is honeycombed with red propaganda—but there is a good supply of ropes, muscles, and lampposts . . . while this world moves, the spirit of liberty will burn in the breast of man."

The man who found these phrases in his mind needs help. He needs a Socrates who will separate the words, cross-examine him until he has defined them, and made words the names of ideas. Made them mean a particular object and nothing else.

For these tense syllables have got themselves connected in his mind by primitive association, and are bundled together by his memories of Christmas, his indignation as a conservative, and his thrills as the heir to a revolutionary tradition. Sometimes the snarl is too huge and ancient for quick unravelling. Sometimes, as in modern psychotheraphy, there are layers upon layers of memory reaching back to infancy, which have to be separated and named.

The effect of naming, the effect, that is, of saying that the labor groups C and M, but not X, are underpaid, instead of saying that Labor is Exploited, is incisive. Perceptions recover their identity, and the emotion they arouse is specific, since it is no longer reinforced by large and accidental connections with everything from Christmas to Moscow. The disentangled idea with a name of its own, and an emotion that has been scrutinized, is ever so much more open to correction by new data in the problem. It had been imbedded in the whole personality, had affiliations of some sort with the whole ego; a challenge would reverberate through the whole soul. After it has been thoroughly criticized, the idea is no longer *me* but *that*. It is objectified, it is at arm's length. Its fate is not bound up with my fate, but with the fate of the outer world upon which I am acting.

Re-education of this kind will help to bring our public opinions into grip with the environment. That is the way the enormous censoring, stereotyping, and dramatizing apparatus can be liquidated. Where there is no difficulty in knowing what the relevant environment is, the critic, the teacher, the physician, can unravel the mind. But where the environment is as obscure to the analyst as to his pupil, no analytic technic is sufficient. Intelligence work is required. In political and industrial problems the critic as such can do something, but unless he can count upon receiving from expert reporters a valid picture of the environment, his dialectic cannot go far.

Therefore, though here, as in most other matters, "education" is the supreme remedy, the value of this education will depend upon the evolution of knowledge. And our knowledge of human institutions is still extraordinarily meager and impressionistic. The gathering of social knowledge is, on the whole, still haphazard; not, as it will have to become, the normal accompaniment of action. And yet the collection of information will not be made, one may be sure, for the sake of its ultimate use. It will be made because modern decision requires it to be made. But as it is being made, there will accumulate a body of data which political science can turn into generalization, and build up for the schools into a conceptual picture of the world. When that picture takes form, civic education can become a preparation for dealing with an unseen environment.

As a working model of the social system becomes available to the teacher, he can use is to make the pupil acutely aware of how his mind works on unfamiliar facts. Until he has such a model, the teacher cannot hope to prepare men fully for the world they will find. What he can do is to prepare them to deal with that world with a great deal more sophistication about their own minds. He can, by the use of the case method, teach the pupil the habit of examining the sources of his information. He can teach him, for example, to look in his newspaper for the place where the dispatch was filed, for the name of the correspondent, the name of the press service, the authority given for the statement, the circumstances under which the statement was secured. He can teach the pupil to ask himself whether the reporter saw what he describes, and to remember how that reporter described other events in the past. He can teach him the character of censorship, of the idea of privacy, and furnish him with knowledge of past propaganda. He can, by the proper use of history, make him aware of the stereotype, and can educate a habit of introspection about the imagery evoked by printed words. He can, by courses in comparative history and anthropology, produce a lifelong realization of the way codes impose a special pattern upon the imagination. He can teach men to catch themselves making allegories, dramatizing relations, and personifying abstractions. He can show the pupil how he identifies himself with these allegories, how he becomes interested, and how he selects the attitude, heroic, romantic, economic which he adopts while holding a particular opinion.

The study of error is not only in the highest degree prophylactic, but it serves as a stimulating introduction to the study of truth. As our minds become more deeply aware of their own subjectivism, we find a zest in objective method that is not otherwise there. We see vividly, as normally we should not, the enormous mischief and casual cruelty of our prejudices. And the destruction of a prejudice, though painful at first, because of its connection with our self-respect, gives an immense relief and a fine pride when it is successfully done. There is a radical enlargement of the range of attention. As the current categories dissolve, a hard, simple version of the world breaks up. The scene turns vivid and full. There follows an emotional incentive to hearty appreciation of scientific method, which otherwise it is not easy to arouse, and is impossible to sustain. Prejudices are so much easier and more interesting. For if you teach the principles of science as if they had always been accepted, their chief virtue as a discipline, which is objectivity, will make them dull. But teach them at first as victories over the superstitions of the mind, and the exhilaration of the chase and of the conquest may carry the pupil over that hard transition from his own self-bound experience to the phase where his curiosity has matured, and his reason has acquired passion.

---

5 · *The Wonders of the Human Spirit*

"Reflections on Gandhi," Today and Tomorrow, *February 3, 1948.*

In the life and death of Mahatma Gandhi we have seen reenacted in our time the supreme drama of humanity. Gandhi was a political leader and he was a seer, and perhaps never before on so grand a scale has anyone sought to shape the course of events in the world as it is by the example of a spirit which was not of the world as it is.

Gandhi was, as St. Paul said, transformed in the renewing of his mind, he was not "conformed to this world." Yet he sought to govern turbulent masses of men who were still very much conformed to this world, and have not been transformed. He died by violence as he was staking his life in order to set the example of non-violence.

Thus he posed again the perennial question of how the insight of the seers and saints is related to the work of legislators, rulers, and statesmen. That they are in conflict is only too plain, and yet it is impossible to admit, as Gandhi refused to admit, that the conflict can never be resolved. For it is necessary to govern mankind and it is necessary to transform men.

Perhaps we may say that the insight of the governors of

men is, as it were, horizontal: They act in the present, with men as they are, with the knowledge they possess, with what they can now understand, with the mixture of their passions and desires and instincts. They must work with concrete and with the plainly and generally intelligible things.

The insight of the seers, on the contrary, is vertical: They deal, however wide their appeal, with each person potentially, as he might be transformed, renewed, and regenerated. And because they appeal to experience which men have not yet had, with things that are not at hand and are out of their immediate reach, with the invisible and the unattained, they speak and act, as Gandhi did, obscurely, appealing to the imagination by symbolic evocation and subtle example.

The ideals of human life which the seers teach—non-resistance, humility, and poverty and chastity—have never been and can never be the laws of a secular society. Chastity, consistently and habitually observed, would annihilate it. Poverty, if universally pursued, would plunge it into misery and disease. Humility and non-resistance, if they were the rule, would mean the triumph of predatory force.

Is it possible that the greatest seers and teachers did not know this, and that what they enjoined upon men was a kind of suicide and self-annihilation? Obviously not. Their wisdom was not naïve, and it can be understood if we approach it not as rules of conduct but as an insight into the economy and the order and the quality of the passions.

At the summit of their wisdom what they teach is, I think, not how in the practical issues of daily life men in society can and should behave but to what ultimate values they should give their allegiance. Thus the injunction to render unto Caesar the things that are Caesar's is not a definite political principle which can be applied to define the relation of Church and State. It is an injunction as to where men shall have their ultimate obligations, that in rendering to Caesar the things that are Caesar's, they should not give to Caesar their ultimate loyalty, but should reserve it.

In the same manner, to have humility is to have, in the last reaches of conviction, a saving doubt. To embrace poverty is to be without possessiveness and a total attachment to things and to honors. To be non-resistant is to be at last non-competitive.

What the seer points toward is best described in the language of St. Paul as the creation of the new man. "And that ye put on the new man, which after God is created in righteousness and true holiness." What is this new man? He is the man who has been renewed and is "no longer under a schoolmaster," whose passions have been altered, as Gandhi sought to alter the passions of his countrymen, so that they need no discipline from without because they have been transformed from within. Such regenerated men can, as Confucius said, follow what their hearts desire without transgressing what is right. They are "led of the spirit" in the Pauline language, and therefore they "are not under the law."

It is not for such men as them that governments are instituted and laws enacted and enforced. These are for the old Adam. It is for the aggressive, possessive, carnal appetites of the old Adam that there are punishments and rewards, and for his violence a superior force.

It is only for the regenerate man, whose passions have been transformed, that the discipline of the law and of power are no longer needed, nor any incentive or reward beyond the exquisite and exhilarating wholesomeness and unity and freedom of his own passions.

"Amelia Earhart," Today and Tomorrow, *July 8, 1937.*

I cannot quite remember whether Miss Earhart undertook her flight with some practical purpose in mind, say, to demonstrate something or other about aviation which will make it a little easier for commercial passengers to move more quickly around the world. There are those who seem to think that an enterprise like hers must have some such justification, that without it there was no good reason for taking such grave risks.

But in truth Miss Earhart needs no such justification. The world is a better place to live in because it contains human beings who will give up ease and security and stake their own lives in order to do what they themselves think worth doing. They help to offset the much larger number who are ready to sacrifice the ease and the security and the very lives of others in order to do what they want done. No end of synthetic heroes strut the stage, great bold men in bulletproof vests surrounded by squads of armed guards, demonstrating their courage by terrorizing the weak and the defenseless. It is somehow reassuring to think that there are also men and women who take the risks themselves, who pit themselves not against their fellow beings but against the immensity and the violence of the natural world, who are brave without cruelty to others and impassioned with an idea that dignifies all who contemplate it.

The best things of mankind are as useless as Amelia Earhart's adventure. They are the things that are undertaken not for some definite, measurable result, but because someone, not counting the costs or calculating the consequences, is moved by curiosity, the love of excellence, a point of honor, the compulsion to invent or to make or to understand. In such persons mankind overcomes the inertia which would keep it earthbound forever in its habitual ways. They have in them the free and useless energy with which alone men surpass themselves.

Such energy cannot be planned and managed and made purposeful, or weighed by the standards of utility or judged by its social consequences. It is wild and it is free. But all the heroes, the saints and the seers, the explorers and the creators partake of it. They do not know what they discover. They do not know where their impulse is taking them. They can give no account in advance of where they are going or explain completely where they have been. They have been possessed for a time with an extraordinary passion which is unintelligible in ordinary terms.

No preconceived theory fits them. No material purpose actuates them. They do the useless, brave, noble, the divinely foolish and the very wisest things that are done by man. And what they prove to themselves and to others is that man is no mere creature of his habits, no mere automaton in his routine, no mere cog in the collective machine, but that in the dust of which he is made there is also fire, lighted now and then by great winds from the sky.

6 · *An Image of Man for Liberal Democracy*

"Man's Image of Man," The Commonweal, *XXXV (1942), 406, an address delivered before the Seventeenth Annual Meeting of the American Catholic Philosophical Association in Philadelphia, Pennsylvania on December 29 and 30, 1941.*

Most of us have, I think, taken it easily for granted that an age of progress was brought to an end by the great war which began in 1914, and we have then attributed to the war itself, as if it were an accidental and extraneous piece of very bad luck, the disorder of this age. Surely that is only the appearance of things. Surely the truth is that our Western civilization was already sick when the war of 1914 broke out, and it is to this sickness, immensely aggravated by war, that we must attribute the failure of the peace and of the reconstruction.

The symptoms of that sickness have been most visible not only in the ensuing catastrophe of revolutionary war but in the widespread sense of personal disorientation which preceded it. Men were increasingly uneasy, unsettled, and unhappy in the years before the great catastrophe of our age.

The moralist may describe this inner disorder as vice and sin. The statesman may describe it as discontent and lawlessness. The physician may describe it as a maladjustment disclosed by such symptoms as confusion, anxiety, depression, frustration, inferiority, persecution, aimlessness, and weariness. The theologian may describe it as godlessness. They are, I believe, talking about the same thing. They are talking about the modern men who have failed to understand and to live in the order to which man, as he is really constituted, belongs. The modern man is a sick man because—misconceiving the nature of man—he has allowed himself to become the kind of man who cannot be happy, who cannot operate the institutions of the

Western world, who cannot find security and serenity in the universe.

For the paramount characteristic of the modern man is that he rejects the classic and traditional conception of human nature, which is, as Plato says, that the soul leads the affections, and as St. Thomas Aquinas says, that the human person exercises "a royal and politic sovereignty" over the desires. The modern view of human nature has been that reason is not the representative within us of the universal order—and therefore the ruler of our appetites—but that reason is the instrument of our appetites—that, as Mr. Bernard Shaw has put it, "it is only by accurate reasoning that we can calculate our actions so as to do what we intend to do—that is, to fulfill our will."

This conception of human nature—one in which desire is sovereign and reason is the instrument for serving and satisfying desire—this conception has become increasingly the accepted image of man in the modern world. It is upon this image of man that our secular education has been based, and our social philosophy, and our personal codes. Our world today is in the hands of masses of people who are formed in this image and regard it as indubitably the true and scientifically correct conception of human nature. Yet the cultural tradition and the great central institutions of the Western world come down to us from men who would have regarded what is now the fashionable image of man as the image of an uncivilized barbarian.

This modern man, as he is turned out by our secular schools and as he is shaped by the prevailing popular culture, is a being whose desires are limited, not by his reason, which represents the universal order of things, but only by the difficulty of getting more and more satisfaction. The desires of the modern man are, as respects his own inner measures of control, illimitable desires. It follows that the desires of the modern man can never be satisfied, and it is the anguish of unlimited and therefore insatiable desire which is the characteristic misery of our age.

For the unending pursuit of the ever-fleeting object of desire means not only that a man must surely fail; it means also —and this is much worse than failure—that his whole effort must seem to him futile. Yet in our age—because we have accepted the secular image of man—our social criterion of progress has been that we must encourage and incite ourselves to be forever unsatisfied, to think nothing is enough, and thus to seek the satisfaction of insatiable needs.

Thus we have made social problems insoluble. For while we talk of a standard of life, in fact we have no standard of life except that each man shall desire more than he has thus far obtained. Under nineteenth-century capitalism the ideal of the successful man was interminable acquisition of wealth and power. Under twentieth-century social democracy the ideal is the same, except that more persons are involved in the interminable acquisition of wealth and power. In neither social philosophy is there any measure of or any means of putting a limit upon what men shall desire and then seek to acquire.

It is precisely here, I believe, that the peculiar social problem of the Western world has been generated. For at bottom the social problem is not that of satisfying men's objective needs; modern technology is able to do that. The social problem of the modern world arises not out of the objective difficulty of providing an adequate material existence but out of men's subjective expectations, which, because they are unlimited and insatiable, cause violence, inequality, hatred, and frustration.

Though we like to tell ourselves that our purpose is to solve the social problem by ministering to men's needs, in practice we have a conception of human nature, and derived from it an educational system and a commercial and political propaganda, which treat all needs as unlimited. No income can therefore be sufficient to satisfy men's needs. For the appetite merely grows from feeding it. No standard of living is a standard. For there is always a more luxurious standard. No prosperity is rich enough. For the statistical curves on the charts might always go higher still. No nation can be big enough and no state can be powerful enough. For until someone has conquered the whole world, it is always possible to be bigger and greater than you are.

Thus there can never be contentment and peace of mind for modern men because their desires are irrational and, therefore, always expanding and forever unsatisfied. Their insatiable desires are an unending torture, like that which the gods inflicted on Sisyphus, in which they hunger though they eat, thirst though they drink, feel they are naked though they are clothed, long for love and cannot consummate it, seek and never find, achieve and always fail. This is the bitter core of the unhappiness of the modern man. He is an unhappy man and, therefore, a dangerous man, because he could not ever be satisfied. His true nature, which is to find peace in the rational measure of things, has been deformed by desire that knows no limit and can find no rest.

This, I believe, is what we have to understand if we are to understand the discontent which is shaking the world. Men cannot remain civilized when they have rejected the culture of their civilization; that is to say, when they no longer think of themselves and their place in the universe, when they no longer discipline themselves and their children in the tradition which comes to them from the prophets and the saints and the teachers and the philosophers and the discoverers who raised Western men out of barbarism. The secular man—the man who obeys his impulses and knows no reason that transcends his wishes—this secular man, now dominant in the world, has for his chief article of faith an ideal of secular progress which is totally alienated from and profoundly opposed to the real character of the human person.

He supposes himself to be a bundle of desires which can be satisfied by becoming richer, more powerful, more famous, more glamorous, more irresistible. For in the secular tradition men are not taught to think that the disciplining of their desires to a rational measure is indispensable if they are ever to be truly satisfied. Thus the modern conception of progress is self-defeating. For it is based on a fundamental misunderstanding of the economy of human existence; the secular theory of progress is an effort to balance the supply of satisfactions and the demand for them by expanding the demand faster than the supply can be increased. And since demand comes from our appetites, which grow by what they feed upon, whereas supply can be increased only by work and sacrifice, a philosophy which fails to insist upon the limitation of desire must make men forever unhappy—forever incapable of being satisfied and therefore forever seeking the unattainable.

We frequently fall into error and folly, says Dr. Johnson, "not because the true principles of action are not known but because, for a time, they are not remembered." The true principle of action, long known but in our century not remembered, is that man is so constituted that his greatest need is not the satisfaction of his desires but that his reason shall impose law and order upon his desires. This is the truth about man without which—had it not been discovered, had it not been revealed—our barbarian ancestors could not have bred more or less civilized descendants. Without the discovery of the truth about the nature of man, the barbarian would not have wished, nor would he have had any idea of how, to raise himself out of barbarism. And, as we can see by looking at the world about us, as soon as men lose hold of this truth, seeing no compelling reason why they should restrain their appetites, they quickly become barbarians again.

The ideal which arises out of the classical image of man is not progress, which merely seeks to multiply the supply of satisfactions, but the good life.

To pursue the good life, as described, for example, by Aristotle, is to cultivate not some but all the human dispositions by limiting each to a Golden Mean; thus the demand for satisfactions, the promptings of appetite, the pressure of ambition, though recognized as natural and normal, are never unlimited. They are disciplined to the reality of things, and having been made moderate, they are not inherently and forever doomed to disappointment and frustration.

As perfected in the religious tradition of the West the good life is an imitation of God—that is to say, the cultivation of the reason, which is an imitation of His omniscience, and of the only true freedom—the freedom to follow the dictates of reason —which is an intimation of His omnipotence.

Men who live in this tradition are capable of brotherhood in a civilized society. They can prefer to do unto others what they would have others do unto them. For men who choose to be ruled by reason are bound together as equals—equals not in the vulgar sense that they have identical or even comparable gifts and talents—but because they seek to reason and to obey reason.

This common potentiality gives them the right to hope that they can discover justice, that they can agree upon what is right. Their common freedom to follow reason by mastering their desires gives them the common hope that they can make and maintain a civilized order.

Thus we see that the golden rule in social relations will work only among men who practice the golden mean in their personal conduct. Without these two elemental laws of human existence—that of the golden mean and that of the golden rule —the good society is impossible. The secular conception of man rejects the golden mean and has therefore made unworkable, even though lip service is still given to it, the golden rule. For where there is no limitation upon desire—no willingness to accept the discipline which the golden mean requires—then the relations of men with one another must become an interminable struggle for domination and survival.

When aggregations of men are "emancipated"—that was

how they described it—when they no longer feel themselves bound by the elemental laws of their own nature, they do not in fact feel that they are free men. For they are oppressed by inner confusion and the anxieties of insecurity. Far from entering into a joyous sense of freedom, they feel themselves at war with one another, and indeed at war within themselves.

That is why, as modern men cast off the bonds of tradition, they were not imbued with the spirit of confident enterprise and exhilarating adventure; the completely secularized modern man has disclosed his true condition within himself by joining in the search for protection and stability, seeking security from the state as he has lost his self-confidence and his self-reliance.

For at bottom the personal life of a man will be a disordered life if he has no rational command over his desires. In this disorder the sources of man's confidence in himself, and with it his peace of mind and his resolution, are impaired. The modern secular way of life is not suited to the real nature of men. For it withholds from them that discipline of their own impulses which is indispensable to their health and their happiness. Because they are deprived of a rational measure upon their desires, they do not conserve their energy but spend it upon unattainable and unsatisfying ends.

Disordered men cannot face life confidently; their impulse must, therefore, be to escape from the pressure of their own insatiable appetites, and from the endless conflicts with other men who also are driven by insatiable appetites. For disordered men there is at last no solace except in a flight from reality. Lacking confidence in themselves they cannot seek refuge in themselves, achieving peace in solitude and meditation. They seek refuge among the masses of their fellow beings, becoming anonymous, faceless, and no longer persons in some one of those mass movements which are so characteristic of our times.

Actuated by their own inner disorder, driven by fear, inspired by fantasies of hope, these masses in movement cannot constitute a society. They are a horde, as Toynbee has put it, arising within our civilization rather than invading it from without. They are a horde of beings without autonomy, of individuals uprooted and so isolated and disordered that they surrender their judgment and their freedom to the master of the horde. Thus out of the chaos to which the evolution of secular individualism leads, there is born the formless mysticism of an irrational collectivism. The dissolution of Western society ends —as we have seen it demonstrated in the lands where it is totally advanced—in an organized barbarism which makes the lives of all who fall within its power "poor, nasty, brutish, and short."

The outcome proves that above all the other necessities of human nature, above the satisfaction of any other need, above hunger, love, pleasure, fame—even life itself—what a man most needs is the conviction that he is contained within the discipline of an ordered existence. Man can bear anything except a sense of his own utter demoralization. As long as he has the support of a discipline which is rational and transcends his immediate promptings, he will endure discomfort, pain, and danger. That is why men with faith can face martyrdom while men without it feel stricken when they are not invited to dinner.

This neglected truth about the nature of man is at the core of the great central tradition of the Western world. In this tradition, man does not fulfill his destiny except as he is ruled by the reason within him which transcends that which is only animal, because it is attached to that which is universal. The tradition is a hard one to live by, and few succeed, and none altogether. But hard as it is, the rule of life it imposes is not an unworldly counsel of perfection. It is the truth about the only way in which men can be happy. That there is so little happiness among men shows only how hard it is for most men to do the hard things that alone can make them happy.

Yet we need not doubt that men will, indeed that men must, rediscover and return to the great tradition in which our civilization was made. We know that the truth will prevail, and we may be sure that it will prevail because, men being what they are, they have within themselves, in the very structure of their own beings, the authentic means and the imperative need to find the indispensable truth. Were this not the fact, they would never have found it.

And so, though we live in a time of trouble in which much, perhaps most, of what we cherish might be destroyed, nevertheless we may be sure that men can, that men must, and that therefore men will, re-create that which matters in that which has perished. For the roots of the good society are not in charters and in buildings but in the men who made them, and, more exactly, in that part of the nature of the human person where resides his reason and his freedom to follow his reason. This part of man is indestructible. For in all men who are born it is reborn.

V

The Public Philosophy

1 · *The Higher Law*

The Good Society (1937), *Chapter 15.*

The rediscovery and the reconstruction of general political standards can be carried forward only, I believe, by developing the abiding truth of the older liberalism after purging it of the defects which destroyed it. The pioneer liberals vindicated the supremacy of law over the arbitrary power of men. That is the abiding truth which we inherit from them. But the law which they vindicated was in many respects the mere defense of ancient privileges and immunities. Thus they made it easy to invoke the supremacy of the law in order to prohibit the improvement of human affairs. In the decadence of liberalism the conception of higher law was used to defend vested rights and obstruct reform. That was its fatal defect and the cause of its downfall. But in the debacle there was swept away not only the mistaken insistence upon the supremacy of the traditional law, but the nobler intuition that liberty and human dignity depend upon the supremacy of the spirit of law.

We can, and I believe that we must, disentangle the general theory of liberalism from its historic identification with the common-law rights and privileges and immunities enjoyed by Englishmen and Americans in the nineteenth century. When Coke told James I that the King was under God and the law, the enduring part of the reply is not to be found in any pretension that the law itself as it happens to be is perfect and immutable; that, for example, the lawful right of the lord of the manor arbitrarily to imprison the villein is not to be challenged. The essential and enduring part of Coke's reply is the denial that the King may act arbitrarily. The denial that men may be arbitrary in human transactions *is* the higher law.

That is the substance of the higher law. That is the spiritual essence without which the letter of the law is nothing but the formal trappings of vested rights or the ceremonial disguise of caprice and willfulness. Constitutional restraints and bills of rights, the whole apparatus of responsible government and of an independent judiciary, the conception of due process of law in courts, in legislatures, among executives, are but the rough approximations by which men have sought to exorcise the devil of arbitrariness in human relations. Among a people which does not try to obey this higher law, no constitution is worth the paper it is written on; though they have all the forms of liberty, they will not enjoy its substance. The laws depend upon moral commitments which could never possibly be expressly stated in the laws themselves: upon a level of truthfulness in giving testimony, of reasonableness in argument, of trust, confidence, and good faith in transactions; upon a mood of disinterestedness and justice, far above anything that the letter of the law demands. It is not enough that men should be as truthful as the laws against perjury require and as reasonable as the rules of evidence compel a clever lawyer to be. To maintain a constitutional order they must be much more truthful, reasonable, just, and honorable than the letter of the laws. There must be more than legal prohibition against arbitrariness, against overreaching, deception, and oppression. There must be an habitual, confirmed, and well-nigh intuitive dislike of arbitrariness; a quick sensitiveness to its manifestations and a spontaneous disapproval and resistance. For only by adhering to this unwritten higher law can they make actual law effective or have criteria by which to reform it.

By this higher law all formal laws and all political behavior are judged in civilized societies. When the principle which Coke affirmed against the King is recognized, then the privileges of the lord of the manor no longer stand impervious to criticism and to reform. If the sovereign himself may not act willfully, arbitrarily, by personal prerogative, then no one may. His ministers may not. The legislature may not. Majorities may not. Individuals may not. Crowds may not. The national state may not. This law which is the spirit of law is the opposite of an accumulation of old precedents and new fiats. By this higher law, that men must not be arbitrary, the old law is continually tested and the new law reviewed.

To those who ask where this higher law is to be found, the answer is that it is a progressive discovery of men striving to civilize themselves, and that its scope and implications are a gradual revelation that is by no means completed. In the beginning of law, men could aim no higher than to keep the peace. They had made a great advance when the injured man agreed to take in vengeance no more than an eye for an eye. They advanced further when the dominion of the strong over the weak was legalized as caste, and bounds were put on their superior strength. They advanced still further when the masters had duties toward as well as rights over their subjects. The advance continued as the rights of the masters were progressively checked and liquidated as having no intrinsic justification.

The development of human rights is simply the expression of the higher law that men shall not deal arbitrarily with one another. Human rights do not mean, as some confused individualists have supposed, that there are certain sterile areas where men collectively may not deal at all with men individually. We are in truth members of one another, and a philosophy which seeks to differentiate the community from the persons who belong to it, treating them as if they were distinct sovereignties having only diplomatic relations, is contrary to fact and can lead only to moral bewilderment. The rights of man are not the rights of Robinson Crusoe before his man Friday appeared. They stem from the right not to be dealt with arbitrarily by anyone else, and the inescapable corollary of the rights of man is the duty of man not to deal arbitrarily with others.

The gradual encroachment of true law upon willfulness and caprice is the progress of liberty in human affairs. That is how the emancipation of mankind has been begun and must be continued. As those who have the power to coerce lose the authority to rule by fiat, liberty advances. It advances by the continual struggle of men against the possessors of arbitrary power.

"The Modern Malady," Today and Tomorrow, *November 3, 1938.*

A few days before the celebrated broadcast by Mr. Orson Welles, a professor, who shall be nameless here, made a speech on the need for "streamlining" education. "The computing machine, interest tables, and other 'fingertip' methods of solving once-hard problems have," said he, "done away with the need for much of the old ' 'rithmetic.' " This is a most illuminating remark. As an indicator of what is most deeply and dangerously wrong with the modern world, the professor's statement could hardly, I think, be more exact.

"In a world of . . . automatic calculators," he explained, "the use of numbers has changed. Eleven gallons of gasoline at 16⁸⁄₁₀ cents a gallon; we know where the attendant finds the answer and we usually know it will be correct." Thus streamlined education means that the customer looks at the dial to see what the automatic calculator registers, and is compelled to rely upon that, never having wasted his precious time learning how to multiply 11 x 16⁸⁄₁₀. Consider what this principle of education means. It means a population which not only uses machines as a convenience, but has been made so entirely dependent upon them that the ordinary man would not know how to find out whether the automatic calculator was accurate or whether it was honest. He could not even go to an expert and ask him to test the machine. For if two experts disagreed, he would not know enough of the elements of arithmetic to have any ground for deciding which expert he ought to believe.

Now it is, I believe, in this everwidening separation from the elementary facts, the elementary truths, and the elementary necessities of human existence, that the profound confusion of modern men originates. All over the world, but most particularly in the countries where civilization is supposed to be most advanced, there are collected in great cities huge masses of people who have lost their roots in the earth beneath them and their knowledge of the fixed stars in the heavens above them. They are the crowds that drift with all the winds that blow, and are caught up at last in the great hurricanes.

They are the people who eat but no longer know how their food is grown, who work and no longer see what they help to produce, who hear all the latest news and all the latest opinions but have no philosophy by which they can distinguish the true from the false, the credible from the incredible, the good from the bad. Is it so surprising that as civilization has become more streamlined, democracy has become more unworkable?

For these masses without roots, these crowds without convictions are the spiritual proletariat of the modern age, and the eruption of their volcanic and hysterical energy is the revolution that is shaking the world. They are the chaos in which the new Caesars are born.

No one need delude himself into thinking that there is a quick and easy remedy at hand, or that one will be found until enough men have mustered up the courage to see the malady without flinching. But we can perhaps discern, though dimly as yet, the direction in which we must go.

We can do this by recovering and remembering the enduring truths about man and his relations with other men, and about the government of men, which in the modern age we have been too sophisticated, too restless, too remote from reality, and too uneducated to comprehend.

Thus it is always true that if the forces of the law are not indisputably stronger than all other forces, the law will perish. It is always true that a society is dissolving in which the privileges of the few are greater than their services, in which the rights of the many are greater than their duties. It is always true that men must earn their living in the sweat of their brows, and that there is no streamlined substitute for this perennial necessity.

It is always true that the object of policy within a state must be to protect individuals and natural communities in the property on which and by which they earn their living, and thus to attach them to the state not by commands and doles and slogans but by their immediate and self-respecting interest. It is always true that the accumulation of property is an evil whether it be in the hands of a plutocracy or of a Socialist or Fascist state. For it is always true that the arrival of masses without property will in the end destroy a civilization.

It is always true that a society of free men is a society of men with secure and sufficient property. It is always true that individuals cannot be free if their community is not independent. It is always true that independence has to be maintained by the willingness to fight and die for it. And finally it is true that men will not have the will to live or the courage to die if they have ceased to believe that they are in communion with things that transcend entirely their personal affairs.

Are these truisms? Or are these truths, enduring truths, that modern men have forgotten, have rejected, and have violated to their own confusion and despair?

It is not the fashion to believe that there are truths, like these, which are indeed fundamental and universal. For the modern man has persuaded himself that nothing is really true, and that all truths are just the convenient opinions of a class or of a nation at a particular moment. But this disbelief in the existence of a central tradition of human wisdom is the philosophy of the spiritual proletariat. This feeling, which pervades the great urban centers, that all things are relative and impermanent and of no real importance, is merely the reflection of their own separation from the elementary experiences of humanity. And the bitter, frustrated, and aimless skepticism of the modern man is itself the consequence of the modern disease of which he is the victim.

2 · *The Higher Law as the Public Philosophy*

The Public Philosophy (*1955*), *Chapter 8.*

The public philosophy is known as *natural law,* a name which, alas, causes great semantic confusion. This philosophy is the premise of the institutions of the Western society, and they are, I believe, unworkable in communities that do not adhere to it. Except on the premises of this philosophy, it is impossible to reach intelligible and workable conceptions of popular election, majority rule, representative assemblies, free speech, loyalty, property, corporations, and voluntary associations. The founders of these institutions, which the recently enfranchised democracies have inherited, were all of them adherents of some one of the various schools of natural law. . . .

To speak of a public philosophy is, I am well aware, to raise dangerous questions, rather like opening Pandora's box.

Within the Western nations, as Father Murray has put it, there is "a plurality of incompatible faiths"; there is also a multitude of secularized and agnostic people. Since there is so little prospect of agreement, and such certainty of dissension, on the content of the public philosophy, it seems expedient not to raise the issues by talking about them. It is easier to follow the rule that each person's beliefs are private and that only overt conduct is a public matter.

One might say that this prudent rule reflects and registers the terms of settlement of the religious wars and of the long struggle against exclusive authority in the realm of the spirit by "thrones or dominations, or principalities or powers."

Freedom of religion and of thought and of speech were achieved by denying both to the state and to the established church a sovereign monopoly in the field of religion, philosophy, morals, science, learning, opinion, and conscience. The liberal constitutions, with their bills of rights, fixed the boundaries past which the sovereign—the King, the Parliament, the Congress, the voters—were forbidden to go.

Yet the men of the seventeenth and eighteenth centuries who established these great salutary rules would certainly have denied that a community could do without a general public philosophy. They were themselves the adherents of a public philosophy—of the doctrine of natural law, which held that there was law "above the ruler and the sovereign people . . . above the whole community of mortals."

The traditions of civility spring from this principle, which was first worked out by the Stoics. . . .

These traditions were expounded in the treatises of philosophers, were developed in the tracts of the publicists, were absorbed by the lawyers and applied in the courts. At times of great stress some of the endangered traditions were committed to writing, as in the Magna Carta and the Declaration of Independence. For the guidance of judges and lawyers, large portions were described—as in Lord Coke's examination of the common law. The public philosophy was in part expounded in the Bill of Rights of 1689. It was re-enacted in the first ten amendments of the Constitution of the United States. The largest part of the public philosophy was never explicitly stated.

Being the wisdom of a great society over the generations, it can never be stated in any single document. But the traditions of civility permeated the peoples of the West and provided a standard of public and private action which promoted, facilitated, and protected the institutions of freedom and the growth of democracy.

The founders of our free institutions were themselves adherents of this public philosophy. When they insisted upon excluding the temporal power from the realm of the mind and the spirit, it was not that they had no public philosophy. It was because experience had taught them that as power corrupts, it corrupts the public philosophy. It was, therefore, a practical rule of politics that the government should not be given sovereignty and proprietorship over the public philosophy.

3 · *The Neglect of the Public Philosophy*

The Public Philosophy (*1955*), *Chapter 8.*

As time went on, there fell out of fashion the public philosophy of the founders of Western institutions. The rule that the temporal power should be excluded from the realm of the mind and of the spirit was then subtly transformed. It became the rule that ideas and principles are private—with only subjective relevance and significance. Only when there is "a clear and present danger" to public order are the acts of speaking and publishing in the public domain. All the first and last things were removed from the public domain. All that has to do with what man is and should be, or how he should hold himself in the scheme of things, what are his rightful ends and the legitimate means, became private and subjective and publicly unaccountable. And so the liberal democracies of the West became the first great society to treat as a private concern the formative beliefs that shape the character of its citizens.

This has brought about a radical change in the meaning of

freedom. Originally it was founded on the postulate that there was a universal order on which all reasonable men were agreed; within that public agreement on the fundamentals and on the ultimates, it was safe to permit and it would be desirable to encourage, dissent, and dispute. But with the disappearance of the public philosophy—and of a consensus on the first and last things—there was opened up a great vacuum in the public mind, yawning to be filled.

As long as it worked, there was an obvious practical advantage in treating the struggle for the ultimate allegiance of men as not within the sphere of the public interest. It was a way of not having to open the Pandora's box of theological, moral, and ideological issues which divide the Western society. But in this century, when the hard decisions have had to be made, this rule of prudence has ceased to work. The expedient worked only as long as the general mass of the people were not seriously dissatisfied with things as they were. It was an expedient that looked toward reforms and improvement. But it assumed a society which was secure, progressive, expanding, and unchallenged. That is why it was only in the fine Victorian weather, before the storm clouds of the great wars began to gather, that the liberal democratic policy of public agnosticism and practical neutrality in ultimate issues was possible.

We come, then, to a crucial question. If the discussion of public philosophy has been, so to speak, tabled in the liberal democracies, can we assume that, though it is not being discussed, there is a public philosophy? Is there a body of positive principles and precepts which a good citizen cannot deny or ignore? I am writing this book in the conviction that there is. It is a conviction which I have acquired gradually, not so much from a theoretical education, but rather from the practical experience of seeing how hard it is for our generation to make democracy work. I believe there is a public philosophy. Indeed there is such a thing as the public philosophy of civility. It does not have to be discovered or invented. It is known. But it does have to be revived and renewed. . . .

In our time the institutions built upon the foundations of the public philosophy still stand. But they are used by a public who are not being taught, and no longer adhere to, the philosophy. Increasingly, the people are alienated from the inner principles of their institutions. The question is whether and how this alienation can be overcome, and the rupture of the traditions of civility repaired.

Needless to say I am not about to argue that the rupture can be repaired by a neo-classical or neo-medieval restoration, or by some kind of romantic return to feudalism, folk-dancing and handicrafts. We cannot rub out the modern age, we cannot roll back the history that has made us what we are. We cannot start again as if there had been no advance of science, no spread of rationalism and secularism, no industrial revolution, no dissolution of the old habitual order of things, no sudden increase in the population. The poignant question is whether, and, if so, how, modern men could make vital contact with the lost traditions of civility.

The appearance of things is quite obviously unpromising. There is radical novelty in our modern ways of life. The climate of feeling and the style of thought have changed radically. Modern men will first need to be convinced that the traditions of civility were not abandoned because they became antiquated. This is one of the roots of their unbelief and there is no denying its depth. Since the public philosophy preceded the advance of modern science and the industrial revolution, how can it be expected to provide a positive doctrine which is directly and practically relevant to the age we live in?

It does, one must admit, look like that, and quite evidently the original principles and precepts do not now provide the specific rules and patterns of a way of life in the circumstances of this age. A rereading of the political classics from Aristotle to Burke will not give the answers to the immediate and concrete questions: to the burning issues of diplomacy, military defense, trade, taxes, prices, and wages. Nor have the classical books anything to say about repairing automobiles, treating poliomyelitis, or proceeding with nuclear fission. As handbooks for the busy man, wanting to know how to do this or that, they are now lamentably out of date. The language is archaic, the idiom is strange, the images are unfamiliar, the practical precepts are addressed to forgotten issues.

But this irrelevance and remoteness might be the dust which has settled during the long time when philosophers and scholars and popular educators have relegated the public philosophy to the attic, when they have treated it as no longer usable by modern and progressive men. It is a neglected philosophy. For several generations it has been exceptional and indeed eccentric to use this philosophy in the practical discussion of public policies.

Neglect might well explain its dilapidated condition. If this were the explanation, it would encourage us to explore the question of a renascence. Could modern men again make vital contact with the traditions of civility? At least once before something of the sort did happen. The traditions were articulated in the Graeco-Roman world, and submerged in the West by the decline and the fall of the Western empire. Later on they were revived and renovated and remade in a great flowering of discovery and enterprise and creativity. The revival of learning did not provide maps for Columbus to use in discovering America. But it did produce much human wisdom which helped Columbus and his contemporaries to discover themselves and their possibilities.

The ancient world, we may remind ourselves, was not destroyed because the traditions were false. They were submerged, neglected, lost. For the men adhering to them had become a dwindling minority who were overthrown and displaced by men who were alien to the traditions, having never been initiated and adopted into them. May it not be that while the historical circumstances are obviously so different, something like that is happening again?

4 · *The Renewal of the Public Philosophy*

The Public Philosophy (*1955*), *Chapter 9.*

The freedom which modern men are turned away from, not seldom with relief and often with enthusiasm, is the hollow shell of freedom. The current theory of freedom holds that what men believe may be important to them but that it has almost no public significance. The outer defenses of the free way of life stand upon the legal guarantees against the coercion of belief. But the citadel is vacant because the public philosophy is gone, and all that the defenders of freedom have to defend in common is a public neutrality and a public agnosticism.

Yet when we have demonstrated the need for the public

philosophy, how do we prove that the need can be satisfied? Not, we may be sure, by exhortation, however eloquent, to rise to the enormity of the present danger, still less by lamentations about the glory and the grandeur that are past. Modern men, to whom the argument is addressed, have a low capacity to believe in the invisible, the intangible, and the imponderable.

Exhortation can capture the will to believe. But of the will to believe there is no lack. The modern trouble is in a low capacity to believe in precepts which restrict and restrain private interests and desire. Conviction of the need of these restraints is difficult to restore once it has been radically impaired. Public principles can, of course, be imposed by a despotic government. But the public philosophy of a free society cannot be restored by fiat and by force. To come to grips with the unbelief which underlies the condition of anomy, we must find a way to re-establish confidence in the validity of public standards. We must renew the convictions from which our political morality springs.

In the prevailing popular culture all philosophies are the instruments of some man's purpose, all truths are self-centered and self-regarding, and all principles are the rationalizations of some special interest. There is no public criterion of the true and the false, of the right and the wrong, beyond that which the preponderant mass of voters, consumers, readers, and listeners happen at the moment to be supposed to want.

There is no reason to think that this condition of mind can be changed until it can be proved to the modern skeptic that there are certain principles which, when they have been demonstrated, only the willfully irrational can deny, that there are certain obligations binding on all men who are committed to a free society, and that only the willfully subversive can reject them.

When I say that the condition of anomy cannot be corrected unless these things are proved to the modern skeptic, I mean that the skeptic must find the proof compelling. His skepticism cannot be cured by forcing him to conform. If he has no strong beliefs, he will usually conform if he is made to conform. But the very fact that he has been forced by the government or by the crowd will prove that the official doctrine lacked something in the way of evidence or of reason to carry full conviction. In the blood of the martyrs to intolerance are the seeds of unbelief.

In order to repair the capacity to believe in the public philosophy, it will be necessary to demonstrate the practical relevance and the productivity of the public philosophy. It is almost impossible to deny its high and broad generalities. The difficulty is to see how they are to be applied in the practical affairs of a modern state.

We are back, in a manner of speaking, before the Roman lawyers worked out the *ius gentium* and related it to the *ius naturale,* back with Alexander the Great, who understood the pressing need for common laws in a plural society, and with Zeno who formulated the higher generalities. Given the practical need, which is acute, and the higher generalities, which are self-evident, can we develop a positive working doctrine of the good society under modern conditions? The answer which I am making to this question is that it can be done if the ideas of the public philosophy are recovered and are re-established in the minds of men of light and leading. . . .

The free political institutions of the Western world were conceived and established by men who believed that honest reflection on the common experience of mankind would always cause men to come to the same ultimate conclusions. Within the Golden Rule of the same philosophy for elucidating their ultimate ends, they could engage with confident hope in the progressive discovery of truth. All issues could be settled by scientific investigation and by free debate if—but only if—all the investigators and the debaters adhered to the public philosophy; if, that is to say, they used the same criteria and rules of reason for arriving at the truth and for distinguishing good and evil.

Quite evidently, there is no clear sharp line which can be drawn in any community or among communities between those who adhere and those who do not adhere to the public philosophy. But while there are many shades and degrees in the spectrum, the two ends are well defined. When the adherence of the whole body of people to the public philosophy is firm, a true community exists; where there is division and dissent over the main principles, the result is a condition of latent war.

In the maintenance and formation of a true community the articulate philosophy is, one might say, like the thread which holds the pieces of the fabric together. . . .

The fabrics in the metaphor are the traditions of how the good life is lived and the good society is governed. When they come apart, as they have in the Western democracies, the result is tantamount to a kind of collective amnesia. The liberal democracies have been making mistakes in peace and in war which they would never have made were they not suffering from what is a failure of memory. They have forgotten too much of what their predecessors had learned before them. The newly enfranchised democracies are like men who have kept their appetites but have forgotten how to grow food. They have the perennial human needs for law and order, for freedom and justice, for what only good government can give them. But the art of governing well has to be learned. If it is to be learned, it has to be transmitted from the old to the young, and the habits and the ideas must be maintained as a seamless web of memory among the bearers of the tradition, generation after generation.

When the continuity of the traditions of civility is ruptured, the community is threatened; unless the rupture is repaired, the community will break down into factional, class, racial, and regional wars. For when the continuity is interrupted, the cultural heritage is not being transmitted. The new generation is faced with the task of rediscovering and re-inventing and relearning, by trial and error, most of what the guardians of a society need to know.

No one generation can do this. For no one generation of men are capable of creating for themselves the arts and sciences of a high civilization. Men can know more than their ancestors did if they start with a knowledge of what their ancestors had already learned. They can do advanced experiments if they do not have to learn all over again how to do the elementary ones. That is why a society can be progressive only if it conserves its traditions. The generations are, as Bernard of Chartres said, "like dwarfs seated on the shoulders of giants," enabled, therefore, to "see more things than the Ancients and things more distant."

But traditions are more than the culture of the arts and sciences. They are the public world to which our private worlds are joined. This continuum of public and private memories transcends all persons in their immediate and natural lives and it ties them all together. In it there is performed the mystery by which individuals are adopted and initiated into membership in the community.

The body which carries this mystery is the history of the community, and its central theme is the great deeds and the high purposes of the great predecessors. From them the new men descend and prove themselves by becoming participants in the unfinished story.

"Where I belong," says Jaspers, "and what I am living for, I first learned in the mirror of history." When the individual becomes civilized he acquires a second nature. This second nature is made in the image of what he is and is living for and should become. He has seen the image in the mirror of history. This second nature, which rules over the natural man, is at home in the good society. This second nature is no proletarian but feels itself to be a rightful proprietor and ruler of the community. Full allegiance to the community can be given only by a man's second nature, ruling over his first and primitive nature, and treating it as not finally himself. Then the disciplines and the necessities and the constraints of a civilized life have ceased to be alien to him, and imposed from without. They have become his own inner imperatives.

"To the First and Last Things," Today and Tomorrow, *May 25, 1940.*

Behind all questions of politics and armaments, of personalities and parties, there is the question whether a self-governing people will impose upon itself a self-discipline strong enough to insure its own defense. The question is put to a final and desperate test in Western Europe today, and in the Americas it is the question on which depends the future of this hemisphere as a hemisphere of freedom. Liberty without discipline cannot survive. Without order and authority in the spirit of man the free way of life leads through weakness, disorganization, self-indulgence, and moral indifference to the destruction of freedom itself.

The tragic ordeal through which the Western world is passing was prepared in the long period of easy liberty during which men forgot the elementary truths of human existence. They forgot that their freedom was achieved by heroic sacrifice; they became so accustomed to freedom that they thought it was as normal as the air they breathe, and they came to believe that the heroic virtues were antiquated and that sacrifice was a bore and bother. They forgot that their rights were founded on their duties, and they thought that to get while the getting was good, whether by private smartness or by collective pressure, was the normal and natural thing to do. They forgot that unless they bear themselves so that the eternal values of truth, justice, and righteousness are perpetually revealed to them, they will not know how to resist the corrosion of their virtue or how to face the trials that life will bring to them upon this earth. They had become too comfortable and too safe and too sophisticated to believe the first things and the last things which men have been inspired to understand through generations of suffering, and they thought it clever to be cynical, and enlightened to be unbelieving, and sensible to be soft.

And so, through suffering, they must rediscover these first and last things again, and be purified once more by repentance.

The free peoples of the Western world have lived upon a great inheritance which they have squandered recklessly. When they were put to the test, they had come to the point where they took the blessings of this inheritance so totally for granted that they no longer knew, and their schools had almost ceased to teach them, and their leaders were afraid to remind them, how the laws and the institutions and the great controlling customs of our civilization were made. They thought that the God whom they believed in dimly or not at all had conferred these blessings upon them gratuitously, that somehow they, as distinguished from their own ancestors and from millions of their fellow beings in less fortunate lands, were exempt from the labors and the sacrifices and the trials of man. They did not know that the products of civilization which they so greedily consumed are not the enduring inheritance of man.

These pleasant things are no more than an estate accumulated by the labor of the father and easily ruined by the dissipation of his son.

They did not believe any longer that the true inheritance of man is the capacity to produce these products, to preserve the estate by remaking it. Only that. All that has been conferred upon man is the capacity to know what is good and the freedom of will to strive for it.

What is left of our civilization will not be maintained, what has been wrecked will not be restored, by imagining that some new political gadget can be invented, some new political formula improvised which will save it. Our civilization can be maintained and restored only by remembering and rediscovering the truths, and by re-establishing the virtuous habits on which it was founded. There is no use looking into the blank future for some new and fancy revelation of what man needs in order to live.

The relevation has been made. By it man conquered the

jungle about him and the barbarian within him. The elementary principles of work and sacrifice and duty—and the transcendant criteria of truth, justice, and righteousness—and the grace of love and charity—are the things which have made men free. Men can keep their freedom and reconquer it only by these means. These are the terms stipulated in the nature of things for the salvation of men on this earth, and only in this profound, this stern, and this tested wisdom shall we find once more the light and the courage we need.

The Public Philosophy (1955), *Chapter 11.*

The revival of the public philosophy depends on whether its principles and precepts—which were articulated before the industrial revolution, before the era of rapid technological change, and before the rise of the mass democracies—depends on whether this old philosophy can be reworked for the modern age. If this cannot be done, then the free and democratic nations face the totalitarian challenge without a public philosophy which free men believe in and cherish, with no public faith beyond a mere official agnosticism, neutrality, and indifference. There is not much doubt how the struggle is likely to end if it lies between those who, believing, care very much—and those who, lacking belief, cannot care very much.

5 · *The Public Philosophy and Private Property*

The Public Philosophy (1955), *Chapter 9.*

Let us put the matter to the test by applying the public philosophy to some of the great topics of our public life.

I shall begin with the theory of private property—before

and after the loss of the public philosophy and the rupture of the traditions. We can do this conveniently by examining what Blackstone, working in the middle of the eighteenth century, does with the theory of private property. Blackstone's mind was formed in the classical tradition. But Blackstone's world was in movement, and he was not equal to the creative effort of using the tradition to cope with the new circumstances.

He had declared that security of the person was the first, that liberty of the individual was the second, and that property was "the third absolute right inherent in every Englishman." But as a civilized man, he had to do more than to assert the absolute right. He had "to examine more deeply the rudiments and grounds" on which it could be justified rationally.

Between the lines of his elegant and stately prose one can see, I think, that Blackstone was puzzled. According to his tradition, the rational justification of property is like a system of corresponding and reciprocal rights and duties. In the public philosophy an absolute right to property, or to anything else that affects other men, cannot be entertained. To claim it is to be outside the law and the bounds of civility. This conception of property is most easily intelligible in a society where the principal forms of private property are in agricultural land. The land is visible and its products are known to all. This lends itself to a definition of the corresponding rights and duties: of the landlord with his tenants and hired workers below him in the hierarchy and above him with the sovereign power, claiming taxes and services.

When the main forms of property are intangible, the difficulty of defining rights and duties is much greater. When Blackstone was writing, England was a rising commercial power and the comparatively simple problems of a society based on landed property were already overtaken by the problems of an economy in which property was owned as money, as commercial paper, as stocks and bonds. It was easy enough to assert rights to intangible property, but difficult to define the duties of intangible property. Yet unless that was done, property would not be under general laws.

Blackstone is in a way a tragic figure in that, thanks to his education, he had the intimation that the right direction was to work toward bringing intangible property under public standards. Yet for one reason or another he did not take it. He was, however, troubled. He knew that "nothing . . . so generally . . . engages the affections of mankind" as that "sole and despotic dominion which one man claims and exercises over the external things of the world, in total exclusion of the right of any other individual in the universe." But as a man steeped in the civilized traditions of the West, he knew too that there must be rational limits put upon the acquisitive and possessive instincts. As a man of the world, that is to say, of his world and of the world that was to come, he knew also how little the rising men of property wished to hear about obligations that would limit their absolute rights.

So, with a certain regret, and perhaps with an intuitive foreboding, he wrote that "Pleased as we are with the possession, we seem afraid to look back to the means by which it was acquired, as if fearful of some defect in our title . . . not caring to reflect that (accurately and strictly speaking) there is no foundation in nature or in natural law, why a set of words upon parchment should convey the dominion of land: why the son should have a right to exclude his fellow-creatures from a determinate spot of ground, because his father had done so before him: or why the occupier of a particular field or of a jewel, when lying on his death-bed, and no longer able to maintain possession, should be entitled to tell the rest of the world which of them should enjoy it after him."

Blackstone thought that these questions which challenge "the sole and despotic dominion" of the property holder, "would be useless and even troublesome in common life." As a man of his world he felt bound to say that "it is well if the mass of mankind will obey the laws when made, without scrutinizing too nicely into the reason for making them." But as one formed in the traditions of civility, he could not ignore the question of whether there was "some defect in our title" to absolute property. And as an exponent of "rational science" he felt bound to expound the classical conception of private property. . . .

The rights of property . . . are a creation of the laws of the state. And since the laws can be altered, there are no absolute rights of property. There are legal rights to use and to enjoy and to dispose of property. The laws define what are the rights to use and to enjoy and to dispose of property, which the courts will enforce. . . .

Conceived in this fashion, private property can never be regarded as giving to any man an absolute title to exercise "the sole and despotic dominion" over the land and the resources of nature. The ultimate title does not lie in the owner. The title is in "mankind," in *The People* as a corporate community. The rights of the individual in that patrimony are creations of the law, and have no other validity except as they are ordained by law. The purpose of laws which establish private property is not to satisfy the acquisitive and possessive instincts of the primitive man, but to promote "the grand ends of civil society"—which comprehend "the peace and security of individuals."

Because the legal owner enjoys the use of a limited necessity belonging to all men, he cannot be the sovereign lord of his possessions. He is not entitled to exercise his absolute and therefore arbitrary will. He owes duties that correspond with his rights. His ownership is a grant made by the laws to achieve not his private purposes but the common social purpose. And, therefore, the laws of property may and should be judged, reviewed, and, when necessary, amended, so as to define the specific system of rights and duties that will promote the ends of society.

This is a doctrine of private property which denies the pretension to a "sole and despotic dominion." When Blackstone, though his conscience was troubled, accepted the sole and despotic dominion, he broke with the public philosophy and the traditions of civility. After his break the recognized theorists developed regressively the conception of private property as an absolute right. For a time they excluded from political philosophy, from jurisprudence and from legislation, almost any notion that property had duties as well as rights.

Absolute private property inevitably produced intolerable evils. Absolute owners did grave damage to their neighbors and to their descendants: they ruined the fertility of the land, they exploited destructively the minerals under the surface, they burned and cut forests, they destroyed the wild life, they polluted streams, they cornered supplies and formed monopolies, they held land and resources out of use, they exploited the feeble bargaining power of wage earners.

For such abuses of absolute property the political scientists and the lawmakers had no remedy. They had lost the tradition that property is the creation of the law for social purposes. They had no principles by which the law could deal with the abuses of property. The individualists of the nineteenth century could not, therefore, defend and preserve the system of private property by reforming it, and by adapting it to the circumstances of the modern age. They knew much about the rights of property and little about any corresponding duties. And so, because there was no legal remedy for the abuses of private property, because the duties which are the rational justification of property were no longer defined and enforced, the idea of private property lost its rational justification.

Between the property holders and the propertyless, who became the majority in many countries, there was, in consequence, no connecting bond, no consensus within the same realm of rational discourse. The proletariat had the duty to respect the rights of owners. But the owners owed no reciprocal duty to the proletariat. There were no obligations in which the proletarians found *their* rights. Thus there arose the ominous phenomenon of "the two nations," the confrontation of those who owned the earth by those who had nothing to lose. The latter were more numerous than the former. As they acquired votes, the main issue in the domestic politics of the democracies became the struggle between the minority who had so much absolute property and the great mass of the electorate who had so little property.

To this conflict there have been and are two possible outcomes: a gradual, cumulative, and perhaps at last a violent expropriation of the men of property—or reforms of the laws of property which restore adequate duties. But for several generations after Blackstone, the very idea of property as a system of duties was obscured. The public philosophy was discarded, and the most humane and enlightened men of the nineteenth century had little notion how rational reforms could be made. The alternatives, it appeared, were to defend absolute property against the growing discontent of the propertyless, or to abolish private property. It was a dangerous and a false dilemma. But in the nineteenth century this became the dilemma. The choice, it was said, was between individualism and collectivism, between Manchester and Marx, between absolute property maintained by the force of the few and absolute property abolished by the dictatorship of the mass.

The case of Blackstone has shown that a different and better theory of property was possible. It was possible *if* he and his successors had adhered to the public philosophy—if they had used, instead of abandoning, the principles which he stated so well. The earth is the general property of all mankind. Private titles of ownership are assigned by lawmaking authorities to promote the grand ends of civil society. Private property is, therefore, a system of legal rights and duties. Under changing conditions the system must be kept in accord with the grand ends of civil society.

Blackstone and his successors did not work out legal propositions from these principles. As I am contending that it would have been better if they had done so, I now ask myself what is the validity of these principles? Are they devices, like the rules of the road, for regulating the traffic? If they are only that, then another set of assumptions could be just as valid, like the rule of the road in Britain that one must drive to the left. One could, and in fact men have, constructed systems of property on quite different assumptions—on the assumption, for example, that the earth is the general property of white men only, or of a master race of white men, or of those castes which have not sinned in a previous incarnation. But if the principles are more than that, if they have a validity which overrides such special claims, what is the virtue which gives them their validity?

They are the laws of a rational order of human society—in the sense that all men, when they are sincerely and lucidly rational, will regard them as self-evident. The rational order consists of the terms which must be met in order to fulfill men's capacity for the good life in this world. They are the terms of the widest consensus of rational men in a plural society. They are the propositions to which all men concerned, if they are sincerely and lucidly rational, can be expected to converge. There could never be a consensus that Africa belongs to the descendants of the Dutch settlers; a property system founded on that pretension cannot be generally acceptable, and will generate disorder. The classical doctrine has a superior validity in that a system of property based upon it may obtain a consensus of support in the community, and would have the prospect of being workable.

When we speak of these principles as natural laws, we must be careful. They are not scientific "laws" like the laws of the motions of the heavenly bodies. They do not describe human behavior as it is. They prescribe what it should be. They do not enable us to predict what men will actually do. They are the principles of right behavior in the good society, governed by the Western traditions of civility.

It is possible to organize a state and to conduct a government on quite different principles. But the outcome will not be freedom and the good life.

6 · *The Public Philosophy and Freedom of Speech*

The Public Philosophy (*1955*), *Chapter 9.*

Only within a community which adheres to the public philosophy is there sure and sufficient ground for the freedom to think and to ask questions, to speak and to punish. Nobody can justify in principle, much less in practice, a claim that there exists an unrestricted right of anyone to utter anything he likes at any time he chooses. There can, for example, be no right, as Mr. Justice Holmes said, to cry "Fire" in a crowded theater. Nor is there a right to tell a customer that the glass beads are diamonds, or a voter that the opposition candidate for President is a Soviet agent.

Freedom of speech has become a central concern of the Western society because of the discovery among the Greeks that dialectic, as demonstrated in the Socratic dialogues, is a principal method of attaining truth, and particularly a method of attaining moral and political truth. "The ability to raise searching difficulties on both sides of a subject will," said Aristotle, "make us detect more easily the truth and error about the several points that arise." The right to speak freely is one of the necessary means to the attainment of the truth. That, and not the subjective pleasure of utterance, is why freedom is a necessity in the good society.

This was the ground on which Milton in the *Areopagitica* opposed the order of Parliament (1643) that no book should be printed or put on sale unless it had first been licensed by the authorities. . . .

The method of dialectics is to confront ideas with opposing ideas in order that the pro and the con of the dispute will lead to true ideas. But the dispute must not be treated as a trial of strength. It must be a means of elucidation. In a Socratic dialogue the disputants are arguing co-operatively in order to acquire more wisdom than either of them had when he began. In a sophistical argument the sophist is out to win a case, using rhetoric and not dialectic. "Both alike," says Aristotle, "are concerned with such things as come, more or less, within the general ken of all men and belong to no definite science." But while "dialectic is a process of criticism wherein lies the path to the principle of all inquiries," "rhetoric is concerned with the modes of persuasion."

Divorced from its original purpose and justification, as a process of criticism, freedom to think and speak are not self-evident necessities. It is only from the hope and the intention of discovering truth that freedom acquires such high public significance. The right of self-expression is, as such, a private amenity rather than a public necessity. The right to utter words, whether or not they have meaning, and regardless of their truth, could not be a vital interest of a great state but for the presumption that they are the chaff which goes with the utterance of true and significant words.

But when the chaff of silliness, baseness, and deception is so voluminous that it submerges the kernels of truth, freedom of speech may produce such frivolity, or such mischief, that it cannot be preserved against the demand for a restoration of order or of decency. If there is a dividing line between liberty and license, it is where freedom of speech is no longer respected as a procedure of the truth and becomes the unrestricted right to exploit the ignorance, and to incite the passions, of the people. Then freedom is such a hullabaloo of sophistry, propaganda, special pleading, lobbying, and salesmanship that it is difficult to remember why freedom of speech is worth the pain and trouble of defending it.

What has been lost in the tumult is the meaning of the obligation which is involved in the right to speak freely. It is the obligation to subject the utterance to criticism and debate. Because the dialectical debate is a procedure for attaining moral and political truth, the right to speak is protected by a willingness to debate.

In the public philosophy, freedom of speech is conceived as the means to a confrontation of opinion—as in a Socratic dialogue, in a schoolmen's disputation, in the critiques of scientists and savants, in a court of law, in a representative assembly, in an open forum. . . .

And because the purpose of the confrontation is to discern

truth, there are rules of evidence and of parliamentary procedure, there are codes of fair dealing and fair comment, by which a loyal man will consider himself bound when he exercises the right to publish opinions. For the right to freedom of speech is no license to deceive, and willful misrepresentation is a violation of its principles. It is sophistry to pretend that in a free country a man has some sort of inalienable or constitutional right to deceive his fellow men. There is no more right to deceive than there is a right to swindle, to cheat, or to pick pockets. It may be inexpedient to arraign every public liar, as we try to arraign other swindlers. It may be a poor policy to have too many laws which encourage litigation about matters of opinion. But, in principle, there can be no immunity for lying in any of its protean forms.

In our time the application of these fundamental principles poses many unsolved practical problems. For the modern media of mass communication do not lend themselves easily to a confrontation of opinions. The dialectical process for finding truth works best when the same audience hears all the sides of the disputation. This is manifestly impossible in the moving pictures: if a film advocates a thesis, the same audience cannot be shown another film designed to answer it. Radio and television broadcasts do permit some debate. But despite the effort of the companies to let opposing views be heard equally, and to organize programs on which there are opposing speakers, the technical conditions of broadcasting do not favor genuine and productive debate. For the audience, tuning on and tuning off here and there, cannot be counted upon to hear, even in summary form, the essential evidence and the main arguments on all the significant sides of a question. Rarely, and on very few public issues, does the mass audience have the benefit of the process by which truth is sifted from error—the dialectic of debate in which there is immediate challenge, reply, cross-examination, and rebuttal. The men who regularly broadcast the news and comment upon the news cannot—like a speaker in the Senate or in the House of Commons—be challenged by one of their listeners and compelled then and there to verify their statements of fact and to re-argue their inferences from the facts.

Yet when genuine debate is lacking, freedom of speech does not work as it is meant to work. It has lost the principle which regulates it and justifies it—that is to say, dialectic conducted according to logic and the rules of evidence. If there is no effective debate, the unrestricted right to speak will unloose so many propagandists, procurers, and panderers upon the public that sooner or later in self-defense the people will turn to the censors to protect them. An unrestricted and unregulated right to speak cannot be maintained. It will be curtailed for all manner of reasons and pretexts, and to serve all kinds of good, foolish, or sinister ends.

For in the absence of debate, unrestricted utterance leads to the degradation of opinion. By a kind of Gresham's law the more rational is overcome by the less rational, and the opinions that will prevail will be those which are held most ardently by those with the most passionate will. For that reason the freedom to speak can never be maintained merely by objecting to interference with the liberty of the press, of printing, of broadcasting, of the screen. It can be maintained only by promoting debate.

In the end what men will most ardently desire is to suppress those who disagree with them and, therefore, stand in the way of the realization of their desires. Thus, once confrontation in debate is no longer necessary, the toleration of all opinions leads to intolerance. Freedom of speech, separated from its essential principle, leads through a short transitional chaos to the destruction of freedom of speech. . . .

7 · *The Articulation of the Public Philosophy*

The Public Philosophy (*1955*), *Chapter 11.*

We come now to the problem of communicating the public philosophy to the modern democracies. The problem has been, to be sure, only too obvious from the beginning. For . . . the public philosophy is in a deep contradiction with the Jacobin ideology, which is, in fact, the popular doctrine of the mass democracies.

The public philosophy is addressed to the government of our appetites and passions by the reasons of a second, civilized, and, therefore, acquired nature. Therefore, the public philosophy cannot be popular. For it aims to resist and to regulate those very desires and opinions which are most popular. The warrant of the public philosophy is that while the regime it imposes is hard, the results of rational and disciplined government will be good. And so, while the right but hard decisions are not likely to be popular when they are taken, the wrong and soft decisions will, if they are frequent and big enough, bring on a disorder in which freedom and democracy are destroyed.

If we ask whether the public philosophy can be communicated to the democracies, the answer must begin with the acknowledgment that there must be a doctrine to communicate. The philosophy must first be made clear and pertinent to our modern anxieties. Our reconnaissance has been addressed to that first need.

But beyond it lies the problem of the capacity and the willingness of modern men to receive this kind of philosphy. The concepts and the principles of the public philosophy have their being in the realm of immaterial entities. They cannot be experienced by our sense organs or even, strictly speaking, imagined in visual or tangible terms. Yet these essences, these abstractions, which are out of sight and out of touch, are to have and to hold men's highest loyalties.

The problem of communication is posed because in the modern world, as it is today, most men—not all men, to be sure, but most active and influential men—are in practice positivists who hold that the only world which has reality is the physical world. Only seeing is believing. Nothing is real enough to be taken seriously, nothing can be a matter of deep concern, which cannot, or at least might not, somewhere and sometime, be seen, heard, tasted, smelled, or touched. . . .

Early in the history of Western society, political thinkers in Rome hit upon the idea that the concepts of the public philosophy—particularly the idea of reciprocal rights and duties under law—could be given concreteness by treating them as contracts. In this way, freedom emanating from a constitutional order has been advocated, explained, made real to the imagination and the conscience of Western men; by establishing the presumption that civilized society is founded on a public social contract.

A contract is an agreement reached voluntarily, *quid pro*

quo and likely, therefore, to be observed—in any event, rightfully enforceable. Being voluntary, it has the consent of the parties. The presumption is not only that one party has acceded to what the other party proposed, but also that, in the original meaning of the word, both parties have consented—that they have thought, felt and judged the matter together. Being a contract, the agreement will, presumably, be specific enough to minimize the quarrels of misunderstanding. It will say what the parties may expect of one another. It will say what are their respective rights and duties. In the field of the contract, their relations will be regulated and criteria will exist for adjudicating issues between them.

These are the essential characteristics of a constitutional system. It can be said to prevail when every man in and out of office is bound by lawful contracts. Without this, that is, without constitutional government, there is no freedom. For the antithesis to being free is to be at the mercy of men who can act arbitrarily. It is not to know what may be done to you. It is to have no right to an accounting, and to have no means of objecting. Despotism and anarchy prevail when a constitutional order does not exist. Both are lawless and arbitrary. Indeed, despotism may be defined as the anarchy of lawless rulers, and anarchy as the despotism of lawless crowds.

The first principle of a civilized state is that power is legitimate only when it is under contract. Then it is, as we say, duly constituted. This principle is of such controlling significance that in the Western world the making of the contracts of government and of society has usually been regarded as marking —historically or symbolically—the crossing of the line which divides barbarity from civility. . . .

Men have been laboring with the problem of how to make concrete and real what is abstract and immaterial ever since the Greek philosophers began to feel the need to accommodate the popular Homeric religion to the advance of science. The theologians, says Aristotle, are like the philosophers in that they promulgate certain doctrines; but they are unlike them in that they do so in mythical form.

The method of accommodation employed by the philosophers has been to treat the materialization in the myth as allegory: as translation of the same knowledge into another language. To converse with the devil, for example, could then mean what literally it says—to talk face to face with the devil, a concrete materialized personage. But it could mean, also, the imitation of a wicked nature without—as the Cambridge Platonist John Smith wrote, "a mutual local presence," that is to say, without meeting a devil in person. This was an accommodation to those who, believing in the wickedness of evil, could not believe in the personified devil. The devil could mean either "some apostate spirit as one particular being," and also "the spirit of apostasie which is lodged in all men's natures." This is the method of plural interpretation; it uses "the language of accommodation." It is justified and legitimate, said John Smith in his discourse entitled "A Christian's Conflicts and Conquests," because "truth is content, when it comes into the world, to wear our mantles, to learn our language, to conform itself as it were to our dress and fashions . . . it speaks with the most idiotical sort of men in the most idiotical way, and becomes all things to all men, as every sonne of truth should do for their good."

But there are limits beyond which we cannot carry the time-honored method of accommodating the diversity of beliefs. As we know from the variety and sharpness of schisms and sects in our time, we have gone beyond the limits of accommodation. We know, too, that as the divisions grow wider and more irreconcilable, there arise issues of loyalty with which the general principle of toleration is unable to cope.

For the toleration of differences is possible only on the assumption that there is no vital threat to the community. Toleration is not, therefore, a sufficient principle for dealing with the diversity of opinions and beliefs. It is itself dependent upon the positive principle of accommodation. The principle calls for the effort to find agreement beneath the differences.

In studying how accommodation is achieved, we may begin by observing that it is the philosophers, using Aristotle's broad terminology, who work out and promote the plural interpretation. They propose the terms for accommodating their immaterial belief to the concrete and materialized imagery of the fundamentalists. Thus it was the Cambridge John Smith who took the initiative about the devil. John Smith was not addressing the fundamentalists who believed in the personified devil; in fact what he said about the whole matter was not meant to trouble the fundamentalists at all. He was addressing men who were unable to believe in the personified devil and yet were still in essential communion with the fundamentalists. For they did believe in the spirit of the devil which, as everyone knows, is in all of us. In this accommodation the Christian Platonists gave up trying to believe what they could not believe. They went on believing that which in its essence their fundamentalist neighbors believed. Thus they could continue to live in the same community with them.

There is an impressive historical example of how by accommodation it is possible to communicate these difficult truths to a large heterogeneous society. In medieval Christendom a great subject of accommodation was the origin and sanction of the public philosophy itself, of the natural laws of the rational order. Otto von Gierke says that despite the innumerable learned controversies of the lawyers, the theologians and the philosophers, "all were agreed that there was natural law, which, on the one hand, radiated from a principle transcending earthly power, and on the other hand was true and perfectly binding law . . . the highest power on earth was subject to the rules of natural law. They stood above the Pope and above the Kaiser, above the ruler and above the sovereign people, nay, above the whole community of mortals. Neither statute nor act of government, neither resolution of the people nor custom could break the bounds that thus were set. Whatever contradicted the eternal and immutable principles of natural law was utterly void and would bind no one."

But though there was agreement on this, there was deep controversy over whether the natural laws were the commands of God or whether they were the dictates of an eternal reason, grounded on the being of God, and unalterable even by God himself. How were men to imagine, to materialize and make concrete the natural law which is above the Pope and the Kaiser and all mortals? As decrees of an omniscient and omnipotent heavenly king? Or as the principles of the nature of things? There were some who could not conceive of binding laws which had to be obeyed unless there was a lawgiver made in the image of the human lawgivers they had seen or heard about. There were others to whose capacity it was not necessary to condescend with quite that much materialization.

The crucial point, however, is not where the naturalists and supernaturalists disagreed. It is that they did agree that there was a valid law which, whether it was the commandment of God or the reason of things, was transcendent. They did agree that it was not something decided upon by certain men and then proclaimed by them. It was not someone's fancy, someone's prejudice, someone's wish or rationalization, a psychological experience and no more. It is there objectively, not subjectively. It can be discovered. It has to be obeyed.

8 · *The Uses of Tradition*

The New Imperative (1935), *Chapter 3, a printed version of the Phi Beta Kappa oration in Sanders Theater, Harvard University, June 21, 1935.*

Here in this university there is perfomed the miracle which distinguishes civilized man from all the other animals. He can transmit from one generation to another the knowledge which he discovers, the skill which he acquires, the wisdom which he perceives. But though man has the faculty of tradition, it is an uncertain one. Oftener than not he has been unable to absorb and to transmit the vital essence of his tradition. Then he has fallen into dark ages when he has lost his inheritance, into dull ages when he is uninterested in it, and into ages of bewilderment when he cries out for it and cannot find it.

So the history of man is heavy with the tragedy of his unrealized possibilities. For had he been able to transmit the human heritage unimpaired in its full vitality from ancient times to the present day, so that no skill was lost and none of the lessons of experience forgotten, the compounded wisdom of mankind would have produced a civilization so splendid as to surpass our ability to imagine it.

But again and again the tradition of the good life has become dim and has been interrupted, and then it has had laboriously to be rediscovered and realized and learned once more.

We live in an age when men are dismayed because they feel that they have lost the tradition of the good life. They are acutely aware of the unrealized possibilities of human societies. The intellectual life of the Western world is distracted, its spirit is impaired, by the paradoxes of poverty when there is plenty, of science triumphant in political disorder, of conscience become sensitive to human dignity in the midst of a reversion to the primitive. To these paradoxes men cannot become resigned. They can accept a fate which it is beyond their power to avert. They can endure pain and hardship and natural calamity. But they will not resign themselves to a failure which originates—so they must believe—in their own behavior and could be remedied by intelligence and courage and good will.

A civilization tormented by these paradoxes is sick, like the Roman world of which Lucretius said that it had a malady of which its masters did not know the cause. For us the point at which the malady is most ominous is when young men come asking us what tradition we possess by which they can confront this contradictory world. The older generation who sit in the seats of authority, and in the nature of things determine the answer, do not have an answer. They do not know what to say when they are asked what ideas they possess which offer the new generation valid purposes and noble duties. They are embarrassed at the question. Though they love their country and believe in it, they cannot put into words, because they do not have it in their minds, a conception of the American commonwealth in which the young men can find direction and meaning for their lives.

Thus we are unable to transmit from our generation to the next a credible and coherent tradition. This is our danger. The nation is secure against conquest. Its resources are ample. Its people are energetic and cheerful and brave. But those who determine what schools and colleges and the press shall transmit as the American tradition do not know what to tell the young men. There is a breach, which is threatening and sinister, between the energy of youth and the experience of age.

This new generation, to whom we can offer skill rather than wisdom and specialized knowledge without philosophy, is cheated and feels it is cheated if we do not know how to offer it a part in some great enterprise. For these men are young and they are not yet tired and they do not yet prefer comfort and security above all other things. They have courage unspoiled by the commitments of maturity and they have not lived until they have known a duty that transcends personal ambition. They must believe that they are needed. They must enter into an idea that will inform and transfigure their private worlds.

But they cannot find this idea in the teachings and the

warnings of those who sit in the seats of authority. Some, therefore, have sought it, and believe they have found it, in the revolutionary fervors and alien faiths of central and eastern Europe. Others (and they are the great majority) go out into the world without political convictions. The consequences are ominous. For they mean that those who will rule the American commonwealth tomorrow are spiritually isolated from those who rule it today. The fathers do not know what their sons will do with the estate and so they cannot act in the present with the conviction of permanence. The sons cannot prepare for the future with the enthusiasm of loyalty. The circuits of tradition, by which purposes are transmitted from one generation to another, are seriously interrupted.

This is the condition, which has preceded so many of the tragedies of history, when the successful and the dominant live for the moment, defensively, dreading the future and not daring to engage it, irresolute because they have lost purpose and intention and the conviction of a great destiny. When this happens, wisdom acquired through many ages is blown about by all the winds of doctrine; then the government of the commonwealth is not in the hands of confident men.

"The Bonds of Affection," Today and Tomorrow, *December 6, 1954.*

A few years ago I would have felt differently than I did last Tuesday morning in London when I had the good luck to see the state opening of Parliament and the tribute to Churchill in Westminster Hall. Anyone at any time would be fascinated by the splendor and brilliance of the ceremony in the House of Lords, and deeply moved by seeing full justice done publicly to the great man. But for an American today there was also, I could not help feeling, a poignant reminder that something at home, which is infinitely precious, is in danger of being lost.

That something is a loyalty to the enduring nation which is so compelling that it keeps party politics, and the competition for votes and for popular applause, in their proper place. That proper place is well below, and far apart from, the high concerns of the state in its dealings abroad and, at home, in the administration of justice. Churchill, in his speech replying to Mr. Attlee, spoke of "that characteristic British parliamentary principle, cherished in both Lords and Commons, 'don't bring politics into private life.' " The principle, so an American can feel, is broader than that. It is not to let politics invade every nook and cranny of public life until the whole institutional framework of the nation is submerged and overwhelmed by ambitious and quarreling men.

The British have their own way of applying the principle that the nation is above politicians and voters and the tides of opinion. Their way is unique, the product of their own history, and impossible, of course, to duplicate. But the principle itself does not depend upon having a radiant Queen to play the central part in an ancient rite. It depends upon the things for which Lincoln on the eve of the Civil War was reaching in the closing paragraph of his first inaugural address. "We are not enemies, but friends. We must not be enemies. Though passion may have strained, it must not break, our bonds of affection. The mystic chords of memory, stretching from every battlefield and patriot grave to every living heart and hearthstone all over this broad land, will yet swell the chorus of the Union when again touched, as surely they will be, by the better angels of our nature."

It is not necessary, as our own history has shown, to have the pomp and circumstance of a monarchy and of an hereditary aristocracy in order to remember that there is a limit beyond which political passions must not go, or they will break the bonds of affection which hold the nation together in time of trouble. Our American unity has been a plainer one than is the British: it has been made up of respect for the principles and the usages and, above all, for the spirit of the Constitution.

"The Coronation of a Queen," Today and Tomorrow, *June 2, 1953.*

Many men who live far beyond the Commonwealth and Empire have come to feel, as the coronation of the Queen drew near, that though they have no part in the gorgeous ceremony, they do participate in the solemn rite. For the British have made out of the forms and usages of their own unique history a great work of art which celebrates the saving truth about the government of men.

It is the truth that in every good society there must be a

common center, known to be legitimate, to which the loyalty and the public love of all men are bound. That center of allegiance may be incarnate in an actual person or, as in a republic, it may be disembodied and have its being in the idea of the constitution and its ideal meaning. But always and everywhere, if a government is to be good, a center of men's allegiance must be recognized that is above the diversities and conflicts of their interests, and that is invulnerable to the pressure of party, faction, class, race, and sect.

And since this center of men's worldly allegiance must be beyond the reach of their worldly passions, it must be founded in, it must be consecrated to, the realm of the spirit. It must be bound to the truths that are more than the private and passing opinions of persons and of crowds, and to the laws that are above their wishes and their impulses.

This is the universal essence which Queen Elizabeth II represents for all mankind when she is recognized, is sworn, is anointed, and is crowned. In the course of the centuries, the British people—the most gifted in government since the Romans and with their genius in poetry—have invested monarchy with the meaning that must be recognized somewhere and somehow in any state—whether or not it has a king—if it is to be governed well.

The ritual itself is an eloquent record of how this has been done, so often against the will of the reigning monarch himself. The ritual looks back upon and sums up the centuries of struggle and of inspiration in which the British have brought all earthly powers—kings, nobles, and all the commoners no less—under the laws. It is a great art to have woven about their hereditary and not always very royal and admirable kings, a web of usages and symbols and ceremonies which—though they are unique for the British people in their concrete and historic circumstance—are none the less true and significant for all peoples and all states.

The truths of this rite are most timely for our day. Our generation would, in any circumstances, be more sensitive and receptive to them than those that have preceded us, even if by great good fortune the central figure were not the young and beautiful Queen attended by her great Prime Minister, so undoubtedly the chivalrous and dauntless champion of freedom and good hope. This is a moment to reaffirm and to celebrate the essential truths. For the future of the free democratic societies hangs in the balance because, confronted with the challenge of their adversaries, they are so weakened by the conflict and confusion within and among themselves.

If the free world is in this great peril, it is not because the adversaries of freedom are so strong or so attractive but because so many, indeed most, of the large democratic states are at the moment so badly governed. In many of them, our own alas included, good government is undermined by the usurpation of the sovereign power by the popular assembly. In the crisis of our Western society this usurpation has brought about a paralysis and panic fear which threaten to wreck the position of the whole free world, and to destroy the freedom and the kindly community of men with one another at home.

"The Living Past," Today and Tomorrow, *April 13, 1943.*

The other evening I saw all but the last act of a play in which Jefferson and Hamilton appear as the champions of two great opposing principles: of liberty and authority, of belief in the perfectibility of human nature as against a knowledge of its defects. Since I could not stay to the end, I do not know whether in the last act the author married the two principles and had them live happily ever after or whether he left Jefferson and Hamilton fighting forever the battle between good and evil. All I can say is that when I left the theater the prospects were not good for a marriage.

If so, it is a pity. For the wisest man of that time, who was Washington, knew that he needed both Jefferson and Hamilton to establish the Republic, and it would be a sad reflection upon our own political sense if he were still unable to feel how indispensable and complementary were these two great men and what they stood for. "It may be," says our own historian, James Truslow Adams, "that without a vision men shall die. It is no less true that without hard practical sense they shall also die. Without Jefferson the new nation might have lost its soul. Without Hamilton it would assuredly have been killed in body."

We have begun to realize in these days how close we have come to separating the coming generation from its heritage in the American past; we are shocked and dismayed to discover how unreal the great Americans have become to them, how the events which have formed the nation are dim, how dangerously close we have come to being a people who inhabit the land with their bodies without possessing it in their souls.

But we must know also that there is no short way to make the past live again in men's minds; it cannot be done by passing a law, or by appropriating money, or by a witch hunt among the professors. The American past can be brought to life again only by men who tell the majestic story once more, aware that they are making history and not merely writing it. When we read the writings of the early Americans we find that, unlike our own generation, the past was continually present in their minds as part of their own experience. They were making a new government, and for their own guidance, for knowledge of what to do, they drew not upon surveys of contemporary opinion and questionnaires but upon precedent and experience.

Nor did the best of them fall into the error, which I thought the playwright was falling into, of accepting the past on its own terms, that is to say, of identifying themselves with the partisan passions of the men of the past. The true study of history is more than a flashback in a movie by which we re-enact with photographic realism what once happened. It should give us more understanding than we could have had if we ourselves had been men of the past. For we see all sides of the past and we know also the outcome.

We have missed the meaning of history, then, if today we are "Jeffersonians" opposed to "Hamiltonians" or vice versa. This robs history of wisdom, which is all that makes history more than dry bones and tittle-tattle. To be partisan today as between Jefferson and Hamilton is like arguing whether men or women are more necessary to the procreation of the race. For it is beyond argument that it was out of the union of the two principles which Jefferson and Hamilton represented that there was born the Republic which has endured.

To perpetuate the Republic in this epoch of war and revolution it is now more than ever necessary that we maintain the marriage of Jeffersonian liberty and of Hamiltonian authority. We can do ourselves no greater injury than to become unconscious of either principle; so enamored of freedom that we do not construct strong lawful authority to contain it and sustain it, or so apprehensive of freedom that we seek to deny it and suppress it.

The conflict of the two principles can be resolved only by uniting them. Neither can live alone. Alone, that is, without the other, each is excessive and soon intolerable. Freedom, the faith in man's perfectibility, has always and will always in itself lead through anarchy to despotism. Authority, the conviction that men have to be governed and not merely let loose, will in itself always lead through arbitrariness and corruption to rebellion and chaos. Only in their union are they fruitful. Only freedom which is under strong law, only strong law to which men consent because it preserves freedom, can endure.

9 · *The Mandate of Heaven*

The Public Philosophy (*1955*), *Chapter 11.*

At the end, then, the questions are how we conceive of ourselves and the public world beyond our private selves. Much depends upon the philosophers. For though they are not kings, they are, we may say, the teachers of the teachers. "In the history of Western governments," says Francis G. Wilson, "the transitions of society can be marked by the changing character of the intellectuals," who have served the government as lawyers, advisers, administrators, who have been teachers in the schools, who have been members of professions like medicine and theology. It is through them that doctrines are made to operate in practical affairs. And their doctrine, which they, themselves, have learned in the schools and universities, will have the shape and the reference and the direction which the prevailing philosophy gives it.

That is how and why philosophy and theology are the ultimate and decisive studies in which we engage. In them are defined the main characteristics of the images of man which will be acted upon in the arts and sciences of the epoch. The role of philosophers is rarely, no doubt, creative. But it is critical, in that they have a deciding influence in determining what may be believed, how it can be believed, and what cannot be believed. The philosophers, one might say, stand at the crossroads. While they may not cause the traffic to move, they can stop it and start it, they can direct it one way or the other.

I do not contend, though I hope, that the decline of Western society will be arrested if the teachers in our schools and universities come back to the great tradition of the public philosophy. But I do contend that the decline, which is already far advanced, cannot be arrested if the prevailing philosophers oppose this restoration and revival, if they impugn rather than support the validity of an order which is superior to the values that Sartre tells each man "to invent."

What the prevailing philosophers say about religion is not itself, in Tillich's terms, religion as an ultimate concern of worship and of love. But if the philosophers teach that religious experience is a purely psychological phenomenon, related to nothing beyond each man's psychic condition, then they will give educated men a bad intellectual conscience if they have religious experiences. The philosopher cannot give them religion. But they can keep them away from it.

Philosophers play the same role in relation to the principles of the good society. These require, as we have seen, the mastery of human nature in the raw by an acquired rational second nature. In the literal sense, the principles of the good society must be unpopular until they have prevailed sufficiently to alter the popular impulses. For the popular impulses are opposed to public principles. These principles cannot be made to prevail if they are discredited—if they are dismissed as superstition, as obscurantism, as meaningless metaphysics, as reactionary, as self-seeking rationalizations.

The public philosophy is in a large measure intellectually discredited among contemporary men. Because of that, what we may call the terms of discourse in public controversy are highly unfavorable to anyone who adheres to the public philosophy. The signs and seals of legitimacy, of rightness and of truth, have been taken over by men who reject, even when they are not the avowed adversaries of, the doctrine of constitutional democracy.

If the decline of the West under the misrule of the people is to be halted, it will be necessary to alter these terms of discourse. They are now set overwhelmingly against the credibility and against the rightness of the principles of the constitutional state; they are set in favor of the Jacobin conception of the emancipated and sovereign people.

I have been arguing, hopefully and wishfully, that it may be possible to alter the terms of discourse if a convincing demonstration can be made that the principles of the good society are not, in Sartre's phrase, invented and chosen—that the conditions which must be met if there is to be a good society are there, outside our wishes, where they can be discovered by rational inquiry, and developed and adapted and refined by rational discussion.

If eventually this were demonstrated successfully, it would, I believe, rearm all those who are concerned with the anomy of our society, with its progressive barbarization, and with its descent into violence and tyranny. Amidst the quagmire of moral impressionism they would stand again on hard intellectual ground where there are significant objects that are given and are not merely projected, that are compelling and are not merely wished. Their hope would be re-established that there is a public world, sovereign above the infinite number of contradictory and competing private worlds. Without this certainty, their struggle must be unavailing.

As the defenders of civility, they cannot do without the signs and seals of legitimacy, of rightness and of truth. For it is a practical rule, well known to experienced men, that the relation is very close between our capacity to act at all and our conviction that the action we are taking is right. This does not mean, of course, that the action *is* necessarily right. What is necessary to continuous action is that it shall be *believed* to be right. Without that belief, most men will not have the energy and will to persevere in the action. Thus satanism, which prefers evil as such, is present in some men and perhaps potential in many. Yet, except in a condition of the profoundest hysteria, as in a lynching, satanism cannot be preached to multitudes. Even Hitler, who was enormously satanic and delighted in monstrous evil, did nevertheless need, it would seem, to be reassured that he was not only a great man but, in a mysterious way, a righteous one.

William Jennings Bryan once said that to be clad in the armor of righteousness will make the humblest citizen of all the land stronger than all the hosts of error. That is not quite true. But the reason the humblest citizen is not stronger than the hosts of error is that the latter also are clad in an armor which they at least believe is the armor of righteousness. Had they not been issued the armor of righteousness, they would not, as a matter of fact, be a host at all. For political ideas acquire operative force in human affairs when, as we have seen, they acquire legitimacy, when they have the title of being right which binds men's consciences. Then they possess, as the Confucian doctrine has it, "the mandate of heaven."

In the crisis within the Western society, there is at issue now the mandate of heaven.

VI

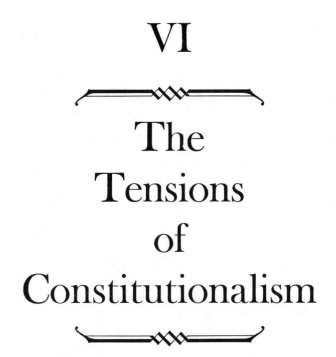

The Tensions of Constitutionalism

1 · *The Uses of Constitutionalism*

"This Democracy," Today and Tomorrow, *November 26, 1936. The angry reaction to the Supreme Court's nullification of critical parts of the New Deal program offered Lippmann an opportunity to examine the significance of constitutionalism in a democracy.*

Through all the comment it is implied, and apparently never questioned, that the American government would be more progressive, more democratic, and more liberal if the courts ceased to interfere with Congress and the state legislatures.

Thus the whole argument assumes that in one way or another the lawmakers ought to have a freer hand, in fact that any temporary majority of elected representatives ought to be able to make the law of the land.

This assumption needs to be examined for it is altogether opposed to the spirit of American Constitutional democracy. In Britain, Parliament is supreme and in theory anything can be done by the act of any Parliament. In theory Parliament can abolish the monarchy, the House of Lords, the courts, the Civil Service, private property, civil liberty. Actually these things are not likely to be done because custom and usage are powerful restraints upon the supremacy of Parliament. But the authors of the American Constitution were establishing a government for a new nation, for a nation in the making, for a nation without a strong and well-defined unwritten law. And being men of great insight into the art of government, they set up a constitution intended by its own provisions to do what the unwritten law does in England.

They made a constitution which deliberately denies that the opinion of a temporary majority is to be regarded as the will of the people. The ultimate authority, of course, is in "the people." But the will of the people is not confused with the opinions of fifty-one per cent of the voters at any particular election. Therefore the whole American system is devised to see to it that in fundamental matters affecting the liberties and the property of individuals, and the rights of local communities, the will of the people shall be thoroughly known before great changes are finally adopted. The authors of the Constitution were interested not only in what two hundred and fifty congressmen think ought to be done, not only in what fifty-one per cent of the voters think they think on election day, but in what these politicians and voters will think when they have cooled off and learned more. The founders were equally interested in the forty-nine per cent, and they meant to see to it that before anything final and radical was done, the minority should have plenty of time to make themselves heard. Nor were they interested only in counting heads. They meant to create a system in which sections and regions could not suddenly override smaller sections and smaller regions.

This is the purpose of the famous system of checks and balances and of Constitutional supremacy and judicial construction. It is based on a refusal to believe that a true democracy means the dictatorship of transient pluralities.

This is a more deeply democratic conception of popular rule than one which gives transient majorities supreme power. Compare it with the kind of popular rule by which Napoleon III made himself Emperor, by which Hitler made himself dictator, by which the people of the Saar voted away their right to vote again on how they shall be governed. There you have the naked result of the doctrine that passing majorities should be supreme. They are so supreme that in one hysterical plebiscite they can vote away their own and their children's right to change their minds. They are so supreme that they can vote away their supremacy. And so Hitler is planning to have the Nazis rule Germany for a thousand years as a result of an election held in the winter of 1933.

This is the *reductio ad absurdum* of popular rule, and our system recognizes no such nonsense. It conceives the people as varied and differing human beings, liable to be swept away by passions but capable of learning from experience and of listening to reason. In great matters the will of the American people is not to be formed overnight, in a whirlwind campaign, in the midst of a passing emergency, but slowly, after prolonged argument, after repeated opportunity to make the opposition effective, by consulting the voters several times and in different ways, by letting Philip sober make up his mind when Philip is no longer drunk. We recognize, in short, the simple truth that we are human, not very wise, not very far-seeing, likely to do foolish things, and that it takes time to find out what we really mean, and to correct our mistakes.

This system is worth defending, particularly by those who believe in democratic government. That does not mean that the Supreme Court is infallible, or that the Court itself has invariably seen the issues clearly and dispassionately, or that enlightened judges are not preferable to unenlightened ones. But it does mean that the system of checks and balances which compel passing majorities to reconsider their opinions and enables minorities to challenge those opinions is more truly democratic than one which allows majorities to do what they want when they want to do it. That other system is not democracy but the dictatorship of the majority. And the dictatorship of temporary majorities leads, as the Constitutional Fathers saw so clearly, to the dictatorship of oligarchs and demagogues.

"The Right of Filibuster," Today and Tomorrow, *February 1, 1938.*

It is generally assumed that it is rather undemocratic and disreputable to carry on a filibuster in the United States Senate. The filibuster is, of course, a weapon of the minority. It is a device for prolonging the debate in order to prevent the majority from voting to pass a bill, and those who feel that democracy means that any majority should be able to do whatever it chooses whenever it chooses naturally condemn the filibuster.

They are, I think, mistaken. It can be shown, I feel sure, that the filibuster under the present rules of the Senate conforms with the essential spirit of the American Constitution, and that it is one of the very strongest practical guaranties we possess for preserving the rights which are in the Constitution.

The apparent objection to the filibuster—that it obstructs the rule of the majority—is easily disposed of. The majority of the Senate has the power to apply cloture at any time. In other words, whenever a majority wishes to stop a filibuster it can vote to stop it, and after that no one may speak more than once or longer than one hour on the pending measure. Therefore, though the filibuster is conducted by a minority it can only be conducted with the consent of the majority. . . .

Behind this more or less technical justification of the filibuster there is a much more substantial justification. Democracy, as we have always understood it in America, has never meant the unrestricted rule of the majority. Our whole Constitutional system is based on a conscious and deliberate rejection of that principle, and the insistence, in place of it, upon the principle that it is not the bare current majority but the great ultimate majority, the majority which is formed after there has been plenty of time for debate, which is sovereign in this democracy. . . .

Thus there is no guarantee in the Constitution—of freedom of conscience, of the press, or even of the prohibition of human slavery—which a great majority of the voters cannot repeal. The final power is in the people and they can, if they decide, amend the Constitution in order to establish a complete despotism. But they cannot do it as the German Reichstag did five years ago when by majority vote it consented to commit suicide. American liberty is ever so much more strongly entrenched, and the majority of the moment cannot vote away the democratic system or the Constitutional rights of the individual.

That can be done in America only if there is an overwhelming majority and then only after the minority has had time to make a thorough appeal to the conscience of the people. That is what is meant by the checks and balances of the American Constitution. That is why we have a Constitution which limits the power of Congress, of the President, of state legislatures and of governors. That is why the Constitution is interpreted by an independent judiciary. That is why this Constitution cannot be amended until an enormous and deliberate majority speaking through two-thirds of both houses of Congress and three-quarters of the states consents to the amendment. And that is why in one of these houses, the Senate, we have the jealously guarded tradition of unlimited debate, and why a majority of the Senate is very reluctant to apply cloture and stop debate.

No frame of government can absolutely guarantee human liberty. But the American system, whatever its other faults may be, is the most ingeniously and elaborately contrived mechanism on earth to make it difficult to abolish liberty in a gust of popular passion.

If we ask ourselves how we are to know when a minority is justified in using the mechanism to obstruct the majority, the answer is, I think, clear enough. Only a minority with deep convictions facing a majority with weak convictions can under the present rules conduct a filibuster.

"Filibusters and the American Idea," Today and Tomorrow, *March 3, 1949.*

In the American system of government the right of "democratic decision" has never been identified with majority rule as such. The genius of the American system, unique I believe among the democracies of the world, is that it limits all power—including the power of the majority. Absolute power, whether in a king, a president, a legislative majority, a popular majority, is alien to the American idea of "democratic decision."

The American idea of a democratic decision has always been that important minorities must not be coerced. When there is strong opposition, it is neither wise nor practical to force a decision. It is necessary and it is better to postpone the decision—to respect the opposition and then to accept the burden of trying to persuade it.

For a decision which has to be enforced against the determined opposition of large communities and regions of the country will, as Americans have long realized, almost never produce the results it is supposed to produce. The opposition and the resistance, having been overridden, will not disappear. They will merely find some other way of avoiding, evading, obstructing, or nullifying the decision.

For that reason it is a cardinal principle of the American

democracy that great decisions on issues that men regard as vital shall not be taken by the vote of the majority until the consent of the minority has been obtained. Where the consent of the minority has been lacking, as for example in the case of the prohibition amendment, the "democratic decision" has produced hypocrisy and lawlessness.

This is the issue in the Senate. It is not whether there shall be unlimited debates. The right of unlimited debates is merely a device, rather an awkward and tiresome device, to prevent large and determined communities from being coerced.

The issue is whether the fundamental principle of American democratic decision—that strong minorities must be persuaded and not coerced—shall be altered radically, not by Constitutional amendment but by a subtle change in the rules of the Senate.

The issue has been raised in connection with the civil rights legislation. The question is whether the vindication of these civil rights requires the sacrifice of the American limitation on majority rule. The question is a painful one. But I believe the answer has to be that the rights of Negroes will in the end be made more secure, even if they are vindicated more slowly, if the cardinal principle—that minorities shall not be coerced by majorities—is conserved.

For if that principle is abandoned, then the great limitations on the absolutism and the tyranny of transient majorities will be gone, and the path will be much more open than it now is to the demagogic dictator who, having aroused a mob, destroys the liberties of the people.

"On This Rock," Today and Tomorrow, *December 10, 1935.*

No doubt it is true that many selfishly stubborn interests use the Constitution to protect their special privileges. Nevertheless, it will be a bad day for democratic government in the modern world if American progressives cease to understand and to stand by the American conception of government as a limited grant of power to public officials. What is the good of denouncing the despotisms of Europe if here at home we cultivate the idea that anything may be done which at the moment seems good to those who are in office? Is it not evident that this is the very doctrine which destroys all the defenses against tyranny? For was there ever a tyrant who did not profess a profound interest in the future of the race or one who did not temporarily persuade a large group of persons that he knew how to insure the welfare of the race?

I am no believer in the literal inspiration of the Constitution or in its rigid interpretation. But those who do not see that liberty and progress in America both depend upon limiting the power of all government, upon preserving its federal nature, upon protecting local authority, are, I believe, tragically blind to the plainest lesson of the world they live in. For once a people lets all power become concentrated at one point, it is like an army trapped in a salient.

The reason why no dictator can seize power in the United States, as Mussolini seized it in Italy when he marched on Rome, is that there is no Rome against which an American dictator can march. He would have to march in forty-nine different directions at once. For there is no one place in the American system where sufficient power can be seized with which to dictate to the whole country. That is what the founders of the Republic intended. This is precisely what they had in mind when they made the central government a government of enumerated powers, when they jealously insisted upon preserving the identity and the substantial sovereignty of the separate states. They understood the mechanism and the strategy of tyranny. They consolidated the defenses against it, and American progressives who have witnessed the revival of despotism in the world ought to be the very last persons to doubt the importance of those defenses or to become lazy and indifferent about keeping them strong.

It is true that if we maintain a limited central government and a federal system of states, progress in good works is slow in that it is necessary to convince each locality that the good works are good. There are many who think that takes too long. But they will do well to remember that if it is a slow business converting each state to good ideas, it is also a slow business converting each state to bad ones. For myself, I would rather wait till Mayor LaGuardia converted New York City to good housing if that means that men like Huey Long have to wait till they have converted forty-eight states to their ideas.

And it does mean just that. The federal government means that the people of each region have to be convinced separately. They cannot be blessed immediately, uniformly, with all that seems good. But also they cannot be cursed immediately and uniformly with the same lunacy.

To insist that except in the direst emergency and then only for the emergency, these principles must take precedence over all other considerations is, it seems to me, the paramount duty of the citizen. He must not be deterred by any outcry that if he does not believe that the federal government should clear the slums, he must believe that people shall be doomed to live in foul buildings. We have had to face this same issue many times. Those who did not believe in the Eighteenth Amendment were charged with desiring drunkenness. Those who do not believe in the Child Labor Amendment are accused of wanting to preserve child labor. Those who do not believe that the federal government should have any control of the schools are accused of favoring ignorance. Those who opposed the N.R.A. were accused of approving of sweated labor and sharp commercial practice.

No doubt it is true that in opposing all these different kinds of centralization they find themselves often in bad company. But nevertheless you cannot have your cake and eat it, too. You cannot have a free government without some abuse of freedom. You cannot have a system of separate states and have uniformly high social standards in all of them. But if the American doctrine is correct, that in freedom mankind can realize its possibilities, then, as Franklin said, in the Bill of Rights of Pennsylvania, "a frequent recurrence to fundamental principles . . . is absolutely necessary to preserve the blessings of liberty and keep a government free." It is not only necessary to recur frequently to these principles, but at all times to defend them.

They must be defended not only against the avowed enemies of liberty but against those who, in their zeal for some particular blessing, forget and abandon the convictions without which there would be no liberty. There is no conviction so vital to the American people as the conviction that no one anywhere at any time shall have a monopoly of unlimited power. It is upon that conviction that the Republic rests. It is in that conviction that the American people have grown great and have remained free. It is that conviction that no one who considers himself a friend of the people should ever for a moment abandon.

"The Voice of the Supreme Court," Today and Tomorrow, *January 10, 1934. The Supreme Court's five-to-four decision upholding the constitutionality of Minnesota's debt moratorium law gave rise to these reflections on the flexibility of constitutional government.*

The details of the statute, of the particular case, and of the argument from precedent we may leave to the lawyers. Our concern is with the general principles which were invoked by Chief Justice Hughes in the majority opinion holding the Minnesota statute Constitutional. For presumably his statement of principles in this case discloses what will be the mind of the majority in considering the body of the new legislation.

The basic principle is that the power exists in American government to protect "the vital interests of the people." "We must never forget," says the Chief Justice, quoting Marshall, "that it is a Constitution we are expounding . . . a Constitution intended to endure for ages to come, and consequently, to be adapted to the various crises of human affairs." The Legislature and the Supreme Court of Minnesota had declared that an emergency existed which threatened many of the people with "the loss of homes and lands which furnish those in possession the necessary shelter and means of subsistence." The Chief Justice finds that the Minnesota estimate of the facts of the situation "cannot be regarded as a subterfuge or as lacking in adequate basis" and that it is "beyond cavil" that there were conditions in Minnesota "urgently demanding relief." In other words, this law to postpone the redemption of mortgages and prevent foreclosure was honest. It responded to a true estimate of the facts. It was not a sly device for enabling debtors to cheat their creditors.

Thus it transpires that the Court holds that extraordinary legislation may be justified, provided it is clear that it deals with a real public need. Apparently the Court will insist upon being convinced that the extraordinary laws are what they profess to be: measures to protect the public interest under extraordinary circumstances. . . .

In recognizing that power exists to deal with the emergency the Court, furthermore, lays down the rule that extraordinary legislation must be "temporary in operation . . . [and] limited to the exigency which called it forth." A legislature, for example, may relieve debtors in a crisis by giving them a moratorium, but it cannot cancel their debts for all time to come. This statute runs until May 1, 1935. "The operation of the statute," says the Court, "could not validly outlast the emergency or be so extended as virtually to destroy the contracts."

This appears to be quite in line with other decisions in recent years which draw a rather sharp line between temporary and permanent legislation. Toward temporary laws to meet a crisis the Court is very liberal: it recognizes that the power exists to do any reasonable thing to meet a crisis, be it war, or earthquake and flood and fire, or an economic convulsion. But laws which are to be permanent it quite evidently intends to scrutinize carefully and to judge by much stricter standards of Constitutional powers and rights.

Although the Minnesota decision is by a narrow majority of five to four, few reasonable people have ever doubted that the Court would uphold emergency legislation that was patently sincere. It would be a strange constitution which prevented a legislature from using its best judgment to protect its people during a great calamity, which bound it so that in the theoretical interest of the creditor, it could not act to prevent a disaster which would overwhelm creditor and debtor alike. But at the same time this decision by the so-called "liberals" of the Court makes it perfectly clear that permanent changes in American institutions cannot be wrought by subterfuges, by exploiting the emergency for ends which, however good in themselves, are not part of the emergency.

This is the genuine liberal doctrine. It contemplates a government of powers adapted, as Marshall said, to the various crises of human affairs. But it contemplates also a government in which permanent changes in institutions must be made only by the considered action of the people, by the people and their representatives when the issues are squarely presented, when they have had the opportunity to know what they are doing, when they are not confused by the pressure of an immediate crisis and are under no compulsion to assent to what they do not really believe in because they are frightened by a great but temporary danger.

A constitution which is flexible enough to enable governments to deal with a crisis and yet strong enough to withstand temptation to scrap essential parts of it in moments of excitement is likely to weather many storms. The Constitution which the Chief Justice has once more expounded is the Constitution which the great mass of the people have believed in.

2 · *The Premises of Constitutionalism*

"In Defense of Liberalism," Vanity Fair, *XLIII (November 1934), 24.*

The liberal philosophy is not to be judged by those who have never experienced it or by those who would douse the lamps that men have lighted because they are not so bright as the sun. The principles of liberalism are not the invention of sentimental theorists. They were not discovered in the eighteenth century. They are not to be confused with the economic policy of the nineteenth-century states. They are the crystallization of years of experience in the government of men. These principles are older than all existing constitutions and are more deeply rooted than any formulation of them that can be put into words. . . .

The liberal philosophy holds that enduring governments must be accountable to someone beside themselves; that a government responsible only to its own conscience is not for long tolerable. It holds that since any government is liable to fail, there is needed a method of changing the governors without wrecking the state. It holds that unless there is a method, be it through elections or otherwise, by which the governed can make their views effective in some proportion to their weight, the nation is at the mercy of violence in the form of terrorism, assassination, conspiracy, mass compulsion, and civil war.

It holds, therefore, that there must be civil liberty so that opinions may be formed and expressed. The liberal faith in civil liberties is due to a realization that rulers need criticism to check them and to inform them, that the ruled need freedom to have ideas and express them in order to contribute what their own experience teaches them, to vent their grievances, to prepare themselves for responsibility.

This is the political justification of liberty; it is founded, however, on a deeper insight into the nature of man and his history. The liberals believe that no rulers are wise enough to plan the destiny of mankind. They maintain therefore that the power of government must be limited, and that beyond those limits government must protect the freedom of men. They rely upon the initiative, the inventiveness, the endurance of individuals who, given opportunity, are challenged by it. They hold that a wide distribution of responsibility is the surest foundation of a society, that self-reliant individuals will sustain the nation when its governors fail, that among those individuals new governors will be trained and recruited.

The Stakes of Diplomacy (*1915*), *Chapter 4.*

Because a whole people clamors for a war, and gets it, there is no ground for calling the war democratic. One might just as well call the subjection of Negroes democratic because the whole white South desires it, or acquiesce in the oppression of Slavs because the Magyars are united in its favor. The mere fact that a whole mass of people is unanimous doesn't make their decision a democratic one. This isn't because democracies are not capable of evil, or because I as a democrat would prefer to call whatever I don't like undemocratic. It is because a thing can be popular and still lack the very essence of democracy. Kings, lynchings, and crusades can be popular, but they are not democratic because the interests of all groups concerned have not entered into the making of them. Democracy is a meaningless word unless it signifies that differences of opinion have been expressed, represented, and even satisfied in the decision.

The Stakes of Diplomacy (*1915*), *Chapter 15.*

The great healing effect of publicity is that by revealing men's motives it civilizes them. If people have to declare publicly what they want and why they want it, they cannot be altogether ruthless. It takes more courage than most men have to be openly selfish and regardless of the judgments of their fellows. A special interest frankly avowed is no terror to democracy. It is neutralized by publicity. The danger democracy has always to guard against is the identification of special interests with the national will, patriotism, humanity. The emotions of the people are easily tapped, and therefore easily exploited. And since the beginning of time they have been exploited in the interests of dynasties, oligarchies, priesthoods, and economic classes. The people have suffered, worked, paid, and perished for ends they did not understand. They have gone to battle with noble words in their hearts, ignorant of the true motives and ambitions which arranged the battle. The great virtue of democracy—in fact, its supreme virtue—is that it supplies a method for dragging the realities into the light, of summoning our rulers to declare themselves and submit to judgment. The enemies of democracies recognize the importance of this power, for they pay it the tribute of hypocrisy. They always put on a good face, they dress up their plans in high-sounding phrases, they touch the heart when they approach the pocket.

"The Forgotten Principle," Today and Tomorrow, *January 30, 1936.*

Though the political campaign is just starting, the speeches already bear a remarkable resemblance to the communiqués from the African war. There is the same disposition to claim everything and to concede nothing. . . .

By their respective supporters, and no doubt by themselves, this kind of talk is probably regarded as evidence that they are men of principle, ready to fight for their convictions, that they are bold, forthright, and uncompromising. I should like to raise the question whether the men who take such absolute positions are entitled to claim that they alone are men of principle, and I should like to ask whether in a nation where the interests are complex and diverse, the principle of toleration, which means a refusal to take an absolutist position, which requires a determination to moderate differences and to reconcile opposing interests, is not in itself a high and necessary principle. . . .

Whether or not we find the principle of toleration attractive, it is at least certain that American society is founded upon it. Here is an order in human affairs where rights and powers are variously distributed. Some are reserved to the individual. Some are reserved to the separate states. Some are granted to the national government. Some may be exercised by Congress, some by the President, and some by the judiciary, some by the state legislatures, some by the governors, some by the state judges, some by cities, some by countries. There are some decisions that can be taken by a majority of the elected representatives, others require more than a majority, still others call for a complicated and lengthy process of popular ratification. One fundamental principle runs through the whole conception, and that is that no man, no group of men, no majority of the voters shall ever be able to enjoy a monopoly of power over all human concerns. The system was created with the express intention to keep power so divided that it would never give anyone, or any group however large, a free hand to govern absolutely.

Now, when power is so thoroughly divided, when there are so many different organs of government checking and balancing each other, it might be supposed that government would be completely ineffective. It would be ineffective if everyone took an absolute view of his interests, and there have been times, as for example, before the Civil War, when the opposing views became too absolute to be reconciled successfully. The system of distributed power and of checks and balances will not work automatically. It can never be made to work by men who have not acquired the habit of compromising and conciliating their differences.

For when men undertake to operate a federal union, they commit themselves to a continual adjustment of state and national powers. When men undertake to operate representative government, they commit themselves to the kind of rule by the majority which respects the interests of the minority. When they undertake to operate a government of co-ordinate powers, they commit themselves to that necessary give and take, which alone will permit separated powers to be co-ordinated. When they undertake to reserve the rights of the individual as against the state, they commit themselves to the necessity of exercising individual rights in such a way as not to impair the general interest.

In short, the principle of toleration, or to state it in its nobler and more positive form, the principle of the golden mean in human conduct, is the premise of the American social order. Toleration is not merely a generous by-product of the American system: it is its essential principle. The kind of government Americans believe they have depends upon their ability to administer their institutions on the moral principle that excess is the character of vice, that moderation, proportion, and catholicity, and not imperiousness, self-righteousness, and assertiveness, are the virtues of a civilized society.

Much has been said and much will be said from now on about preserving American institutions. It will be well to remember, when the rhetoric is hottest, that the men who can conduct themselves tolerantly are the men who are most likely to understand the inner nature of those institutions.

"The Vindication of Democracy," Today and Tomorrow, *July 5, 1934.*

A great deal of scorn has been poured out upon the endless talking done in representative parliaments. It is often tiresome. In great emergencies it may be dangerous. But this endless talking marks a very great advance in civilization. It required about five hundred years of constitutional development among the English-speaking peoples to turn the pugnacity and the predatory impulses of men into the channels of talk, rhetoric, bombast, reason, and persuasion. Deride the talk as much as you like, it is the civilized substitute for street brawls, gangs, conspiracies, assassinations, private armies. No other substitute has as yet been discovered.

The doctrine preached by the Fascists that a nation can think and feel with one mind and one heart, except on details, is contrary to all human experience. For a short time, in a mood of exaltation or under the crushing power of terrorism, a nation may appear to be of one mind. But that cannot possibly last, and among highly civilized people it has neither been expected nor desired. It is assumed that people will think differently and will have opposing interests and views. Unanimity is not desired, because people have learned that no man is omniscient and that therefore no man should be omnipotent. An opposition is just as much a part of the government as the party in power. Since unanimity is neither desirable nor for the long run possible, instead of suppressing the opposition, civilized countries guarantee it representation and opportunity to express its views.

Once a nation abandons these principles it is inevitably driven to the disorders which constitutional government gradually overcame. The idea that these armies of Black Shirts and Brown Shirts represent some great new twentieth-century invention can be entertained only by those who have never read any history. They are unmistakably a reversion to political practices which prevailed in western Europe up to about the seventeenth century. That they often have patriotic ideals, that they are often inspired by great zeal is nothing new. Caesar Borgia also saw visions of national greatness and the armies of the Pretender felt they were saving England.

But the progress of civilization has required that they be suppressed. Our democratic principles are the product of this experience in overcoming the disorders of government by plot, intrigue, assassination, and partisan armies. Democracy is not the creation of abstract theorists. It is the creation of men who step by step through centuries of disorder established a regime of order. The forms of representative government may vary. They may be amended. But for its essential principle, that opposition is legal, and that it may win control of the government, there is among modern people no alternative except terrorism, assassination, and the continual threat of civil war.

"Opposition and Criticism," Today and Tomorrow, *December 22, 1933.*

Our form of government does not provide any way of changing the Administration when it has lost the confidence of the people. Yet there is nothing so dangerous in a troubled time as a government which has lost the power to govern.

For that reason it is the manifest disposition of responsible men to discourage and dissipate organized opposition from any quarter which might threaten to bring about a political deadlock this winter. That does not mean dumb assent to the whole Administration program. Nor does it mean lack of conviction on matters of principle. It means, as I see it, the recognition that there is a greater principle at stake than that which is involved in any particular measure, that it is more important that the national government should be strong and effective to act than that it should be infallible according to your views or my views or anyone else's.

In reasonably settled times there is more to be gained than lost by the uncompromising advocacy of particular policies. That is the way the nation is educated, and in the process new habits are formed. But in times like these it is far more necessary that the government should be strong for the unforeseeable emergencies, that it should represent a well-united people who know it is strong, than that it should or should not do this or that. For political paralysis is ever so much worse than any error. Nothing seems to me clearer from the experience of democratic governments than that impotence in the presence of factions and organized minorities and special interests, and then the despair which the sight of impotence arouses, is their undoing. In critical times a nation can get along, and find its way out, under a strong Tory government like that in Great Britain, or under a strong progressive government like ours, but under a feeble government it will drift into confusion and disorder.

It is obstruction and deadlock, then, that are to be avoided, not criticism and debate. There is a great difference between the two. Under a strategy of obstruction the opposition seeks to stop the government and force it to go another way; under a strategy of criticism it forces the government to hear complaint and to account for itself, but it does not seek to deprive it of power or responsibility. The Republican Congress which was elected in 1918 sought to strip President Wilson of authority to conduct the government. The Democratic Congress elected in 1930 brought President Hoover's Administration to a standstill last winter. In neither of these Congresses was there argument. There was political war, and it is this that sensible men will seek to prevent.

Criticism is a wholly different thing. It is most necessary. Any administration which has exercised as much power as this one needs criticism for its own good. It needs to hear the objections. It needs the clarification which comes from having to explain what it is doing. It needs protection from its own courtiers, from the delusions of its own unexamined premises, from the conceit that sooner or later afflicts the human animal when everybody around him says yes. It needs, in short, a series of great debates in which the principles and measures it is using are thoroughly aired, thoroughly questioned, and thoroughly explained. If the Republicans will provoke such debates, they will do the country a service.

"The Indispensable Opposition," The Atlantic Monthly, *CLXIV (1939), 186.*

The essence of freedom of opinion is not in mere toleration as such, but in the debate which toleration provides; it is not in the venting of opinion, but in the confrontation of opinion. That this is the practical substance can readily be understood when we remember how differently we feel and act about the censorship and regulation of opinion purveyed by different media of communication. We find, then, that, in so far as the medium makes difficult the confrontation of opinion in debate, we are driven toward censorship and regulation.

There is, for example, the whispering campaign, the circulation of anonymous rumors by men who cannot be compelled to prove what they say. They put the utmost strain on our tolerance, and there are few who do not rejoice when the anonymous slanderer is caught, exposed, and punished. At a higher level there is the moving picture, a most powerful medium for conveying ideas, but a medium which does not permit debate. A moving picture cannot be answered effectively by another moving picture; in all free countries there is some censorship of the movies, and there would be more if the producers did not recognize their limitations by avoiding political controversy. There is then the radio. Here debate is difficult: it is not easy to make sure that the speaker is being answered in the presence of the same audience. Inevitably, there is some regulation of the radio.

When we reach the newspaper press, the opportunity for debate is so considerable that discontent cannot grow to the point where under normal conditions there is any disposition to regulate the press. But when newspapers abuse their power by injuring people who have no means of replying, a disposition to regulate the press appears. When we arrive at Congress we find that, because the membership of the House is so large, full debate is impracticable. So there are restrictive rules. On the other hand, in the Senate, where the conditions of full debate exist, there is almost absolute freedom of speech.

This shows us that the preservation and development of freedom of opinion are not only a matter of adhering to abstract legal rights, but also, and very urgently, a matter of organizing and arranging sufficient debate. Once we have a firm hold on the central principle, there are many practical conclusions to be drawn. We then realize that the defense of freedom of opinion consists primarily in perfecting the opportunity for an adequate give-and-take of opinion; it consists also in regulating the freedom of those revolutionists who cannot or will not permit or maintain debate when it does not suit their purposes.

We must insist that free oratory is only the beginning of free speech; it is not the end, but a means to an end. The end is to find the truth. The practical justification of civil liberty is not that self-expression is one of the rights of man. It is that the examination of opinion is one of the necessities of man. For experience tells us that it is only when freedom of opinion becomes the compulsion to debate, that the seed which our fathers planted has produced its fruit. When that is understood, freedom will be cherished not because it is a vent for our opinions but because it is the surest method of correcting them.

The unexamined life, said Socrates, is unfit to be lived by man. This is the virtue of liberty, and the ground on which we may best justify our belief in it, that it tolerates error in order to serve the truth. When men are brought face to face with their opponents, forced to listen and learn and mend their ideas, they cease to be children and savages and begin to live like civilized men. Then only is freedom a reality, when men may voice their opinions because they must examine their opinions.

The only reason for dwelling on all this is that if we are to preserve democracy we must understand its principles. And the principle which distinguishes it from all other forms of government is that in a democracy the opposition not only is tolerated as constitutional but must be maintained because it is in fact indispensable.

The democratic system cannot be operated without effective opposition. For in making the great experiment of governing people by consent rather than by coercion, it is not sufficient that the party in power should have a majority. It is just as necessary that the party in power should never outrage the minority. That means that it must listen to the minority and be moved by the criticisms of the minority. That means that its measures must take account of the minority's objections, and that in administering measures it must remember that the minority may become the majority.

The opposition is indispensable. A good statesman, like any other sensible human being, always learns more from his opponents than from his fervent supporters. For his supporters will push him to disaster unless his opponents show him where the dangers are. So if he is wise he will often pray to be delivered from his friends, because they will ruin him. But, though it hurts, he ought also to pray never to be left without opponents; for they keep him on the path of reason and good sense.

The national unity of a free people depends upon a sufficiently even balance of political power to make it impracticable for the administration to be arbitrary and for the opposition to be revolutionary and irreconcilable. Where that balance no longer exists, democracy perishes. For unless all the citizens of a state are forced by circumstances to compromise, unless they feel that they can affect policy but that no one can wholly dominate it, unless by habit and necessity they have to give and take, freedom cannot be maintained.

3 · *The Balance of Functions*

The Public Philosophy (*1955*), *Chapter 3.*

The Western liberal democracies are a declining power in human affairs. I argue that this is due to a derangement of the functions of their governments which disables them in coping with the mounting disorder. I do not say, indeed it is impossible to know surely, whether the malady can be cured or whether it must run its course. But I do say that if it cannot be cured, it will continue to erode the safeguards against despotism, and the failure of the West may be such that freedom will be lost and will not be restored again except by another revolution. . . .

When I describe the malady of democratic states as a derangement in the relation between the mass of the people and the government, I am, of course, implying that there is a sound relationship and that we should be able to know what it is. We must now examine this assumption. We are looking into the relation between, on the one hand, the governing or executive power and, on the other hand, the elected assembly and the voters in the constituencies. The best place to begin is in the simple beginnings of our constitutional development—in the medieval English Parliament—before the essential functions and their relations had become complicated by their later development.

No relationship, sound or unsound, could exist until the functions of execution and representation had become differentiated. In primitive societies they are not differentiated. Under the Norman and Angevin rulers the differentiation had not yet occurred. These rulers "judged and legislated as well as administered." But by the thirteenth century the differentiation is already visible, and the essential relation in which we are interested can be recognized. There is a writ issued under Henry III in 1254, summoning Parliament. The sheriff of each county is ordered to "cause to come before the King's Council two good and discreet Knights of the Shire, whom the men of the county shall have chosen for this purpose in the stead of all and of each of them, to consider along with knights of other shires what aid they will grant the King."

Let us note the dualism. There is the government, which means the King and his Council of prelates and peers. Then there are the Knights of the Shires, representing the men of the counties. They are to meet, and the King will ask the Knights what aid they will grant to him. This is the basic relationship. The government can act. Because it can act, it decides what action should be taken, and it proposes the measures; it then asks the representatives of those who must supply the money and the men for the means to carry out its decisions. The governed, through their representatives, the two Knights of the Shire from each county, give or withhold their consent.

From the tension and the balance of the two powers—that of the ruler and that of the ruled—there evolved the written and the unwritten contracts of the constitution. The grant of aid by the ruled must be preceded by the ruler's redress of their grievances. The government will be refused the means of governing if it does not listen to the petitions, if it does not inform, if it does not consult, if it cannot win the consent of, those who have been elected as the representatives of the governed.

The executive is the active power in the state, the asking and the proposing power. The representative assembly is the consenting power, the petitioning, the approving and the criticizing, the accepting and the refusing power. The two powers are necessary if there is to be order and freedom. But each must be true to its own nature, each limiting and complementing the other. The government must be able to govern and the citizens must be represented in order that they shall not be oppressed. The health of the system depends upon the relationship of the two powers. If either absorbs or destroys the functions of the other power, the constitution is deranged.

There is here a relationship between governors and governed which is, I would contend, rooted in the nature of things. At the risk of reasoning by analogy, I would suggest that this duality of function within a political society has a certain resemblance to that of the two sexes. In the act of reproduction each sex has an unalterable physiological function. If this function is devitalized or is confused with the function of the other sex, the result is sterility and disorder.

In the final acts of the state the issues are war and peace, security and solvency, order and insurrection. In these final acts the executive power cannot be exercised by the representative assembly. Nor can it be exercised after the suppression of the assembly. For in the derangement of the two primary functions lie the seeds of disaster.

The Public Philosophy (*1955*), *Chapter 5.*

During the nineteenth century good democrats were primarily concerned with insuring representation in the assemblies and with extending the control of the assemblies over the executive power. It is true that the problem of the inadequate executive, overridden and dominated by the assembly, was very much in the minds of the Founding Fathers, at the Philadelphia convention, and it has been a continuing concern of the critics and opponents of democracy. But until the twentieth century the problem was not sharply and urgently posed. That there was such a problem was well known. But it was not the immediate problem.

For some generations before 1914, the West enjoyed fine political weather. Moreover, the full force of the coming enfranchisement, emancipation, and secularization of the whole population had not yet worked its consequences. Governments still had authority and power, which were independent of the assemblies and the electorates. They still drew upon the traditional sources of authority—upon prescription, hereditary prerogative, and consecration.

Yet the need to protect the executive and judicial powers from the representative assemblies and from mass opinion has long been understood. Many expedients have been devised to soften, to neutralize, to check and to balance the pressure of parties, factions, lobbies, sects. The expedients have taken, says Bryce, two general forms, the one being to put constitutional restrictions upon the assembly and the other, "by a division of the whole power of the people," to weaken it. This has been done by electing the legislature and the executive separately, or by having the legislative bodies elected by the differing constituencies and at different times.

The constitutional mechanisms have never themselves been sufficient to protect the executive. And much invention and reforming energy have been applied to finding other ways to insulate the judicial, the executive and the administrative functions from the heavy pressures of "politics" and "politicians." The object has been to separate them from the electoral process. The judiciary must be independent of fear and favor. There must be no connection between the judgment of the courts and the election returns. The civil service, the military services, the foreign service, the scientific and technical services, the quasi-judicial administrative tribunals, the investigating commissions, the public schools and institutions of learning should be substantially independent of the elections. These reforms were inspired by the dire effects of the spoils system, and they were pushed as practical remedies for obvious evils.

Yet implicit in them there is a principle which, if it can be applied deeply enough, gets at the root of the disorder of modern democracy. It is that though public officials are elected by the voters, or are appointed by men who are elected, they owe their primary allegiance not to the opinions of the voters but to the law, to the criteria of their professions, to the integrity of the arts and sciences in which they work, to their own conscientious and responsible convictions of their duty within the rules and the frame of reference they have sworn to respect.

The implied principle may be defined in other terms by saying that while the electors choose the ruler, they do not own any shares in him and they have no right to command him. His duty is to the office and not to his electors. Their duty is to fill the office and not to direct the officeholder. I realize that, as I have stated it, the principle runs counter to the popular view that in a democracy public men are the servants (that is, the agents) of the people (that is, of the voters). As the game of politics is played, what I am saying must seem at first like a counsel of perfection. . . .

If we look closely at the matter, we find, I believe, this must be the principle of election when the electors are choosing, not someone to represent them to the government, but the governors themselves. Though it is not too well recognized, there is a radical difference between the election of an executive and the election of a representative. For while the executive is in honor bound not to consider himself as the agent of his electors, the representative is expected to be, within the limits of reason and the general public interest, their agent.

This distinction has deep roots in the political experience of Western society, and, though unrecognized in principle, it is implicit in our moral judgments. Everyone who has a case in court is entitled, we believe, to be represented by a lawyer who, within the law and the code of professional practice, is expected to be the partisan and advocate of his client. But this presupposes not only that his opponent will be effectively represented too, but that the case will go to a court where the judge is not an advocate and has no clients. The judge is bound by his judicial vows. The same ethical standards are recognized, though they are applied less rigorously, in the executive branch of the government. No president or head of a department could afford to admit that he was using his office to further the interests of a client or of a pressure group, or even his party. His acts must be presented as taken in obedience to his oath of office, which means taken disinterestedly and rationally. He must never in so many words admit that in order to gain votes he sacrificed the public good, that he played "politics." Often enough he does just that. But fealty to the public interest is his virtue. And he must, at the very least, pay it the homage of hypocrisy.

When we move over to the representative assembly, the image is different, and the ethical rule is applied, if at all, loosely and lightly. The representative is in some very considerable degree an agent, and the image of his virtue is rather like that of the lawyer than of the judge. There are, of course, occasions when he is in fact the holder of one of the great offices of state—as when he must speak and vote on a declaration of war and the ratification of a treaty. But in the general run of the mundane business which comes before the assembly, he is entitled, indeed he is in duty bound, to keep close to the interests and sentiments of his constituents, and, within reasonable limits, to do what he can to support them. For it is indispensable to the freedom and the order of a civilized state that the voters should be effectively represented. But representation must not be confused with governing.

4 · *The Derangement of Functions*

The Public Philosophy (1955), *Chapter 1.*

1917 was the year of the two Russian revolutions. It was the year of the American involvement which brought with it the declaration of the Wilsonian principles. For Italy it was the year of Caporetto. For Austria-Hungary it was the beginning of the end under the successor of Francis Joseph. For Germany it was the year of the July crisis and of the need of the Prussian monarchy to listen to the Reichstag and its demand for a negotiated peace. For France it was the year of the mutinies, and for Britain the year of moral peril from the submarine. In eastern and central Europe tortured and infuriated masses brought down the historic states and the institutions of the old regime. In western Europe and in North America the breakthrough took the form—if I may use the term—of a deep and pervasive infiltration. Behind the façade, which was little changed, the old structure of executive government with the consent of a representative assembly was dismantled—not everywhere and not in all fields, but where it mattered the most—in the making of high policy for war and peace.

The existing governments had exhausted their imperium—their authority to bind and their power to command. With their traditional means they were no longer able to carry on the hyperbolic war; yet they were unable to negotiate peace. They had, therefore, to turn to the people. They had to ask still greater exertions and sacrifices. They obtained them by "democratizing" the conduct and the aims of the war: by pursuing total victory and by promising total peace.

In substance they ceded the executive power of decision over the strategical and the political conditions for concluding the war. In effect they lost control of the war. This revolution appeared to be a cession of power to the representative assemblies, and when it happened it was acclaimed as promising the end of the evils of secret diplomacy and the undemocratic conduct of unpopular wars. In fact, the powers which were ceded by the executive passed through the assemblies, which could not exercise them, to the mass of voters who, though unable also to exercise them, passed them on to the party bosses, the agents of pressure groups, and the magnates of the new media of mass communications.

The consequences were disastrous and revolutionary. The democracies became incapacitated to wage war for rational ends and to make a peace which would be observed or could be enforced.

Perhaps, before going any further, I should say that I am a liberal democrat and have no wish to disfranchise my fellow citizens. My hope is that both liberty and democracy can be preserved before the one destroys the other. Whether this can be done is the question of our time, what with more than half the world denying and despairing of it. Of one thing we may be sure. If it is to be done at all, we must be uninhibited in our examination of our condition. And since our condition is manifestly connected with grave errors in war and peace that have been committed by democratic governments, we must adopt the habit of thinking as plainly about the sovereign people as we do about the politicians they elect. It will not do to think poorly of the politicians and to talk with bated breath about the voters. No more than the kings before them should the people be hedged with divinity. Like all princes and rulers, like all sovereigns, they are ill-served by flattery and adulation. And they are betrayed by the servile hypocrisy which tells them that what is true and what is false, what is right and what is wrong, can be determined by their votes.

If I am right in what I have been saying, there has developed in this century a functional derangement of the relationship between the mass of the people and the government. The people have acquired power which they are incapable of exercising, and the governments they elect have lost powers which they must recover if they are to govern. What, then, are the true boundaries of the people's power? The answer cannot be simple. But for a rough beginning let us say that the people are able to give and to withhold their consent to being governed—their consent to what the government asks of them, proposes to them, and has done in the conduct of their affairs. They can elect the government. They can remove it. They can approve or disapprove its performance. But they cannot administer the government. They cannot themselves perform. They cannot normally initiate and propose the necessary legislation. A mass cannot govern. The people, as Jefferson said, are not "qualified to exercise themselves the Executive Department; but they are qualified to name the person who shall exercise it . . . They are not qualified to legislate; with us therefore they only choose the legislators."

Where mass opinion dominates the government, there is a morbid derangement of the true functions of power. The derangement brings about the enfeeblement, verging on paralysis, of the capacity to govern. This breakdown in the Constitutional order is the cause of the precipitate and catastrophic decline of Western society. It may, if it cannot be arrested and reversed, bring about the fall of the West.

The Public Philosophy (*1955*), *Chapter 5.*

We cannot take popular government for granted, as if its principles were settled and beyond discussion. We are compelled to agree with Sir Henry Maine, who wrote, some seventy years ago, that "the actual history of popular government since it was introduced, in its modern shape, into the civilized world," does "little to support the assumption that popular government has an indefinitely long future before it. Experience rather tends to show that it is characterized by great fragility, and that since its appearance, all forms of government have become more insecure than they were before."

We have been dwelling upon the devitalization of the executive power as the cause of the fragility that Maine speaks of. It is, I have been saying, the disorder which results from a functional derangement in the relationship between the executive power on the one hand, the representative assemblies and the mass electorates on the other hand.

Democratic states are susceptible to this derangement because congenitally the executive, when dependent on election, is weaker than the elected representatives. The normal drainage of power in a democratic state is away from the governing center and down into the constituencies. And the normal tendency of elections is to reduce elected officers to the role of agents or organized pluralities. Modern democratic governments are, to be sure, big governments, in their personnel, in the range and variety of their projects, the ubiquitousness of their interventions. But to be big is not necessarily to be strong. They are, in fact, swollen rather than strong, being too weak to resist the pressure of special interests and of the departmental bureaucracies.

As a rule competition in the electoral market works like Gresham's law: the soft money drives the hard money out of circulation. The competitive odds are heavily against the candidate who, like Burke with the electors of Bristol, promises to be true to his own best reason and judgment. The odds are all in favor of the candidate who offers himself as the agent, the delegate, the spokesman, the errand boy, of blocs of voters.

In a modern democratic state, the chief executive office must be elective. But as heredity, prescription, consecration, rank, and hierarchy are dissolved by the acids of modernity, the executives become totally dependent on election. They have no status and no tenure which reinforce their consciences, which invest them with power to withstand the tides of popular opinion and to defend the public interest.

They hold their offices for a short time, and to do this they must maneuver and manipulate combinations among the factions and the pressure groups. Their policies must be selected and shaped so as to attract and hold together these combinations. There are moments, the "finest hours," when communities are lifted above their habitual selves in unity and fellowship. But these moments are rare. They are not the stuff of daily life in a democracy, and they are remembered like a miracle in a dream. In the daily routine of democratic politics, elected executives can never for long take their eyes from the mirror of the constituencies. They must not look too much out of the window at the realities beyond. . . .

In the effort to understand the malady of democratic government I have dwelt upon the underlying duality of functions: *governing*, that is, the administration of the laws and the initiative in legislating, and *representing* the living persons who are governed, who must pay, who must work, who must fight and, it may be, die for the acts of the government. I attribute the democratic disaster of the twentieth century to a derangement of these primary functions.

The power of the executive has become enfeebled, often to the verge of impotence, by the pressures of the representative assembly and of mass opinions. This derangement of the governing power has forced the democratic states to commit disastrous and, it could be, fatal mistakes. It has also transformed the assemblies in most, perhaps not in all, democratic states from the defenders of local and personal rights into boss-ridden oligarchies, threatening the security, the solvency, and the liberties of the state.

In the traditions of Western society, civilized government is founded on the assumption that the two powers exercising the two functions will be in balance—that they will check, restrain, compensate, complement, inform, and vitalize each one the other.

In this century, the balance of the two powers has been seriously upset. Two great streams of evolution have converged upon the modern democracies to devitalize, to enfeeble, and to eviscerate the executive powers. One is the enormous expansion of public expenditure, chiefly for war and reconstruction; this has augmented the power of the assemblies which vote the appropriations on which the executive depends. The other development which has acted to enfeeble the executive power is the growing incapacity of the large majority of the democratic peoples to believe in intangible realities. This has stripped the government of that imponderable authority which is derived from tradition, immemorial usage, consecration, veneration, prescription, prestige, heredity, hierarchy.

At the beginning of our constitutional development the king, when he had mastered the great barons, was the proprietor of the greatest wealth in the realm. The crown was also the point from which radiated the imponderable powers to bind and to command. As the king needed money and men for his wars, he summoned representatives of the counties and the boroughs, who had the money and the men he needed. But the imponderable powers, together with very considerable power in land and in men, were still in the king's own hands. Gradually, over the centuries, the power of the Parliament over the supplies of the government grew larger. They had to appropriate a larger proportion of a much greater total. At the same time, in the white light of the enlightenment and the secularization of men's minds, the imponderable powers of the crown diminished.

Under the stress and the strain of the great wars of the twentieth century, the executive power has become elaborately dependent upon the assemblies for its enormous expenditures of men and of money. The executive has, at the same time, been deprived of very nearly all of his imponderable power; fearing the action of the representative assembly, he is under great temptation to outwit it or bypass it, as did Franklin D. Roosevelt in the period of the Second World War. It is significant, I think, certainly it is at least suggestive, that while nearly all the Western governments have been in deep trouble since the First World War, the constitutional monarchies of Scandinavia, the Low Countries, and the United Kingdom have shown greater capacity to endure, to preserve order with freedom, than the republics of France, Germany, Spain and Italy. In some measure that may be because in a republic the governing power, being wholly secularized, loses much of its prestige; it is stripped, if one prefers, of all the illusions of intrinsic majesty.

The evaporation of the imponderable powers, a total dependence upon the assemblies and the mass electorates, has upset the balance of powers between the two functions of the state. The executive has lost both its material and its ethereal powers. The assemblies and the mass electorates have acquired the monopoly of effective powers.

This is the internal revolution which has deranged the constitutional system of the liberal democratic states.

"Presidential Power and Congressional Control," Today and Tomorrow, *February 8, 1941.*

Once again, in dealing with the lease-lend bill, we are confronted with the perennial difficulty of the American government. It is how to relate the presidency and the Congress so that the Executive may have adequate power and the Legislature may have adequate control.

Never have we found, except temporarily, a definitely workable solution. Since Washington's second term the pendulum has swung back and forth from one extreme to another—between strong presidential authority and Congressional supremacy—from the presidency as conceived by men like Washington, Hamilton, and Marshall, like Jackson, Lincoln, Theodore Roosevelt, Wilson, and Franklin Roosevelt to the presidency as conceived by Whigs like Clay and Webster, by the Republicans who fought Lincoln, by Thaddeus Stevens, or as administered by such Presidents as Pierce, Buchanan, Arthur, Harrison, Taft, Harding, Coolidge, and Hoover. There is nothing new in the pleas now being uttered against granting powers to the President; they have been made against every strong President in American history. "No one at a distance," says George W. Julian in his memoirs, "could form any conception of the hostility of the Republican members of Congress to Lincoln at the time of the final adjournment" of the Thirty-seventh Congress in 1863; "it was the belief of many that our last session of Congress had been held in Washington. Senator Wade said the country was going to hell, and that the scenes witnessed in the French Revolution were nothing in comparison with what we should see here."

Lincoln's Administration is, in fact, a classic example of how our failure to work out a satisfactory relationship between the President and Congress will cause the pendulum to swing violently. As Professor Lovejoy has just reminded us, Lincoln was at war for weeks before he called Congress in session. He set up a limited conscription before Congress authorized it. He suspended the writ of habeas corpus without Congressional ratification. He pledged the consent of the United States and paid out money without appropriation. He waited till Congress had adjourned and then issued the Emancipation Proclamation. And while this was going on, Congress was trying to run the war through a joint committee which undertook to force the appointment and removal of generals, and to interrogate the commanders on their strategic plans. And when Lincoln was dead, the pendulum swung and the country had inflicted upon it a dictatorship from Congress which brought about the black history of reconstruction.

No one can read the record of the unending conflict between the President and Congress without realizing, it seems to me, that the lack of a working arrangement between them exposes our government to continual trouble. We have not found a way to give the President his necessary powers without impairing the control of Congress. And we have not found a way to give Congress control without depriving the President of essential power.

This difficulty can be resolved, but only by the display of self-restraint, objectivity of mind, and magnanimity which are rare indeed in public life. The difficulty will never be restored by those who, if they like the President, are for him regardless, who if they do not like him, incite Congress to resist him. President Roosevelt has a bad record in his dealings with Congress; the impartial historian will surely say that he drove Congress in the days when it would have been just as easy and far wiser to win the confidence of Congress. But though this explains, it does not justify, the opposition who now, when it is necessary to vest him with certain powers, would rather risk the failure of a policy they approve than give the President authority to execute it.

Nor will the problem be made soluble by developing an ideology, historically quite false, on the line now being taken by ex-President Hoover and those who share his views. They are suffering from the fundamental misapprehension that our civil liberties and the essentials of representative government can be preserved only if the presidency is a weak office. They start with the conviction, which Mr. Hoover expressed before he became President, that "if we examine the fate of wrecked republics over the world, we shall find first a weakening of the legislative arm," and seeing that Hitler, Mussolini, and Stalin have dismissed the legislature, they conclude that whatever weakens the executive, whatever aggrandizes the legislature, makes for the preservation of liberty.

This is, I submit, a misreading of history. The contemporary dictatorships have not evolved, as Mr. Hoover assumed, out of a strong executive and a weak legislature. On the contrary, both Mussolini and Hitler overthrew a weak executive surrounded by a legislature which had all the power there was but could not exercise it. Dictatorship does not evolve out of strong, coherent, decisive government; it is the result of a reaction against a government which is so weak that it cannot act effectively at home or abroad. Anarchy, disorder, impotence, paralysis, and humiliation are the seed bed of dictatorship. Weak government has never been favorable to liberty. For a government which cannot govern must in the nature of things give way to a government which can govern.

Nor are weak Presidents over here the ones who preserve and promote the proper authority of Congress. The situation which existed when Lincoln overrode Congress was prepared by the feeble Presidents who preceded him. In our own time the weakness of Taft in dealing with Congress brought about the division of his party and opened the way to the strong presidency of Wilson; the weakness of Hoover in dealing with Congress led directly to the political overturn which has produced the first third-term President. It is not true, as the old Whigs once believed, as the Taft and Hoover Republicans now believe, that Congress grows strong in its proper authority by weakening the President's powers or by installing in the office a weak man.

A sound relation will exist only when Congress takes the view that the way to exercise its functions is not to deprive the President of power but to increase the power of Congress to hold him accountable. Congress will never grow strong by weakening the President but only by strengthening itself. This it has never done successfully and adequately.

Thus Congress has two great powers of control over the Executive—the power of the purse, which is the control of expenditures, and the power of the sword, which is the control over the raising of the armed forces, the conduct of foreign relations, and the declaration of war and peace. But the American Congress has no effective means of exercising either of these powers. In money matters, it authorizes and appropriates. But it lacks any effective procedure, such as exists in the House of Commons, for a regular accounting and audit of the money it appropriates. If such a procedure existed, Congress would be in a position to exercise the control which a representative legislature ought to exercise.

In military and diplomatic affairs Congress is even more inefficiently equipped to exercise an effective control. These great committees, composed of men who rise to the top by seniority and not because they are the chosen and trusted representatives of their parties, are quite incapable of consulting continually and effectively with the President and his Secretary of State. There was a time not long ago when they actually refused to listen to the Secretary of State in executive session. Yet only an innocent or a demagogue can suppose that it is possible to deal with foreign affairs by broadcasting everything affecting them. The fact that Congress lacks a regular and reliable means of keeping its trusted leaders informed about foreign affairs means that co-ordination and co-operation between the two branches of the government are almost impossible.

Yet there is no other way to establish proper control over the Executive. It is no good depriving him of necessary power. It is no good arguing that mechanical provisos and limitations are a real substitute for consultation, common council, and continuing accountability.

The two branches of the government will quarrel endlessly at the expense of the nation, depriving it of the unity it needs and the collective wisdom it should have, as long as the responsible men at both ends of Pennsylvania Avenue deal with one another suspiciously and at arm's length.

"Democracy in Trouble," Today and Tomorrow, *January 5, 1956.*

France is the victim of a political disease to which all democracies are susceptible. It is that the popularly elected legislature will become all-powerful, thus reducing the executive to impotence. Experience seems to show that the democratic system is extremely unstable, and liable to fall down into dictatorship, if the executive is wholly the creature of, is wholly dependent upon, the legislature. It is almost certainly no accident that—excepting only Switzerland, which has a special and ancient tradition—the successful Western democracies are either constitutional monarchies as in Great Britain, in the leading members of the commonwealth, in the Low Countries, and in Scandinavia, or are like the United States, where the executive is separately elected and has a popular mandate separate from that of the legislature.

The French system, which has been described as that of the "enthroned legislature," lacks the essence of executive authority—an executive possessing a legitimate mandate of its own.

Although our own system was designed to avoid the dangers of the enthroned legislature and the impotent executive, we cannot take our own system for granted. Between 1950 and 1954, in the last years of Truman and the first years of Eisenhower, this country suffered a much milder but nonetheless a painful and debilitating attack of the same disease which afflicts France.

During this time the President's Constitutional powers to conduct foreign relations were gravely impaired by a Congressional usurpation—of which McCarthy was the spear-point. It was not until after the elections of 1954 that the President recovered most of his constitutional powers. It has been since then and only since then, by the way, that the country has thought of Mr. Eisenhower as a successful President. The last two years of Truman and the first two years of Eisenhower were an inglorious and dangerous period in our history. They were a period of what Woodrow Wilson called Congressional government, by which he meant Congressional usurpation of the executive power of government.

This being an election year, the fundamental question before the country is whether and how and by whom the presidential office is to be maintained in its full powers within our system. A weakness in the presidency, a vacancy in the presidential office, threaten that balance between the Congress and the executive which is the inner principle of our Constitution. The role of the President in our system is such that, in so far as human beings can take precautions for the future, it is their duty not to gamble and not to take imprudent risks.

For, as we can see by looking around the world, democracy is a difficult form of government and its future is not yet assured. It is more than ever necessary that in America democratic government should be able to govern effectively. Seeing to that is the main business before the American people.

"Nightmare in Washington," Today and Tomorrow, *May 3, 1954. In Senator McCarthy's investigation of the Army, Lippmann found a dramatic illustration of the derangement of functions.*

Disgraceful and damaging as is the whole squalid business, it would only make matters infinitely worse to close down or to interrupt the hearings. This is a committee acting under the authority of the Senate and before it are high officials in the executive branch of the government. The country had better be shown to the bitter end, no matter how long it takes, what grave damage McCarthyism has done to America.

The damage cannot be repaired by smothering the Senate's inquiry. The confidence of our own people is profoundly shaken. Our prestige in the world and our claim to be the leader and defender of free peoples have been hurt by McCarthy, as they never were hurt by the world-wide apparatus of the Communist propaganda.

The heart of the damage is the fact that the government has allowed itself to be intimidated by an ambitious and ruthless demagogue. This damage, permitting ourselves to be intimidated, can be repaired only when it has been proved to ourselves and to the world abroad that nobody is afraid any longer.

As we watch the spectacle of a great government in disorder, we ask ourselves what is it that has gone so wrong. The Constitution, the government, American institutions, the churches, the schools and universities, the press are all still there, and yet the sanity and the security of the country, its self-respect and its liberties are shaken and impaired.

The immediate answer to the question of why we are so stricken leads directly, I believe, to the remedy for the trouble. McCarthy's power is built not upon the Constitutional right of Congress to investigate but upon a flagrant abuse of that right. The abuse of that right is unchecked because the Senate is not observing faithfully its Constitutional obligations and because of an unnecessary, unwarranted, and, in the spirit at least, an unconstitutional acquiescence by the President in the abuse.

The abuse lies in the taking over by a Congressional committee of powers which belong to the executive and to the judicial branch. Take, for example, McCarthy's investigation at Fort Monmouth. Just what was it that the Senate had a right and duty to investigate there? The Army was already investigating the possible security risks before McCarthy got into the act.

For what purpose did he get into the act? Was he presuming to substitute himself for the Army in judging each specific case? Was he questioning the good faith of the Army, which was dealing with the allegations of security risk? What was McCarthy doing at Fort Monmouth? Was there any legislation contemplated or required? Was there any allegation that the Army was itself tainted with disloyalty and was not trying to eliminate the security risks which it, not Senator McCarthy, had found it necessary to examine?

What, I repeat, was the Senate investigating at Fort Monmouth? The answer is that it was not investigating anything that was its business as a legislature which makes the laws and then inquires into whether they are faithfully and efficiently and honestly administered and enforced. The Fort Monmouth cases were entirely within the prerogative and the responsibility of the executive branch of the government. If after that, there had been, which there was not, any case of espionage, it was the duty of the Executive to take the case to the courts. The McCarthy investigation in all this is a usurpation of power which belongs to the executive branch of the government.

Why does not the Senate forbid its own committees to commit this usurpation of power and to bring the government of the United States into such disorder and disrepute? There are, I would argue, many contributing but only one central and decisive reason for the Senate's behavior.

One of the contributing reasons is that the party bosses have regarded McCarthy as a political asset. Another is that a large number of the senators have been afraid of him, afraid of being attacked personally or politically by him. Another contributing reason is that many senators have not known how to meet the charge that only Communists are opposed to McCarthy, and have reluctantly had to admit to themselves that the cheapest and easiest way not to look red or pink was to be yellow.

But these are not the decisive reasons for the pusillanimous failure of the Senate to curb McCarthy. The decisive reason is that in this hard world and under the American system of government, which is designed for the kind of hard world that the world is, the abuse of power is not often curbed unless the abuse is resisted.

McCarthyism is an invasion of the prerogatives of other branches of the government, particularly the executive branch. It is for the Executive to repel the invasion, to resist the usurpation, to defend its Constitutional prerogatives. It would be nice, no doubt, if in a nicer world the Senate would observe the self-restraint which would make it unnecessary for an amiable and peace-loving President to fight for the rights of his office. But the Senate is not that nice, and so it will tolerate and connive at the abuses of McCarthy until and unless the President, whose Administration is being abused, stands up and says so far and no further.

"The Conduct of American Foreign Policy,"
Today and Tomorrow, *May 6, 1939.*

Many things are being done these days in Washington to reorganize the machinery of government, but there is one part of the machinery about which nothing is being done. Yet it is now the most dangerously defective part of the whole government mechanism, the part that most urgently needs to be reorganized. This is the mechanism for conducting foreign relations.

The center of the trouble lies in the relation between the President and the two houses of Congress. Under the Constitution they have separate and co-ordinate powers in foreign relations. But obviously they have a joint responsibility. Thus the President appoints ambassadors. The Congress must confirm them. The President negotiates treaties. The Senate must ratify them. The President is commander in chief of the armed forces. The Congress alone has the power to raise and support armies. The President can break off diplomatic relations. The Congress alone has power formally to declare war. But the President has the power, which Lincoln exercised in April, 1861, to recognize the existence of a state of war even though war has not been formally declared. The President can bring a war to its conclusion. But the Congress must ratify the treaty of peace.

It is evident that in conducting foreign relations the two branches of government are not only co-ordinate but interlocking. It is clear that the mechanism will not work unless the two branches of the government have access to the same information, are able to consult continuously, and are able to know before either commits itself irrevocably that it has the support of the other. Without a machinery of unbroken consultation, and a confirmed habit of using it, the President and Congress tend to pull apart, to work at cross-purposes, each to suspect the other of usurping rights, and to divide the country in those very times of crisis when it is most necessary that the United States should deal with the outer world consistently, firmly, and with dignity.

But no effective machinery of consultation now exists. It is the root of our present difficulties. It is most dangerous. It may have profoundly tragic consequences. The fact is that the two branches of government, on whose joint action depends the safety of the American people, are so far apart that it might almost be said that they are not on speaking terms. Certainly they are not able to speak to each other with the candor and confidence that should exist among men who have a joint responsibility for the lives, the fortunes, and the honor of the nation.

Congress and the President are very active about American foreign affairs. They ought to be. The situation throughout the world is more critical than it has been within the memory of any living man. But the fact is that in the face of this situation the Congress and the President are not consulting one another, are not examining the issues together, are not trying with all their power to learn from one another, and to judge together what the United States should do. This is the trouble at the bottom of all the trouble.

It can be corrected if the people want it corrected.

What is the issue, for example, in regard to the Neutrality Act? In the first instance, it is whether Congress shall fix the rules of neutrality by mandatory legislation or whether the President shall fix them by executive discretion. But why should this issue have arisen at all? Why should the country have to choose between making rigid Congressional rules that may not fit the practical situation and giving to one man unlimited personal discretion?

If it were the established practice of the President to keep the leaders of both parties fully and currently informed, and to act only after consultation with them, there would be no need to choose between cast-iron laws and unfettered personal discretion. The two organs of the government would be co-ordinated as they were meant to be co-ordinated. Congress would exercise continuous supervision over foreign policy, and the President would be required and would be able to provide Congress continuously with the information that is necessary if Congress is to know what it is doing.

But as things go now, Congress gets its information from the newspapers and from the rumors that circulate in the lobbies. It has no means of knowing from day to day what information is coming to the State Department. It never really understands in advance what the President is doing or why he is really doing it. And at the other end of Pennsylvania Avenue the President deals with Congress at arm's length, passing out scraps of information, hints of his intentions to this visitor of that, knowledge which gets distorted by gossip, sensationalized, misunderstood, at times misrepresented. That is why Congress wants to legislate wholesale, once-and-for-all, rigidly, and in generalities, and that is why this President, like almost every other President since Washington, wants to get rid of Congress and take charge personally.

Behind the issue of mandatory legislation versus presidential discretion there has arisen, of course, the much more momentous issue of an active policy versus a passive policy. This is a real issue. There is a real difference of opinion as to whether the best interests of the United States will be served by positive intervention to prevent war, and if war breaks out, by favoring the Anglo-French side, or whether American interests will be served better by a policy of indifference to the fate of Europe, and of non-intercourse with all the nations that may go to war.

But these differences of opinion are being sharpened beyond all reason by the conflict between Congress and the President. It is being made to appear as if the country had to choose between joining the grand alliance and conscripting another army to fight in France and, on the other hand, sealing itself up hermetically and renouncing all its rights, all its interests, all provision for its larger security. Surely, the very essence of a good foreign policy would be to steer this country through the crisis and between the extremes, without running it on to the monster Scylla or into the whirlpool of Charybdis.

That can be achieved only by men of very cool judgment and with very firm purpose, who know what they are doing and know that they have the means to do it. The Congress alone obviously cannot do that. The President alone cannot do it. In an atmosphere of conflict, rivalry, oratory, broadcasts, press interviews, declarations, resolutions, endless debates, hearings, nobody can do it. The wisest men and the greatest statesmen of all time, if they were gathered together, could not do it.

Yet this is what is now in prospect for ourselves and for the world. We are not promised a thorough, loyal, candid, painstaking attempt by Congress and the President to shape American policy in the greatest crisis of modern history. We are promised an interminable debate and agitation, with charges and countercharges, propaganda and counterpropaganda, all mixed up with domestic policies, and personal grudges, and ambitions for 1940, and heaven only knows what manner of masked intrigue fomenting the confusion from abroad.

The American people deserve something better than that from their government. They are entitled to be protected against the consequences of so reckless and so irresponsible a method of dealing with issues of life and death. They ought to insist now that before anything else is done the President call in the leaders of both parties and of all factions and come at once to an understanding with them that they will arrange to inform one another and to consult, to receive confidences and to keep them, and thus discharge together their joint responsibility.

It can be done. It requires no legislation. It is done in England, it is done in France, it is done in every working democracy. It can be done here. All it requires is the will to do it, and the capacity of the men in Washington to rise to the occasion, putting aside all little things in order that they may be equal to their immense responsibilities.

5 · *The Ideal of Representative Government*

"The Ideal of Representative Government," Today and Tomorrow, *May 17, 1932.*

The last ten years have been a period of disillusionment with the working of elected governments. Both in the crisis of the war and in the crisis of the reconstruction the democratic system has seemed again and again to present almost insuperable difficulties to wise and prompt decisions. That has been the universal experience, and the behavior of Congress during the last few months has added new distrust to the doubts which were already in the air.

The chief complaint against Congress, and it is well founded, is that it does not succeed in representing the national interest, that its members are preoccupied with their own special interest in re-election, and that to this end, in the effort to placate, cajole, and even to bribe their constituents, they will as a general rule sacrifice every other consideration. Thus it has been plain throughout the debates on the tax bill and on the appropriations that what was moving the individual members was not loyalty to the national interest as a whole but an extreme sensitiveness to the demands and wishes of groups of voters.

Many explanations have been current as to why this demoralization prevails. It has been suggested that the term of office is too short, that a congressman is no sooner seated than he must start preparing for re-election. It has been suggested that the direct primary has shattered party responsibility and made Congress a place where each member must shift for himself. It has been pointed out that the custom of selecting congressmen solely from the districts where they live deprives the country of the services of able men.

These are, it seems to me, sound criticisms of our system,

and no doubt it would be improved if the term of office were longer, if the party system were revived, and if able men could be elected from districts in which they do not necessarily reside. But the trouble is really deeper than these reforms imply. The trouble is that the country has abandoned the conception of representative government and is trying to deal with enormous complex problems through an assembly of mere delegates. The American people has forgotten that if it is to have good government it must elect men, not to perform errands for their constituents, but to use their judgment freely, and freely to speak and act upon that judgment.

The real problem at Washington today was stated with perfect clearness by Edmund Burke some years before the American Republic was founded. This is a good time to turn back to Burke, who was one of the wisest men of his century and among the profoundest political thinkers of the tradition which we inherit. Burke's constituency was the city of Bristol and in 1774 he and Cruger were the two Whig candidates. Cruger had told the voters that if they elected him he would do what they desired. Burke abjured this doctrine and in his speeches plainly told the voters that he would not be their slave. He was anxious to meet their wishes. He would prefer their interest to his own. But "his unbiased opinion, his mature judgment, his enlightened conscience he (as a representative) ought not to sacrifice to you, to any man, or to any set of men living. These he does not derive from your pleasure; no, nor from the law and the constitution. They are a trust from Providence for the abuse of which he is deeply answerable. Your representative owes you, not his industry alone, but his judgment; and he betrays, instead of serving you, if he sacrifices it to your opinion."

That is the heart of the matter. This conception of the relation between the representative and his constituents rested upon Burke's conviction as to what a national legislature ought to be: "Parliament," he said, "is not a *congress* of ambassadors from different and hostile interests; which interests each must maintain, as an agent and advocate, against other agents and advocates; but parliament is a *deliberative* assembly of *one* nation, with *one* interest, that of the whole; where, not local purposes, not local prejudices, ought to guide, but the general good, resulting from the general reason of the whole. You choose a member, indeed; but when you have chosen him, he is not a member of Bristol, but he is a member of *parliament.* If the local constituent should have an interest, or should form an hasty opinion, evidently opposite to the real good of the rest of the community, the member for that place ought to be as far, as any other, from any endeavor to give it effect."

This is the ideal of representative government. You may say that it is suitable to a race of heroes and of saints. Perhaps. But this is the ideal, and as long as we profess to be living under representative government it is useful to recall it.

VII

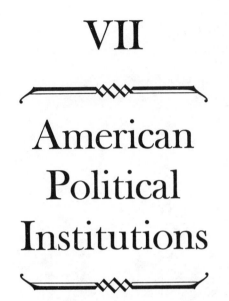

American Political Institutions

1 · *Some Rules for Presidents*

A Preface to Politics (*1913*), *Chapter 1.*

Our desperate adherence to an old method has produced the confusion of political life. Because we have insisted upon looking at government as a frame and governing as a routine, because, in short, we have been static in our theories, politics has such an unreal relation to actual conditions. Feckless—that is what our politics is. It is literally eccentric; it has been centered mechanically instead of vitally. We have, it seems, been seduced by a fictitious analogy; we have hoped for machine regularity when we needed human initiative and leadership, when life was crying that its inventive abilities should be freed.

Roosevelt in his term did much to center government truly. For a time natural leadership and nominal position coincided, and the administration became in a measure a real sovereignty. The routine conception dwindled, and the Roosevelt appointees went at issues as problems to be solved. They may have been mistaken; Roosevelt may be uncritical in his judgments. But the fact remains that the Roosevelt regime gave a new prestige to the presidency by effecting through it the greatest release of political invention in a generation. Contrast it with the Taft Administration, and the quality is set in relief. Taft was the perfect routineer trying to run government as automatically as possible. His sincerity consisted in utter respect for form; he denied himself whatever leadership he was capable of, and outwardly at least he tried to "balance" the government. His greatest passions seem to be purely administrative and legal. The people did not like it. They said it was dead. They were right. They had grown accustomed to a humanly liberating atmosphere in which formality was an instrument instead of an idol. They had seen the Roosevelt influence adding to the resources of life—irrigation, and waterways, conservation, the Panama Canal, the "country life" movement. They knew these things were achieved through initiative that burst through formal restrictions, and they applauded wildly. It was only a taste, but it was a taste, a taste of what government might be like.

The opposition was instructive. Apart from those who feared Roosevelt for selfish reasons, his enemies were men who loved an orderly adherence to traditional methods. They shivered in the emotional gale; they obstructed and the gale became destructive. They felt that, along with obviously good things, this sudden national fertility might breed a monster—that a leadership like Roosevelt's might indeed prove dangerous, as giving birth may lead to death.

What the methodically-minded do not see is that the sterility of a routine is far more appalling. Not everyone may feel that to push out into the untried, and take risks for big prizes, is worth while. Men will tell you that government has no business to undertake an adventure, to make experiments. They think that safety lies in repetition, that if you do nothing, nothing will be done to you. It's a mistake due to poverty of imagination and inability to learn from experience. Even the timidest soul dare not "stand pat." The indictment against mere routine in government is a staggering one.

For while statesmen are pottering along doing the same thing year in, year out, putting up the tariff one year and down the next, passing appropriation bills and recodifying laws, the real forces in the country do not stand still. Vast changes, economic and psychological, take place, and these changes demand new guidance. . . .

Statesmen who had decided that at last men were to be the

masters of their own history, instead of its victims, would face politics in a truly revolutionary manner. It would give a new outlook to statesmanship, turning it from the mere preservation of order, the administration of political machinery, and the guarding of ancient privilege to the invention of new political forms, the prevision of social wants, and the preparation for new economic growths.

"Democracy and Dictatorship," Today and Tomorrow, *February 24, 1933.*

Some observers profess to see evidence . . . that Congress can be brought by the pressure of public opinion to deal so promptly and decisively with great issues that no change of procedure is required for the period of the emergency. I believe they are mistaken. The repeal of the Eighteenth Amendment was a simple issue upon which a clear popular verdict had been rendered. Yet it took Congress two months to act. The issues which the incoming Administration must deal with are complex and controversial. Unlike prohibition they have not been debated for ten years; unlike prohibition they involve considerations that are outside the normal experience of most men. They have, moreover, to be acted upon more or less as a whole if the measures proposed are to be effective, not one at a time after long delays and with the fate of other measures, organically related to them, in doubt. It is no reflection upon Congress to say that the characters of the issues and the normal legislative procedure are incompatible one with the other.

The emergency calls for changes which will concentrate in the President the widest administrative and ministerial powers possible under the Constitution, and in matters of policy the reinforcement of his leadership by the party caucus and by cloture on debate. The object to be gained by extending the President's powers is to reduce the power of the individual congressman over, and to relieve him of, the responsibility for as many decisions as possible affecting patronage, pork subsidies, and bonuses. These questions are at the heart of the government's financial problem, and they cannot be dealt with promptly or adequately by a body of men subject to pressure and reprisal in an election within eighteen months. For the individual legislator these questions are matters of political life and death. Only the President is sufficiently secure in his office to take the responsibility of action.

The object of the caucus and of cloture is to confirm the President's leadership in questions of policy in order that he may be able to proceed confidently with a national, and necessarily complex, program. Neither caucus nor cloture deprives Congress of its Constitutional powers, nor does it destroy the right of debate, of criticism, and of opposition. But caucus and cloture do subordinate local and special views to a national view. Under caucus and cloture the individual congressman is sheltered from the pressure of lobbyists and in some degree at least from the reprisals of minorities. In losing some of his power he sloughs off some of his personal accountability. He is able to say to the lobbyists that in a national emergency patriotism required him to work with the majority and to follow the leadership of the President chosen by overwhelming vote of the people.

Proposals of this sort have loosely been described as designed to establish a dictatorship. This is an abuse of the plain meaning of words. A dictatorship is a wholly different thing, as one can readily see by looking at the dictatorships in Europe.

The basic fact in a dictatorship is that the regime holds its power not by the votes of the people, but by the force of a body of armed men. This is the essential difference between dictatorship and democracy. A democracy which freely grants extraordinary powers to the Executive, but retains the power to recall them at will, is still in every sense of the word a democracy. Under dictatorship the extraordinary powers cannot be recalled by vote of the people or their genuine representatives. For these powers rest not upon votes, but upon bayonets, upon the regular army, as in Japan; upon more or less irregular armies, like the Black Shirts in Italy and the Brown Shirts in Germany.

Under dictatorship civil liberties are either suspended or granted at the pleasure of the dictator. Thus he can and does suppress the opposition by force, is able to govern by decree, and to perpetuate his regime until it is overthrown by force or it disintegrates from within.

There is thus no analogy whatever between a dictatorship and these American proposals for a concentration of authority during the emergency. The only connection there is between the two conceptions is the knowledge that a democracy which fails to concentrate authority in an emergency almost inevitably falls into such confusion that the ground is prepared for the rise of a dictator.

It is no accident that dictatorships have been set up in those countries where the democracy was too inexperienced to deal effectively with a crisis. There are no dictatorships in mature democracies like the British, the French, or the Scandinavian. It is in the countries where the people have not had the knowledge or the courage to make popular government work effectively that the dictators have had their triumphs. Dictators do not overthrow governments. They take the powers which have fallen from the hands of impotent and demoralized politicians.

Thus the dictatorship came in Russia after the pitiable weakness of the Kerensky regime; in Italy after the confusion and corruption of the Giolitti regime; in Germany after repeated elections and parliamentary maneuvers had shown that the party system was deadlocked and paralyzed by the internal divisions of the German nation. Dictatorship is the reaction of a people to the weakness of democracy in a crisis.

The proposals for a concentration of authority in the United States, and for the raising of a standard around which a national public opinion can rally, are proposals which are designed to cure those very weaknesses of democracy which in a long and severe crisis become finally intolerable. There is nothing in these proposals which the sincerest believer in democracy need be ashamed to advocate. They do not approach the powers that have been conferred upon Presidents in time of war. They are not so great as the powers which mature democracies, like the British, normally confer upon the government of the day. . . .

We cannot duplicate the British system and it would be foolish to try. But within the framework of our own institutions and without violation of their spirit we can and should achieve that concentration of authority without which it is so improbable as to be virtually impossible that we can carry out a program of recovery.

"On Reforming the Presidency," Today and Tomorrow, *April 14, 1938.*

American Presidents drift into trouble . . . because they are never quite sure whether they are primarily the chief magistrates of the Republic or the leaders of their party. As chief magistrate it would be the President's first duty to see that the Executive was able to represent and to lead a true working majority in Congress. As chief of state he would see to it that the co-ordinate branches of the government were in fact co-ordinated. But as a party or, even, as a factional leader, the President takes a different view and thinks of himself as a man whose personal honor depends upon being ready to stand and fall for his personal convictions.

The American system of government is peculiar in that it requires a President who is both chief magistrate and party leader. These two functions are compatible at the beginning of a new term when the President's authority, his patronage, and his personal prestige are fresh. But they become incompatible when, as is now the case, the President as party leader no longer commands a working majority in Congress. Then there is struggle and a deadlock and the government is unable to govern.

This difficulty was not envisaged by the founders of the American government because they conceived the President as primarily the chief magistrate. Washington acted on that theory. Both Hamilton and Jefferson were members of his cabinet. It seems clear that if the American form of government is to work effectively in the very critical times through which we are living, it is to the Washingtonian rather than to the Jacksonian conception of the presidency that we must return. For there must be a government that can govern. And therefore, the President cannot afford to be a factional leader alone, laying himself open to the fate of factional leaders, which is that they may be destroyed by the opposing faction.

The President, if we are to maintain the division of powers and a system of representative democracy, must hold himself above and beyond the ties of faction and party and personal doctrine, and think of himself primarily and in all crucial matters as the chief of state. For a party leader who is irremovable when he can no longer lead is dangerous, like a derelict ship in a stormy sea.

"The President," Today and Tomorrow, *April 19, 1941.*

In this tremendous time the American people must look to their President for leadership. They are not getting leadership from the President. They are not being treated as they deserve to be treated and as they have a right to be treated. They are not being treated as men and women but rather as if they were inquisitive children. They are not being dealt with seriously, truthfully, responsibly, and nobly. They are being dealt with cleverly, indirectly, even condescendingly, and nervously. They are asked to put their trust in the President, which indeed they must, for he is the President; but in return they must have his trust and they must have his confidence and they must have his guidance.

Only the President, because he is the Chief Executive, is in a position to know all the facts. Only the President and his advisers are in a position to weigh all the facts. Therefore, the President alone can lead the country. It is impossible for the country to lead the President. The newspapers do their honest and their courageous best to report the facts. But they are obstructed by an almost impenetrable censorship in all the critical quarters of the world. Editors, orators, writers do their best to discern the significance of the facts which happen to be available to them. But the policy of a government in a time of supreme crisis cannot be shaped by such partial judgments on insufficient evidence. Yet that is all that can come from private committees, from mass meetings, editorials, and speeches. The policy of the government must rest on the support of the nation. But the nation must first be informed, and always it must be dealt with squarely.

There is not the slightest reason to doubt that the American people will in the future as they have in the past do whatever they are convinced they must do to preserve their independence, their liberties, and their honor. Once convinced, they have authorized expenditures for defense which in fact are limited only by the country's capacity to produce. Once convinced, they have adopted conscription. Once convinced, they have committed themselves to aid their friends. Once convinced, and as soon as they are asked, they will pay taxes, they will save, they will forgo business as usual and their luxuries and conveniences. They are working, and they will work harder, and they will forget petty differences—once they are convinced and are seriously asked to do so.

This people is made of better stuff—is more ready to face the truth, more ready to rise to the occasion—than the President implies by his cleverness and his maneuvers and his devices and his casual comment on great issues. Because the President is underestimating the American people, he is separating himself from the American people, denying to them the guidance which is their right and depriving himself of the support of the people's convictions which is the government's indispensable need. In the presence of such momentous events—involving momentous decisions whatever may be the course of events—there is no substitute among free men for lucidity and courage and the simplicity of a noble spirit.

The President of the United States cannot administer the whole effort of the nation. The reason why Mr. Roosevelt is failing to inform the people and guide them, and is thus becoming separated from them, is that he is exhausting his energies on tasks that no one man can possibly do well, and that no President in such a time as this ought to attempt.

It is absurd, for example, for him to think he can decide, as he did the other day, whether the steel capacity of the country is sufficient. It is absurd for him to think that he can, as is now proposed, settle the coal strike in the Southern fields. It is absurd for him to think that the lend-lease program can be administered personally from the White House. Yet if he attempts all these things, and a thousand others besides, he will never have the time or the nervous energy or the physical strength to do well the great things a President must do—to anticipate the future, to determine the great issues of policy, to select the right men to execute the policies, and never to cease explaining to the people—directly and publicly and also privately and continually through their chosen leaders what the government is doing and why.

If the President is to do the things which only the President can do, he will have to give up doing the things that others could do better, and would if they had the chance. He must trust the people, must guide them and depend upon them. And he must trust individuals in the vast undertaking of the government, and if there are men who cannot carry the responsibility, they must be replaced and others found who can carry it. Instead, Mr. Roosevelt is playing with the people, and in his own

Administration he will not give adequate authority to the competent and he takes upon himself the unnecessary burden of carrying along the incompetent.

That is not the way to make democracy work and prove itself in the greatest test to which it has ever been subjected. To fail to inform the people, waiting for them to lead him, is not democracy but demagoguery. To act as if the people had to be manipulated is to deny the very virtues on which rests the hope of democracy; it is to think that free men will shrink from the truth and flinch in their duty. To fail to call into his councils men of all parties and factions is to cut himself off from the sources of wisdom and to close the only way to that union which is a nation's strength. To refuse to displace the incompetent, to hold back from giving authority to the efficient, to clutch in his hands so many strings that they must become tangled, is to deal in a trivial fashion with a great occasion.

"The Chief Magistrate," Today and Tomorrow, *September 29, 1953.*

The President must have been thinking of the hard months immediately ahead of him when he said in his Boston speech that "we face and make decisions" in the belief that "we—this American society . . . are not some perilously balanced equation of political convenience in which labor plus farm plus capital plus management equals America."

There, surely, he was speaking from the heart, protesting against the "calculating self-interested . . . conflicting classes and sections" that press upon him every day. America should not be, he was saying, the perilously balanced equations that come up to him for his approval as Administration policy: the equation between a balanced budget with lower taxes on the one hand, and on the other hand more military security; the equation in military security between the Air Force and the older services; between deterrent and passive defense; the equation between Durkin and Weeks, between Benson and the farm bloc, between McKay and the rural consumers of electric power, between the creditor and exporting interests and the protected industries, etc., etc.

It is undoubtedly true that most "problems" come up to the President for his decision in the form of an "equation" which is meant to balance conflicting interests. The President, quite rightly, feels that this is not the way great affairs of state should be carried on. But I am afraid that all experience is against him if he supposes that he can by preaching and persuasion make the many interests, groups, sections less "calculating," less "self-interested," or less conflicting.

In fact the President's troubles can only increase as long as the impression exists that the eventual policy decided upon will register the wishes of those who exert the greatest pressure. This impression does prevail because of Mr. Eisenhower's own personal theory that virtually all great problems can be settled by bringing the conflicting interests together and telling them to work out an agreement. This theory—that the policy will be whatever comes out of the conference of conflicting interests—usually means either no agreement at all, or an agreement to divide the pie in equal slices. Often at least one interest would rather do nothing at all than that which the others would accept; in other cases, notoriously for example in the military budget, the result has been a policy of equal shares for each service.

The fallacy is in the notion that the President is a kind of presiding officer—rather like the Vice-President when he is in the Senate—who keeps order while his Cabinet officers and the agents of interests debate, deliberate, and decide; he intervenes only to break a tie. In fact, however, the President is the chief magistrate who must render judgment on the contentious issues before him and must see to it that the judgment is carried out.

This is not the way in which calculating, self-interested, conflicting interests are subordinated to the "peace and well-being of our whole people." It is done by governing them. To govern them is to establish the certain knowledge that while the conferences and the commissions of the conflicting interests will be heard carefully and honestly, the national policy will not be the equation that they might agree upon. It will be the judgment of the President after he has heard all the arguments and has consulted his advisers and his party leaders.

As long as the conflicting interests involved in the issue are encouraged to think that they will decide it, that they are not merely claimants but are going to be the makers of the policy, just so long will they be incited to exert more and more pressure and to become more and more demanding.

"The National Consensus," Today and Tomorrow, *January 12, 1956.*

The real contest and conflict in our modern politics is not about legislative measures. It is about the administration of the government. It is about the way farm policy, the military establishment, fiscal affairs, the welfare and protective measures are in fact conducted and operated. That is why the presidency has become so paramount in our system. For the presidential office is the fountainhead of administration. This may also be the explanation of why the investigative power of Congress, which has to do with administration, has tended to become so much more controversial and important than the legislative powers of Congress.

"Candidate and Leader," Today and Tomorrow, *July 10, 1956.*

The relations between the President and his party in Congress are remarkable. His enormous popularity and prestige have made him, as he was far from being in 1952, the undisputed choice of the party for President. Yet he is as little able today, as he was when he took office, to unite and lead his party in support of his policies. The issues on which the party will not unite behind him are not small issues. They are the crucial and major issues of foreign policy, defense, education. What takes some explaining is how, though he and they are divided in Congress, they can be united for the presidential election.

This is possible because in General Eisenhower's conception of the American government, the President is not the leader of the system who makes it work but the officer who presides over the Executive branch. He exhorts, he preaches, he proposes measures, he pleads for them. But he does not lead the Congress. In his book there are no rewards for men, like Senator Wiley, who take risks in order to follow him; there are no penalties for those who, like Senator Knowland, so often oppose him. Yet in order to lead a party it is necessary not only to talk but also to use a discipline of rewards and penalties.

It is General Eisenhower's unwillingness to insist upon

party discipline, his virtual neutrality between those who oppose him and those who support him, that account for his inability to lead Congress. His personal popularity, which is his party's prime asset, is freely available to all Republicans without any reciprocal obligation on their part. So the Republicans opposed to Eisenhower want him for President, being under no obligation to follow him.

The American political system has never worked well when the President is passive and unable to give a strong lead to Congress. For the American Congress is like other legislative bodies, as, for example, the French National Assembly. It is almost incapable of dealing successfully with big questions except under the leadership, which includes the discipline, of the Executive. On measures where the national interest is more than the net sum of opposing local interests, the Executive, that is, the President, must be the active political force.

He cannot drop the big measures into the legislative assembly, making an occasional public comment and doing some private lobbying, but on the whole standing aside in an attitude of respectful neutrality. For the big measures are almost certain to be ground to bits by congressmen responding to local pressures from their constituents. These measures can be saved and carried through the Legislature only if the representatives can feel behind them, and can point to, a national pressure which is stronger than the local pressures. Except when there is an upheaval of popular sentiment, only the President can generate the national pressure.

"The President and the People," Today and Tomorrow, *March 7, 1961.*

As of now, there are many more people who like John Kennedy, and his appointments, and his style of operating in office, than there are people who understand and believe in what he is committed to doing. He will have to close this gap; he will have to persuade the large majority who like him that they must also believe in him. Until this is done, the important constructive measures of his Administration are headed for serious trouble in Congress. For Congress is not now feeling the pressure of a large convinced Kennedy majority.

Such a majority cannot, I venture to think, be rallied

wholly or in the main by personal popularity. As measured by the Gallup poll, Mr. Kennedy probably is about as popular as was General Eisenhower after his first month in the White House. But his situation is radically different from General Eisenhower's. He is committed to positive programs that require new laws and new appropriations and perhaps new taxes. His predecessor was primarily interested in undoing rather than in doing. High personal popularity with a passive and negative program makes for an easy life. But personal popularity is not enough to carry with it an active and innovating program.

The President will have to find ways of communicating his own convictions to a working majority of the people. Is he not doing that? Not adequately, so it seems to me. There is a missing element in his press conferences, his speeches, and his public appearances, and for lack of it he receives much approval without creating sufficient conviction.

That missing element is, I think, the willingness to take the time and to take the trouble to explain, to expound, to describe, in a word, to teach. John Kennedy is already proving himself to be an extraordinary Chief Executive. He has very great gifts of precise analysis and judgment, he has a rare combination of courage and political sophistication. Indeed, he has all the makings of a great President. But if he is to be a great President, he must be not only executive, organizer, politician, and popular leader. He must also be a popular teacher.

The greatest leaders are also great teachers.

The instinct to teach, to make himself understood because he has explained himself, has not yet shown itself in the President. I say not yet because I have no doubt that this instinct to teach is in him. It is in every man who has deep convictions and a passion to realize them.

"The President at Yale," Today and Tomorrow, *June 14, 1962.*

At Yale the President made a most important address—for the domestic economy the most significant, it seems to me, since he was inaugurated. In it he described, as he has never before done so explicitly, what it is that is new in the New Frontier.

Unlike President Franklin D. Roosevelt's New Deal, the Kennedy Administration is not working for a change in the balance of social forces within the country. Mr. Roosevelt used the power of the federal government to increase the influence of agriculture and of labor, as compared with the influence of business, and of the underdeveloped South and West as compared with the Northeast.

The battles of the New Deal era were in the classic pattern of social struggle, of the havenots against the haves. These battles were won by Mr. Roosevelt and a new balance of forces was firmly established. This was proved during the eight years of President Eisenhower when there was no attempt to repeal and undo the New Deal.

The Kennedy Administration begins where General Eisenhower left off. It is not seeking another change in the structure of American society but, on the contrary, to make more efficient the existing balance of forces. It is confronted, however, with a cultural gap; that is to say, with popular beliefs about the economy which are a generation out of date.

With rare exceptions the leaders of both parties hold to economic doctrines which have long since been abandoned as antiquated by all the progressive and advanced countries of the world.

Governor Rockefeller understands modern economic doctrine, but men like General Eisenhower and Senator Byrd talk as if they had never read a book on economic matters which has been written since the great depression of 1929.

If President Kennedy is to fulfill his promises, if he is to raise the American economy from the creeping stagnation which has come upon it in the second half of the fifties, if he is to recover the industrial pre-eminence which we once had and have now lost, the Administration will have to do a mighty job of public re-education.

If our leaders do not learn to understand modern economics, we shall not be able to operate successfully the modern economy. It is this work of re-education which the President began at Yale. It was a very good beginning.

But, of course, one speech will not do what needs to be done—which is to close the cultural gap and put American public opinion and American political debate in touch with the realities of the modern age.

This re-education is not a fight between good men and bad men, between rich men and poor men, between Republicans and Democrats. It is, like all education, a search for enlightenment in which all who participate bravely will be the winners.

2 · *The Plight of Congress*

Public Opinion (1922), *Chapter 18. Although Lippmann has always insisted that Congress restrict itself to its proper function, he has nevertheless expressed concern over the steady decline in its prestige.*

Some critics have traced this to the custom of sending only local celebrities to Washington. They have thought that if Congress could consist of the nationally eminent men, the life of the capital would be more brilliant. It would be, of course, and it would be a very good thing if retiring Presidents and Cabinet officers followed the example of John Quincy Adams. But the absence of these men does not explain the plight of Congress, for its decline began when it was relatively the most eminent branch of the government. Indeed it is more probable that the reverse is true, and that Congress ceased to attract the eminent as it lost direct influence on the shaping of national policy.

The main reason for the discredit, which is world wide, is, I think, to be found in the fact that a congress of representatives is essentially a group of blind men in a vast, unknown world. With some exceptions, the only method recognized in the Constitution or in the theory of representative government, by which Congress can inform itself, is to exchange opinions from the districts. There is no systematic, adequate, and authorized way for Congress to know what is going on in the world. The theory is that the best man of each district brings the best wisdom of his constituents to a central place, and that all these wisdoms combined are all the wisdom that Congress needs. Now there is no need to question the value of expressing local opinions and exchanging them. Congress has great value as the market place of a continental nation. In the coatrooms, the hotel lobbies, the boarding houses of Capitol Hill, at the tea parties of the Congressional matrons, and from occasional entries into the drawing rooms of cosmopolitan Washington, new vistas are opened, and wider horizons. But even if the theory were applied, and the districts always sent their wisest men, the sum or a combination of local impressions is not a wide enough base for national policy, and no base at all for the control of foreign policy. Since the real effects of most laws are subtle and hidden, they cannot be understood by filtering local experiences through local states of mind. They can be known only by controlled reporting and objective analysis. And just as the head of a large factory cannot know how efficient it is by talking to the foreman, but must examine cost sheets and data that only an accountant can dig out for him, so the lawmaker does not arrive at a true picture of the state of the union by putting together a mosaic of local pictures. He needs to know the local pictures, but unless he possesses instruments for calibrating them, one picture is as good as the next, and a great deal better.

The President does come to the assistance of Congress by delivering messages on the state of the Union. He is in a position to do that because he presides over a vast collection of bureaus and their agents, which report as well as act. But he tells Congress what he chooses to tell it. He cannot be heckled, and the censorship as to what is compatible with the public interest is in his hands. It is a wholly one-sided and tricky relationship, which sometimes reaches such heights of absurdity that Congress, in order to secure an important document, has to thank the enterprise of a Chicago newspaper, or the calculated indiscretion of a subordinate official. So bad is the contact of legislators with necessary facts that they are forced to rely either on private tips or on that legalized atrocity, the Congressional investigation, where congressmen, starved of their legitimate food for thought, go on a wild and feverish man hunt, and do not stop at cannibalism.

Except for the little that these investigations yield, the occasional communications from the executive departments, interested and disinterested data collected by private persons, such newspapers, periodicals, and books as congressmen read, and a new and excellent practice of calling for help from expert bodies like the Interstate Commerce Commission, the Federal Trade Commission, and the Tariff Commission, the creation of Congressional opinion is incestuous. From this it follows either that legislation of a national character is prepared by a few informed insiders, and put through by partisan force; or that the legislation is broken up into a collection of local items, each of which is enacted for a local reason. Tariff schedules, navy yards, army posts, rivers and harbors, post offices and federal buildings, pensions and patronage: these are fed out to concave communities as tangible evidence of the benefits of national life. Being concave, they can see the white marble building which rises out of federal funds to raise local realty values and employ local contractors more readily than they can judge the cumulative cost of the pork barrel. It is fair to say that in a large assembly of men, each of whom has practical knowledge only of his own district, laws dealing with translocal affairs are rejected or accepted by the mass of congressmen without creative participation of any kind. They participate only in making those laws that can be treated as a bundle of local issues. For a legislature without effective means of information and analysis must oscillate between blind regularity, tempered by occasional insurgency, and logrolling. And it is the logrolling which makes the regularity palatable, because it is by logrolling that a congressman proves to his more active constituents that he is watching their interests as they conceive them.

This is no fault of the individual congressman's, except when he is complacent about it. The cleverest and most industrious representative cannot hope to understand a fraction of the bills on which he votes. The best he can do is to specialize on a few bills, and take somebody's word about the rest. I have known congressmen, when they were boning up on a subject, to study as they had not studied since they passed their final examinations, many large cups of black coffee, wet towels, and all. They had to dig for information, sweat over arranging and verifying facts, which, in any consciously organized government, should have been easily available in a form suitable for decision. And even when they really knew a subject, their anxieties had only begun. For back home the editors, the board of trade, the central federated union, and the women's clubs had spared themselves these labors, and were prepared to view the congressman's performance through local spectacles.

Liberty and the News (1920), *Chapter 2.*

Parliamentary action is becoming notoriously ineffective. In America certainly the concentration of power in the Executive is out of all proportion either to the intentions of the Fathers or to the orthodox theory of representative government. The cause is fairly clear. Congress is an assemblage of men selected for local reasons from districts. It brings to Washington a more or less accurate sense of the superficial desires of its constituency. In Washington it is supposed to think nationally and internationally. But for that task its equipment and its sources of information are hardly better than that of any other reader of the newspaper. Except for its spasmodic investigating committees, Congress has no particular way of informing itself. But the Executive has. The Executive is an elaborate hierarchy reaching to every part of the nation and to all parts of the world. It has an independent machinery, fallible and not too trustworthy, of course, but nevertheless a machinery of intelligence. It can be informed and it can act, whereas Congress is not informed and cannot act.

Now the popular theory of representative government is that the representatives have the information and therefore create the policy which the Executive administers. The more subtle theory is that the Executive initiates the policy which the Legislature corrects in accordance with popular wisdom. But when the Legislature is haphazardly informed, this amounts to very little, and the people themselves prefer to trust the Executive which knows, rather than the Congress which is vainly trying to know. The result has been the development of a kind of government which has been harshly described as plebiscite autocracy, or government by newspapers. Decisions in the modern state tend to be made by the interaction, not of Congress and the Executive, but of public opinion and the Executive.

Public opinion for this purpose finds itself collected about special groups which act as extra-legal organs of government. There is a labor nucleus, a farmers' nucleus, a prohibition nucleus, a National Security League nucleus, and so on. These groups conduct a continual electioneering campaign upon the unformed, exploitable mass of public opinion. Being special groups, they have special sources of information, and what they lack in the way of information is often manufactured. These conflicting pressures beat upon the executive departments and upon Congress, and formulate the conduct of the government. The government itself acts in reference to these groups far more than in reference to the district congressmen. So politics as it is now played consists in coercing and seducing the representative by the threat and the appeal of these unofficial groups. Sometimes they are the allies, sometimes the enemies, of the party in power, but more and more they are the energy of public affairs. Government tends to operate by the impact of controlled opinion upon administration. This shift in the locus of sovereignty has placed a premium upon the manufacture of what is usually called consent. No wonder that the most powerful newspaper proprietor in the English-speaking world declined a mere government post.

No wonder, too, that the protection of the sources of its opinion is the basic problem of democracy. Everything else depends upon it. Without protection against propaganda, without standards of evidence, without criteria of emphasis, the living substance of all popular decision is exposed to every prejudice and to infinite exploitation.

"Liberty and the Bonus," Today and Tomorrow, *March 16, 1934.*

In modern times the power of the purse has developed far beyond this original conception of it. Congress and other American legislative bodies have not been content to grant funds to the Executive, to say how much he may spend. They have proceeded to force funds upon the Executive, to tell him what he must spend. Thus we have arrived at the curious position where Presidents, governors and mayors are almost continually engaged in trying to persuade the representative body not to appropriate money. In former days the king went, hat in hand, so to speak, to the legislature asking for funds; today the Executive in a democracy goes, hat in hand, to the Legislature, asking it not to make him spend, not to tax the people so much, so that he may preserve the public credit.

A situation has now developed in which Constitutional liberty calls for restraint upon the power of the legislature to appropriate just as in former days it called for restraint upon the power of the Executive to spend. For a legislature can squander the liberties of the people. If it forces expenditure in the interest of organized minorities, it affects the interests of the unorganized majority. If it destroys the public credit, as it has done in many American cities, as it might do in the nation, it jeopardizes the jobs and the savings of the people. If the despotism of minorities is carried far enough to cause a general financial disaster, even the forms of free government may be overwhelmed in a mass movement clamoring for the efficiency of a dictatorship.

The power of the legislature to force expenditure upon the executive is a perversion of representative government. It is an example of how a good principle, the power of the purse, can be carried to a point where it becomes a bad principle. If Constitutional liberty is to be preserved, if representative government is to work satisfactorily, it will be necessary to redefine the power of the purse. It is not difficult to do this. It should be the duty of the Executive to ask for funds. It should be the duty of Congress to grant or to refuse them. The Executive should have no right to spend what Congress has not appropriated. Congress should have no right to appropriate funds which the Executive does not ask for.

Only by the power of the purse can the representative body keep the Executive effectively accountable to the popular will. That is the lesson of the long past. The lesson of the recent past is that only by leaving to the Executive the power to initiate expenditure, can the national interests as a whole be effectively protected against the pressure of minorities. In the equilibrium between these two powers, of the Executive to ask and the Legislature to grant funds, lies the hope of Constitutional liberty.

This has been recognized for two hundred years in England, where free government has had its longest and surest development. It is recognized in the United States. But unfortunately this reform which is of absolutely fundamental importance to the preservation of democracy, is known by the prosaic and uninspiring name of the executive budget. Yet it is not an exaggeration to say that in its moral and spiritual consequences in the realm of liberty, the movement to limit the power of minorities in the Legislature is the complement of the refusal to submit to taxation without representation.

"And Now Congress," Today and Tomorrow, *September 30, 1939.*

No one need spend any further effort arguing whether Congress should remain in Washington for the duration of the war. The question is settled. The bill reported to the Senate disposes conclusively of the idea that the direction of American policy is to be left to the discretion of the President. The bill is so drawn that Congress could not, even if it wished to do so, adjourn and go home. For the bill will impose new and drastic embargoes on American shipping to virtually all parts of the world and upon American finance and commerce in the bulk of its foreign transactions. The administration of the embargoes, in order to make them workable, in order to protect American interests from unnecessary injuries, and in order to mitigate the losses, will require continual and detailed attention by Congress. The Legislature will have to be at hand, not for the purpose of making speeches every day, but for the purpose of watching the practical effects and of understanding the real situation as it develops and of consulting about the actual operation of the law. A procedure will have to be worked out by which the Administration and Congress can effectively discharge their common responsibility.

But while it is now settled that the President is not to have a free hand in foreign policy and that he can exercise his powers only by remaining closely accountable to Congress, it is not yet clearly settled that Congress is fully prepared to play its great part. That will not be settled until it has been made perfectly evident in the coming debate that the Congress really means to accept the responsibility of debating and deciding great issues. The country has made plain that it does not wish to leave its destiny to the personal judgment of the President; but it would be jumping out of the frying pan into the fire to submit the decision of these great issues to the letter writers, the radio speakers, the lobbyists, and the organizers of mass meetings and parades and demonstrations.

The Congress has accepted its Constitutional responsibility for the peace and security of the American people; it will not be equal to that responsibility unless it reaches its decisions by the conscientious and fearless examination of the evidence and the argument presented in the actual debates. Congressmen must listen to their constituents who express their opinion, but if they are to be worthy of the respect of their constituents, each congressman will have to say what Edmund Burke said to his constituents, that "his unbiased opinion, his mature judgment, his enlightened conscience he ought not to sacrifice to you, to any man, or to any set of men living. . . ."

This conception of the duty of the elected legislator is the very heart and soul of representative government. Let the legislator abdicate to the Executive, and there is personal government; let him abdicate to the pressure of crowds, and there is government by agitators and demagogues. The legislator cannot, without betraying free government, abdicate his right *and* his duty to follow his own best judgment in the light of his own conscience.

Happily, that is the view adopted by the American Legion in its convention in Chicago, that it is the task of the citizens to say that they want neutrality, and non-involvement, and a wholly adequate armament, but that it is the task of the Congress and the Administration jointly to determine the means. The Legion has given the people a wise example. It has recognized that citizens can declare, for example, in favor of increased national defense, but that citizens cannot make blueprints for new battleships; it has recognized equally that citizens can declare for a policy of neutrality, but that they are in no position to determine whether, for example, an embargo on finished arms or an embargo on ships and finance is the better means. The character of the armaments and the structure of the neutrality legislation cannot be determined by letter writers and by the radio audience; that is responsible and technical work which calls for first-hand information, for study and reflection, and for thorough discussion among men who are able to know all the facts.

It is a work that Congress cannot evade by counting letters, reading the result of polls, and trying to make its decisions conform to the winds of opinion. The people can speak to Congress about what they want accomplished; as to how it is to be accomplished, Congress must use its judgment, and in so far as any bloc in Congress seeks to incite pressure which prevents the congressmen from using their judgment, that bloc is violating the spirit of representative government.

Much is at stake in this debate: not least among these things is whether representative government is to prove itself equal to the great task which has to be done. If the debate is protracted into a filibuster, if it ceases to be honest deliberation and becomes a contest in the incitement of popular emotion and the encouragement of pressure groups, then whatever the final outcome, the country will suffer. It will suffer because it will have to face the grave perils that lie ahead without a government that can be relied upon, without leadership that it can confidently trust, without the unity that is the one final, sure guarantee of its security.

That must not happen. It will not happen if Congress will debate the measure before it, decide the issue when every responsible legislator has had his say, and then remain continually on guard to deal with the effects of its measure and with developments that cannot now be foreseen.

"The President's Return," Today and Tomorrow, *December 21, 1943.*

For about sixty days the Congress, which is now taking a recess, has had a fairly free hand in dealing with affairs on the home front. The President has made no serious attempt to lead Congress; except in support of the war, there has been a bi-partisan majority opposed to the President, and he himself has been abroad, or busy with the preparations for going abroad.

No national policy on domestic issues has thus far been shaped by Congress. On the contrary, Congress has left for its holiday with nothing decided on the interrelated questions of taxes, prices, and wage control, which are the paramount questions on the home front. The record in fact is worse than that; the net combined effect of the actions of Congress has been to threaten a breakdown of the whole wartime control of inflation. Congress has voted *against* taxes and other measures to stabilize; when Congress has voted *for* anything, it voted for increased prices and increased wages. Moreover, there has come from Congress a chorus of voices which have in substance invited the people to complain and feel aggrieved about, rather than to accept cheerfully and bear proudly, the unavoidable inconveniences and sacrifices of war.

If in practical matters this leaderless Congress has been negative, in its moral example it has been simply deplorable—so deplorable that there must be a prompt and thorough restoration of the national purpose and the public spirit in order to sustain our people in the tremendous ordeal of battle which the winter and the spring will bring.

These are hard words. But few careful observers of the Washington scene will dispute them. They have nothing to do with party politics, the next election, the fourth term, the New Deal, Mr. Willkie, Governor Dewey, the old guard; in fact, those who feel, and I happen to be one of them, that the time is at hand for a change of Administration are among those who feel most deeply how intolerably dangerous it would be if this destructive paralysis of government is not halted.

These sixty days in Congress have demonstrated once more a truth which is as old as the American government: that without strong national leadership by the President, Congress—though it is elected by the people—soon ceases to represent the nation. The votes of this Congress have not represented the real views of the American nation. We have only to compare the newspapers of the country and the various polls of opinion with the actions of Congress to see that organized pressure groups and not the views of the great majority of the people have prevailed.

There is no mystery about this. The ordinary elected representative hears from the pressure groups, which are led by professionals. The great majority of his constituents leave him alone except on those rare occasions when they are aroused by, and respond to, a national leader. That is why presidential leadership is so indispensable in our system of government: the President is the man who speaks for the great but ordinarily silent majority, and only when he is leading that majority is the ordinary congressman able to point to the real majority and say no to the pressure groups. For that same reason a congressman who is deeply concerned with the national interest will always desire strong leadership by the President.

Strong Presidents usually make big mistakes, and after a while the country grows tired of them. But never for long can the country do without a strong President; if it does not like the one it has it must find another one. The bad patches of our history have been the periods when the Presidents were weak and the center of power was in Congress—the decade just before the War Between the States, the two decades after Lincoln's death, the time of Harding.

Some day we may find a way to remedy this crucial defect of our government, which is that there is no satisfactory, workable system of striking a good balance between Congress and the Executive. We have not yet found it, and therefore we are compelled, especially in time of war and great crisis, to prefer the strong national leadership of the President, even when we disagree with many of his measures, to the logrolling of pressure groups in an unled, undisciplined Congress.

"Senators and Scientists and Secrecy," Today and Tomorrow, *May 23, 1949.*

Underlying all the incidents, like that of the young Communist student who got a fellowship of $1,600 for a year's graduate work in theoretical physics, there is a riddle to which no one can hope to find the perfect answer. It is how to guard a vital military secret—like production of atomic weapons—without destroying the conditions which made possible the discovery of the secret of producing them, and of other secrets that remain to be discovered.

At bottom, in so far as there is misunderstanding between so many senators and most scientists, it turns on this: the senators are worried lest the monopoly of the atomic bomb be lost, and the whole precarious balance of power in the world be upset; the scientists are worried lest an understandable but misguided zeal in protecting the monopoly retard the progress of scientific discovery in America, and leave us some day hugging an obsolete weapon.

That, they say, could happen to us. For though the bomb is now an American monopoly, the crucial scientific discoveries and the massive research and the creative reasoning which developed these discoveries were not an American monopoly in the first place, and are not now an American monopoly. And therefore, they contend, if in guarding, as we must, the military secret that has been discovered, we also discourage the process by which discoveries are made, we shall suffer what all nations have suffered where original and creative thought has withered away.

This is a matter on which laymen, including senators, must, if they are conscientious, seek guidance from men who have themselves participated in the discoveries and have lived all their lives with other men who labor to find out a little more of what no one has ever known. The Congress has never before had to deal seriously with men like these. It is used to dealing with many kinds of people, including engineers, applied scientists, inventors. But never before have the interests of government become entangled with men who work at the farthest reaches of the human mind. Misunderstanding is unavoidable, and only humility and common sense—there is no neat formula—can keep the misunderstanding within manageable bounds.

That is all that we can expect to do—to pick our way through the conflict between the military need for secrecy and the scientific need for freedom. But as we pick our way we ought never to forget that the great military weapon was not made by military men or by public officials but by scientific men from all parts of the country and from many parts of the world. They know more about it than any one else. If they told all they knew, only men like them would really understand them. They are the best, in fact the only, judges of what is really secret—a secret from their own peers—and what is merely not understood by the great mass of people who know nothing of the subject anyway. For to all but the very few everything that is written about nuclear physics might as well be written in Chinese.

The effort of laymen, who know virtually nothing about nuclear physics, to determine what is a secret and how to guard it, is rather like what would happen if, say, Senator Hickenlooper woke up one morning and found he had been appointed the censor of the Chinese Nationalist press. I hope I do him no injustice in assuming that his ability to read Chinese is no greater than his knowledge of the science of nuclear physics.

Now to Senator Hickenlooper—assuming him to be illiterate in Chinese—everything published in the Chinese papers would be an absolute secret, a complete and total mystery. How then would he proceed to make sure that nothing was published in the Nationalist press which would be of benefit to the Communists? One way, of course, would be to suspend publication of all papers. If that did not seem feasible, he might get all the Chinese reporters, copyreaders, and printers to sign their names to an oath not to reveal secrets. But that could not satisfy him because how could every Chinese reporter and copyreader know whether any particular piece of information was a secret or not?

So eventually—to continue, but with apologies to Senator Hickenlooper—he would have to call in Chinese who can read Chinese and Chinese who happen to know all the military secrets of the Chinese. With their help he might make a reasonably efficient censor. Without their help, the best he could hope for when the record of his service was made up would be to get an "A" plus for effort and an "A" minus—because he had all the virtues except humility—for character.

"The Usurpers," Today and Tomorrow, *January 17, 1952.*

All those who, being in it or near it, have something to do with this Congress, are agreed in expecting a sorry show. There is no evidence as yet for thinking that they may be wrong and there is nothing else to rely upon to prevent this sorry show unless it is the very faint and, perhaps, fatuous hope that more and more will realize, assisted by the press and radio, that the biggest news that anyone could make would be good news, and that—to judge by the men who in fact seem to be the most liked in the country—the best way to be popular is not to be, in the strict and refined sense of the old word, a slobberer over the public interest.

The prospect, however, is not too bright for a session of Congress which will make Americans proud of their institutions, and will cause the world not only to respect our power and to seek our help but also to admire and be moved by our example. Why, we must ask ourselves, should the prospects be so poor? Why, to say it plainly here as it is being said in so many other places, should the leader of the free nations feel that it is doomed to make an exhibition of itself because it is about to perform the greatest of the functions of a free and democratic people?

There is something absurd and repulsive, and I would think unnecessary, in taking this humiliation for granted. It is much as if a man were to say: "Tomorrow is my wedding day and I shall be at the church at the right time. . . . But you must not hold it against me when I come up the aisle reeling from the barroom brawls I shall have taken part in on my way to the church."

To say that we are in the letdown which always follows a war is of course true. But it does not say very much about how men who do not like this letdown might begin to overcome it. I would suggest that the reason for the very bad relations between Congress and the President—and for the general feeling that nothing can be done about them—is in a critical breakdown of the Constitutional relations between the two branches of the government. There have been serious invasions and usurpations by each against the other, and the violence of the struggle between the Executive and the Congress is due in large measure to the fact that their relations are unregulated at the present time by respect for, and loyalty to, the spirit and intent of the Constitution.

Many years ago, F. S. Oliver wrote that "the spirit of the nation is a great force, but it is one which cannot always be on the alert, and while it sleeps, the part of noble institutions is to keep watch." In the field of war and peace it is the part of noble institutions to watch over the balance of independence and responsibility between the President and the Congress. In the past two years—I would say since the last illness of Senator Vandenberg—neither Truman nor Taft has shown a proper respect and loyalty where the Constitution was meant to be supreme.

Senator Taft's book has an impressive and cogent chapter called "The Place of the President and Congress in Foreign Policy." The chapter is an argument that the President exceeded his authority when he committed an army to the Korean War and again when he committed another army to NATO, without the authorization of Congress. I think, and in fact have thought from the beginning, that Senator Taft is right—that in the true intent and purpose of the Constitution the President's action has been a usurpation of the power of Congress.

But what I find deplorable is that Senator Taft should pass over in complete silence the unprecedented usurpations by Congress of the President's powers in the conduct of foreign affairs. The most clearly identifiable has been the seizure by the Senate Foreign Relations Committee, which I understand is actually acknowledged in writing by the State Department, of a veto on the President's Constitutional right to recognize governments. But the usurpation of the President's powers has gone far beyond that. Congress has invaded and infiltrated not only the making of policy, not only negotiation with foreign states, but the very administrative detail of every part of American foreign relations.

One can argue whether theoretically the American system of government with its separated powers is as good as would be a parliamentary government. But what is not seriously arguable, I think, is that the only way to make this government of ours work well is to be faithful to its own Constitutional principle and to preserve the spirit and meaning of the separation of powers.

That, I contend, is what the Truman Administration and the Republicans under the leadership of Taft have flagrantly failed to do—ever since they have no longer been kept in order by the moderating effect of Vandenberg, with his passionate Constitutionalism. Neither Truman nor Taft has acted with the scruple and restraint, with the loyalty and the devotion to the spirit of American institutions which their responsibilities and the great occasion called for.

That is why the Congress, the administrative officials, and the correspondents who have to watch it and write about it are so unanimous in thinking that we are in for a series of cheap and nasty brawls.

"The Power to Investigate," Today and Tomorrow, *January 4, 1955.*

It is possible, I think, to draw a fairly clear line between the proper and the improper use of the Congressional power of investigation. I do not contend that the rule I am suggesting would apply everywhere and always and in all conceivable cases. But the rule will work most of the time and particularly in the cases which have caused so much anguish, bitterness, and dissension.

The rule is that when Congress is investigating the Executive branch of the government, the political head of a department or agency should accept full responsibility for his subordinates and be held accountable for them. The evil reflected by the case of General Zwicker, which was only one case among many, was not merely that this officer was abused by McCarthy. It was that he, an officer under orders, rather than the Secretary of the Army who was his political chieftain, was made answerable for a question of Army administration. Stevens was answerable to Congress and he was responsible for Zwicker. It is a grave abuse of the legislative power of investigation if Congress holds Zwicker, rather than Stevens who is responsible for Zwicker, answerable.

The rule that political chiefs—and not civil servants and military men—are answerable to Congress is fundamental to good administration and to a sound and workable relationship between the Executive and the Legislature. In the field of subversion and security risks and corruption the Congressional power to investigate should be limited to the responsible political chiefs and it should be addressed to the question of whether they are exercising their responsibilities so as to justify the confidence of Congress.

If they are not, they should be replaced by other political chieftains. They cannot be replaced, and no attempt should be made to replace them, by the chairman of a Senate investigating committee. That is to change these committees from being instruments for holding the Executive accountable into irregular courts, exercising without rules or restraint the police power and the judicial power. The chief of a Senate investigating committee cannot reach over the head of the department chief and seize a subordinate in order to put him on trial, without destroying the discipline and the morale of the department.

Public opinion is not likely to go far wrong if it applies this rule to legislative investigations: who is being questioned? Is he the boss, who is responsible, or is he someone down the line? If he is the boss who is being questioned, the committee may be acting rightly or wrongly, wisely or foolishly. But it is within its proper limits, and it is not abusing its power.

But if the committee goes after the subordinate, if it places him on trial for his political life, it is usurping the authority of the political chieftain to judge his own subordinates, to choose them, to promote them, to fire them, and to lead them. Then the system is deranged, and the result is the mess we have been seeing.

3 · *The Restraining Hand of the Supreme Court*

"The Function of the Supreme Court," Today and Tomorrow, *January 25, 1936.*

Recently on several occasions the Supreme Court has felt called upon to explain what it does when it holds a statute to be unconstitutional. In these cases "the judicial branch of the government has only one duty," said Mr. Justice Roberts—"to lay the article of the Constitution which is invoked beside the statute which is challenged and to decide whether the latter squares with the former. . . . This Court neither approves nor condemns any legislative policy. Its delicate and difficult office is to ascertain and declare whether the legislation is in accordance with, or in contravention of, the provisions of the Constitution; and having done that its duty ends." The same view was stated by Mr. Justice Stone: "Courts are concerned only with the power to enact statutes, not with their wisdom."

The Court would not perhaps feel called upon to reiterate this doctrine so frequently if it were not aware that the doctrine is not universally understood and accepted. The plain fact of the matter is that the doctrine is not wholly intelligible to the lay mind. The ordinary man finds it hard to understand why, if, as the court seems to be saying, it has no concern with wisdom, but has only to compare two texts, its office is so "delicate and difficult"; nor why judges themselves often differ so sharply about the texts; nor why, for example, it did not become clear until the year 1936 that Hamilton and Story rather than Madison had the "correct" view of the "general welfare" clause. It is a very real question whether the doctrine as presented to the lay mind is sufficiently convincing to withstand the strain of a long series of decisions that challenge the actions of Congress.

When Mr. Justice Stone says that courts are concerned only with the power to enact statutes, not with their wisdom, he will be understood by many as implying that the powers of Congress and the powers reserved to the states are clearly defined. But is it not the essence of the matter that there is a large area in which the respective powers of Congress and the states are not defined—are not defined in language so plain that Congress and the President can have no reasonable doubt? Surely, this is the actual situation in the controversial matters. The Constitution calls for a federal union in which some powers belong to Congress and others to the states. But the Constitution, as originally written, does not and could not have anticipated all the powers that government would exercise in the course of a century and a half, and therefore it did not and could not have distributed every conceivable power precisely as between Congress and the states.

If, by some miracle of prophetic insight, the authors of the Constitution had been able to define and distribute precisely every power of government, these particular questions would present no difficulty to the Court. The reason why men differ honestly and with conviction, the reason why opinion in these matters is not unanimous in Congress or even in the Supreme Court itself, is that there is a large area in which the distribution of powers is not defined. And what the Court has to do when a controversy arises in this disputed area is to determine how power shall be distributed.

This determination, as the Court insists, ought not to depend on whether the judges think the statute is wise. But must the Court not inevitably decide whether it thinks that such a distribution of novel powers is wise? Some organ of the government has to decide such questions. For, lacking an exhaustive definition of all the conceivable powers that government may wish to exercise, these questions must continually be raised.

Obviously Congress cannot be the judge of its own powers as against the states. For in that event the states would be at the mercy of Congressional majorities. The individual states cannot be the judges. For in that event there would be no union. Somebody must arbitrate these disputes about the distribution of power. And if the Supreme Court did not exist to arbitrate them, some other tribunal would have to be created to fulfill precisely the same function.

Now the decision as to how powers not already defined shall be distributed cannot be deduced by a kind of automatic logical process from the words of the Constitution. The decision has inevitably to be a judgment of how novel power can be most wisely distributed in the kind of government which exists in America.

In these high and ultimate questions the Court cannot, of course, decide in accordance with the personal view of the judges as to what sort of government they might like to see. When they are not bound by the letter of the Constitution, they are bound by its spirit. That is the reason why their office is so "delicate and difficult." They cannot rely upon the letter of a text. If they could, their office would be neither delicate nor difficult. They have to rely upon the spirit, the intent, the genius of American institutions.

In this final duty which they perform they have to exercise the highest kind of political wisdom. They have to determine whether in a matter where a definitive text is lacking, some novel development of government powers is consistent with the living principle of the government as a whole.

If this is the real function of the Court, would it not perhaps be better to recognize it and to trust the people to see how indispensable and how rational it is? I know that there are some who hold that popular respect for the courts would be undermined if the people were not taught to believe that in the realm of Constitutional construction the Court merely "finds" the law that is there. My impression is that, on the contrary, popular respect is being diminished by a continual insistence that the Court merely finds the law though Congress and even some of the justices cannot find it. Is not all this a little too much like the effort to preserve the chastity of a youth by refusing to tell him the facts of life? Would it not be better to take the adult view that the truth is the best of all ways of defending the Constitution and the Court?

It seems to me that the American people are quite capable of understanding that the Constitution does not precisely define the distribution of all powers—that someone must arbitrate in disputed questions—that Congress cannot be the final judge of its powers—that the states cannot be the final judges of their powers—that, if there is to be a federal government, an agency must exist which is the final judge, subject of course to the right of the people to amend the Constitution. If this view were popularly accepted, the question of five-to-four or six-to-three decisions would cease to be troublesome. For men would say that the question had to be decided, that some decision is better than none, and that while men may honestly differ, the majority must rule.

There is every reason to think, I am convinced, that such an appeal to their reason would strengthen rather than weaken the people's loyalty to the Court. As matters stand today, their reason is often bewildered and dissatisfied, on occasions at war with their loyalty. It is evident that the people wish to believe in the Court. That wish is not, if I read the popular temper correctly, derived merely from blind reverence for authority. On the contrary, it is derived from a vividly renewed sense of the importance of law as against arbitrariness, and it can be reinforced by an appeal to their reason.

For this generation has learned again what the authors of the Constitution knew so well. They, too, lived in a period of war, revolution, and despotism. They saw, as Jefferson put it, that "a single consolidated government would become the most corrupt government on earth." The people today see how true that is, and that is why they approve, even when they dislike a particular verdict of the Court, the spectacle of a mighty government with all its force compelled to submit to the restraints imposed by nine elderly men who command no force of their own. They realize, as they could not possibly have realized it thirty years ago, that this power to restrain government itself is —though it may at times be inconvenient and confusing—the very foundation of a civilized society.

"Judges as Presidential Candidates," Today and Tomorrow, *June 13, 1935.*

The authority of the Court is one of the most extraordinary things in the history of government. Here are nine men who, without physical power of any kind, can, under certain conditions, override the will of Congress and the President. Their verdicts are obeyed absolutely. On what does the power of the Court rest? It rests on the conviction of the people that the Court interprets the disinterested and considered and permanent judgment of the people as against the momentary, impulsive, expedient, and short-sighted opinions of temporary majorities. In the annals of democracy the Court stands forth as a unique institution. For the first time in the history of popular government the people themselves have imposed upon themselves a comprehensive restraint to which they willingly submit. This is a very great thing. The Court represents the people's own moral conviction that they must not act hastily or arbitrarily, that there must always be an appeal from Philip drunk to Philip sober, that the voice of reason must in the end prevail over the prompting of appetite and of impulse.

All of this depends upon the people's own belief that the Court is above all ordinary worldly temptation. Everything has been done to give the justices independence, inviolability, and prestige so that they may be, and so that they shall be believed to be, beyond the daily struggle in political affairs. And yet now the fervent defenders of the Constitution are seriously considering the nomination as an opponent of the New Deal of a judge who must sit in judgment on the New Deal.

The mere talk about this boom creates mischief so serious that it may require some decisive action to dispose of it. The Court is adjourned for the summer. But if, when the court reconvenes in the autumn, the boom has not been completely deflated, Mr. Justice Roberts will be compelled to take notice. No one knows better than he, a man of the highest judicial integrity and sensibility, that he cannot sit in judgment on the Democratic Administration and continue to be discussed as a Republican candidate. If the boom is not destroyed first by responsible Republican leaders, his choice will be to destroy it himself or to resign from the bench.

There ought not to be any real hesitation about the proper course. Now is a very good time to put an end once and for all to the idea that justices of the Supreme Court are available candidates for political office. This would make a very good first plank in a program to defend the Constitution and the Supreme Court as its final interpreter. A man who accepts appointment to the Supreme Court should be regarded as having forever renounced all other worldly ambitions. The nature of the institution demands that candidates for appointment, the justices who are appointed, and the nation, should look upon the Court as the summit of a career beyond which there is nothing in the way of office, honor, or material gain to be won or lost.

"On Selecting a Successor to Holmes," Today and Tomorrow, *January 21, 1932.*

In the vast range of his powers there are few in which the President exercises so far-reaching an influence on the nation's history as in the selection of judges of the Supreme Court. When he makes these appointments he deals not with the emergencies of the moment but with the future which no man can clearly foresee. For though the business of the Court is to decide particular cases before it, it is through these cases that it adjusts not only the relations of the individual to the separate states and to the United States, of the states to one another and to the Union, of the three branches of the government to each other, but also acts as the guardian and promoter of acceptable and workable compromise between the claims of the past and the needs of the present, between settled traditions and the evolution of public purposes.

It is not enough, therefore, that the Court should be composed of competent and upright judges. It is essential that its deliberations should be infused with prophetic and creative willingness to administer the Constitution, as Mr. Justice Holmes has said, "not simply by taking the words and a dictionary but by considering their origin and the line of their growth," realizing that these legal texts "have called into life a being the development of which could not have been foreseen completely by the most gifted of its begetters," and that, therefore, cases "must be considered in the light of our whole experience and not merely in that of what was said a hundred years ago."

Thus there are no mechanical rules which can measure qualifications for work of this sort. The selection of judges of the Supreme Court calls for the exercise of the highest kind of intuitive judgment upon the reach and subtlety and learning and disinterestedness of the available men. It calls for an understanding on the part of a President that it is not the conveniences of his own term in office but events after his own term which he is helping to determine.

At this moment it is important it be not forgotten that we stand upon the threshold of great changes in American life. There is a crisis in the world and for the time being our energies are absorbed in meeting it. But a crisis cannot be permanent; it must resolve itself somehow—whether according to our plans or by sheer force of brute circumstances will depend upon the amount of intelligence, courage, and collective discipline that can be mustered in time. The crisis will, nevertheless, pass. And however it passes, it will leave us with the urgent necessity and the compelling desire to reconsider many established things and to experiment with new forms of collective effort. For only the blind imagine that we shall find ourselves back where we were in the postwar "normalcy" or in the prewar innocence. The processes of history are cumulative and irreversible, and when the tension of the crisis relaxes, we shall find ourselves in one of the great eras of reorganization and pioneering.

It would be naïve to think that men can or will be satisfied with the kind of life which they now have. They know, and every one knows, that invention and technical skill have opened up possibilities of security and plenty which are to a grievous extent unused or perverted. The awful paradox of our time, that there should be want in the midst of abundance, is self-evident proof that the prevailing political and economic arrangements and policies and methods of administering affairs are deeply and seriously at fault. A period of great changes is not merely indicated. It is certain.

In such a period it is crucial whether or not change is continuous with the past, whether there is a sudden break with established wisdom or the use of that wisdom to season new enterprise. Of all the Western peoples the English-speaking nations have been the most successful in finding ways to preserve and yet to change. Their secret is their sense of the law, which in their great periods they have looked upon not as an iron frame, but as a garment which can be cut and altered so that it always covers them and yet allows them to move freely.

It is the business of the Court in our political system to oversee this cutting and alteration of the garment that it may always fit comfortably and endure. That has been the work of the judges from Marshall to Holmes, and those who see ahead ought to hope ardently for a true successor in that great line.

4 · *The Parties and the Political Process*

"Concerning Parties," **Today and Tomorrow**, *January 31, 1934.*

It is of the very essence of despotism that it can never afford to fail. That is what distinguishes it most vitally from democracy. In a despotism there is no organized opposition which can take over the power when the Administration in office has failed. All the eggs are in one basket. Everything is staked on one coterie of men. When the going is good, they move more quickly and efficiently than democracies, where the opposition has to be persuaded and conciliated. But when they lose, there are no reserves. There are no substitutes on the bench ready to go out on the field and carry the ball. That is why democracies with the habit of party government have outlived all other forms of government in the modern world. They have, as it were, at least two governments always at hand, and when one fails they have the other. They have diversified the risks of mortality, corruption, and stupidity which pervade all human affairs. They have remembered that the most beautifully impressive machine cannot run for very long unless there is available a complete supply of spare parts.

So it is a symptom of national health that the Republicans have begun to take seriously their role as an opposition party.

Their task is not an easy one. When a party has been defeated, as the Democrats were in 1920, 1925, and 1928 and the Republicans in 1932, it seems almost unbelievable that it can ever revive. After a crushing defeat its principles are discredited, its leaders are in eclipse, the rank and file of party workers dismayed and demoralized. Our political customs accentuate the difficulty of organizing the opposition. For those most competent to lead it, namely, those who have held responsible posts in the previous Administration, are forced into complete retirement. It is a wasteful and inherently absurd arrangement which deprives the nation of the services of those most able to criticize, and produces such spectacles as the attempt of Republican senators to debate the Money Bill though they do not understand it, while Mr. Hoover and Mr. Ogden Mills, who have the equipment to understand it, are not heard in the debate.

Nevertheless, though it is difficult for an opposition to organize quickly after a bad defeat, it does in the course of time get itself organized. It is always a mistake to assume that either of the two American parties is dead, however divided and crushed it may seem to be. Herbert Croly used to say that the two parties were virtually indestructible: they were low-grade organisms which had neither a brain or a heart that could be stopped, and so you could cut them in half and the two halves would wiggle on and somehow grow together again. This idea ought to be a great comfort to Republican politicians. It was until quite recently a great comfort to the Democrats. And it will be again.

So unimpressive a view of American party life is often discouraging to men who would like to think of parties as associations of men committed to great principles. But our own history seems to show that we never have developed a system of parties based on permanent conflicts of principle. There is a reason for that, I think, and a good one. America is too extensive and too diversified to be divided permanently by any one conflict of interests, and of principles which rationalize those interests. We have class conflicts, but they are localized. We have regional conflicts, but there are many regions and the issues are continually shifting. For that reason America is the despair of all those who like their politics to be neat and logical; of Marxians, for example, and rugged individualists and planners, and upholders of *laissez faire,* and all others who have an internally consistent social philosophy.

Yet the key to the mystery of American politics is there for anyone to see who will look at it simply as it is. The United States is not a compact nation like the European nations, among whom political science, as we know it, was first developed. It is a continental nation of a kind hitherto unknown in history, the kind of nation conceivably that the whole of Europe might have become had Latin become its universal language and had Europe found a bond of union. The American Republic is not merely federal in its constitutional form; it is federal in its social and economic structure.

Once that is understood, the true character of American parties is apparent. They are loose federations of regional parties. The real issues are made in the local parties, but when these local parties federate for national purposes, principles and issues have to be compromised to form a workable union. There is such a thing as New England Republicanism which corresponds to the European notion of parties. There is such a thing as a Democracy of the cotton states. There is such a thing as a Democracy of the great cities. There is such a thing as Republicanism of the prairies. But however much keynote orators proclaim the national principles of the Republican Party or of the Democratic, there are not any except temporarily for the purposes of forming a working union among the regional components.

Far from being a bad thing, this tendency of national parties to stultify local issues is in the long view a very good thing. It accomplishes what the authors of the Constitution saw to be necessary, namely, the subduing of partisan fury and factionalism, though it accomplishes it in a way that they did not foresee. They tried to "refine the will of the people" by the Electoral College and various other devices. Our unprincipled parties somehow achieve the same result. They confine intransigent politics, which so often has destroyed states, within regions where it can do no irreparable damage, and they compel those who govern the nation to work through compromise and conciliation. And the result, though it is frequently inglorious and often sordid enough in all conscience, is almost certainly humanly more tolerable and more likely to endure than government by the opinionated and the omnipotent.

"In Praise of the Parties," Today and Tomorrow, *April 4, 1936.*

A new way of disqualifying men for public office has recently come into favor. It is no longer necessary to ask what the candidate himself stands for. The important question it: Who stands for him? Then if someone you do not like can be found supporting the candidate you do not like, so much the worse for the candidate.

Thus it has recently been said that Senator Borah received "the kiss of death" when Dr. Townsend gave him his blessing. Governor Landon has received the kiss of death because Mr. Hearst is for him. Senator Vandenberg has received the kiss of death because someone took it into his head to say that Mr. Hoover is for him. Mr. Hoover was kissed to death long ago because he may have been for Mr. Hoover. Colonel Knox has been repeatedly kissed to death because certain not too savory Illinois machine politicians are for him. . . .

There is no way of arranging it so that membership in a party is an exclusive privilege enjoyed only by those whose views seem to us sound, pure, and righteous. And that being the case, it will not do to hold it against Governor Landon because Mr. Hearst came out to see him in a private car, or against Senator Borah because Dr. Townsend finds him the least objectionable, or against Colonel Knox because the Illinois politicians are for him. After all, it is asking a good deal of a candidate that he should go to the people saying: I should like you to vote for me, but here is a blacklist of people whose vote I distinctly do not want.

It would seem to be a good deal fairer to judge him as he is, by what he is, by what he has done, by what he proposes to do, rather than by the hitchhikers on his bandwagon.

As a matter of fact, there are few more genuinely reassuring phenomena in American politics than these hitchhikers. For if everyone with some political influence went off and founded a political party of his own, if the only persons supporting a candidate were those who agreed with him one hundred per cent, we should have fifty parties and no party government. We should have factions instead of parties, and we should be cursed with that very impotence and discordance which brought democratic government to a standstill in a large part of Europe.

Far from being a bad sign, the behavior of these hitch-hikers is a symptom of the constitutional vigor of the American political system. For it means that with entire freedom to agitate any cause, when it comes down to choosing their governors, Americans are still able to coalesce sufficiently to provide the indispensable requisite: a sufficient working majority of reasonably like-minded men.

So for myself I much prefer to see Mr. Hearst following Governor Landon, Dr. Townsend following Senator Borah, Father Coughlin following someone, to seeing each of them trying to become the little leader of a little faction of his own. For while pressure groups and organized minorities exercise more influence than they ought to exercise, it is still a comfort to know that they become submerged in the old parties when a national Administration is to be elected.

To the observer of the checkered history of popular government in the modern world, it is a comfort, too, to reflect that the major parties in America are almost completely without sharply defined intellectual convictions. I know that there are many who think that the two parties ought to find irreconcilable principles on which to divide, and that each election ought to be the most momentous since 1861, since 1776, since Armageddon. For myself, I think the best elections are those which are not momentous, and the best party system is one in which both parties are in fundamental agreement, differing only as to methods, ways and means, incidental measures, and personalities.

This is not because principles are not important. It is because great parties in a nation with forty million voters can fight on fundamental principles only at the risk of tearing the nation apart. No principle that will do that ought to be made a partisan issue. Under our marvelously clumsy party system no principle of that sort can, thank heavens, become a partisan issue.

In other countries, wherever it has been tried, whenever fundamental principles have been made partisan issues, the result has been disastrous, and we ought to be duly grateful that our national parties and our candidates fight, when the issue is really joined, about relatively superficial issues.

In American politics the real fights on basic issues take place within the parties. They do not follow party lines. . . .

The net effect of this beneficent confusion is that all sorts of persons who do not agree in principle find themselves working together in practice. And that, in the perspective of what happens when men become isolated in their principles, is all to the good.

"The Deepest Issue of Our Time," Vital Speeches of the Day, *II* (*1936*), *602, an address delivered at the University of Rochester on June 15, 1936.*

No one can attend many American political conventions, and I have been going to them more or less regularly for twenty years, without having at times some doubts as to whether they provide the best method of selecting the governors of a great nation. The confusion, the noise, the milling about of large crowds, the hasty conferences, the bargains, the compromises are such that toward the third or fourth day of it you begin to ask yourself whether a nation can afford to entrust its destiny to all this ballyhoo and hullabaloo.

It is then that it is most incumbent upon us to see things in perspective and to remember what are the alternatives. There are only two other ways of selecting the rulers of a state, and however irrational our democratic method may seem when you watch the delegate from Oklahoma bellowing into the ear of the delegate from New York, it is the least irrational method of choosing the head of a government yet devised by men. You can make the head of the state the son or the daughter of the head of the state. You can have hereditary rulers, but since the Mendelian law operates in royal families no less than in others, hereditary government is based on a pure gamble. Or you may let the head of the state be the man who can seize supreme power by physical force or by conspiracy and intrigue. That surely is extremely irrational.

So our method, which is a mixture of deliberation and ballyhoo, of argument and political trading, of common judgment and popular excitement, shines by comparison when we consider the alternative. That it is not so bad a method as it seems at four in the morning on the third day of a convention has been demonstrated by experience. For by this method the American people have operated a government under the same Constitution longer than any other people in the world today.

"The Election Explained," Today and Tomorrow, *November 3, 1952.*

The other day I found myself insisting to a visitor from abroad that an American election is a whole lot better than it sounds. He did not think so. There were no clearly defined issues which were being debated, he said, and moreover, as the campaign went on and on, everyone seemed to be getting more and more vehement about less and less.

That, I admitted, was quite true. But he was mistaken, I argued, in thinking that this was the defect of the American system. On the contrary, this was its enormous virtue. In the tremendous uproar of the primaries, the conventions, and the election campaign, the system works toward the reduction rather than the aggravation of the differences between the parties. It is not an elegant process. It does not sound intelligent when you listen to it. Much of it is tiresome, annoying, and embarrassing. But since no one invented it, since it has grown up unintentionally out of our experience, Americans may say without boasting that it is one of their greatest blessings.

What is unique about the American political system is that here the principles and institutions of freedom and democracy have been made to work on a continental scale. There are countries where the liberties of the individual are more securely protected than they are here. There are countries where the government is more efficient, where it is more honest, where it is more truly representative.

But on the other hand, there has as yet been no other country in the history of the world where so many people, so diverse in their origins and in their interests, have on so vast a territory governed themselves so long and preserved their freedom. No other nation of comparable size on a land of comparable extent has as yet succeeded in maintaining a government based on free elections and in a society which respects the rights of men.

This is the American achievement—to have shown that the principles of a free society can be made to work in a great society. This is not something that can be taken for granted—that so vast a country can be kept free under one government. That is why our bigness and our size, which we boast so much too much about, are also our preoccupation and our worry. We have had a civil war, which has left an indelible mark upon the

American mind, and the problem of union, over and above the problems of democracy and of freedom, is never entirely settled and forgotten among us.

The American political system, as it works in the primaries and the conventions and the election campaign, is addressed—not by intention but empirically—to the problem of the union. We have developed out of our experience a process by which the conflicts and diversities of sections, of classes and sects are assuaged and mollified, are purged and cooled, so that the nation can live with them and the government be carried on.

That, said I to my helpless, astounded, and bewildered guest, is the reason in the madness you have been seeing.

"Party Politics," Today and Tomorrow, *September 13, 1955.*

As the American party system works today, there are in each party two main groups of professional politicians. They have differing primary interests. The one group is made up of the senior senators of the party together with those members of the House who have sure seats and long service and high seniority. They might be called the Congressional faction. Among the Democrats they are, of course, from the Solid South. Among the Republicans they come in the main from the northern Middle West.

A significant fact about this group of professional politicians is that they do not retire to private life even if their party loses the presidential election. They are never out of office. Moreover, they may actually be in power, as are the Congressional Democrats today, though the Administration belongs to the other party. Whether or not they have the majority in either house, and therefore the committee chairmanships, they make the party's public record in between elections. There is no higher authority on the party's principles and programs than theirs, and there is no politician on the outside who can lead them or can speak for them.

Their primary personal interest is not to elect a President. It is to fortify their own position in Congress, in their constituencies, and in the control of the party organization. They would like best, of course, to be the senior members of a party that controlled both ends of Pennsylvania Avenue. But it is against their interest to have a President of their own party who ignores them or, worse still, might challenge them.

The other group of professional politicians is drawn from the state capitals and the big cities. The Congressional group are centered in the rock-ribbed constituencies. The other group are centered in the doubtful states and the highest contested districts. They look toward the White House and toward national, rather than a regional, leadership. For their elections are hard-fought and they need help from the national party. They might perhaps be called the presidential group.

Their primary interest in national politics is the presidency. Based as they are in the doubtful states, they are far more keenly aware than are the Congressional group of the role of the independent voter. This causes them to favor a national rather than a regional, a broad rather than a narrow, a moderate rather than an extreme, party program.

"The Senate Inquisition," Forum and Century, *LXXXIV (1930), 129. An investigation of lobbying practices by Senator Caraway of Arkansas gave Lippmann an opportunity to comment on the difficulties that attend congressional attempts to regulate the activities of pressure groups.*

In any event, it is necessary to recognize that the record of the Caraway Committee raises a larger question than the manners and morals of Senator Caraway. It is whether the pressure of organized groups upon government can be decently and effectively regulated. It is an enormously difficult question—perhaps the paramount question with which those inquiries we hopefully call political science have to deal in a modern democracy. I do not know the answer to the question, but it seems to me useful to recognize that we are actually witnessing in the conduct of the Caraway Committee an *ad hoc* and somewhat befuddled attempt to solve the problem. This committee is operating on one of the frontiers of democracy. In a realm of affairs where there is as yet no settled law or any particular respect for the traditional code of morals, Senator Caraway has set up a vigilance committee to improvise justice and, as is usually the case in such proceedings, to work off grudges.

There is little hope, I should suppose, that Congress can

devise a body of law which will effectively and decently regulate the pressure of the lobbies. By formal legislation it can hardly go further than to declare certain general principles, such as that the names of lobbyists, their backers, their receipts and expenditures must be published. Legislation of this sort is not self-enforcing and the premium upon evasion is high. Our experience in attempting to make political parties accountable for money spent in elections is not encouraging. It would be very much more difficult to obtain an honest accounting from the countless organizations which spend money to manufacture public opinion and to influence government. There is not, I am satisfied, a real accounting of the money spent by the two parties. The corrupt practices acts are coarse nets which catch the whales but not the sharks.

What happens—and I believe it happened in 1928—is that a large part of the money spent never passes through the hands of the officials who are formally responsible. For example, there has never been any accounting of the vast sums spent on the subterranean campaign against Al Smith. In the light of that experience it would be naïve to suppose that a private interest pursuing a selfish purpose will voluntarily destroy its own influence by disclosing its own secrets. The admonitions of the President and our best citizens on the virtue of observing the law because it *is* the law would, in this field of human affairs, be insufficient to melt a pound of butter.

The rough methods of the Caraway Committee have their basis in these circumstances. The regulation of lobbying and propaganda would call for a nice balance between public and private rights; between the right of the generality, on the one hand, not to have the processes of government distorted by the pressure of private groups, and the right of the citizen, on the other hand, to work for his interests and his convictions. It is very difficult to say, even as a matter of pure theory, where one right ends and the other begins, to define the difference between freedom of speech and the kind of lobbying and propaganda which needs somehow to be regulated.

In practice the discrimination is even more difficult. There is no consensus of opinion on the principles which ought to govern, and we have no knowledge as to how effectively to apply the principles on which we might agree. While this confusion lasts, we must therefore expect continual trespass back and forth, by pressure groups on the public interest, and by public men on individual privacy.

The problem is not one which is likely to be solved by an ingenious idea. The American people have been experimenting with ingenious ideas in this field for fifty years. They have passed bushels of laws and have enforced some of them somewhat. We have learned something in the process, but we have not learned how to solve the problem. Nor shall we learn, I think. My own guess is that the problem does not lie on the plane of formal lawmaking, but on the plane of the *mores* of the nation.

We do not have, as yet, a body of intellectual and moral habits, customs, and attitudes to fit the realities of modern popular government. Our political consciences are the deposit of a simpler age when opinion was regulated by the traditions and the decisions of church and state and class. There is as yet no alternative public conscience suited to the present age in which opinion is free and the circulation of opinion so much determined by the supply and demand of accidental popular interest and so subject to the power of money and the control of mechanical resources.

A public conscience cannot be improvised. It is the product of wont and use, of adaptation by trial and error, and of their clarification by criticism. I would not, therefore, wish to abolish the Caraway Committees; nor would I wish to submit to them. The inquisition is necessary if we are to keep the propagandists and lobbyists within any bounds whatever.

On the other hand, resistance to the inquisition is no less necessary if we are to stop the never-ending audacity of elected persons from peeping through every keyhole. It is likely that the courts will, to some degree, define more clearly than they have yet done the rights of the individual against the inquisitorial powers of legislative bodies; but, essentially, the case is one in which good precedents must be made by the legislative bodies themselves as a result of the give and take of opposing interests. These good precedents will emerge from the present disorder provided there presides over this conflict of interests a vigilant, disinterested public opinion.

"On the Strength of Democracy," Today and Tomorrow, *November 5, 1940.*

When the returns are in, just about half the people, those who voted for the loser, will have to ask themselves how seriously they believe the campaign orators who told them that democracy was lost if their opponents won the election. Much will depend on how the losers answer this question. If they believe seriously that Mr. Willkie is the head and front of an unholy alliance of reactionaries and revolutionists or that Mr. Roosevelt is the center of an effort to set up a dictatorship and establish national socialism, then the loser cannot accept the result of this election as Americans have always, with the dreadful exception only of the election of 1860, accepted the results of all their elections.

But as a matter of fact the nation will accept the result because accepting the result is the deep habit of this, the oldest and most solidly established democracy on earth. The nation will accept the result because the people know in their hearts that the rhetorical threats and the rhetorical promises which they have just been hearing belong to the routine of campaigning in the month of October before election, and that for every grain of truth these political words contain there are ten grains of buncombe. Were it not for this habitual common sense, which rests upon three centuries of experience on this soil with lawful and responsible government, elections here would not be elections; they would be, as in so many other lands where democracy is not deeply rooted in habit, the prelude to civil war. This common sense will now prevail. Though the flaming charges of the past ten days would, if they were seriously believed, leave the nation hopelessly divided and, therefore, paralyzed, the event will show, I believe, a great popular rally to the President-elect and no popular amiability to the losers who sulk or for winners who remember their grudges.

The charge that one party would destroy and the boast that the other party alone can save democracy rests upon a misunderstanding of democracy. For it is not political parties that save democracy, but, on the contrary, it is the democratic system which saves the nation from the excesses of the political parties.

5 · *The Public Service*

"Servant Trouble at the White House," Today and Tomorrow, *April 28, 1949.*

Mr. Truman painted a heart-rending picture of life in Washington when he remarked at his press conference last week that public officials had to be iron men with an elephant hide and that their pay is not worth the ribbing they have to take. If that is the way things are, Mr. Truman is going to have his worst trouble in working out a proper scale of payments. For iron men can be found. Those who were not born with elephant hides can grow them. But how to figure out the pay is a puzzle; perhaps the best way will be to renegotiate the salaries at the end of each month, letting those who have been glorified by Fulton Lewis, Jr., pay consolation to those who have been ribbed by Drew Pearson.

All this will not be what the storybooks say about the ideal public servant who has the iron of conviction in his soul and wears the armor of a good conscience. But this is a great country even in its less glamorous moments.

Much has been said in recent years about the difficulty of getting and keeping able men in public life. Now there is no doubt that the pay is too low, especially for officials who have no private income, who have a growing family, and who ought in order to do their work well to be able to meet other public men outside their offices. But while salaries ought to be increased, they can never be increased to the point where these abler men can earn as much working for the government as they could earn in private life.

As a matter of fact, the difficulty of getting or keeping the able men is not usually a matter of money. The difficulty of getting them is to recognize ability when it has not yet been demonstrated by some obvious worldly success. This is a great gift and a rare one: to see who is going to be eminent before he has made a reputation, and then to want him and then to back him. This was one of the conspicuous achievements of Stimson and Marshall during the war, that they were able to discern the qualities of men, who have since become famous, while these men were still unknown and obscure.

The difficulty of keeping men has not often, I believe, been caused by money. Much more often than not that has been the ostensible reason, so to speak, the diplomatic reason, why men have resigned and have gone back to private life. There may have been some who had to go and earn money though they would have preferred to stay in office, though they were actually asked to stay in office. But many more have gone, announcing that they had to earn money, when in fact they were being eased out of office or were being refused the promotion which they felt they had earned.

Rarely have they refused to come back, even though they could not possibly have had time to recoup their fortunes, if they were offered something sufficiently important and interesting to do. The joys of private life, which they thought they yearned for amidst the frustrations of public life and amidst the ribbing from Congress and the press, have usually palled on them quickly. For the truth is that public life, once a man has been infected with its excitement and importance, is something that few ever get over. They are homesick for it ever after, and even the Congressional investigations and Drew Pearson's broadcasts are, like the pangs of childbirth, soon forgotten.

Mr. Truman's main difficulty, in fact his only real difficulty, is that he has not always wanted to keep, or been willing to promote, the ablest men who learned to be public servants during the past decade.

The greatest waste in the public service is that just about when men have learned how to govern, they are retired because someone else wants their job, or because they feel they must be promoted. Therefore, a man who has done well in one post but probably has gone stale in it and ought to move out of it, is rarely offered a different post.

He can only go up or go out. If he has been an Assistant Secretary of State he feels that he cannot be an Assistant Secretary of Commerce because the Department of Commerce is not so high in the hierarchy of rank as is the Department of State. So just when he would make an excellent Assistant Secretary of Commerce he retires—largely because his dignity demands that he be made Under Secretary of State.

If only these customs could be changed, it would do more than anything that can be done with money, to improve the public service.

"Mr. Hoover and J. Q. Adams," Today and Tomorrow, *June 2, 1949.*

Mr. Hoover's career illustrates an important aspect of the problem of government on which his commission has just completed its massive report. Mr. Hoover retired from public office seventeen years ago. During those seventeen years of the New Deal and of the war the functions of government expanded enormously, creating that very complexity, confusion and waste which the new Hoover blueprints are designed to cure.

In all that time Mr. Hoover was only an eminent private citizen, an outsider who had no opportunity and no right to take part in preventing the disorders as they were being produced by ill-considered laws and executive orders. He could make complaining speeches and he could issue statements criticizing the work of his successor. But being an outsider, he could not speak with the constructive authority of real knowledge of the crisis in which the government was expanding, and therefore he was discounted as a partisan critic. How much better it would have been if during those seventeen years the ex-President had had as a matter of right a responsible part in the government about which he had learned so much. Then he would have been able to deal with the efficiency of government continuously over seventeen years, not merely in one encyclopedic report which almost no one will ever even read the whole of. . . .

There is an inherent absurdity in the American practice of discarding ex-Presidents, and indeed other high officials, just when by the hardest and surest way they have acquired wisdom in government and public affairs. This absurdity has nothing to do with the Constitution. It is simply a bad habit which can be corrected whenever the American people wake up to the fact that the quality of a government like the quality of an army is maintained by bringing the raw recruits into contact with seasoned troops. The blueprints of reorganization, like the manuals of drill, are useful. But what really counts the most is that those who have fresh energy but are without experience should mix with those who, though they are beginning to be tired, have learned the facts of life.

One ex-President, and so far as I know only one, has shown how unreasonable and unnecessary it is to discard our high officials. John Quincy Adams, after one term, was not only overwhelmingly defeated by Andrew Jackson in the election of 1828, but his party, the Federalist, was split, and Adams found himself repudiated by a large section of it. He retired to his home in Quincy, Massachusetts, where he tried to find something to do by reading books, tending to his farm, and planning to write history. Then about 1830 he was asked to run for Congress. Unlike all other ex-Presidents, and indeed most ex-senators and ex-Cabinet officers, John Quincy Adams did not think it beneath his dignity to become a member of the lower House.

He was elected, and then re-elected eight times, serving, as it happened, for seventeen years. His biographer, W. C. Ford, says that in those seventeen years after his defeat for the presidency "he entered upon years of influence and combat which made his Congressional service unique and quite the most important part of his career. . . . At the time of his election no member had sat in the House who possessed such varied experience and appropriate qualities. He was familiar with the inside political history of forty years abroad and at home."

Why, it is interesting to ask, has no one else followed the example of John Quincy Adams? I can think of only two reasons, which may be aspects of the same underlying reason. It is that men who have had the great dignities of very high office think it beneath them to take a lower office, and in any event beneath them to scratch for votes to get themselves elected to a lower office.

But that could be cured by giving ex-Presidents a seat, without voting rights, in the Senate. And perhaps—if it is not too daring an idea—we could go further and give ex-Cabinet officers, who have served with distinction, a seat without voting rights in the House—let us say on a nomination by the President which was approved by the House.

Somehow or other we must find ways to recognize distinction, to use experience and not to discard it. Until we find ways to do that we shall not only waste good public servants, when they are most fit to serve, but we shall never recruit great talents that are so desperately needed. For the younger men of great talent, seeing what happens to men who take high office, shrink from a government which will so ruthlessly retire them in mid-career—will retire them just when they are prepared to do their best, just when it is too late for them to make a new and different career for themselves.

"The Official and the Partner," Today and Tomorrow, *August 2, 1955. The misuse of the high office of Secretary of the Air Force in the granting of government contracts led Lippmann to ponder the "conflict of interests" problem.*

The mystery of the Talbott case is how he managed to act so foolishly, and the best explanation would seem to be that he has been two men, public official and private promoter, inhabiting the same body. The Secretary of the Air Force and the Mulligan partner have lived and worked side by side in the Pentagon, each more or less uncontrolled by the other. The Secretary did not serve the partner corruptly. But neither did he rule the partner properly.

There is no evidence, I believe, that Mr. Talbott used his power as Secretary of the Air Force to induce or compel defense contractors to give profitable business to the Mulligan firm. There is no evidence, that is to say, that he meant to act corruptly. On the contrary, the evidence, including his own admission of his mistakes, shows that the Secretary was not really aware of what the Mulligan partner was doing. Had he realized it, had he been acting consciously and corruptly, he would have taken the trouble, as a competent villain would, to cover his tracks. The last thing he would have done was what Talbott actually did do, which was to promote his private business from his office in the Pentagon and with the help of Air Force personnel and on Air Force stationery.

There is no obvious explanation of such extraordinary foolishness. There is no doubt that he has been proud and happy to be Secretary of the Air Force, and that he is deeply attached to his high and honorable office. There is no doubt that he is a rich man to whom $60,000 is not important money, and that it could buy him nothing remotely so precious as his public office. There is no doubt, on the other hand, that his Mulligan activities, once they were known, were obviously bound to ruin his public career. There is no doubt, moreover, that his activities will hurt badly the Mulligan firm itself.

The whole performance makes no sense except on the theory that Talbott was two men, and that when the Mulligan partner was in charge of his body, the Secretary of the Air Force was sleeping and unconscious. For no Secretary of the Air Force who was functioning at all could have supposed that it was right to promote from his office in the Pentagon a profitable private business on the fringes of the national defense. In this case the Secretary did not veto the partner's activities. Neither did he hide his activities. So I say that the public official must have been suppressed and asleep.

The question, then, is why the Secretary of the Air Force did not govern the promoter, why he did not enforce the standards of public behavior upon the private business man. There is here a great and persistent ethical question which has been discussed since the days of the Greek moralists. Can a man who knows what is right do wrong—can he knowingly give in to his appetite, say for the Mulligan profits? Socrates held that no one acts against what he knows to be the right—that men act wrongly from ignorance.

But Aristotle disagreed with Socrates, pointing out that a man may do what is wrong if his convictions about what is right are confused and weak, not clear and strong. In this deplorable case we must, I believe, side with Aristotle and say that as compared with the avarice of the Mulligan partner the moral convictions of the Secretary were confused and weak.

It has been pointed out that the Talbott case poses the problem of the workability and the fairness of the old statute about "conflict of interests." There is, of course, such a problem, and it is a very difficult one. But the Talbott case bears only indirectly, in my view, on that problem. For no matter how much the statutes were liberalized, it could never be stretched to the point of tolerating the use of a public office to promote a private business that is closely related to the public business. The law might be revised, for example, to permit a man to keep his old securities, and to receive the dividends. But nobody would suggest that it could be made lawful for him to use the facilities of public office to enhance the value of his securities.

The essence of the problem of "conflict of interests" is that only the most elementary rules can be fixed in the law, that all the rest lies in what Lord Moulton once called "the domain of manners," which includes "all the things that a man should impose upon himself from duty to good taste." It is possible to say in the law that an official must not make a private profit out of his public actions. But it is not possible to set down in the law just how he must decide the more complicated issues where his private interest, though it is involved, cannot be measured in dollars and cents. His moral duty is to decide every question on public grounds alone, regardless of whether this hurts or helps him, his family, his partners, his friends, or his political party. But here, not the law but only an instructed conscience can help him make the decision.

In the case of a high and conspicuous public official, who must not only do his job but cannot help setting an example, the sovereign rule is never to give his private interests the benefit of any doubt. Talbott seems not to have understood that rule. . . .

The wider problems of the conflict of interests need to be re-examined and reconsidered. There is a complicated cluster of problems. One of them, though only one, arises from the fact that for many business executives the holding of a public office is not a new career but an interlude in their normal careers. The question is whether a temporary public servant can be expected, or should be required, to reorganize his private affairs as if he were a federal judge or a foreign security officer or a civil servant in a lifetime career. Many men refuse the temporary public assignment because they are unwilling to make the big personal sacrifice which the existing rules now demand. And, on the other hand, in so far as the temporary officials are intending to return to their old business, can it truly be said that there is not, in the intent of the statute, a conflict of interests?

We must, I think, ask ourselves whether, except in the emergency of war, it is good public policy to rely so much on temporary officials. For myself I do not think it is. For no matter how able the business executive, it will take him a long time to learn the public business. The Pentagon has seen a continuing stream of civilian officials, coming in with no knowledge of the Pentagon and going out just about when they have acquired some knowledge. Does not the public business of national defense require civilian as well as military officers who make the national defense the work of their lives?

Sometimes I wonder whether the President is not mistaken in thinking that a trained private executive and a trained public official are interchangeable. For instead of building up a corps of high career officials, he seems to be trying to get along with men borrowed temporarily from the official hierarchy of the private corporations.

"The McElroy Affair," Today and Tomorrow, *March 3, 1959.*

The news that Secretary McElroy may be resigning in a few months raises a serious question about the prevailing standards of public service.

It appears that when the President approached Mr. McElroy about appointing him to what is surely one of the most difficult and most responsible offices in the government, they came to an understanding that Mr. McElroy might serve for a very limited period only. The reason for this seems to have been that Mr. McElroy could take only so much leave of absence from his business without sacrificing certain financial benefits for which he is eligible.

When we remember that what is at stake is the office of Secretary of Defense, it is necessary to ask whether Mr. McElroy should have laid down, or that the President should have agreed to, the conditions under which his appointment was made.

For this limited period of service was just about long enough to enable Mr. McElroy to begin to learn to be Secretary of Defense. He is a bright and intelligent man, but when he took office he had had no background of experience in the military establishment and no important experience in public life.

The Defense Department is an enormously complex organization, and the great issues on which the Secretary must pass are highly technical ones in the field of strategy, tactics, engineering, production, and research. Moreover, the Secretary of Defense is the key man in the relations between the armed services and the Congress.

Eighteen months are perhaps enough for a reasonably good introduction to the work of the office. But as Mr. McElroy's recent testimony before the Congressional committee showed, while he has learned many lessons, yet he is far from having mastered the job.

Now, with the problem of American armed power at the center of the world situation, Mr. McElroy is looking forward to leaving in order to go back home and make more money. A successor must be found who can then look forward to about eighteen months in office before he goes home. Mr. McElroy expects to leave the job just as he is about ready to do it. His successor, if he comes from the outside, may be able to learn about the job just as the time comes for him to leave the job; if his successor is promoted from within the Department of Defense, he is more likely than not to be a caretaker and not much more.

All this adds up to the fact that with so much at stake a very serious office has not been treated seriously enough. This is against the national interest, which requires a highly competent Secretary of Defense, and it is a bad example of how the public service should be valued by our people.

Broadly speaking, there are two kinds of opinion as to how the highest offices of the government should be recruited. There are those who believe that for the most part—although there are exceptions to all such rules—the big offices can be filled most successfully by men who have made a success in private business. The theory here is that there is no great difference between public and private life, and that experience in business is not really different from experience in government. With the conspicuous exception of Secretary Dulles, who has combined a lifetime of public service with a highly successful law practice, President Eisenhower has shown a predilection for successful corporate executives.

The other school of opinion holds that the public service is in itself a vocation and a professional career and that it cannot be treated, like Sunday painting or Sunday golf, as an interlude for amateurs. Those who think this way regard it as a fundamental fallacy to suppose that success in corporate business is preparation for success in the public business. They believe that, on the whole, it is better to fill the higher offices with men whose main work in life has been in politics and the public service.

Those of us who take this view believe that public service is a profession and an art which must be acquired by long experience in public life. For the art of governing men is a great art itself—perhaps the greatest, as it surely is the most momentous, of all the arts, and a lifetime is not too long a time in which to learn it.

"Something Off My Chest," Today and Tomorrow, *March 14, 1942.*

If there is any one who thinks the government's publicity is successful, I have not happened to meet him. Indeed, it is fair to say that, far from earning public confidence, the elaborate and costly publicity offices are managing to get themselves disliked and distrusted. I venture to believe that the rapidly mounting irritation with the public-relations experts is due to the fact that they operate on a theory which is inherently insincere, and that, as the temper of the people hardens because they face the issues of life and death, they find this insincerity more and more repellent.

The profession of publicity experts is a new one. Its forerunners were, I suppose, P. T. Barnum and the theatrical press agents of our age of innocence. But in its modern, serious, respectable, elaborately organized, and "scientific" form, the profession of publicity expert has developed in the last thirty-odd years. He "sells" ideas, and unfortunately he has succeeded in selling the idea to public men that they can hire publicity experts to sell them and their actions to the public. I call this conception of publicity inherently insincere because it assumes that the public aspect of a person can be fabricated by men who have specialized in the art of manipulating public opinion. Along with so many other things that were shoddy, this notion of public relations flourished in that interval between the two wars when the people were unwilling to face the first and last things of human existence.

This notion is now being burned up in the fires of war. For when free men and women stake their lives, their fortunes, and their dearest hopes in their country's cause they will not stomach a fabricated, manipulated, synthetic public mask covering the faces of their leaders.

The core of the matter can best be examined by considering the employment of professional writers to prepare speeches for high officials to deliver. No one is concerned about the men who prepare information from government departments in a convenient form for publication. The real question arises only when they prepare important addresses in which the people are supposed to hear directly from a responsible leader what he thinks and why he does what he does.

Therefore, to be specific and quite frank, because the leadership of the President himself is involved, let us consider the extraordinary and, to my old-fashioned mind, the astounding thing that now happens when the announcement is made that the President will deliver an important address. The papers report that a number of professional writers, men not responsible for shaping or carrying out the policies he will discuss, are gathering at the White House to write the words which the President will utter.

It will be said that all Presidents, and indeed all public men, are assisted by others in preparing their addresses. That is true. And it is entirely necessary and proper. But there is this great difference between the new procedure at the White House and that which was employed by Mr. Roosevelt himself in the earlier days, in the days of the brain trust. Whatever one may think of the brain trust, they were a group of men actively and continually at work in the shaping of policy. They were not a group of ghost writers lacking first-hand knowledge of, and personal responsibility for, the things they helped the President put into words. And that, I am profoundly convinced, is a principal reason why the earlier speeches of the President were less rhetorical but far more effective, having then—what in recent times they have lacked—the feeling of action rather than of literary comment and special pleading.

The address of a President should be an event and not a lecture or a public reading, and the decision about when he should speak and what needs saying can be wisely made, not by supposed experts on public opinion, but only by men participating in the action he is going to talk about. There is all the difference in the world between being assisted by his official family and being assisted by ghost writers. The artists who now help the President with his speeches ought to be the first to understand this, that authentic words are not like a coat of paint sprayed on a building that someone else has built. "The style is the man himself." The style of the President's recent speeches has been the style of men brought in from the outside who know only by hearsay, not by their own acts, what the government is doing. It does not require training as a literary critic for the people to feel this and to be put off by it. There is in most men, as indeed in children, and even in animals, an instinctive sense of the real and the phony when they are spoken to.

The vice of the new publicity expert and ghost-writer system in public life is that it proceeds to create a synthetic public man in front of the actual public man. And since the public is increasingly aware of this system and of how it operates, the system destroys the bonds of confidence between leaders and the people. The actual man is no longer face to face with the people. He wears a disguise which has been contrived for him. This masquerade will not work in serious times among a free people, who are curious, inquisitive, and quickly repelled if they feel they are being fooled.

A public man can and needs to be supplied with material and advice and criticism in preparing an important address. But no one can write an authentic speech for another man; it is as impossible as writing his love letters for him or saying his prayers for him. When he speaks to the people, he and not someone else must speak. For it is much more important that he could be genuine, and it is infinitely more persuasive, than that he be bright, clever, ingenious, entertaining, eloquent, or even grammatical. It is, moreover, a delusion, fostered into an inferiority complex among executives by professional writers, that in an age of specialists some are called to act and some are called to find the right words for men of action to use. The truth is that anyone who knows what he is doing can say what he is doing, and anyone who knows what he thinks can say what he thinks. Those who cannot speak for themselves are, with very rare exceptions, not very sure of what they are doing and of what they mean. The sooner they are found out the better.

VIII

The Role of Government

1 · *The Possibilities of the State*

A Preface to Politics (1913), *Chapters 8 and 9.*

It is perfectly true that that government is best which governs least. It is equally true that that government is best which provides most. The first truth belongs to the eighteenth century; the second to the twentieth. Neither of them can be neglected in our attitude toward the state. Without the Jeffersonian distrust of the police we might easily grow into an impertinent and tyrannous collectivism; without a vivid sense of the possibilities of the state we abandon the supreme instrument of civilization. The two theories need to be held together, yet clearly distinguished.

Government has been an exalted policeman; it was there to guard property and to prevent us from quarreling too violently. That was about all it was good for. Yet society found problems on its hands—problems which Woodrow Wilson calls moral and social in their nature. Vice and crime, disease, and grinding poverty forced themselves on the attention of the community. A typical example is the way the social evil compelled the city of Chicago to begin an investigation. Yet when government was asked to handle the question, it had for wisdom an ancient conception of itself as a policeman. Its only method was to forbid, to prosecute, to jail—in short, to use the taboo. But experience has shown that the taboo will not solve "moral and social questions"—that nine times out of ten it aggravates the disease. Political action becomes a petty, futile, mean little intrusion when its only method is prosecution.

No wonder then that conservatively-minded men pray that moral and social questions be kept out of politics; no wonder that more daring souls begin to hate the whole idea of government and take to anarchism. So long as the state is conceived merely as an agent of repression, the less it interferes with our lives, the better. Much of the horror of socialism comes from a belief that by increasing the functions of government its regulating power over our daily lives will grow into a tyranny. I share this horror when certain Socialists begin to propound their schemes. There is a dreadful amount of forcible scrubbing and arranging and pocketing implied in some socialisms. There is a wish to have the state use its position as general employer to become a censor of morals and arbiter of elegance, like the benevolent employers of the day who take an impertinent interest in the private lives of their workers. Without any doubt socialism has within it the germs of that great bureaucratic tyranny which Chesterton and Belloc have named the Servile State.

So it is a wise instinct that makes men jealous of the policeman's power. Far better we may say that moral and social problems be left to private solution than that they be subjected to the clumsy method of the taboo. When Woodrow Wilson argues that social problems are not susceptible to treatment in a party program, he must mean only one thing: that they cannot be handled by the state as he conceives it. He is right. His attitude is far better than that of the Vice Commission; it, too, had only a policeman's view of government, but it proceeded to apply it to problems that are not susceptible to such treatment. Wilson, at least, knows the limitations of his philosophy.

But once you see the state as a provider of civilizing opportunities, his whole objection collapses. As soon as government begins to supply services, it is turning away from the sterile tyranny of the taboo. The provision of schools, streets, plumbing, highways, libraries, parks, universities, medical attention, post offices, a Panama Canal, agricultural information, fire protection—is a use of government totally different from the ideal of Jefferson. To furnish these opportunities is to add to the resources of life, and only a doctrinaire adherence to a misunderstood ideal will raise any objection to them. . . .

Confronted with a novelty, the first impulse is to snub it, and send it into exile. When it becomes too persistent to be ignored, a taboo is erected and threats of fines and condign punishment are made if it doesn't cease to appear. This is the level of culture at which Sherman Anti-Trust acts are passed, brothels are raided, and labor agitators are thrown into jail. If the taboo is effective it drives the evil under cover, where it festers and emits a slow poison. This is the price we pay for the appearance of suppression. But if the problem is more heavily charged with power, the taboo irritates the force until it explodes. Not infrequently, what was once simply a factor of life becomes the dominating part of it. At this point the whole routineer scheme of things collapses, there is a period of convulsion and Cæsarean births, and men weary of excitement sink back into a newer routine. Thus the cycle of futility is completed.

The process bears as much resemblance to statecraft as sitting backward on a runaway horse does to horsemanship. The ordinary politician has no real control, no direction, no insight into the power he rides. What he has is an elevated, though temporary, seat. Real statesmanship has a different ambition. It begins by accepting human nature. No routine has ever done that in spite of the conservative patter about "human nature"; mechanical politics has usually begun by ignoring and ended by violating the nature of men.

To accept that nature does not mean that we accept its present character. It is probably true that the impulses of men have changed very little within recorded history. What has changed enormously from epoch to epoch is the character in which these impulses appear. The impulses that at one period work themselves out into cruelty and lust may at another produce the richest values of civilized life. The statesman can affect that choice. His business is to provide fine opportunities for the expression of human impulses—to surround childhood, youth, and age with homes and schools, cities and countryside that shall be stocked with interest and the chance for generous activity.

Government can play a leading part in this work, for with

the decadence of the church it has become the only truly catholic organization in the land. Its task is essentially to carry out programs of service, to add and build and increase the facilities of life.

"Law and Order," Metropolitan, *XLII* (*August 1915*), 32.

Our statute books are cluttered with legislation that represents somebody's good intention, rather than a real insight into what is possible. And these laws cannot be enforced in a country where the sense of democracy is strong. The law to be more than a sham must represent the real desire or obtain the consent of the biggest portion of the community. It does no good to legislate a morality which only the angels practice; it does only harm to pass bills which run counter to the deepest tendencies of the age. Yet many of our laws about sex and about business are so utterly unrelated to the ordinary lives of the American people that breaking the law is almost a national habit.

This lawlessness will continue until we make up our minds that legislation in a democracy is, first of all, a series of common rules which enables us to live together without too much friction; then, that law is a way of spending money for our cities and countryside so that we shall all have a better chance to live. Law is not a method of making us perfect. Perfection cannot be legislated at Albany or Washington. Neither is it a method of protecting property in the hands of people who happen to have it. Nor is it a method of strangling everything that is new, and of putting a damper on all aspirations. In order to be effective, law in a democracy must be elastic, not brittle; it must be capable of changing and adapting itself to growth; it must set no impossible ideals; it must be satisfied at any particular moment with the best that is possible under the circumstances. So far as morals go, the law is concerned with the minimum. It sets the standard below which civilization should not sink, but it cannot pretend to say how the best of men should live.

"The Underworld," Today and Tomorrow, *April 1, 1932. Contemplation of the problem of organized crime evoked these observations on the reach of the law.*

We may quite pertinently ask ourselves what there is in our national life which paralyzes our efforts to deal with this problem. We cannot expect, I think, that a nation of pioneers and immigrants, who have lost touch with the established habits of the past and are still restless and unsettled in their constantly changing environment, should have attained the degree of order and discipline that exists among some of the older nations of the West. But we might reasonably hope that we would not sink into a defeatist attitude before the barbarism in our midst. There must be some reason why we are so continually frustrated when we seek to arouse ourselves into action.

My own notion is that we are constantly frustrated by two traditions which we deeply cherish.

The first is our almost instinctive belief that the laws must represent not merely a reasonable adjustment of human interests but what the majority of the voters regard as the highest and noblest ideals. Thus American lawmaking makes no concession to the weakness of human nature. Our laws are written by men who have pleased their constituents by writing into law innumerable declarations of moral faith, and taken as a body the American statute books are an encyclopedia of moral perfection. They outlaw not only all crimes and frauds but also all the vices and peccadillos and impure thoughts of man.

So thoroughly imbued are the American people with the idea that the law must express moral perfection that a proposal to modify prohibition is widely regarded as propaganda for drunkenness, a proposal to modify the laws against other sins is regarded as an invitation to a carnival of licentiousness. As a result, the American people have insisted upon outlawing human propensities in which they rather generally indulge. They have pushed into the underworld activities which in all other civilized countries are regulated by custom and law. And by their moral fervor as lawmakers they have made a large part of the people allies and clients of lawbreakers.

But not only do the American people insist that the written law shall be uncompromising with unrighteousness; they insist at the same time that the government which executes these laws shall be weak. The same voters and the same lawmakers who enact laws that no despotism has ever been able to enforce are jealous to the point of absurdity at intrusting the Executive and Judiciary with power. It is fair to say, I think, that we have the strongest laws and the weakest government of any highly civilized people. Nowhere else, I think, are the police of a great city like New York under the control of politicians who are locally elected. Nowhere else, I think, are judges so tied to fluctuating political majorities and nowhere else are they so ignominiously entangled with legislative rules.

The American distrust of the Executive and of the Judiciary, which expresses itself in a refusal to give them authority and dignity, is, I suppose, an inheritance from the struggle of the colonies against the crown. Whatever its origin, there can be little doubt that Americans unconsciously think that the preservation of their liberty is bound up with the weakness of the Executive and the Judiciary.

These two ingredients of our national mind account in large measure, I think, for the rise of the underworld and for our impotence in combating it. By passing excessive laws we put a premium on lawlessness; by refusing power to the government we stultify the execution of the laws. These, too, are the reasons why our efforts at reform expire so quickly. Any reform that amounts to anything requires modification of laws which embody exorbitant moral aspirations and a grant of power which must look like an infringement of liberty.

The American people are as yet unprepared to give up their right to have laws which express their faith in moral perfection. They are unprepared to establish governments which have authority and power if that means giving up a measure of liberty and democracy. But until they are prepared to alter their basic prepossessions in these respects they will continue to have majestic laws and immense lawlessness.

"Lawlessness," Today and Tomorrow, *December 5, 1933.*

Today there comes to an end the attempt to impose upon a whole people an absolute rule of personal conduct. The authors of the Eighteenth Amendment had seen the evils that alcohol can produce. They knew about the drunkard who ruins himself and brings disaster to his family. They knew how the efforts to regulate the liquor industry in the interest of temperance had corrupted public life. They concluded that an appetite which had caused so much misery should be suppressed, that a trade which had caused so much dishonesty should be outlawed.

What they overlooked was the conscience of the great mass of people who did not drink immoderately and had no part in the political corruption. These were the men and women who resisted prohibition and defeated it. They refused to give up a pleasure which did them no harm in order to save the drunkards who abused it. They resented a rule of conduct which treated everyone as if he were an instinctive drunkard. So they rebelled. The law was at odds not only with their appetites but with their consciences. They made prohibition unenforceable. They encouraged the bootlegger and the speakeasy by patronizing them. They nullified enforcement by discrediting it.

In the course of time all the evils which had led to prohibition were flourishing under prohibition, and in addition a monstrous hypocrisy and corruption peculiar to it. Sometime within the past two years the demonstration had convinced the people that the Eighteenth Amendment could not and should not be enforced, that not to repeal it and not to enforce it was intolerable.

The Eighteenth Amendment will long be remembered as a conspicuous example of a law that produced lawlessness because it traversed the working conscience of the great mass of the people. This generation of Americans, at least, has learned from it a more certain feeling for the truth that legislation, however noble in purpose, cannot effectively become the law unless its purpose is the actual purpose of the great mass of a community. Our forefathers would have said that the law must conform to the will of the people, and by that phrase they would have meant the abiding will, not the momentary opinion or the excited whim which propaganda or demagoguery or a spectacular event may arouse. They would have meant the will of the people which is founded in habits, needs, and experiences that change so slowly that for the practical purpose of the moment they are unchanging. To that will all laws and all reforms and all schemes must in the long run conform. . . .

The struggle against lawlessness is the struggle for civilization itself. It is the herculean effort to bring under control the persistently primitive nature of men, their greed and lust and animal violence, so that their energies shall not destroy them.

The laws can perhaps do only what is most temporary and expedient for the moment; religion and education and morals are the radical forces, since they seek to transmute and regenerate rather than to regulate and police the energies of men, to make them inwardly civilized rather than to restrain them from without. The civilizing effort as a whole has therefore no one method on which it can rely exclusively. It is like the effort to subdue the fierce rebellion of the great waters of the Mississippi. No one device will work along the whole course; at this point there must be dikes, at that one a new channel, at another a reservoir, and on the slopes where the headwaters gather it is necessary to plant trees with faith and understanding, and sow the earth with seeds that the ground may be made firm.

"America Must Grow," The Saturday Evening Post, *CCXXXIII (November 5, 1960)*, 36.

To those who say that the government cannot affect growth, the answer is that it can and that it does. Thus it can promote growth by varying taxes, the tightness of money and its spending, so as to keep total private, plus public, spending in balance with capacity.

It can promote growth by altering taxes to bear more on consumption and less on saving, by permitting rapid amortization and by making money cheaper, so as to shift the composition of spending in favor of private investment and against private consumption.

It can promote growth by using taxes to release resources for public investment. Spending on roads and laboratories, on airports and on urban transport, all add to the productive capacity of the economy.

It can promote growth, at least in the longer run, by supporting research, improving the quality of education, and promoting public health.

It can promote growth by a number of indirect measures. It can make it easier for people to change jobs and move from areas of labor surplus. It can disseminate information about high-productivity techniques. It can campaign against the more serious rigidities in big business and big labor. It can rationalize its own agricultural program. It can reduce tariffs and allow foreign competition to encourage greater efficiency.

The capacity of the government to promote growth cannot be disputed. The truth is that government cannot be neutral even if it wants to be. By the way it makes use of its traditional instruments of policy, it will inevitably affect growth. Those of us who believe that we must speed up growth are proposing that in making its decisions about taxes and spending, tariffs and interest rates, the government should take into account their effect on growth and exploit its own power for stimulating growth.

2 · *The Method of Freedom*

The Method of Freedom (*1934*), *Part 2.*

It is often assumed in current discussion that all the nations must make an exclusive choice between the old theoretically neutral state on the one hand and some form of absolute collectivism and a directed economy on the other. The militant partisans have done their best to narrow the choice to these alternatives. Yet there exists a radically different method which is actually in use in most of the free countries. It does not as yet have a spectacular name, a great dialectical apparatus, a magniloquent philosophy, perfervid oratory, or mass emotion. But it is the method of those people who have had the largest experience in the art of self-government and the conduct of modern economic enterprise. That gives the method great authority, and the time has come, I believe, to recognize that there has appeared, principally among the English-speaking peoples, a method of social control which is not *laissez faire*, which is not communism, which is not fascism, but the product of their own experience and their own genius.

I shall call it the method of free collectivism. It is collectivist because it acknowledges the obligation of the state for the standard of life and the operation of the economic order *as a whole*. It is free because it preserves within very wide limits the liberty of private transactions. Its object is not to direct individual enterprise and choice according to an official plan but to put them and keep them in a working equilibrium. Its method is to redress the balance of private actions by compensating public actions.

The system of free collectivism originates not in military necessity but in an effort to correct the abuses and overcome the disorders of capitalism. In the first instance it takes the form of measures which set limits within which private initiative is confined and fix standards to which it must conform. This part of the system has a long history and is well understood. It is based upon a recognition of the fact that initiative may be evil as well as good, and that it is the duty of the state to encourage initiative when it is socially beneficent and to discourage it when it is not.

Thus it comprises measures to prevent fraud as between buyers and sellers: honest weights and measures, the enforcement of equitable contracts, the suppression of counterfeiting, and the misrepresentation of goods. It comprises measures to equalize the bargaining power of the consumer and of the employee: the regulation of public utilities, factory laws, and minimum wage laws. It comprises measures to break up monopolies, to discourage harmful enterprises, to prevent nuisances, to retrict speculation, to repress a too rampant individualism in the use of property. It comprises measures to insure the weak against the hazards of existence and to restrain the strong from accumulating excessive wealth and power.

The body of laws which regulates enterprise is enormous, and however foolish or unworkable some of these laws may be, no one imagines that all these laws are unnecessary. In fact, there is every reason to think that if a regime of free transactions is to be preserved, even more searching and comprehensive standards will have to be set for it. It is more than likely, for example, that secrecy in corporate accounting will have to be abolished, that all large enterprises will have to submit to publicly instituted systems of bookkeeping, and that their whole financial structure will become as visible as that of a railroad or a municipal corporation. For it is only by making publicly available to everyone the whole position of these enterprises that the relations of capital and labor, of corporation and investor, of industry and consumer can be lifted to a plane where transactions are really free because all the relevant facts are known. To preserve the reality of free contract it will almost surely be necessary to abolish the sham freedom of corporate secrecy.

But all of this does not go to the heart of the matter. It can prevent abuses. It does not reach the vital defect of individualism, which is that the multitude of individual decisions is not sufficiently enlightened to keep the economy *as a whole* in working order. Regulation is essentially negative. In the main it merely forbids this or that. But it is not possible to prohibit by laws the cumulative errors which produce the cycles of boom and depression. The state cannot make laws against the excessive optimism of prosperity or the panic pessimism of the ensuing crash. Yet it is in this cycle that the supreme danger arises. For the social order has now become so intricate that any serious breakdown in its economy will unloose forces that may destroy it.

Not only is it impossible to control the rhythm of capitalism by regulating laws but the very attempt to do it is as likely as not to accentuate the violence of the maladjustment. The experience of the postwar years has shown with great conclusiveness that the effort to control depression at some particular point, say, at the price of wheat, or at the price of gold, or at the wage rate in some sheltered industry, or at a threatened bank or railroad—merely makes a part of the economy rigid and forces the rest of it to bend all the more.

The postwar economic cycle demonstrated clearly that individual decisions were not sufficient to create a lasting prosperity and that individuals could not endure the remedy of individual readjustment. The classical theorists overestimated the enlightenment which is based on self-interest and the fortitude based upon self-reliance. The event has shown that the individual judgment upon which they relied exclusively has in the crucial cases meant that the individual followed the crowd. Imitation, the herd instinct, the contagion of numbers, fashions, moods, rather than a truly enlightened self-interest, have tended to govern the economy.

This submerging of individualism in mass behavior is the consequence of the increasing complexity of the economic order. The data for a "sound" judgment are not any longer available to most men. For an integral part of every judgment is now a speculation on what other speculators will do. Take, for example, a banker who makes a loan to a reliable individual for a useful project on ample security at existing values. By every conventional rule it is a sound loan. Yet it may be a bad loan for no other reason than that too many bankers have made too many equally sound loans to too many reliable individuals for too many similar projects. The algebraic sum of a great number of reputable transactions may easily prove to be a disaster for all. We have seen this illustrated again and again in recent years. We have seen it in another phase of the cycle, when the individual decision to call a loan and make himself liquid becomes a collective disaster if the whole mass of individuals is stricken with prudence at the same time.

It follows that if individuals are to continue to decide when they will buy and sell, spend and save, borrow and lend, expand and contract their enterprises, some kind of compensatory mechanism to redress their liability to error must be set up by public authority. It has become necessary to create collective power, to mobilize collective resources, and to work out technical procedures by means of which the modern state can balance, equalize, neutralize, offset, correct the private judgments of masses of individuals. This is what I mean by a Compensated Economy and the method of Free Collectivism. . . .

To anyone steeped in the tradition of *laissez faire* there may at first appear to be little difference between a directed economy and a compensated economy. Both call for the exercise of vast powers by the state, for continual and deep intervention in the economic order. Both are collectivist in that both rest on a recognition that the standard of life and the management of the economy as a whole are a collective responsibility and not solely an individual one.

Yet between the two conceptions there is a radical difference. Under absolute collectivism, be it of the Fascist or Communist type, the government is in fact the master, the citizen a subject and a servant. Under free collectivism, the government in its economic activities is in effect a gigantic public corporation which stands ready to throw its weight into the scales wherever and whenever it is necessary to redress the balance of private transactions. The initiative, throughout the whole realm of production and consumption, excepting only public utilities and public works reserved as instruments of compensatory control, remains in individual hands.

This initiative is subjected not to an official plan and to administrative orders, but to the play of prices representing the judgments and preferences of producers, consumers, and investors. Within extremely wide limits, enterprise is free. Men decide for themselves, guided chiefly by their estimates of the profits they may obtain, what they will produce; guided chiefly by the opportunities available and their own aptitudes, they decide at what they will work; guided by their needs and tastes in relation to their incomes, they decide what they will consume and how much they will save.

These choices are not made for them by officials exercising the power of the state. Thus economic progress is determined by technological advance, by private enterprise, and by what might be described as the perpetual plebiscite of the markets. The object of the state's intervention is not to supplant this system but to preserve it by remedying its abuses and correcting its errors. The intervention takes the form not of commands and prohibitions but of compensatory measures.

The purpose of the intervention is not to impose an official pattern upon all enterprise, but to maintain a working, moving equilibrium in the complex of private transactions. In substance, the state undertakes to counteract the mass errors of the individualist crowd by doing the opposite of what the crowd is doing; it saves when the crowd is spending too much; it borrows when the crowd is saving too much; it economizes when the crowd is extravagant, and it spends when the crowd is afraid to spend; it contracts when the crowd is expansive; it becomes enterprising when the crowd is depressed; it buys in sellers' markets and sells in buyers' markets; it taxes when the crowd is borrowing, and borrows when the crowd is hoarding; it becomes an employer when there is private unemployment, and it shuts down when there is work for all. Its ideal is to prevent excess; its general principle is not to impose a social order conceived by officials but to maintain in a changing order, worked out by the initiative and energy of individuals, a golden mean.

In the practice of statesmanship the compensatory method is, I believe, an epoch-making invention. For generations it has been supposed that an exclusive choice had to be made between collectivism and the freedom of private initiative, that the management of affairs had either to be left to individuals or assumed by the state. Whichever way one looked at these alternatives, the prospect was unsatisfactory. To concentrate initiative in officials was a certain way to kill initiative and liberty and to establish a state which in the ordinary course of events was bound to be despotic and inefficient. On the other hand, to let individualism run loose in a complex social order was to let it run wild and thus to produce disorder and injustice.

This dilemma is being resolved not by the arguments of collectivists and individualists but by the gradual uncovering of a new social principle. It provides both for individual initiative and collective initiative. The one is not the substitute for the other. The two are complementary. It is the method of freedom. The authority of the government is used to assist men in maintaining the security of an ordered life. The state, though it is powerful, is not the master of the people, but remains, as it must where they have liberty, their servant.

The New Imperative (*1935*), *Chapters 1 and 3.*

It has, I think, been clearly established that government must henceforth hold itself consciously responsible for the maintenance of the standard of life prevailing among the people. This is, I believe, a new imperative which takes its place alongside the older imperatives to defend the nation against attack and to preserve domestic peace. If this is true, it is important. If it is true, it is desirable to grasp it as a general idea apart from the bewildering details of the particular measures in which for the moment it happens to be embodied. Thus, for example, opinions differ about the immediate objectives of foreign policy and even more about such instruments of policy as treaties, battleships, cruisers and submarines. But all debate about these matters starts from the common premise that it is a duty of government to defend the safety of the nation. In respect to domestic peace there is no dispute that government must maintain law and order however much men may differ about particular laws or about how to organize the police and the judiciary. But in this new and unexplored realm the basic idea has not yet been accepted into the tradition of government. It is entangled with superficial differences about highly debatable particular measures. Yet experience in the postwar era has shown, I am convinced, that the ability to protect the popular standard of life is an indispensable condition of the survival of political institutions. . . .

It has been said that to place upon government responsibility for the defense of the popular standard of life is to ask of it more than it can do; the rulers of men are not wise enough or brave enough or disinterested enough to fulfill this new imperative. That may be. My thesis is that they have to attempt it whether or not they succeed. We have on the one hand an economic order incapable of maintaining itself by individual adjustments alone; we have on the other hand the political power of the masses of the people. When an intricate capitalism is combined with popular sovereignty the people will turn to the state for help whenever capitalism is unable to satisfy their habitual expectations. The skeptics may be right in saying that no government can satisfy those expectations. But the democracy will not believe them and it will follow leaders who at least promise to try.

A clear and unprejudiced view of this new imperative is rendered difficult because it is, for the moment, fashionable to think of all political change in terms of ideas borrowed from the revolutions of central and eastern Europe. If this meant only that every innovation was met by an outcry about bolshevism, and every resistance by an outcry about fascism, it might be said that this habit of thought was unimportant. There will always be many whose minds come to rest in a slogan, and if they did not have the phrases about bolshevism and fascism to draw upon, they would find others, no less irrational, in which to vent their prejudices. But the spell cast by the European revolutions is wider than that. To a very high degree the whole discussion of current American events is imprisoned within these same stereotypes.

They are used as criteria of ideas, proposals, and measures, as yardsticks to determine whether the direction of policy is an advance toward, or a retreat from, the Communist or the Fascist scheme of things. It is assumed, as if it were axiomatic and self-evident, that social change in all countries, the United States among them, is in the direction of communism or of fascism, and that there is no other direction in which it is possible to go. The underlying assumption is that there is one highway for mankind and that on that highway the United States can stand still, it can move forward to Moscow, or it can move backward to Berlin. . . . Theoretically, of course, it is conceivable that in Russia, Germany, and Italy we can see the prototypes of our struggles and the anticipation of our destiny. But there is no reason why we should accept the notion as self-evident.

It takes for granted something which is extremely improbable, namely, that nations which have had different histories will henceforth have the same future, that dissimilar causes will produce similar results. Many theorists in the nineteenth century, notably Karl Marx, did suppose that there was one historical pattern which governed the evolution of all societies. But this theory cannot, except by torturing the evidence, be reconciled with the history of the nations of the Western world, much less with the history of all the peoples of the earth. . . .

The basic question is not whether we ought to have state socialism, regimentation, inflation, or a flexible and competitive economy. It is whether we can have any coherent and working economy by having no conscious policy, allowing those who are strong to escape automatism in their own efforts and to subject others to its intensified consequences. The truth is that in the modern state even a policy of *laissez faire* would have to be deliberately administered, the free play of supply and demand would have to be deliberately maintained. This would be my own deepest preference. I should rather have economic liberty than centralized direction and command. But if we are to have economic liberty we must accept the ancient truth that liberty is not the natural state of man, but the achievement of an organized society. Liberty is a right which only vigilant and wise governments can provide. It is the artificial product of civilized effort and is lost almost instantly when the primitive passions of men are unleashed.

The association between liberty and the absence of purpose in government is merely a temporary coincidence due to the fact that in the nineteenth century the English-speaking peoples had an open frontier in America and a head start in the export of manufactures from England. The coincidence will not be repeated in this century. We have to govern the great interests of the commonwealth or we perish. We have to govern them or we lose our liberties. We have to teach young men to govern them or we shall not teach the young men their inescapable duty. But we cannot begin until we have said farewell to the assumption that Utopia is in the old American frontier and in the Lancashire of Cobden. We cannot begin until we have renounced the illusion that in a world of highly organized national states, with gigantic corporate organizations within those states, the vital interests of the whole economy will be automatically self-regulating. We shall be utterly confused, we shall mumble and fumble when the young men examine us, we shall be defensive and impotent and without moral authority until we reconcile our philosophy with our practice.

The issue of automatism as against governing is obsolete. The real issue is not whether the major interests of the commonwealth shall be matters of conscious policy. It is what the policy shall be and by what means it shall be applied. I am not pleading that we indoctrinate young men with a belief that all social arrangements should be planned and directed by highly centralized government. Far from it. On that question I shall be in the ranks with those who think no government is wise enough or good enough to be trusted with so much power, with those who will fight as best they can for the utmost that is possible in decentralization and in voluntary agreement. But it is precisely because this great issue of the omnivorous state confronts us that it is so urgent to rid ourselves of the fictitious and distracting issues raised by the automatists with their program of know-nothing and do-nothing. . . .

If we are not to be swallowed by an imperious state socialism in some one of its many possible forms, then we have to govern successfully this capitalist democracy. Ungoverned, it will not drift through stormy seas into safe harbors. Those who say that it cannot be governed without sacrificing personal liberties to the authority of the state are in effect saying that our civilization is doomed. I do not believe them. They have never given the problem their undivided attention. They cannot see the way because they have not the will. They are like the men who once thought it sacrilegious to examine the constitution of the universe. Like those men they are able to learn little about the constitution of the universe. For the progress of scientific knowledge is the work of men who have believed that it was noble to seek for truth and possible to find it.

So it is with those who believe in the fatalism of human affairs and the impossibility of human intervention. It is imperative that we find a true balance between liberty and authority in the modern state. The fatalists do not find it today because they are not looking for it. They are afraid to look. They think it disreputable to look. They would like nobody to look. The only result of this obscurantism is to inhibit the minds of men from seizing and working upon a problem which historic necessity compels them to face.

We must answer the question that young men put to us. We must tell them that they will have to manage the social order. We must call them to the study, not warn them away from it, of how to achieve the healthy balance of a well-ordered commonwealth. We must call them to the task of preserving the integrity of our civilization as against proletarianism and plutocracy and the fatal diseases of concentrated power and concentrated wealth. We must call them to the defense of freedom, now imperiled throughout the world, by showing them not only its value but the method of its defense. We must dedicate them by rededicating ourselves to the promise of American life which is that men can govern a state in order to enlarge and to preserve the rights of men.

The Good Society (*1937*), *Chapter 9.*

Obviously, it is the duty of a liberal society to see that its markets are efficient and honest. But under the *laissez-faire* delusion it was supposed that good markets would somehow organize themselves or, at any rate, that the markets are as good as they might be. That is not true. The improvement of the markets must be a subject of continual study in a liberal society. It is a vast field of necessary reform. In its first phase it is merely the elaboration of a principle universally accepted from earliest times, that it is the function of government to see that weights and measures are honest. Applied to the complexities of the modern exchange economy, where goods are made by technical processes which only experts understand, the principle of honest weights and measures must mean a drastic modification of the old rule, *caveat emptor*. The buyer is no longer able to judge the technological honesty of the goods he is offered in the market. He does not know whether they are what they are advertised to be. So it becomes necessary to make the seller liable for an untruthful presentation of his wares, to make it unlawful to sell harmful products, to stipulate that only goods of the same quality shall bear the same label, to provide the purchaser with effective means of finding out whether he is getting the best that can be had for the money.

Along with measures to make the markets genuine it is necessary to take steps to reduce the evil of necessitous bargaining. Thus a liberal state cannot be neutral as between those who have too little bargaining power and those who have too much power. It must, by its own principles, encourage and protect the co-operative organization of producers, such as farmers and workingmen, who must sell at once, and at any price offered, and in ignorance of the true supply and demand if they bargain individually. Just as the state, by granting the privilege of incorporation with limited liability, has made possible the collective employment of individual savings, so it might well devise a form of incorporation which would create collective rights and corresponding duties for organizations of farmers, workingmen, and consumers.

That such organizations would be under the temptation to become monopolies in restraint of trade is obvious. We know this from the fact that business corporations do so often yield to that very temptation. Thus an indispensable principle of liberal policy is to outlaw monopoly and the unfair trade practices which lead to monopoly. There is a rather general impression that all business tends toward a condition of monopoly, and that may be true in a society which is drifting without a clear conception of the nature of its own economy. But once men take seriously the idea that they are committed to a mode of production which can be regulated only in free markets, they will reexamine the laws under which monopoly flourishes. They will find, I am convinced, that few effective monopolies have ever been organized and that none can long endure except where there is a legal privilege. It may be a franchise, or the exclusive possession of a limited natural product, or a patent, or a tariff, or simply an exploitation of the corporate device. But if monopoly depends upon a privilege that the law concedes, then monopoly can be destroyed and prevented by changing the law.

Still we have not come to the end of our survey of the fields in which liberal policy must operate in order to adapt the social order to the exchange economy. By its very nature the economy is dynamic—that is to say, the technic and the localization of production is in continual change. Industries die and others are born, and within industries some enterprises are growing and others declining. Industries which were established in one place are replaced by industries in another place, sometimes halfway around the world. In the long view this is industrial progress, but in the close view its human evil is tragic. At no point, perhaps, were the latter-day liberals more insensitively doctrinaire than in the complacency with which they accepted the human costs of industrial progress.

Yet there is nothing whatever in the necessities of the new economy which compels society to be indifferent to the human costs. There is no reason whatever why some part of the wealth produced should not be taken by taxation and used to insure and indemnify human beings against their personal losses in the progress of industry. If technological improvement increases wealth—and, of course, it does—if society as a whole is richer when an industry moves from a place where costs are high to one where they are lower, then some part of that increased wealth can be used to relieve the victims of progress. It can be used to tide them over while they are changing their occupations, to re-educate them for new occupations, to settle them in new places if they have to move.

Not only is there no reason why a liberal state should not insure and indemnify against its own progressive development, but there is every reason why it should. For if it is properly devised, such a system of social insurance would facilitate the necessary technological changes, and reduce the very human resistance which comes from those who now see themselves the appointed victims of progress. No one can blame a man for hating a machine that will place him in the bread line and unfit him for the only job he has learned to do.

It is not only the industrial workers, however, who suffer from industrial progress. All producers are subject in some degree to the same risk when new processes are invented, when more efficient competitors arise, or when tastes change. To be sure, they cannot all be insured and indemnified out of the public treasury. But their losses can be reduced. How that is to be done is a problem of great complexity which I would not pretend to be able to solve. But the character of a possible solution may be indicated by suggesting that business enterprise would be better able to face the risks of industrial progress if corporations were required to amortize their capital debts within the efficient life of the machines and processses that the capital has bought, and were required to obtain new capital in the money market rather than out of accumulated profits. This would no doubt make for smaller corporations. But smaller corporations are more mobile than big ones. They can dissolve more easily and new ones can be created more easily. Such corporations would be more efficiently adapted to a dynamic economy, and they would not raise the problems and the tragedies of semi-obsolete corporate leviathans that are unable to live and unable to die.

It will be seen that the agenda of liberalism is long and yet I should make no claim that mine is complete. The adaptation of the social order to the division of labor is of necessity an immense undertaking since it is the finding of a new way of life for mankind. In all its ramifications it must, therefore, transcend the understanding of any man who lives in the midst of it, or the program of any party, or the reforming energies of any one generation. I have sought only to indicate the more urgent and obvious points at which modern society is maladjusted to its mode of production, and then to illustrate the unfinished mission of liberalism. The agenda refute the notion that liberalism is the sterile apologetic which it became during its subjection to the dogma of *laissez faire* and to the misunderstanding of the classical economists. The agenda demonstrate, I believe, that liberalism is not the rationalization of the status quo, but the logic of the social readjustment required by the industrial revolution.

3 · *The Dimensions of Modern Government*

"The Dream of Troubled Spirits," Today and Tomorrow, *January 20, 1949.*

Two or three of the half-dozen senators who voted against Mr. Acheson revealed, no doubt in a rather uninhibited way, a troubled spirit with which almost everyone, including, I should suppose, Mr. Acheson himself, is touched. They were worried and out of sorts at the enormous complexity and cost of the American government today. They were homesick for the old times of Coolidge, McKinley, and Cleveland when the government minded its own business, and did not have much business to mind.

And yet they were suspicious of Mr. Acheson, and indeed of General Marshall, and of Franklin D. Roosevelt and Winston Churchill before him, for having recognized that there are large parts of the world in which our principles are not regarded as self-evident and our will is not supreme.

There is in all of us a good deal of Wherry—that is to say, of the global isolationists, who would like to shape the destiny of mankind on a budget of about seven billion dollars—who would like to live as we did under Calvin Coolidge and yet to exercise an influence on the world which would have seemed presumptuous to Augustus Caesar. This daydream in which we retain our old privacy and yet exercise universal influence will pass. There are only a very few left in the Senate who do not know that it is a daydream.

But for them, and for all who hanker for it, as most of us do, it is a cause of unhappiness. For in the distortion of the dream, the tremendous events of this age are made totally unintelligible.

They become a little less unintelligible only as we are able to see ourselves, our problems, and our necessities in the perspective of time and place. The effort to do this alone can teach us not to suppose that we can escape history at home, as Mr. Wherry would like to do, or determine, as he would also like to do, the whole course of history abroad.

Thus it is not possible, I think, to understand the first New Deal, or the Truman edition of it, without remembering and realizing that its controlling principle—the idea which separates it from the American past—was developed and enunciated, not by Roosevelt and his "brain trust," but by President Herbert Hoover. This is an historic fact which gives no pleasure to the Democrats or to the Republicans. But it is a fact, and it is most significant.

The sovereign idea of what became known as the New Deal is that the government is charged with the responsibility for the successful operation of the economic order and the maintenance and improvement of the standard of life for all classes in the nation. Though one could find an anticipation of this revolutionary idea in the Square Deal of President Theodore Roosevelt and in the New Freedom of President Woodrow Wilson, it was not until the great depression during the Hoover Administration that it became the established American doctrine.

It would never have occurred to Grant in 1873 or to Cleveland in 1893 or to Harding in 1921 that the federal government could or should, tell farmers, bankers, businessmen, debtors and creditors, employers and employees what to do to restore prosperity—or that public officials had the right to use all the powers of the government and to draw upon all the national resources to protect the standard of life. Until the Hoover Administration the business cycle was supposed to be like the seasons and the weather, something you talked about but did nothing about—while the unemployed walked the streets, the insolvent debtors were foreclosed, the bankrupt went bankrupt, and nature took its course.

On August 11, 1932, President Hoover made an address, accepting the Republican nomination, which is certainly one of the most important, as it is one of the most neglected, public documents of this century. He declared that when "the forces of destruction"—that is to say, the great depression—invaded the American economy and brought about "bank and business failures, demoralization of security and real property values, commodity prices and unemployment . . . two courses were open. We might have done nothing. That would have been utter ruin. Instead, we met the situation with proposals to private business and the Congress of the most gigantic program of economic defense and counterattack ever evolved in the history of the Republic."

Mr. Hoover, in language which was then unprecedented, declared that "the function of the federal government in these times is to use its reserve powers and its strength for the protection of citizens and local governments by support to our institutions against forces beyond their control." That was the beginning of the era in which we live, and of which no one of us will see the end. That was the commitment, born of dire necessity and of hope, by which government is held responsible in respect to the standard of life of the people. No one since then who was President, or sought to be, has ever challenged or renounced this commitment.

"The Big Money," Today and Tomorrow, *March 10, 1952.*

There is an agreeable story going around about a conscientious congressman, a freshman in the House, who went home last summer and found that he could not explain to his constituents the fabulous billions which he had just voted to appropriate. He was much troubled. It was embarrassing to let the voters see that he knew so little about so much public money. But he is a good man, and concerned with more than the appearance of things. So he began to reproach himself that he had not worked hard enough at the job to which he had been elected. While he was feeling that way, he saw in the newspaper that the state university was offering a course in the federal budget. He was not too proud to learn and so he enrolled and went back to school to find out from the professor what he had voted for in Washington.

There must be others, not only congressmen who must do the voting but also those who are expected to write and talk about the budget, lots of us that is to say, who are uneasy. On the one hand we feel that it ought to be possible somewhere in the stupendous sums to save some money. It just isn't likely that every last lieutenant (j.g.) and every colonel has foreseen and calculated accurately what is necessary to the military power of the United States. On the other hand, we are afraid to take the responsibility of cutting any particular item—lest it turn out later that the lieutenant (j.g.) and the colonel were right and that for want of that item the battle was lost.

That is why the oyster forks, the ping pong balls, and the toenail clippers for dogs are such a godsend to us all. We can work off on them our passion for economy and never have to worry that we shall be accused of having disarmed the United States.

The most instructive lesson I ever had in the problem of economy was when the librarian of the university appeared before a board of which I was a member to explain why he needed to build a new wing to house the books. There was a hard-boiled member of the board present who decided to give the librarian a going-over.

"You have several million books," he said strenly, "have you not?"

"Yes, sir, we have," replied the librarian.

"Can you deny, will you have the nerve to deny to this board, that two-thirds of the books are utterly worthless, and that no student, and not even the most crackpot of your professors, will ever open any of these millions of useless books on which you now want to spend millions of dollars?"

The librarian, who seemed to be standing up better than one might have expected, said meekly: "No, sir, at least two-thirds of our books are of no interest to anyone." Then he added: "But the trouble, sir, is that I cannot think of any way of deciding which are the books in our collection that are of no interest to anyone."

This story contains, I believe, the true explanation of why the military budget is so enormous—and of why it would not be safe, without more knowledge than anyone possesses now, to reduce it by any important sum.

The reason the military budgets have become so enormous is that the defense establishment is trying to prepare not for a particular kind of war but for many kinds of war. It is much cheaper to prepare for a particular kind of war in a particular place. What costs like all get-out is trying to have a navy that can fight all kinds of wars on the sea, under the sea, in the air, and on the land—and also an air force that can by itself win any global or local war that can be imagined—and then besides all that, an army which can roll over and jump over and annihilate any army that might get in its way.

Ever since the President decided suddenly to alter the basic American strategy and to fight a land war in Asia, which we had expressly and deliberately decided we would not do, the Pentagon has been acting on the assumption that you never can tell, that it must be prepared for all kinds of wars. That is what is making the whole operation so very, very expensive.

It is like going out shopping to buy clothes for the winter, determined to be the well-dressed man no matter whether the little woman decides to spend the winter on the beach at Miami, or skiing in Norway, or hunting elephants in darkest Africa.

"Big Money," **Today and Tomorrow,** *January 2, 1962.*

As we look forward to the annual midwinter debate on government spending, it is useful if we look at the figures in perspective. To do this we must look not only at federal spending, but at all government spending. The best present estimate is that the total expenditure by federal, state, and local governments will be about $150 billion in the coming year. This is a huge sum. It will be about 27 per cent of a predicted Gross National Product of $568 billion. This large sum must be compared with the growth of our population and the growth of the economy. It must be seen in the light of our responsibilities in the world.

It is a bearable burden. Of the money spent by all government for goods and services, roughly one-half goes for national security. Except for the spectacular rise in the spending for national security, there has been no radical increase in the burden of government spending during the past twenty years. In 1939 government spending (minus defense) amounted to 13.4 per cent of the Gross National Product. In 1960 it was 12.3 per cent. It is interesting to note that in 1929, before the New Deal and the Second World War, government spending (minus defense) was 7.5 per cent of the Gross National Product.

The reason why the share of the Gross National Product spent by all government on non-defense items has not increased is that the total Gross National Product has increased so spectacularly. The country is spending more than it used to, but it has much more money to spend.

It is often said that these large government purchases of goods and services are "creeping socialism." The facts do not, I believe, support this charge. For the goods which are purchased are not being produced, as they would be under socialism, by government-owned and -operated industries. They are being purchased from private firms operated for private profit. In 1960 some 53 per cent of all government purchases were of goods and services produced by private firms. The other 47 per cent went to wages and salaries for government employees. The proportion of government funds was somewhat lower thirty years ago. In 1929 government purchases from private firms accounted for only 39 per cent of government purchases. Thus there has been no decline in the role of private enterprise in government spending. It is evident that creeping socialism has not crept very far.

What has crept along during the twentieth century has been our rapidly growing population which has been moving away from the farms and villages into big cities. People collected in big cities need more public expenditure than do people who live in the open country. This simple and obvious truth is often forgotten by the orators. But the people living in the urban centers are continually aware of the truth. They cannot get along in the cities, as could their grandfathers in the country, with private wells, private cesspools, unpaved streets, no police force, a volunteer fire department, private transportation. They must have the facilities and the amenities that are essential once they have moved from the country into the city.

The so-called socialism which is supposed to be creeping up on us is in fact nothing more than the work of making life safe and decent for a mass society collected in great cities. Through the federal, state, and local governments we spend on these civilian necessities—no doubt with some waste and shenanigans —less than a sixth of all the wealth we produce. We spend an equal amount on the task of containing the Soviet Union and Red China and the Communist movement from expanding any further. The sums are large. We are, in a word, paying the price of having become a modern great power.

4 · *Some Functions of a Modern Government*

"Polio Vaccine and Public Policy," Today and Tomorrow, *May 10, 1955.*

It is established public policy that medical advertising shall not be misleading. It was the duty of the federal government, and specifically of Mrs. Hobby's department, to have frowned upon and to have prevented the theatrical exploitation of Dr. Salk's work. The National Foundation for Infantile Paralysis, which sponsored the experimentations and the development of the vaccine, sponsored also the publicity attending the announcement. The Foundation has done great and necessary things in its field. But it is dependent upon voluntary popular subscription. This requires promotion and publicity which should have been kept carefully distinct from the publication of medical news.

Quite apart from the question of whether the federal government should have asked specific legislation in regard to polio vaccine—and in view of the short supply it should have—the federal government had a general public duty to protect the people against being misled on a burning question of public health. The consultations it has been holding in the past ten days should have been going on for months—ever since the decision was taken to manufacture the vaccine on a large scale.

I do not know why the federal government did not assume the direction of this great public health operation as soon as enough was known about last year's tests to start the pharmaceutical firms making the vaccine. But it would seem as if the inaction of the federal government was due in some considerable degree to theoretical misconceptions—to unexamined and false notions of the general principles of free enterprise, voluntary co-operation and decentralization—and to the strange prejudice that the only way the federal government can assume direction and control of anything is to build up a vast bureaucracy.

The principles of free enterprise and voluntary co-operation are beneficent and widely applicable. They are the rule in our society and a departure from them should be regarded as an exception from the rule. But not all public principles in this workaday world can be applicable at all times and under all circumstances. They are beneficent and are workable only if we apply them with good sense—only if we apply them when conditions make them applicable, and do not apply them when conditions do not make them applicable. As politics is a crude art, and not a mathematical science, there are many borderline cases where it is a close question whether to rely upon free competition and voluntary co-operation or to assume central government direction and control.

But the case of the Salk vaccine was not a borderline question. The vaccine was bound to be in short supply at least for this season; its proper use touched the vital interests of the families of the nation. There should, therefore, have been no more doubt here than there has been in Canada that the public authorities were in control.

"Discovered in Our Time," Today and Tomorrow, *May 20, 1944.*

Men have always, of course, deplored unemployment and wanted good and profitable work, and they have struggled and fought for it. But in this century, bloody and violent though it has been, mankind has made an epoch-making discovery. It is that involuntary mass unemployment in a modern industrial nation is an unnecessary and preventable evil.

Economists, industrial leaders, public officials are by no means entirely agreed which among the many measures are the best. But never again will they or the mass of the people accept the view, which was the common view thirty years ago, that public policy has nothing to do with and can do nothing effective about the maintenance of reasonably full employment. In the two great wars of our generation and in the depression between the two wars it has been demonstrated, one may hope even to the satisfaction of the most unreconstructed minds, that mass unemployment is not inevitable and that it is, therefore, intolerable.

The discovery of new principles of public policy is so rare that we find it difficult to recognize them when they are discovered. We are used to new discoveries in medicine and engineering and we are, if anything, overcredulous about, let us say, the sulfa drugs and penicillin, about flying or the newer alloys and the plastics. In government and public policy there are few great new discoveries and there are no panaceas; most of the problems of international politics were anxiously examined by Thucydides, and there are few fundamental problems of government that were not studied by Aristotle.

Yet when we look back we can see that the world we were born into was profoundly affected by the discovery in the eighteenth century of the principle of the international division of labor. From the very earliest times there had been international trading. Nevertheless, the wide application of this principle as a means of increasing the wealth of nations rested on a new discovery which men like David Hume and Adam Smith were able to define and to explain.

In our epoch the principle of the division of labor has been modified and supplemented by the discovery that large nations with big resources, skilled labor, and progressive management can, if they insist on it, regulate the cycle of booms and depressions. Since the discovery has been made, the public will no more tolerate a failure to apply it than they would tolerate hospitals which refused to use sulfa drugs and penicillin.

If we can absorb this idea, that by a successful policy of maintaining full employment here at home we make our fundamental contribution to economic stability and prosperity abroad —if we grasp this idea, then all sorts of vexatious issues will fall into their proper perspective. Here is the real answer to the notion that prosperity depends upon cutthroat competition for international markets; with full employment at home we shall have no frantic desire to export furiously. Here is the real answer to the notion that we can or should restore world prosperity by some kind of vast philanthropy; if the American economy, which is such an immense factor in the world economy, is kept working steadily at reasonably full capacity it will set up a demand for goods which will contribute enormously to prosperity almost everywhere else.

"On the Grandchildren's Future," Today and Tomorrow, *July 4, 1957.*

The American social order has changed greatly in this century, so greatly that terms like capitalism and free enterprise and competition, which come down to us from the nineteenth century, no longer describe our economy intelligibly.

There have been the wars, and the rise of the United States as a world power with a great military establishment. There has been the fabulous, indeed explosive, increase of the American population. There has been not only the deep and wide technological development, but, with the organization of scientific research, a radically new pace in the application of science.

There has been also, so at least it seems to me, a nonviolent but nevertheless revolutionary change in the inner principle of our own social economy. This is the new principle, which goes by the prosaic name of "full employment"—the imperative that the government must use the fiscal and other powers of the state to keep the demand for labor at least equal to the supply.

Until the present generation this principle was unknown to, much less was it the policy of, the United States or any other capitalist nation. Its adoption marks a profound change. It would not in my view be an exaggeration to say that it has brought about a revolution in the West which has made the Communist revolutionary propaganda irrelevant and antiquated.

For when the government is committed to the maintenance of full employment, the bargaining power of labor is underwritten. This means a decisive change in the balance of forces within our society.

The new principle of full employment was formulated during the great depression between the two world wars. Its technique is based on the discovery during the First World War that a government can promote production, regardless of the gold supply, by managing credit and the currency. The impulse to apply the technique of war finance to the peacetime economy came from the huge unemployment and the vast misery of the great depression. The commitment to the new policy comes from the voters who, having learned that unemployment can be prevented, will not tolerate any government which does not prevent it.

"Regulating the Labor Unions," Today and Tomorrow, *May 29, 1958.*

The principle is now settled . . . that labor unions are like all other powerful interests—subject to public inspection and public regulation. It is a very good thing that this principle is not in dispute. For if it were, if organized labor were making the claim so often made by other interests, that it is private and immune, there would be serious trouble ahead.

For no special interest can exercise the kind of power which the unions possess and then deny that there is a public interest in the way it conducts its affairs. . . .

In the past twenty-five years they have been fostered by privileges created and protected by federal statutes. No other kind of private association exercises so much power over the livelihood of its individual members, over their opportunities, and over the routine of their daily lives. Individual employees may not lawfully negotiate with their employers and they are legally bound by the terms and conditions of employment which a union, certified as the sole official bargaining agent for a given shop or company, may negotiate. Furthermore, in the case of many contracts the law in effect requires the compulsory payment of initiation fees and dues into the union treasury. This legally granted power of the unions to set the terms and conditions of work also affects the rights and interests of management and of the general consuming public. Unions are also granted special immunity from the anti-trust monopoly laws and, as non-profit voluntary organizations, they have exemption from the income tax.

There is, therefore, no longer any argument that federal regulation is justified in principle and necessary in practice. The question is what kind of regulation is most likely to work well. Broadly speaking, there are two types of regulation. The first, on which there is now very general agreement, is that the financial affairs of the unions shall be made public, and their officers legally made accountable for the honest administration of these affairs. . . .

The other type of regulation, now under consideration, is aimed at regulating labor unions by compelling them to adopt more compelling procedures. The theory is that if there were more democracy inside the unions they would be better governed. That may be. But it is a question whether in fact the federal government can make democracy compulsory in private associations, and whether, if it were to try to do so, it would not be biting off more than it can chew.

There are in this country some two hundred national unions and some sixty thousand local unions, and it is not probable that the federal government can really superintend their charters and regulate their internal elections. There is not much value in attempting to do what almost certainly cannot be done. It is likely to lead only to disrespect of the law.

My own view is that the compulsory disclosure of the financial affairs of the unions is a possible though not an easy kind of law to enforce. In so far as it is efficiently enforced, it may help to do many of the things which are supposed to be accomplished by compulsory democracy.

"'Fact Finding' and Steel," Today and Tomorrow, *July 21, 1959.*

Among the many big questions posed by the steel strike, perhaps the most important is what should be the role of the federal government. For there is much confusion about this. The strike is taking place just as Congress is working on a law for the regulation of labor unions, a law which calls for comprehensive and far-reaching federal intervention in the internal affairs of the unions. Yet on the steel strike there are many, including now the President himself, who want no federal intervention and wish to see the issue settled by the test of economic power. . . .

Last week, at his press conference on July 15, the President had had the matter studied. He had learned that "as far as a fact-finding board is concerned, I believe that all the facts are pretty well known. . . . In all our reports, in the labor statistics and the commerce and other figures that are published, some quarterly, some monthly, they are all there. . . ."

Whoever did the studying of the question for the President did not understand the question, or he did not want the President to understand it. For while it may well be true that the "facts" are "all there" in some of the many reports that are published, how is the public to know, how is Congress to know, how are newspaper editors to know which of the facts are important and relevant? The task of finding the facts that matter and of judging how they matter is a semi-judicial function. It cannot be done without a specialized inquiry by trained minds.

If there is no impartial tribunal to find the facts, then there can be no such thing as an enlightened public opinion. And if there is no enlightened opinion that can be brought to bear upon it, a strike of this magnitude must become a test of power in a whirl of propaganda and of prejudice.

When the President rejected the idea of a "fact-finding" which he had thought rather well of a month before, he affirmed a new doctrine: "I believe that we have got thoroughly to test out and use the method of free bargaining." Where great and vital interests are involved how much free bargaining do we really believe in?

In the steel controversy today, the companies happen to have the stronger bargaining position, their customers have large stockpiles, public opinion is stoutly opposed to another round of wage and price increases. The union appears to be far from solid within itself.

But this favorable balance to the companies will not always be the case, and I wonder whether it is wise and prudent for them to set it up as a *principle* that in these great controversies involving the national interest the issue shall be decided by a contest of power?

I do not believe it is true, as has been said recently, that this is "one of the ways in which freedom functions." If freedom is to function it must insist that the struggle of powerful interests be regulated by rational and just procedure. Freedom does not mean that the powerful interests shall fight it out as best they can.

We live in a time when the vital industries and services of the nation are in the hands of giant companies and giant unions. We cannot entrust the interests of the nation to a combination of the companies and the unions, which is what we have had for some years until recently in the steel industry. Nor can we entrust the interests of the nation to a power struggle between the unions and the companies, however much this struggle be prettified by calling it "free bargaining."

In these great conflicts the national interest must be represented and asserted by the federal government. The place to begin this is by a clarification of the contending claims. This alone may be enough to provide the basis of an opinion on which the government can exert its influence, and to which the public can rally.

"Fiasco in Steel," Today and Tomorrow, *October 13, 1959.*

At the beginning of the steel strike in July, the President declared that he would not intervene because "I believe that we have got thoroughly to test out and use the method of free bargaining." . . .

Now three weeks later he has set in motion the machinery of the Taft-Hartley Act, and everyone is hoping that board of inquiry under that act will somehow succeed in avoiding the need to invoke the act, and that it will somehow be able to mediate a settlement. If the board does not succeed, the steel strike will be suspended for eighty days and then may be resumed at the onset of winter.

It is a dreary outcome for what was to have been a test of "the method of free bargaining." The test has gone on since July, and the method of free bargaining has failed in the task. Why did it? It failed because the issues of the steel strike were not ones to which the method of free bargaining applies. The President did not understand the nature of the steel strike. He failed to see that the issues were not those which collective bargaining can resolve.

On the side of labor the ultimate issue is its right to share in the larger profits of the companies. On the side of management the ultimate issue is to put a stop to the spiral of wage increases since the Second World War and to recover some of the ground lost to labor since that time.

Here then is a case of industrial warfare between giant business and giant labor. It is a test of power and of will in which the two parties are not bargaining and will not compromise their differences.

When the President chose to regard the steel strike as one which could be settled by "free bargaining," there was not involved a true principle based on the reality of things but a sentimental illusion. . . . The steel strike is a spectacular example of the fact that, far from being a completed and perfected society, there is in our society much that is primitive, irrational, and increasingly intolerable. It is not a jolly thing to have the basic industry of the country close down for three months with no settlement in sight just because we have not learned how to substitute law and order for unconditional industrial warfare.

The claim that a strike of these dimensions and of such consequences is a private affair, not a proper subject of national intervention, is entirely untenable. It was untenable in July when the Administration approved the claim that this was a private affair and it is untenable in October when the Administration has had to intervene.

The national interest is not only that a settlement should be reached and production resumed. There is a prime national interest in the terms on which the strike is settled. The day is past when this country can tolerate "free" bargaining by which labor gets higher wages and management puts up the prices. The national interest demands that the major industrial conflicts be settled under conditions which are good for the economy as a whole. That being the case, some agency has to have the authority to speak for the national interest when a conflict arises.

In the last analysis what this means is that the great basic industrial settlements, though they are reached by the method of voluntary bargaining, must be in harmony with the verdict that would be reached by arbitration by an authoritative national agency charged with the health of the economy as a whole. This will, I suppose, horrify a great many. But I have put it bluntly and brutally because only in that way do we get away from sentimentality and double-talk and down to the hard realities.

The lesson of the strike is that the country needs to make a new advance into the region where the government can impose peaceful settlements in accordance with the national interest upon the giant corporations and the giant unions. The government should have full power to arbitrate and to impose a settlement.

If it has that power, it can use it best to promote, to induce, and to persuade labor and management to write into their contracts rules for settling their differences by bargaining if possible, by voluntary arbitration if necessary. In the end, however, if they fail to do this, there must be the possibility of a resort to compulsory arbitration.

The big stick should be in the government's possession. If it is there, it will, except on the rarest occasions, be left in the closet.

"The Crux of the Farm Problem," Today and Tomorrow, *February 22, 1962.*

Both we and they, the free societies and the Communists, are contending with a farm problem. But their problem is how to produce enough and ours is what to do with too much.

They are finding that under regimentation and control the farmers lack the incentive to produce. For some thirty years we have been using government controls and subsidies to hold up prices in an effort to protect the farmers' incomes from the consequences of too much supply and too little demand. The overall result has been still more supply resulting in lower incomes for most farmers and huge, costly and unmanageable surpluses in the government's hands.

The farm problem, as we have known it since the time of Coolidge and Hoover, is not confined to the United States. It exists in western Europe and it is the most difficult of all the issues which will have to be settled if there is to be a degree of economic unity in the free world. It is the agricultural questions which make it most difficult to work out some form of economic union—for the six countries in the Common Market, the so-called Outer Seven, the British Commonwealth, the United States, Latin America, and Japan.

The movement toward free trade in industrial products is achieving great momentum, and there do not appear to be any insuperable difficulties to a wide free trade area market. But a wide common market for agricultural products, both temperate and tropical, faces obstacles which will not easily be overcome.

In dealing with unsolved problems, the first step toward an eventual solution is to isolate and define the crux of the problem. The economists have done that. But it may be some time before public men, who have to face the voters, will think it prudent to publish the bad news from the economists. The bad news is that there are more farmers trying to make a living on the land than our modern scientific agriculture requires. Underneath the crop surpluses there is a surplus of farmers. The essence of the farm problem is how to take care of the farmers who, because they are not needed, cannot make a decent living. . . .

We are faced with the brutal fact that there are . . . nearly twice as many farmers as are needed for efficient production. And in the years to come, as more and more scientific means are applied to agriculture, the number of farmers that are needed will decline still more.

I have called this a brutal fact even though it means that for us an age of plenty has arrived. It is a brutal fact because farming is not only the production of food and fiber. It is a way of life which Americans have always believed nourishes the spirit. Yet just as the cities are swallowing the villages, and the metropolis is swallowing the cities, so the industrial farms with their machines and technology are swallowing the traditional farms. We are in the midst of an agricultural revolution which is epochal in its consequences.

This revolution cannot be stopped or turned back by any farm program that Congress could vote or that the Treasury could possibly afford. In view of the many demands on our national strength, we cannot, even if we wished, indulge in the waste of precious human resources represented in the production of crops at high prices for storage. We need that energy spent on real work, not make-work. Gradually, we shall have to recognize the fact that the true purpose of a farm policy is to reduce the hardships of the victims of the agricultural revolution, and to protect and help the unneeded farmers in changing over to other occupations.

If we call things by their right names, a realistic farm policy is not an attempt to rig the market, or to insulate it from competition. In reality it will have to be a welfare program for the retiring farmers and their children, and for the lands which must also be retired from agriculture. We need to encourage the young people from less productive rural areas to leave farming for other occupations. Education plays the leading role. Direct incentives can be offered to encourage the shift away from farming; Denmark, for example, gives special scholarships to young people from the country. As industry becomes more evenly distributed among the states, a move from farming to another industry will less often entail a geographic move. A rural redevelopment program can help provide new uses for the land and new jobs for people retired from farming, softening the impact of the technological revolution in agriculture.

The prospect of more food from less crop land offers us a new freedom to use land as we wish to use it. We have hardly begun to realize the opportunities opened to us by the new processes of agriculture—the opportunity to conserve the soil and wildlife and to reforest and to set aside land for recreation and for esthetic purposes.

So the farm problem should be approached not as an annoying and somewhat tragic muddle, but as a great opportunity.

"The School Crisis," Today and Tomorrow, *February 5, 1957.*

It is often asserted that all the subsidies and grants which appear in the federal budget are there because of the special interests of pressure groups. There is, of course, some truth in this. But as a generalized rule, it is untrue and grossly unfair. In the case of federal aid for schools, it is truer and fairer to say that the opposition comes from pressure groups, whereas the support is truly national and public spirited. There is no special interest which is going to be favored specially by the adoption of these proposals. The demand for them comes from teachers and from school superintendents, from parents and from civic leaders who are worrying about our failure to provide a large part of the coming generation with adequate schooling.

Indeed the support of education—by the localities, the states, and the federal government—is like the support of the national defense. It is a public and patriotic duty which this generation owes to the next. Can we afford to support American education? The answer is that we cannot afford not to support it. Do we have the money to support it? Well, in the past twenty-five years the national income has risen $300 billion while the amount we spend on education has increased by little more than seven or eight billion.

The truth is that it is absurd to say that the richest country in the history of mankind cannot afford both to defend itself and to educate its children.

5 · *Public Need and Private Pleasure*

"Public Need and Private Pleasure," Today and Tomorrow, *September 5, 1957.*

The country has been left with the impression, which will dominate almost every great problem, that if we could cut expenditures by a few more billion dollars, it would be possible to reduce the income tax. This is a dangerous untruth to propagate at this time. Yet both parties are propagating it. The Democrats are said to be planning to pass a tax cut in the next session. The President, who knows that it is wrong to cut taxes when there is such a big inflation, has, nevertheless, encouraged the notion that with a little more budgetary economy, he too might favor tax reductions.

What the country needs to hear from the President is not softness about private self-indulgence but a stern and austere reminder that our public responsibilities must come ahead of our private pleasures.

There is no prospect now in sight of an agreement to slow down the race of armaments. There is, on the contrary, much evidence that the race is swifter. It is no use, then, to tell our people that we can stabilize the military budget at thirty-eight billion dollars.

It is impossible for the country to taper off and to cry quits in providing economic aid to the under-developed countries. We shall not in our time see the end of the need for such aid, and it cannot be the policy of the United States to resign from Asia and Africa. It is no use, then, to go toward the elections of 1958 with a spreading feeling among politicians that if they could abolish foreign aid, there would be a big enough surplus to justify a tax reduction.

Nor can we escape the consequences of the fact that our population is increasing at a prodigious rate—and that almost every necessary public facility is overburdened. This is true of the public schools, the colleges, and the universities, where as the school population rises, the quality of education is deteriorating. The school problem is all the more poignant because, now that the law of the land calls for integrated schools, money will have to be found to replace the generally inferior Negro schools.

In the great urban conglomeration much new public money, not all of it of course federal money, will have to be spent on parks and recreation facilities, and on hospitals, highways, housing, and communications.

We are running counter to the facts of our military and diplomatic position in the world, and of the expansion of our people at home, when we allow politicians to beguile us with talk about tax cuts. What we should be hearing from Washington, and talking about ourselves, is not tax cuts, not how to be able to buy on borrowed money more and more longer and wider and faster motorcars, but how to meet our responsibilities and to do our duty.

"The Incoming Tide," **Today and Tomorrow**, *November 20, 1958.*

What is this tide which has brought in both Mr. Rockefeller and a great Democratic majority? It is propelled, I believe, by the growing conviction, based on personal experience of living in countless American communities, that our public needs are not being adequately met. The face of America has changed since Dwight Eisenhower was a boy in Kansas. We have become in large part a mass society living in congested urban agglomerations. One-half of our people live in metropolitan areas; in the six northeastern states four-fifths of the people live close together in such metropolitan areas.

This is not the only reason, but it is an important and a sufficient reason, why the country today is compelled to spend on civilian projects more public money than it used to spend. Out in the country or even in small villages, the individual can do many things for himself which in the city must be done by public enterprise. There is no need to labor the obvious. When a community grows from, let us say, 10,000 inhabitants to 100,000, the cost of the public services required is bound to go up more than ten times. For the larger community requires extensive facilities—as for example wider roads and underpasses—which the small town does not have to have at all.

Because of the great cost of the Second World War and the very large cost of the cold war, this country, which is a very different country from what it was twenty years ago, is in a predicament. It is rich in the things that money can buy and it is, speaking comparatively, poor in the services and the facilities that private enterprise cannot supply.

From now on, barring a great war, our internal politics will be dominated, we may be reasonably certain, by this predicament.

In it lies the real problem of "spending." The problem is whether the productivity of our economy can be increased so that public spending can be increased without forcing a decrease in private spending, perhaps even while permitting an increase in private spending. This will be the subject of a great debate in the years ahead of us.

There are, no doubt, many different conclusions to be drawn from all this. But the first conclusion I would draw is that the President should look not only at his $80,000,000,000 budget and its $12,000,000,000 deficit. He should look also at the problem of the economy, which is still running below capacity. And last but not least, he should look squarely at the vast complex of difficulties which are being caused by the lag in our public services, and at the human strain to which this lag subjects our people.

For the future, which he must face for another two years, will be greatly concerned with this lag. It will be concerned with the lag in the provision of schools and colleges, with the lag in hospitals and medical services, with the deficiency of highways and the backwardness of much of our transportation, and with city planning and slum clearance. The future will be concerned with the conservation and the development of our natural resources, with the water supply of large areas of the country, with the contamination of the air, and with many other consequences of the extraordinary growth of our population, its conglomeration in big urban masses, and with the shaking up of the people's habits due to the application of modern science.

"Crucial Internal Question," Today and Tomorrow, *December 11, 1958.*

In its essence, the question is whether the United States can afford to do the things which it needs to do. Can it afford to run successfully in the race of armaments? And can it also afford a foreign policy which sustains our alliances and helps to finance the undeveloped countries? And can it also pay for the schools, hospitals, roads, airports, the reclamation and the conservation and the other public services and facilities which our rapidly expanding urbanized population requires? And can it also make it possible for the people as private individuals to raise their personal standard of life?

The obvious answer at the present time is that the pie is not big enough to be cut into such big slices. The issue . . . is whether the pie can be made larger, more exactly whether the average rate of economic growth, which has been about 3 per cent a year during this century, can be raised to 5 per cent a year.

If the rate of growth can be raised to 5 per cent, then the country will be able to afford what it needs to do. If the rate cannot be raised, it will have to cut back . . . on all the essential public needs, including defense. . . .

The problem of increasing the rate of our economic growth is difficult and complex. It involves the budget and the tax structure and credit policy and labor union practices and corporation price practices and many other things besides. But while all these things are debatable, one thing is certain. This country must solve the problem in the years ahead of us. If it does not, it will be in great danger and as a power in the world and as an example of the free and democratic society, it will enter into its decline.

It is not at all an exaggeration to say that the grim competitive challenge with which we are confronted can be met only by a hard and sustained effort to increase the productivity of our economy. This is the way in which the Soviet Union is challenging us—by their own hard and sustained effort over the coming seven to ten years to surpass this country in per capita productivity. The Communists will win this competition unless our productivity is raised rapidly beyond what it is now.

The real challenge which confronts us cannot be met by

balancing the budget at a rate of production which is far below the country's potentiality—and by cheese-paring on defense, and by cheese-paring on the development of under-developed nations, and by hugging the illusion that Communist China and Communist Russia and Communist East Germany are all going to disappear if we dig in where we are and make grim faces at them.

In the real world we are up against great mass societies of powerfully disciplined people, and unless we can restore and concentrate our own energies to outdo them, it will not matter at all how many adjectives we hurl at them in the battle of words.

"The Size of the Problem," Today and Tomorrow, *March 8, 1960.*

Here at home the overriding question is how to pay for the public needs of our growing population in an era when our social order is relentlessly challenged. These public needs include not only the rising costs of the race of armaments and the competition among the underdeveloped nations. They include also the rising costs of scientific research, of better public schools, of more adequate hospitals and public health services, public works, roads, water supply and sewage disposal, slum clearance and urban renewal.

There are some who will say that we cannot meet all our public needs without abandoning the freedom of our society. There are others of us who say that we must meet these needs, that we can meet them without sacrificing our liberty, and indeed that by meeting them we shall strengthen our liberty. This is the central issue of our time, and no one who is interested in public life can ignore it.

An excellent newspaper, which I read regularly and greatly respect, *The Wall Street Journal,* said recently in an editorial that to argue, as I have done, that our public needs have to be met is "to invite us to start surrendering our liberties in panic." For to meet the needs will cost a lot of money, and this will put us on the "dreary road of statism" and "when the individual must face the faceless state, he has only as much free choice as the state chooses to grant."

This would indeed be monstrous if it were allowed to happen. How are we to make up our minds whether it will happen if we decide to devote to defense and to other public needs enough of our wealth to pay for them? One way to go about deciding it is to look at the problem quantitatively and concretely, and not abstractly and in generalities. Let us then look at some figures.

I am taking my figures from the Fourth Report of the Rockefeller Brothers Fund which was issued in 1958. It covers all government expenditures, federal, state, and local, which are for the purchase of goods and services. It omits transfer payments which, like the interest on public debts, "do not make a direct claim on our production of goods and services." The report contains figures for the year 1957 and estimates for the year 1967. The report is, by common consent I believe, expert, disinterested, and obviously it is not partisan.

In 1957 all government purchases of goods and services came to $86.4 billion. In 1967, if we meet the public needs for defense and other things which the authors of the report are agreed upon, the cost will be $153 billion (in 1957 dollars). This gives us an idea of the dimensions of the problem. The question then is whether the expenditure for public purposes of $153 billion in 1967 would revolutionize our society.

In 1957, when we spent $86.4 billion publicly, we were taking 20 per cent of our national production, leaving 80 per cent in private hands. What would be the situation in 1967 if we carry out the programs to meet public needs which are recommended in the Rockefeller Report? The answer to that question will depend on our rate of growth in the next ten years.

The Rockefeller estimates show that on the feasible assumption that our gross national product can grow at a rate of 4 per cent per year, the share taken for public purposes in 1967, if their recommendations as to what is desirable are followed, would be only 24 per cent, and the share left in private hands would be 76 per cent. This would mean that the rise in private consumption, which on the average has been 2 per cent per year, would drop to 1.4 per cent. We would not be raising our private standard of life quite so fast as we are now. But we would be raising our public standard and we would be doing it with three-quarters of our product still in private hands. No one can say that on these fairly conservative assumptions we would not still be a free society.

These figures make the assumption that we can grow only at a rate of 4 per cent. If, however, we could raise the rate of growth to 5 per cent, the position would be changed substantially. We would then be spending for public purposes 22 per cent, which is not much more than the present share of our spending, and there would still be left in private hands 78 per cent. At the same time consumption would be rising at 2.8 per cent, which is above the average.

It is evident then, that the argument of *The Wall Street Journal* is based on an assumption which is not stated. The assumption is that the United States economy, in this age of automation, cannot increase its productivity fast enough to support our growing public needs. The figures I have cited indicate that if we can now achieve a growth rate equal to that of the years 1947 to 1953, that is to say an annual rate of growth of 4.7 per cent, instead of the 2.3 per cent rate of the years since then, we shall be able to provide the needed public services while maintaining approximately the same ratio of public to private spending as we have today.

I am sorry to use so many figures. But they are necessary in order to put in its true perspective the size of the great problem of our era. When we look at this problem quantitatively, comparing our growing needs with what can be our economic growth, we may conclude that our tasks are big, which makes them interesting, but that they are quite within our capacity.

6 · *The Diplomatic Function*

"The Undiplomatic Department," Today and Tomorrow, *January 13, 1954.*

Money and power are, of course, indispensable in the conduct of a foreign policy. But without diplomacy to prepare the way and to soften the impact and to reduce the friction and allay the tension, money and military power are double-edged instruments. Used without diplomacy they may, and usually they do, augment the difficulties they are employed to overcome. Then more money and more power are needed.

The American people are now supporting a large military establishment, and they will be asked, quite rightly, to enlarge it. They are being asked also, because it is necessary, to support a large program of economic rehabilitation. Thus the managers of our foreign relations will have much money and much power at their command. They will also have worked out plans for their policies. But money, power, and plans will not be enough if they do not recover soon the lost art of diplomacy, and begin to practice it.

For we shall not be able to buy the way to peace. We shall not be able to force our way to peace. Above all we shall not be able to declaim and orate our way to peace. We shall have to negotiate the way to peace, using all the arts of diplomacy to find the way and to smooth the path.

"The Dangerous Amateurs," Today and Tomorrow, *February 5, 1952.*

Harold Nicolson once said that the art of diplomacy, as that of water colors, has suffered much from the fascination which it exercises upon the amateur. In Washington today there is one way of identifying easily the amateur who causes our suffering diplomacy to suffer unnecessarily. He is the man who feels that he ought to announce publicly and in no uncertain terms what the government will do and what it will never do on all issues in all quarters of the globe.

He cannot seem to understand that the more rigidly he binds our own government the more he reduces its influence, the more he diminishes its power to negotiate—that the more he sets our own policy on one unalterable course, the more numerous the options among which our antagonists and rivals can choose their course.

These are the amateurs, some of them wearing uniforms, who think they can solve the Far Eastern problem by a series of public commitments. They would like to announce what the Air Force will do, what the Navy will do, if an armistice in Korea is signed and is then broken, if an armistice is not signed and is not broken, if Indo-China is invaded by the Chinese, if Indo-China is infiltrated by the Chinese, if Indo-China is supplied a little, if it is supplied more than a little, from China. They would like to cross all the bridges over all the rivers ahead of them and to burn them all behind them. They believe that the way to impress your enemy is to go Wilson—with his open covenants openly arrived at—one better, and to plump for open war plans openly arrived at.

What they succeed in doing in their clamor for public commitments of this kind is: (a) to embarrass the serious and well-informed soldiers and civilians who know what it would mean and what it would cost to make good on all these threats; (b) to alienate great multitudes of the people of Asia and of Europe who fear and distrust a nation which talks so much and on so many different occasions about the terrible destruction and human agony it can and may cause; (c) to imprison our diplomacy in the formula of all or nothing—in a self-inflicted strait jacket where it can do nothing by negotiation because that is by definition appeasement and it can do nothing by the big threats because that—in their own sober second thoughts—is suicide. . . .

There is no reason to doubt that all of this, or at least much of it, is actuated by the best of intentions. Those who want to leave the Communists in no doubt whatever about our reaction to another aggression are hoping to apply one of the great lessons of the two world wars; namely, that if Germany had known America would intervene at once and on a grand scale, she would not have begun those wars. They are right in insisting that Moscow and Peiping should not think that we would have a long and interminable debate about whether we would intervene against military aggression. Where they go wrong is in wanting to specify how we would intervene, in wishing to publish what is tantamount to a blueprint of the horrors that would follow our intervention.

That is to cross the thin, the subtle, but the fateful line between a guarantee and a threat, and between a diplomatic strategy which is designed to deter and one that is calculated to terrorize. It is in the region of that line that the amateurs need most particularly to be restrained, indeed to hold their tongues and be silent. For a great power can be deterred, and believe that by renouncing big ambitions it can still have peace and security for itself, and that therefore it has nothing to gain by war and everything to lose. But if a great power is terrorized, it may come to believe that war is inevitable, and that everything depends on not losing it.

"When Diplomacy Is Too Open," Today and Tomorrow, *December 22, 1932.*

Mr. Hoover's proposal to set up a commission to deal with war debts, armaments, currencies, and tariffs raises a number of important questions about the conduct of diplomacy among democracies. It is a subject about which little is known. For democratic diplomacy is a new thing in the world. Until the war the voters and their elected representatives played a small part in international affairs. British diplomacy was the province of the British ruling class and of the permanent officials of the Foreign Office. On the continent of Europe the power exercised by the German, Austrian, and Russian empires was wielded by a relatively small number of men. The United States had not yet become a world power; its foreign policy, largely confined to the region of the Pacific and of the Caribbean, was not of much interest to the people at large.

The war brought the people into diplomacy by showing them how their fortunes and their lives were involved in the consequences of diplomacy. But there did not exist, and there does not yet exist, a workable system of democratic diplomacy. A very large part of the history of the world since the peace conference at Paris has been determined by the fact that masses of voters in many countries could not understand each other quickly enough to allow their governments to deal realistically with reconstruction after the devastation of the war. The discovery of ways in which democratic diplomacy can be conducted is one of the great tasks of our generation. The discovery is not an easy one. It will be made, no doubt, by the slow and painful process of trial and error.

The ideal of democratic diplomacy was stated by Woodrow Wilson in his Fourteen Points. It was not invented by Mr. Wilson; historical circumstances had made the participation of the people in diplomacy a certainty when Mr. Wilson wrote his Fourteen Points: what he did was to put in words the necessary logic of events. It is interesting to recall the language of this great statement.

> Open covenants of peace, openly arrived at, after which there shall be no private international understandings of any kind, but diplomacy shall proceed always frankly and in the public view.

Like almost all statements of principle this one can be understood only in the light of the actual conditions which prompted it. Mr. Wilson was denouncing the secret treaties which had played such a part in the alignment of Europe into two hostile coalitions and he was denouncing also the secret treaties made both by the Allies and by the Central Powers to divide up the spoils of victory. That was the target at which he was shooting. But, as so often happens in declarations of principle, Mr. Wilson said a little more than he really meant. The words "openly arrived at" and the dictum that diplomacy should always proceed "in the public view" seemed to say that confidential negotiations were to be prohibited.

Mr. Wilson had soon to correct this. When the time arrived to arrange the armistice with Germany, the American representative, Colonel House, was called upon to explain to Clemenceau, Lloyd George and the other Allied statesmen what each of the Fourteen Points meant. For the purposes of this explanation he used a memorandum, approved by President Wilson, in which the point about open covenants was interpreted as follows:

> The purpose is clearly to prohibit treaties, sections of treaties or understandings that are secret. The phrase "openly arrived at" need not cause difficulty. In fact, the President explained to the Senate last winter that his intention was not to exclude confidential diplomatic negotiations involving delicate matters, but to insist that nothing which occurs in the course of such confidential negotiations shall be binding unless it appears in the final covenant made public to the world.

Thus it is plain that Mr. Wilson, the apostle of open diplomacy, was under no illusion about the necessity of confidential negotiations as the preliminary stage in diplomacy.

The experience of the postwar years has amply proved how indispensable to diplomatic success is preliminary confidential exploration, preparation and understandings. The world has witnessed, it has been said, nearly a hundred international conferences since the war; it would be difficult to name one which achieved anything where the main conclusion had not been tentatively agreed to before the floodlights of publicity were turned on.

Our own experience on this point is ample. The most successful diplomatic achievement of the Hoover Administration was, I suppose, the settlement of the Anglo-American dispute about naval parity. That success was prepared by confidential negotiations which preceded Mr. MacDonald's famous visit to the Rapidan. The visit advertised an agreement which in all its essentials had already been arrived at. No successful confidential negotiations preceded the London Naval Conference. No understanding was arrived at with France and Italy. And as a result the London Naval Conference did little more than to register the agreement reached before Mr. MacDonald went to Rapidan.

The Hoover Moratorium is a classic example of the danger of open diplomacy without confidential preparation. The failure to consult France at that time, though France was the principal creditor apart from ourselves, not only ruined the effects of the moratorium but set in motion a train of events which are the real cause of the present French default. For the French became unanimously convinced that the moratorium broke irreparably Germany's will to pay, and that without being consulted, they were deprived of the assets they had counted upon to meet their own debts. There can be little doubt in retrospect that those Americans were right who advised the President to consult France in June 1931.

In the light of this history it is hard to see what good could be accomplished by setting up immediately a commission authorized to settle virtually all the great unsettled questions of the Western world. Nothing can be done, I believe, by creating commissions and calling conferences until substantial agreement on all the main points is reasonably certain. For an international conference in its public aspects is either a show in which the diplomats publish agreements already arrived at, or it is an arena in which they aggravate their disputes by proclaiming them to the world. No one who has any first-hand acquaintance with international conferences would, I think, hesitate to say that unless publicity is reserved for the end of a negotiation, it renders agreement on vital issues virtually impossible.

For great masses of people cannot negotiate. They can no more negotiate than they can make love or write books or invent. They can approve or disapprove the results, but if they participate in the negotiation itself they merely shout themselves hoarse and fall into a hopeless deadlock.

That is why it is the part of wisdom at the present time to return to the ordinary processes of diplomacy.

"Quiet Diplomacy," Today and Tomorrow, *January 10, 1961.*

The fiasco last year, which ended in Paris but did not begin there, has taught us a lesson. If the kind of understanding which the world so badly needs is to become possible, it cannot be had without far deeper study and preparation than have as yet been given to the problem. We know now that had Eisenhower and Khrushchev met at the summit in May, they would have been grossly unprepared to go beyond generalities.

This labor of study and preparation makes it necessary to resort to quiet diplomacy and to stay away from spectacular actions.

The great task of quiet diplomacy is to work out ways and means of keeping the critical questions—Laos, the Congo, Algeria, Cuba—from reaching the point of irreparable decision. In these critical places we are particularly involved in Laos and in Cuba, and in both places our immediate objective must be to avoid a sudden showdown.

It sounds brave and dashing to say that we must take the lead and act decisively to solve the problems of Laos and of Cuba. But the fact is that these problems are, in the present state of the world, insoluble. There is no conceivable way in which Laos, which has two Communist states on its frontiers, which is a country of trackless jungles, can be made finally secure against infiltration and guerrilla fighting. We cannot seal off Laos from the Communist states which it touches. And there is no conceivable way in which we can deal with Castro except to contain him gradually with the growing collaboration of the other American states. We cannot exorcise the revolutionary spirit of Fidelism.

By open diplomacy, which only too often means loudmouthed diplomacy, we can do little to assuage, indeed much to exacerbate these crisis. For then one side or the other has to back down if there is to be any accommodation. But in quiet diplomacy, there is no loss of face if a country backs away from an extreme position which has proved to be untenable.

For this reason, quiet diplomacy is for the time being the hope of the world.

"Rusk on Quiet Diplomacy," Today and Tomorrow, *January 26, 1961.*

Secretary Rusk's statement that the Administration will "use freely the diplomatic channel" has naturally enough raised the question whether this means that the public will come to know and understand less of what is going on. The question is a perennial one in a democratic society. For true negotiation is impossible if it has to be done publicly and yet a free people cannot be left in the dark. As Mr. Rusk says, "The value of the diplomatic channel depends on its privacy." But the public has the right and the need to know what is being done.

The problem can be stated so that it sounds insoluble. But as a matter of fact it is not at all impossible, although it requires the gifts of leadership, for a competent government to keep the public well informed without destroying the privacy which is essential to diplomatic negotiations. It can be done by periodic talks, one might almost say lectures, given by the President and the Secretary of State explaining the situation and how it got to be what it is, and what are the difficulties and the issues which have to be dealt with.

This is what Churchill did in his great war speeches. He rallied men not only by the eloquence and beauty of his words but even more, I venture to believe, by convincing them that on the issues of life and death they were in the know. Not many can be so eloquent as Churchill. But the Democratic leaders can tell the story. There is no need for Mr. Lincoln White, for example, to tell the newspapers what Mr. Khrushchev said to Mr. Thompson when they met at the Kremlin, or what Mr. Macmillan said to Mr. Kennedy in a message passed on by the ambassador. The indispensable privacy of diplomatic intercourse can be preserved if the leaders know how to talk informatively to the people on the issue of policy.

To talk informatively is in the main to narrate the history, and to be very sparing of pious generalities and of the old stereotype of exhortation and defiance. For if the leaders will interest and do not bore the public, there will be less interest in keyholes and in eavesdropping and leaks.

Quiet diplomacy must not be identified with withdrawal from the public view, with the withholding of knowledge, with locking the door and pulling down the blinds. In a democratic society quiet diplomacy is possible and can be fruitful only if at the same time there is an increase of communication on foreign affairs between the Chief Executive and the public.

Moreover, it can be said, I think, that diplomatic intercourse can be kept quiet and private only if it becomes routine and commonplace. Mr. Khrushchev's interview with Ambassador Thompson is not a true example of quiet diplomacy. For the meeting is not quiet when it is announced to the whole world, and the proof that it was not quiet is that there are leaks about it all over the place. There will not be effective quiet diplomacy until in Moscow and in Washington, diplomatic meetings are so habitual that they are not public events.

Let us hope that we shall get to this. For the great questions which have eventually to be negotiated cannot be resolved by arms-length pronunciamentos. They can be resolved only if intimate and informal talks open the way for formal negotiations.

"The Knight With the Wooden Sword," Today and Tomorrow, *February 24, 1938. Foreign Secretary Anthony Eden's resignation from the Chamberlain Cabinet in February 1939 moved Lippmann to draw lessons for the diplomatic posture of the liberal democracies.*

I can see many persuasive reasons for thinking that Mr. Eden's resignation is a necessary step in the education of the democratic peoples, and that it may prove to have been the only way in which these peoples can be made to clarify their purposes in face of the dangers that beset them. . . .

The crux of the matter, it seems to me, is that ever since the Ethiopian affair Mr. Eden has been in an impossible position. Instead of being the defender of the principles with which he has been associated, he has been driven step by step to compromises which threaten to end in the complete discredit of those principles. The reasons for this are evident. At no moment since the League set out to apply sanctions to Italy has Mr. Eden been able to make his principles effective by convincing Mussolini that Great Britain was ready to fight.

Yet nothing else had the smallest chance of impressing Mussolini. Great Britain has not been ready to fight for the principles that her Foreign Secretary was proclaiming. Great Britain has not felt herself to be well enough armed. She has not felt sure enough of her allies. The British people have not had the will to fight. And no one knew this better than Mussolini.

That being the case, the Last Knight of Europe has had to go forth to fight the infidels brandishing a wooden sword.

The failure of Mr. Eden's conduct of British foreign policy is due in the last analysis to the fact that the democracies have wanted policies for which they were not prepared to pay the price. Mr. Eden has voiced their aspirations. But he has not controlled their behavior. They have been unwilling to admit that the adversaries of democracy are ready to kill and to be killed in order to achieve their purposes, and that as against men who are in this mood, words, moral attitudes, economic threats and blank cartridges are altogether unavailing.

What is more, the democracies have not realized that to take the high moral attitude with the dictators when the dictators believe that it is a pious bluff is the most dangerous of all courses which a government can pursue. For the high sentiments do not restrain the aggression, and the constant yielding encourages it. It arouses the kind of contempt which Hitler displayed on Sunday, and in the end is almost certain to lead to some incident where the government is trapped and compelled to fight anyway.

Mr. Eden's resignation brings the democracies to a point where they have to make up their minds to fish or cut bait. If they are going to stand by Mr. Eden's principles, then in the world as it now is they must convince themselves to begin with, and then the dictators, that at some definite point they will stand and fight for those principles. In dealing with these warrior statesmen the democracies must not delude themselves with the idea that there is any bloodless, inexpensive and pleasant substitute for the willingness to go to war. Collective security, economic sanctions, moral pressure can be made effective only by nations known to be willing to go to war if necessary.

If that willingness to fight does not exist, then Mr. Chamberlain is right when he concludes that he must try to make tolerable terms with the dictators. It is one thing or the other. For more than three years Europe has been denouncing aggression and retreating before it, and this disparity between principles and practice is so utterly demoralizing that, if it continues much longer, the contempt of the dictators for the democracies will become so great that they will become utterly reckless and their actions without bounds.

"Dulles and the Churchmen," Today and Tomorrow, *November 27, 1958.*

Last week at Cleveland before a conference of Protestant churchmen, Secretary Dulles ended his address on a note which was novel and interesting. "Today," he said, "when despotism rides high, our society is closely observed. Many find us lacking." In terms of works, we seem to be confusing freedom with moral license and our productive power is often devoted to frivolities. "In some respects, we seem to be as materialistic as the Communists but without their supporting philosophy and efficiency." But, said Mr. Dulles, there is one other way, and that the most important, in which we are lacking. "In terms of faith, we seem unable to articulate a basic philosophy for our times which carries deep conviction and strong appeal."

This is a remarkable thing for Mr. Dulles to admit. For the President and he, and he particularly, have certainly been untiring in their attempts to articulate a basic philosophy. It is rare indeed that either of them discusses a public question without wrapping it up in the confident claim that the position they have taken is derived directly from the moral order of the universe. How then, has it come about that Mr. Dulles, despite all the basic philosophy that he has articulated for so many years, finds that his use of philosophy does not carry "deep conviction and strong appeal?"

The clue to the answer to this question is to be found in the fact that the very gathering he was addressing has made it manifest that it does not accept the notion that is Mr. Dulles' constant theme. It does not believe that his policies in foreign affairs are derived from and founded upon "a moral order which is fundamental and eternal." Many of the churchmen attending the conference disagreed with the Dulles China policy, and all of them appear to have rejected the notion that any specific Dulles policy has somehow the authority and sanction of religion and of the moral order which religion sustains.

Yet the incessant claim that our policies are more than human, and have about them an aura of divinity, has been having a devastating effect on our prestige in the world. Mr. Dulles, who carries a very big stick with our weapons and our wealth, seems curiously insensitive to the fact that he should therefore speak softly. In the face of the outer world he, even more than the President, is the wielder of great material power and, if only he could see himself as others see him, he would be humble and would not wield this power with moral dogmatism and any suggestion of special righteousness.

There is no surer way for a leader in the free world to repel free men than to let it seem that in our foreign policies we make the assumption of infallibility, that what finally emerges from the vast bureaucracy which forms these policies, is hedged with divinity, and that only the blind, the ignorant and the wicked can disagree with whatever the policy finally happens to be.

It is right here, so I have come to believe, that lies the source of the irritation which is frustrating the hopes of the President and of Mr. Dulles that they can rally the people of the world in a moral crusade against communism. For far from articulating a basic philosophy which is different from communism, the pretense to know and to speak for the universal order of things is, when seen at a distance, in Asia and even in Europe, too painfully similar to the central vice of the Communist philosophy. For the Communists, when they are true believers, are certain that they know the inner secrets of all human experience, and that whatever they happen to be doing is a manifestation of destiny.

The tendency to transform our mundane and secular matters, as for example what to do about Quemoy or Berlin, into religious and moral dogmas is an old and a bad habit of the human race. Freedom has one of its deepest roots in the realization that the business of states is the business of fallible and altogether human persons, that tariffs and budgets and military establishments and what to do in Lebanon and Cyprus and the rest, cannot be deduced directly and neatly and obviously from the moral principles of any religion. The spirit of freedom is an emanation of the human experience in which men have learned to distrust politicians who, lacking humility, are too sure of themselves, and pretend to have some special kind of inspiration.

"The Grace of Humility," Today and Tomorrow, *September 24, 1957.*

What with Little Rock, Cyprus, Algeria, Kashmir, and so forth, the work of the American propagandist is not at present a happy one. It is hard to keep bright and convincing the image of America as the leader of the free nations and the liberator of the captive. For we are a long way short of having learned to practice all that we preach. Yet we preach incessantly about justice and freedom, law and order.

At home, there is the stark fact that there exists among us a caste system based on the color of a man's skin. It mocks us and haunts us whenever we become eloquent and indignant in the United Nations. It mocks us and haunts us when we sprinkle our speeches and writings with advice and warnings and exhortations. There is no use fooling ourselves. The caste system in this country, particularly when as in Little Rock it is maintained by troops, is an enormous, indeed an almost insuperable, obstacle to our leadership in the cause of freedom and human equality.

Abroad, we find ourselves caught in a series of dilemmas—France and the Arabs, Israel and the Arabs, Pakistan and India—where we are damned if we choose and damned if we shrink from choosing and where neither alternative is so noble and so fine as we like our position to be.

My own view is that much of this, though not the whole of it, is, so to speak, in the nature of things, and beyond our control. It is one of the facts of life that no country, which is as powerful and as rich as is the United States, can expect not to be feared, distrusted, envied, and widely disliked. But I think also that all this is much worse than it needs to be. It is more damaging than it would be if those who represent us, particularly the President and the Secretary of State, displayed more of the wisdom that should direct, and of the grace that should sweeten, the possession of great power and great wealth.

There exists a remedy, though not a cure, for the excess of our unpopularity and for the abnormal dislike that exists abroad for Mr. Dulles. The remedy is a strong and, for those who need it, a bitter medicine. It calls for a change in the moral posture which the President and Secretary Dulles habitually adopt when they address mankind. It is a change which would require on their part a humility, that is now lacking, about our moral grandeur, and a new candor. For our faults and our sins seem all the bigger when they are seen by the world against the excessively self-righteous picture that is our official version of ourselves.

In their speeches and press conferences, the President and the Secretary are too noble about our ideals, and never humble at all about our human, our very human, failures and faults.

This alienates, indeed enrages, those who are by national interest our friends and allies, at least the prouder ones among them, who do not in the hope of favors to come, lick our boots. For with great power, which is always suspect, there should go a decent humility and there should be no pretense, no intimation, no implied assumption, not a whisper or a nod that we are not only stronger and richer than our neighbors but quite a bit better.

The President himself is not an arrogant or a proud man. But he is a naïve man in that he believes sincerely that the enunciation of moral ideals will somehow bring about the realization of those ideals. Not long ago he came very near to saying that it was his mission to express the aspirations of this country, leaving it to Mr. Dulles to adjust those aspirations to the realities. This is a novel conception of what it means to be the head of a government. The net practical effect has been to make the world think that the President preaches one thing and that Mr. Dulles does something else.

Mr. Dulles is in action a tough and realistic operator in the realm of expediency. But in speech he is a moralizer, the invariable and confident exponent of all that is righteous. His great handicap, which might be removed by a searching of soul, is that he lays down the moral law without humor and humility, as one of the righteous speaking down to the unrighteous.

This lack of the grace of humility does not make for affection or understanding, or even for charity, as when in Little Rock we, like other nations, fall far short of our professed ideals. It makes, rather, for a kind of unholy satisfaction, human nature being what it is, that we who have not been humble, have been humiliated, and that we who have held our heads too stiffly and too high, have stumbled and fallen on our faces.

IX

The Pattern of Society

1 · *The Plural Society*

A Preface to Politics (1913), *Chapters 3, 4, and 9.*

If "politics" has been indifferent to forces like the union and the trust, it is no exaggeration to say that it has displayed a modest ignorance of women's problems, of educational conflicts and racial aspirations; of the control of newspapers and magazines, the book publishing world, socialist conventions, and unofficial political groups like the single-taxers.

Such genuine powers do not absorb our political interest because we are fooled by the regalia of office. But statesmanship, if it is to be relevant, would obtain a new perspective on these dynamic currents, would find out the wants they express and the energies they contain, would shape and direct and guide them. For unions and trusts, sects, clubs, and voluntary associations stand for actual needs. The size of their following, the intensity of their demands are a fair index of what the statesman must think about. No lawyer created a trust though he drew up its charter; no logician made the labor movement or the feminist agitation. If you ask what for political purposes a nation is, a practical answer would be: it is its "movements." They are the social *life*. So far as the future is man-made it is made of them. They show their real vitality by a relentless growth in spite of all the little fences and obstacles that foolish politicians devise.

There is, of course, much that is dead within the movements. Each one carries along a quantity of inert and outworn ideas—not infrequently there is an internally contradictory current. Thus the very workingmen who agitate for a better diffusion of wealth display a marked hostility to improvements in the production of it. The feminists too have their atavisms; not a few who object to the patriarchal family seem inclined to cure it by going back still more—to the matriarchal. Constructive business has no end of reactionary moments—the most striking, perhaps, is when it buys up patents in order to suppress them. Yet these inversions, though discouraging, are not essential in the life of movements. They need to be expurgated by an unceasing criticism; yet in bulk the forces I have mentioned, and many others less important, carry with them the creative powers of our times. . . .

If this nation did not show an unmistakable tendency to put men at the center of politics instead of machinery and things; if there were not evidence to prove that we are turning from the sterile taboo to the creation of finer environments; if the impetus for shaping our destiny were not present in our politics and our life, then essays like these would be so much baying at the moon, fantastic and unworthy pleas for some irrelevant paradise. But the gropings are there—vastly confused in the tangled strains of the nation's interests. Clogged by the confusion, half-choked by stupid blockades, largely unaware of their own purposes, it is for criticism, organized research, and artistic expression to free and to use these creative energies. They are to be found in the aspirations of labor, among the awakened women, in the development of business, the diffusion of art and science, in the racial mixtures, and many lesser interests which cluster about these greater movements. . . .

Creative statesmanship requires a culture to support it. It can neither be taught by rule nor produced out of a vacuum. A community that clatters along with its rusty habits of thought unquestioned, making no distinction between instruments and idols, with a dull consumption of machine-made romantic fiction, no criticism, an empty pulpit, and an unreliable press, will find itself faithfully mirrored in public affairs. The one thing that no democrat may assume is that the people are dear good souls, fully competent for their task. The most valuable leaders never assume that. . . .

The politics of reconstruction require a nation vastly better educated, a nation freed from its slovenly ways of thinking, stimulated by wider interests, and jacked up constantly by the sharpest kind of criticism. It is puerile to say that institutions must be changed from top to bottom and then assume that their victims are prepared to make the change. No amount of charters, direct primaries, or short ballots will make a democracy out of an illiterate people. Those portions of America where there are voting booths but no schools cannot possibly be described as democracies. Nor can the person who reads one corrupt newspaper and then goes out to vote make any claim to having registered his will. He may have a will, but he has not used it.

For politics whose only ideal is the routine, it is just as well that men shouldn't know what they want or how to express it. Education has always been a considerable nuisance to the conservative intellect. In the southern states, culture among the Negroes is openly deplored, and I do not blame any patriarch for dreading the education of women. It is out of culture that the substance of real revolutions is made. If by some magic force you could grant women the vote and then keep them from schools and colleges, newspapers and lectures, the suffrage would be no more effective than a blue law against kissing your wife on Sunday. It is democratic machinery with an educated citizenship behind it that embodies all the fears of the conservative and the hopes of the radical.

Culture is the name for what people are interested in, their thoughts, their models, the books they read and the speeches they hear, their table talk, gossip, controversies, historical sense and scientific training, the values they appreciate, the quality of life they admire. All communities have a culture. It is the climate of their civilization. Without a favorable culture political schemes are a mere imposition. They will not work without a people to work them.

The real preparation for a creative statesmanship lies deeper than parties and legislatures. It is the work of publicists and educators, scientists, preachers, and artists. Through all the agents that make and popularize thought must come a bent of mind interested in invention and freed from the authority of ideas. The democratic culture must, with critical persistence, make man the measure of all things. I have tried again and again to point out the iconoclasm that is constantly necessary to avoid the distraction that comes of idolizing our own methods of thought. Without an unrelaxing effort to center the mind upon human uses, human purposes, and human results, it drops into idolatry and becomes hostile to creation.

The democratic experiment is the only one that requires this willful humanistic culture. An absolutism like Russia's is served better when the people accept their ideas as authoritative and piously sacrifice humanity to a non-human purpose. An aristocracy flourishes where the people find a vicarious enjoyment in admiring the successes of the ruling class. That prevents men from developing their own interests and looking for their own successes. No doubt Napoleon was well content with the philosophy of those guardsmen who drank his health before he executed them.

But those excellent soldiers would make dismal citizens. A view of life in which man obediently allows himself to be made grist for somebody else's mill is the poorest kind of preparation for the work of self-government. . . .

What I have called culture enters into political life as a very powerful condition. It is a way of creating ourselves. Make a blind struggle luminous, drag an unconscious impulse into the open day, see that men are aware of their necessities, and the future is in a measure controlled. The culture of today is for the future an historical condition. That is its political importance. The mental habits we are forming, our philosophies and magazines, theaters, debates, schools, pulpits, and newspapers become part of an active past which, as Bergson says, "follows us at every instant; all that we have felt, thought, and willed from our earliest infancy is there, leaning over the present which is about to join it, pressing against the portals of consciousness that would fain leave it outside."

"The Deepest Issue of Our Time," Vital Speeches of the Day, *II* (1936), 602, *an address delivered at the University of Rochester on June 15, 1936.*

If we ask ourselves why our democracy has worked, why it has endured the trials of a century and a half, why it survives and is vigorous, we shall be greatly deceived if we think that this is due to the magic of the party system and to the infallible wisdom of elected majorities. American democracy has worked, I am convinced, because of two fundamental reasons.

The first is that government in America has not, hitherto, been permitted to attempt to do many things. Its problems have been kept within the capacity of ordinary men. The second reason why democracy has worked in America is that outside the government and outside the party system, there have existed independent institutions and independent men. Foremost among the independent institutions has been the judiciary, with its power to review the actions of the Legislature and the Executive. But the judiciary has not stood alone outside the political government and the parties. There have been others, notably the free churches, the free press, the free universities, and, no less important to the preservation of democracy, free men with sufficient secured property of their own, farms, factories, shops, professions, savings, which were protected by the law and not dependent upon the will of elected or appointed officials. It has been because the courts, the churches, the press, the schools, and private property have existed independently of government that the nation has remained the master, that it has not become the servant of its government.

The deepest issue of our time is whether the civilized peoples can maintain and develop a free society or whether they are to fall back into the ancient order of things when the whole of men's existence, their consciences, their science, their arts, their labor, and their integrity as individuals were at the disposition of the rulers of the state. The world is faced with a stupendous reaction, and what makes that reaction peculiarly dangerous is that those who are leading this reaction are for the most part convinced that they are the leaders of progress. Not to believe that government must regulate all human affairs is currently regarded as stupidly reactionary by those who imagine themselves the pioneers of a new world. No one these days can, it would seem, conceive a project for the improvement of men's condition except by magnifying and intensifying the activity of governments.

But governments are composed of men, not supermen, not geniuses, mere men, imperfectly educated, not wholly disinterested, with very limited wisdom. Such men can operate only a government of limited powers, and no greater delusion has ever cast its spell upon the human imagination than that a group of mortal men can plan the future of a society and direct the affairs of a whole civilization. It is the presumption of ignorance to believe that; to attempt it is to take the road to ruin. For when governments attempt more than men with their abilities are fitted to do, the more they attempt, the worse they will do it. The men who said that this must be a government of limited powers were men who understood mankind.

Not only must a government limit its functions if it is to be successfully operated, but it must jealously guard the independence of the people, their courts, their churches, their press, their universities, and their property. It must guard them against dependence upon the government and subjection to it and against private privilege, private monopoly, and private lawlessness. For that reason we are called upon to preserve against all attack the absolute independence of the universities.

They must not be the creatures of the government. They must not be terrorized by politicians and by newspapers. They must not be ruled by those who give them money. But for the same reason they must guard their own independence by refusing to become entangled in the making of policy and the administration of government. Those of you who have responsibility as trustees and administrators know that in the application of this principle hard cases arise and that you could not if you wished, and would not if you could, apply the principle with dictatorial precision. But the important thing is not the exceptional and spectacular case: it is the gradual clarification of the principle.

And that principle, it seems to me, is this: the reason why we must guard the freedom of the universities is that only in freedom can knowledge advance. It is only knowledge freely acquired that is disinterested. It is only on such knowledge that a democracy, seeking guidance, can rely. When, therefore, men whose profession it is to teach and to investigate become the makers of policy, become members of an administration in power, become politicians and leaders of causes, they are committed. Nothing they say can be relied upon as disinterested. Nothing they teach can be trusted as scientific.

It is impossible to mix the pursuit of knowledge and the exercise of political power and those who have tried it turn out to be very bad politicians or they cease to be scholars. My own conviction is that this choice has to be faced in American universities and that if the professors try to run the government, we shall end by having the government run the professors. The safety both of the government and of the universities, and their value to each other, depends, I believe, upon their separation in independent spheres of activity.

It took centuries to achieve the separation of Church and State, the separation of the press and the state, the separation of learning from the state, the separation of the judiciary from the executive. And in this separateness the modern progress of mankind has taken place. Let us, therefore, be on guard against a reaction, masquerading as enlightment and progress, which would amalgamate them all again and undo the hard won achievements of the emancipators of mankind.

2 · *The New Economy*

Drift and Mastery (*1914*), *Chapter 2.*

I am not speaking in chorus with those sentimentalists who regard industry as sordid. They merely inherit an ancient and parasitic contempt for labor. I do not say for one instant that money is the root of evil, that rich men are less honest than poor, or any equivalent nonsense. I am simply trying to point out that there is in everyday life a widespread rebellion against the profit motive. That rebellion is not an attack on the creation of wealth. It is, on the contrary, a discovery that private commercialism is an antiquated, feeble, mean, and unimaginative way of dealing with the possibilities of modern industry.

The change is, I believe, working itself out under our very eyes. Each day brings innumerable plans for removing activities from the sphere of profit. Endowment, subsidy, state aid, endless varieties of consumers' and producers' co-operatives; public enterprise—they have been devised to save the theater, to save science and invention, education and journalism, the market basket and public utilities from the life-sapping direction of the commercialist. What is the meaning of these protean efforts to supersede the profiteer if not that his motive produces results hostile to use, and that he is a usurper where the craftsman, the inventor, and the industrial statesman should govern? There is no sudden substitution of sacrifice for selfishness. These experiments are being tried because commercialism failed to serve civilization; the co-operator intrenched behind his wiser organization would smile if you regarded him as a patient lamb on the altar of altruism. He knows that the old economists were bad psychologists and superficial observers when they described man as a slot machine set in motion by inserting a coin.

It is often asserted that modern industry could never have been created had it not been given over to untrammeled exploitation by commercial adventurers. That may be true. There is no great point in discussing the question as to what might have happened if something else had happened in the past. Modern industry was created by the profiteer, and here it is, the great fact in our lives, blackening our cities, fed with the lives of children, a tyrant over men and women, turning out enormous stocks of produce, good, bad, and horrible. We need waste no time arguing whether any other motive could have done the work. What we are finding is that however effective profit may have been for inaugurating modern industry, it is failing as a method of realizing its promise. That is why men turned to co-operatives and labor unions; that is why the state is interfering more and more. These blundering efforts are the assertion of all the men and all those elements of their natures which commercialism has thwarted. No amount of argument can wipe out the fact that the profit system has never commanded the whole-hearted assent of the people who lived under it. There has been a continuous effort to overthrow it. From Robert Owen to John Stuart Mill, from Ruskin through Morris to the varied radicalism of our day, from the millionaire with his peace palaces to Henry Ford with his generous profit-sharing, through the consumer organizing a co-operative market, to the workingmen defying their masters and the economists by pooling their labor, you find a deep stream of uneasiness, of human restlessness against those impositions which are supposed to rest on the eternal principles of man's being.

There is scarcely any need to press the point, for no one questions the statement that endowment, co-operation, or public enterprise are attempts to employ motives different from those of the profiteer. The only dispute is whether these new motives can be extended and made effective. It is, I think, a crucial question. It lies at the root of most theoretical objection to socialism in the famous "human nature" argument. Far from being a trivial question, as Socialist debaters like to pretend—it is the hardest nut they have to crack. They are proposing a reconstruction of human society, and in all honesty, they cannot dodge the question as to whether man as we know him is capable of what they ask. Persian, Mexican, Turkish and Chinese experience with constitutional democracies ought to show how easy it is, as Macaulay said, for a tailor to measure the clothes of all his customers by the Apollo Belvedere. In a matter like this, there is little to choose between the Socialist who is sure his plan will work and the "anti" who is sure it will not. The profit motive is attacked, that is certain; that more or less successful attempts are made to supplant it, is obvious, but how far we can go, that remains an open question. We cannot answer it by analogy; it does not follow from the success of a co-operative grocery that the Steel Trust can be governed on the same plan. If our expectations are to have solidity we must find evidence for them in those great private industries which seem to be completely in the hands of profit. That is where the issues join. The theater has always been a stamping ground for "queer" people; scholars are notoriously incompetent in "business"; scientific research pays so well, is so undeniably valuable, that few dare grudge it a subsidy; public utilities, like the highways, are by tradition not business propositions; and co-operatives have had a stormy history. There are, of course, the Army and Navy, which no man wishes to see organized by private individuals on the make. The most conservative have doubted recently whether armaments should be manufactured for profit. Yet such analogies, impressive as they are, offer nothing conclusive. But if we find that in the staple industries like steel and oil a silent revolution is in progress, then we have a basis for action. If there the profit motive is decadent and new incentives ready, then perhaps what look like irresponsible outcries and wanton agitation will assume the dignity of a new morality.

A Preface to Morals (1929), *Chapter 12.*

It is my impression that when machine industry reaches a certain scale of complexity it exerts such pressure upon the men who run it that they cannot help socializing it. They are subject to a kind of economic selection under which only those men survive who are capable of taking a somewhat disinterested view of their work. A mature industry, because it is too subtly organized to be run by naïvely passionate men, puts a premium upon men whose characters are sufficiently matured to make them respect reality and to discount their own prejudices.

When the machine technology is really advanced, that is to say, when it has drawn great masses of men within the orbit of its influence, when a corporation has become really great, the old distinction between public and private interest becomes very dim. I think it is destined largely to disappear. It is difficult even today to say whether the great railways, the General Electric Company, the United States Steel Corporation, the bigger insurance companies and banks are public or private institutions. When institutions reach a point where the legal owners are virtually disfranchised, when the direction is in the hands of salaried executives, technicians, and experts who hold themselves more or less accountable in standards of conduct to their fellow professionals, when the ultimate control is looked upon by the directors not as "business" but as a trust, it is not fanciful to say, as Mr. Keynes has said, that "the battle of socialism against unlimited private profit is being won in detail hour by hour."

In so far as industry itself evolves its own control, it will regain its liberty from external interference. To say that is to say simply that the "natural liberty" of the early businessman was unworkable because the early businessman was unregenerate: he was immature, and he was therefore acquisitive. The only kind of liberty which is workable in the real world is the liberty of the disinterested man, of the man who has transformed his passions by an understanding of necessity. He can, as Confucius said, follow what his heart desires without transgressing what is right. For he has learned to desire what is right.

The more perfectly we understand the implications of the machine technology upon which our civilization is based, the easier it will be for us to live with it. We shall discern the ideals of our industry in the necessities of industry itself. They are the direction in which it must evolve if it is to fulfill itself. That is what ideals are. They are not hallucinations. They are not a collection of pretty and casual preferences. Ideals are an imaginative understanding of that which is desirable in that which is possible. As we discern the ideals of the machine technology we can consciously pursue them, knowing that we are not vainly trying to impose our casual prejudices, but that we are in harmony with the age we live in.

"Big Businessmen of Tomorrow," The American Magazine, *CXVII (April 1934), 18.*

It is impossible to be a good leader in anything and be very much interested in building up a private fortune. It cannot be done in public life. It cannot be done in the scientific professions. It cannot be done by writers, artists, teachers, and ministers. And now we begin to realize that it cannot be done in finance and industry. A leader, a man who exercises great power in the financial and commercial life of the nation, ought to be well enough paid so that he need not worry about money, and after that he ought not to be much interested in money.

To say this sounds at first very strange. But big business is not ordinary business on a larger scale; it is a wholly different kind of business. And the head of a business big enough to make of him a public character must expect to be judged as such.

Why does bigness make such a difference? Because so many people are affected.

A big corporation employs a very large number of men. If it does not treat them properly, the standard of life of an important part of the community is lowered. If the men strike, the whole community suffers. In a small business, if the employee is badly treated he can, in normal times, leave and find a better job. He has a choice. In any case, the public is unaffected. But the labor policy of a big business does affect the public interest.

A big business supplies a large part of the output of some particular kind of goods that the people need. It can therefore go a long way toward making the price and determining the quality. A small business is in competition with many other small businesses. The buyer can shop around. The larger the business, the narrower is the buyer's freedom to choose. So the sales policy of a big business affects the public.

The capital used in a big business is not provided by its officers and directors—no great part of it, at least. It is supplied by the public which buys its stocks and bonds, by banks which lend it depositors' money. The big businessman is a trustee of other people's money.

Now anyone responsible for labor, sales, and financial policies affecting the vital interests of thousands of workers, consumers, investors, and depositors is in a position radically different from that of a man operating with his own money, with few employees, and in a highly competitive market. The big business is by its very bigness no longer private business, and the rules which apply to it are those which apply to public officials.

What are these rules? They are that responsible heads must have no private interest which interferes with their public duties. An officeholder must not own stock in, or take a retainer from, a railroad or a public utility which he is regulating, or have a stake in a contract which he awards, or speculate in real estate or stocks because he has inside knowledge.

The time is coming when big businessmen will be judged by the same standard. Today many successful men reach a point where they wish to retire from business and to enter the public service. They become ambassadors or cabinet officers, or presidents of colleges. As I see it, in the days to come, men who are about to become heads of great banks or large corporations will look upon themselves as having retired from the business of money-making. Young men who aspire to high positions in the economic world will arrange their personal lives, their scale of personal expenditures, the way honorable men entering public life now have to arrange their lives.

They will expect to be comfortable, but not enormously rich; they will work for honor, for distinction, for promotion, for the interest and excitement and satisfaction of the work itself. Many will try to make themselves financially independent *before* they take the responsible posts. For, in the future, to make a fortune will be considered as improper for the head of a big business as for the President of the United States or the mayor of a city.

This is the new moral standard which is being set up in the conscience of the American people. It will never be expressed completely in laws, though there will be attempts, many of them blundering, to do so. In things like this, the true law is custom, and it seems to me that we can see before our eyes the growth of a new custom, of a new understanding of what the nation must expect of those who are its economic and financial leaders.

Those who have read history will recognize that the extension of the rules of public life to big business is merely a step in an evolution which has been going on for centuries. There was a time when tax-collecting was a private business, when the king's ministers were expected to enrich themselves by taking over the estates of their political enemies, when offices were bought and sold as so much private property. Gradually, very gradually, the conception of public office as a public trust has got itself established in men's minds as the proper ideal; we are still far from having reached a complete observance of the ideal. Nevertheless, it is accepted as the standard, and by it the public judges an Albert B. Fall and a James J. Walker. What we are now witnessing is the gradual extension of that ideal to include business which is so big that it is public business.

That, it seems to me, is what all the investigating of recent times means. That is the moral significance of the New Deal for the big businessman.

Drift and Mastery (*1914*), *Chapter 5.*

The fact is that nothing is so stubbornly resisted as the attempt to organize labor into effective unions. Yet it is labor organized that alone can stand between America and the creation of a permanent, servile class. Unless labor is powerful enough to be respected, it is doomed to a degrading servitude. Without unions no such power is possible. Without unions industrial democracy is unthinkable. Without democracy in industry, that is where it counts most, there is no such thing as democracy in America. For only through the union can the wage-earner participate in the control of industry, and only through the union can he obtain the discipline needed for self-government. Those who fight unions may think they are fighting its obvious errors, but what they are really against is just this encroachment of democracy upon business.

Now men don't agitate for democracy because it is a fine theory. They come to desire it because they have to, because absolutism does not work out any longer to civilized ends. Employers are not wise enough to govern their men with unlimited power, and not generous enough to be trusted with autocracy. That is the plain fact of the situation: the essential reason why private industry has got to prepare itself for democratic control.

I don't pretend for one moment that labor unions are far-seeing, intelligent, or wise in their tactics. I have never seen a political democracy that aroused uncritical enthusiasm. It seems to me simply that the effort to build up unions is as much the work of pioneers, as the extension of civilization into the wilderness. The unions are the first feeble effort to conquer the industrial jungle for democratic life. They may not succeed, but if they don't their failure will be a tragedy for civilization, a loss of co-operative effort, a balking of energy, and the fixing in American life of a class structure.

The unions are struggling where life is nakedly brutal, where the dealings of men have not been raised even to the level of discussion which we find in politics. There is almost as little civil procedure in industry as there is in Mexico, or as there was on the American frontier. To expect unionists then to talk with velvet language and act with the deliberation of a college faculty is to be a tenderfoot, a victim of your class tradition. The virtues of labor today are frontier virtues, its struggles are for rights and privileges that the rest of us inherited from our unrefined ancestors.

Men are fighting for the beginnings of industrial self-government. If the world were wise that fight would be made easier for them. But it is not wise. Few of us care for ten minutes in a month about these beginnings or what they promise. And so the burden falls entirely upon the workers who are directly concerned. They have got to win civilization, they have got to take up the task of fastening a worker's control upon business.

No wonder they despise the scab. He is justly despised. Far from being the independent, liberty-loving soul he is sometimes painted, the scab is a traitor to the economic foundations of democracy. He makes the basic associations of men difficult. He is an indigestible lump in the common life, and it is he who generates nine-tenths of the violence in labor disputes. Democracies of workingmen have to fight him out of sheer self-protection, as a nation has to fight a mutiny, as doctors have to fight a quack. The clubbing of scabs is not a pretty thing; the importation of scabs is an uglier one. It is perhaps true that there is . . . no such thing as peaceful picketing. There is no such thing as a peaceful coast defense or a gentlemanly border patrol. The picket line is to these little economic democracies the guardian of their integrity, their chief protection from foreign invasion.

"The Strike at General Motors," Today and Tomorrow, *January 7, 1937.*

Anyone who studies the position of the leaders on both sides will be forced to conclude, I think, that they are not thinking solely about just and orderly industrial relations in the General Motors

Corporation but about something else. And what is that something else? That something else is, I think, what might be called the sovereign power in industry. Mr. Sloan and his associates wish to fix the basic labor policy of the corporation. Mr. Martin and Mr. Lewis wish to fix the basic labor policy of the corporation. Though both sides say they believe in collective bargaining, each is really asking for arbitrary authority.

No tolerable system of industrial relations can be developed out of these intrinsically arbitrary claims. For the essence of any peaceable relationship in human affairs is that nobody shall have arbitrary power. No doubt the phrase "collective bargaining" is awkward and ambiguous but the underlying intention is clear enough. It means that decisions affecting industrial relations shall be arrived at by consulting those affected, by argument, evidence, persuasion, not by commands or by threats.

But judging by their public statements, neither the management nor the union understands collective bargaining or is actuated by the spirit which collective bargaining requires. If they understood the principles which they both profess, Mr. Sloan would not be issuing proclamations announcing that General Motors "will" do this and "will not" do that. That is the language of authority, not of a constitutional democracy; and Mr. Martin would not be "demanding" that his organization be established arbitrarily as the sole representative of 200,000 human beings.

There is a third party to this dispute, the general American public, and it will have renounced its rights and neglected its own vital interests if it does not at once rise up and assert that it will not tolerate a devastating struggle for arbitrary power in this great industry. This is too important an industry to be made the center of a struggle for power. This is too big a business to be considered as a private affair. It is a business which because of its size and its ramifying connections with the whole American economy must be held to the standards of a public enterprise. In a public enterprise all who engage in it must find for themselves, or else have imposed upon them by law, methods of operating the business without serious interruption and without disorder and violence. For in an enterprise so thoroughly affected with the public interest as in General Motors, nobody, not Mr. Martin, not Mr. Lewis, not Mr. Knudsen, not Mr. Sloan, can be permitted to exercise arbitrary authority, and when they seek it, they must, this being a democracy, be brought to reason by an aroused public opinion.

3 · *Some Notes on the Press*

The Stakes of Diplomacy (*1915*), *Chapter 4.*

It is small wonder that newspapers are, in the main, instruments of irritation between peoples. I leave out of account here the deliberately pacifist press as well as the reptile press of the war parties. It is the ordinary middle-class newspapers which I have in mind, the papers run as commercial enterprises. With all their faults admitted, no one can possibly assert that their owners are criminal enough to provoke war. Yet in almost every crisis the tension is increased by the newspapers.

The reason is in part that war is more sensational than peace—the possibility of conflict is a cheaper and more obvious form of news. It is hard to conceive of a newspaper breaking out into lurid headlines to announce in time of peace that "good will between Japan and the United States is on the increase." It would sound silly. The press cannot shout about the aggression that will not take place, or announce with joy the markets that are not coveted. Indeed, any attempt to do it would be regarded as suspicious. Men would say that the news was intended to conceal something. No one has discovered a way of making good will, harmony, reasonableness easily dramatic. In overwhelming measure the news of the day is the news of trouble and conflict. Those journals which devote themselves to telling of the real advances of mankind—the technological progress, the administrative triumphs, the conquests of prejudice—are not popular. They lack the "punch."

To this condition of news-reporting, international affairs have to conform. As the negotiations of governments are conducted with loaded weapons at hand, and with the pretension to sovereignty by both sides, almost any international situation contains news of trouble. At the same time the editor is publishing his paper for a community in which the opposition is probably not represented. It is easy and natural for him to take a "strong" stand. A "strong" stand is the least dangerous, for it flatters everybody, produces an exhilarating sense of importance, risks no offense to any significant section of his readers. A "weak" stand, a reasonable, complicated desire for adjustment, is a costly and thankless task for an editor. It means that he appeals to thought which is pale rather than to lusts which are strong. He appears academic, mugwumpish, unmanly. And though it requires the highest kind of courage to run against patriotic sentiment, he is likely to be called a coward.

Sympathy for foreigners is the most disinterested and civilized form of sympathy. It is not difficult to understand why editors display so little of it. There is almost no incentive to understand foreign peoples. They are distant. They speak a foreign language. They do not often reward their friends in another land. At home, the editor faces the fact that ignorance and distrust of the alien is the most natural and the cheapest channel into which high passion and united feeling can flow. It is the greatest object of uncorrected enthusiasm, the greatest drama in which the villain is neither an advertiser nor a reader of the newspaper. It is one field of interest where people are at once unanimous and excited, and not many editors have the strength to resist cultivating that field. Then, too, the editor is himself a member of the community subject to the same influences. He is a good American or a good Britisher, sometimes a somewhat professionally good patriot. In following the easiest way, which is the way of irritation, he is not guilty of any malevolent plan. He does it with a good conscience, for the human conscience is never so much at ease as when it follows the line of least resistance. Only saints, heroes, and specialists in virtue feel remorse because they have done what everybody was doing and agreed with what everybody was thinking.

Public Opinion (1922), *Chapter 24.*

It is possible and necessary for journalists to bring home to people the uncertain character of the truth on which their opinions are founded, and by criticism and agitation to prod social science into making more usable formulations of social facts, and to prod statesmen into establishing more visible institutions. The press, in other words, can fight for the extension of reportable truth. But as social truth is organized today, the press is not constituted to furnish from one edition to the next the amount of knowledge which the democratic theory of public opinion demands. This is not due to the Brass Check, as the quality of news in radical papers shows, but to the fact that the press deals with a society in which the governing forces are so imperfectly recorded. The theory that the press can itself record those forces is false. It can normally record only what has been recorded for it by the working of institutions. Everything else is argument and opinion, and fluctuates with the vicissitudes, the self-consciousness, and the courage of the human mind.

If the press is not so universally wicked, nor so deeply conspiring, as Mr. Sinclair would have us believe, it is very much more frail than the democratic theory has as yet admitted. It is too frail to carry the whole burden of popular sovereignty, to supply spontaneously the truth which democrats hoped was inborn. And when we expect it to supply such a body of truth we employ a misleading standard of judgment. We misunderstand the limited nature of news, the illimitable complexity of society; we overestimate our own endurance, public spirit, and all-round competence. We suppose an appetite for uninteresting truths which is not discovered by any honest analysis of our own tastes.

If the newspapers, then, are to be charged with the duty of translating the whole public life of mankind, so that every adult can arrive at an opinion on every moot topic, they fail; they are bound to fail; in any future one can conceive, they will continue to fail. It is not possible to assume that a world, carried on by division of labor and distribution of authority, can be governed by universal opinions in the whole population. Unconsciously the theory sets up the single reader as theoretically omnicompetent, and puts upon the press the burden of accomplishing whatever representative government, industrial organization, and diplomacy have failed to accomplish. Acting upon everybody for thirty minutes in twenty-four hours, the press is asked to create a mystical force called Public Opinion that will take up the slack in public institutions. The press has often mistakenly pretended that it could do just that. It has, at great moral cost to itself, encouraged a democracy, still bound to its original premises, to expect newspapers to supply spontaneously for every organ of government, for every social problem, the machinery of information which these do not normally supply themselves. Institutions, having failed to furnish themselves with instruments of knowledge, have become a bundle of "problems," which the population as a whole, reading the press as a whole, is supposed to solve.

The press, in other words, has come to be regarded as an organ of direct democracy, charged on a much wider scale, and from day to day, with the function often attributed to the initiative, referendum, and recall. The Court of Public Opinion, open day and night, is to lay down the law for everything all the time. It is not workable. And when you consider the nature of news, it is not even thinkable. For the news, as we have seen, is precise in proportion to the precision with which the event is recorded. Unless the event is capable of being named, measured, given shape, made specific, it either fails to take on the character of news, or it is subject to the accidents and prejudices of observation.

Therefore, on the whole, the quality of the news about modern society is an index of its social organization. The better the institutions, the more all interests concerned are formally represented, the more issues are disentangled, the more objective criteria are introduced, the more perfectly an affair can be presented as news. At its best the press is a servant and guardian of institutions; at its worst it is a means by which a few exploit social disorganization to their own ends. In the degree to which institutions fail to function, the unscrupulous journalist can fish in troubled waters, and the conscientious one must gamble with uncertainties.

The press is no substitute for institutions. It is like the beam of a searchlight that moves restlessly about, bringing one episode and then another out of darkness into vision. Men cannot do the work of the world by this light alone. They cannot govern society by episodes, incidents, and eruptions. It is only when they work by a steady light of their own, that the press, when it is turned upon them, reveals a situation intelligible enough for a popular decision. The trouble lies deeper than the press, and so does the remedy. It lies in social organization based on a system of analysis and record, and in all the corollaries of that principle; in the abandonment of the theory of the omnicompetent citizen, in the decentralization of decision, in the co-ordination of decision by comparable record and analysis. If at the centers of management there is a running audit, which makes work intelligible to those who do it, and those who superintend it, issues when they arise are not the mere collisions of the blind. Then, too, the news is uncovered for the press by a system of intelligence that is also a check upon the press.

That is the radical way. For the troubles of the press, like the troubles of representative government, be it territorial or functional, like the troubles of industry, be it capitalist, co-operative, or communist, go back to a common source: to the failure of self-governing people to transcend their casual experience and their prejudice, by inventing, creating, and organizing a machinery of knowledge. It is because they are compelled to act without a reliable picture of the world, that governments, schools, newspapers, and churches make such small headway against the more obvious failings of democracy, against violent prejudice, apathy, preference for the curious trivial as against the dull important, and the hunger for sideshows and three-legged calves. This is the primary defect of popular government, a defect inherent in its traditions, and all its other defects can, I believe, be traced to this one.

"Two Revolutions in the American Press," The Yale Review, XX (*1931*), *433*.

I do not feel that as a working newspaperman I can speak with any authority about newspapers. I do not say this to gain the appearance of modesty. For heaven knows there is nothing modest about journalism as such, least of all about the particular branch of it which I happen to practice. There are few current concerns of mankind on which my colleagues and I do not have something to say; yet the newspaper itself, which is our medium, almost certainly imposes unrealized presumptions, loyalties, and interests, and reservations, upon any newspaperman's discussion of his own craft. The last word, therefore, must lie with the detached student, who can by imagination and sympathy and observation know all that we know without our entanglements.

Certainly it is not easy for one engaged in the practice of daily journalism to feel any confidence in his ability to express more than his own working philosophy, to indicate the general ideas which seem to him to provide rational basis for what he is doing, and to give him his general sense of direction. For it is a first fact in the whole situation of modern newspapers that there does not exist any generally accepted public philosophy about them. . . .

The popular commercial press of the second half of the nineteenth century and down to our own times has had as its central motive the immediate satisfaction of the largest number of people. Its proprietors and editors had, of course, their own convictions, but the working principle which actuated their publications was to catch the daily interest of their potential readers. Thus this press, escaped from the tutelage of government, fell under the tutelage of the masses. It was not a free press in the sense that it was moved by the convictions of its writers, but a kind of freedmen's press, which, lacking the positive qualities of a liberal existence, found support and profit in serving the whims and wishes and curiosity of the people.

I have heard this type of journalism defended eloquently on the ground that in a democracy the press, like the government, should give the public what it wants. A sounder justification for it can, I think, be found, which is that if the publication of news and opinion was ever to be genuinely freed of control by the ruling powers of the state, it had to find its first support in powers which were a match for the ruling powers. The popular commercial press, because it is popular and profitable, has finally broken the ancient monopoly of intelligence, and has at least opened the way to much more substantial liberties.

It could be demonstrated, I think, that however much the laws may seem to grant political freedom, they are ineffective until a country has for some considerable time accustomed itself to newspapers which are highly profitable and immediately powerful because of their skill in enlisting, in holding, and in influencing a great mass of readers. When there is no prosperous and popular press the liberty of publication is precarious. Publications are likely to be either controlled or venal, or else they eke out a miserable and fairly negligible existence. It will be found, I think, that the area of free publication in the world today is on the whole coterminous with the area in which commercial newspapers circulate widely. Based upon the support of literate and relatively well-to-do masses, they dare to be independent of the political power and can afford to be independent of special interests.

Largely because our population provides the broadest base of this kind in the world, the American press has, I believe, become freer from hidden control than any in the world. This is the great service performed by what I have called the popular commercial press, otherwise known as yellow journalism, and in its latest and perhaps last manifestation as tabloid journalism. It is the first politically independent press which the world has known. . . . I do not mean to say that the popular commercial press has won the battle of freedom, but rather that as the frontiers of freedom advance, it is this popular press which first effectively occupies the new territory and consolidates the ground that has been won. Without its massive power new Constitutional liberties are difficult to hold when the fervor of the emancipation has passed.

This type of journalism is not, I believe, enduring. It contains within itself the seeds of its own dissolution. For its actuating principle is to attract daily the most vivid attention of a large mass. Its object, therefore, is not to report events in their due relationships or to interpret them in ways that subsequent events will verify. It selects from the events of the day those aspects which most immediately engage attention, and in place of the effort to see life steadily and whole it sees life dramatically, episodically, and from what is called, in the jargon of the craft, the angle of human interest. This is highly effective—for a while. But the method soon exhausts itself. When everything is dramatic, nothing after a while is dramatic; when everything is highly spiced, nothing after a while has much flavor; when everything is new and startling, the human mind just ceases to be startled. But that is not all. As the readers of this press live longer in the world, and as their personal responsibilities increase, they begin to feel the need of being genuinely informed rather than of being merely amused and excited. Gradually they discover that things do not happen as they are made to appear in the human interest stories. The realization begins to dawn upon them that they have been getting not the news but a species of romantic fiction which they can get much better out of the movies and the magazines. I think I am not mistaken in believing that the popular press has a transient circulation, that its readers pass through it on their way to maturity, and that it can continue to prosper on its original pattern only while there is a continuing supply of immature readers who have not yet felt the need of something else.

As time goes on, therefore, one of two things happens to the popular commercial press. If its owners lack foresight and energy and know only how to repeat the original formulae, the newspaper gradually fails. If, on the other hand, they understand the nature of the process I am describing, they gradually transform the paper itself, making it more and more sober, less and less sensational, increasingly reliable and comprehensive.

In the extreme case, even of tabloid journalism in New York, one can see the growing respectability of the successful one and the steady degeneration of the disreputable one.

The necessity of meeting these conditions has begun to work another revolution in the history of journalism. It has not been heralded as such, but I believe that it dates roughly from the profound revulsion among educated people and among newspapermen themselves at the orgy of lying which the war propaganda let loose. Be that as it may, the most impressive event of the last decade in the history of newspapers has been the demonstration that the objective, orderly, and comprehensive presentation of news is a far more successful type of journalism today than the dramatic, disorderly, episodic type.

This new journalism is even more independent than the popular commercial press which it is crowding into the corner. For it has just as broad a base in the number of its readers, and because it obviously enlists a more sustained attention it is more profitable as an advertising medium. Its real independence lies, however, in the fact that it is not only so self-sufficient that it can be free of hidden control, but that since the commodity it deals in primarily is the approximation to objective fact, it is free also of subserviency to the whims of the public.

The strength of this type of journalism will, I think, be cumulative because it opens the door to the use of trained intelligence in newspaper work. The older type of popular journalism was a romantic art dependent largely on the virtuosity of men like Bennett, Hearst, and Pulitzer. It succeeded if the directing mind had a flair for popular success; it failed if the springs of genius dried up. The newer objective journalism is a less temperamental affair, for it deals with solider realities. There will be place in it always, of course, for originating minds; the recording of human events cannot be standardized into a routine. But it is bound, I think, to become less Napoleonic at the top and less bohemian at the bottom, and to take on the character of a liberal profession.

For the ability to present news objectively and to interpret it realistically is not a native instinct in the human species; it is a product of culture which comes only with knowledge of the past and acute awareness of how deceptive is our normal observation and how wishful is our thinking. I do not know much about the schools of journalism, and I cannot say, therefore, whether they are vocational courses designed to teach the unteachable art of the old romantic journalism or professional schools aiming somehow to prepare men for the new objective journalism. I suspect, however, that schools of journalism in the professional sense will not exist generally until journalism has been practiced for some time as a profession. It has never yet been a profession. It has been at times a dignified calling, at others a romantic adventure, and then again a servile trade. But a profession it could not begin to be until modern objective journalism was successfully created, and with it the need of men who would consider themselves devoted, as all the professions ideally are, to the service of truth alone.

"The Departure of the Lindberghs," Today and Tomorrow, *December 28, 1935.*

The Lindberghs, let it be said squarely, are refugees from the tyranny of yellow journalism. They have fled to England to escape it, and in fleeing they have made their resounding protest. They have been denied their human, their inalienable right to privacy. And in their protest they speak for the conscience of all civilized men.

They have brought to a head the question of how the liberties of the press can be accommodated to the liberties of the individual. It is the ancient and the everlasting problem of humanity, how to combine liberty with order. It is a problem that is insoluble by those who take an absolutist position in human affairs, by those who, for example, seeing the evils of liberty make a fetish of order, or those who, seeing the horrors of unrestrained authority, will recognize no restraints on liberty. The civilized world has known since the Greek thinkers first discovered the principles of human association in a free society that the supreme social principle is moderation in all principles.

The Lindberghs are the immediate victims of criminals, cranks, and journalistic panderers, but finally they are the victims of our failure to have made dominant in the moral tradition of this country the ancient wisdom of the humanists—that excess is the essential characteristic of vice and that in all truth, beauty, and goodness there is proportion, moderation, and restraint. Thus a journalist who respects his own liberties will respect the liberties of others, knowing that on any other terms his freedom will become a tyranny to his fellow men. There is no shorter cut than this to a remedy for the condition which drove the Lindberghs away. It cannot be remedied by catching a villain, by passing new laws, by excited declamation on the front pages of the newspapers. It can be remedied only by a change of the public philosophy, by acquiring the conviction that such things as the Lindberghs have been subjected to are indecent, intolerable, and inhuman.

That conviction must exist at the top, among those who represent the good repute of our civilization, and it must be the real conviction of men who will resent the invasion of their own privacy and will not connive at the violation of the privacy of others. It is no use, for example, to deplore the departure of the Lindberghs and then to turn to some keyhole columnist to find out the details of someone else's private life. Genuine respect for human privacy does not exist among us today. What with those who wish to be in the limelight at any cost, those who are afraid to stand up for their rights, and those who have an infantile curiosity to learn the inside story of the inside story of the facts of life, there has gone out of the public taste the capacity to realize and to resent the treatment of personal lives as a spectacle for the mob.

The commercialized and, it may be added, the political violation of privacy cannot be dealt with by libel suits or even by the horsewhip, though I have seen men writhing with anger and wondering whether respect for their own manhood did not compel them to use a horsewhip. Undoubtedly it is the truth that the only certain answer to yellow journalism is the example and the effective competition of honest journalism. But that example would be greatly fortified if at last the people who are now so horrified and humiliated could continue to be angry long enough to make it dangerously unprofitable to prostitute the liberties of the press.

"Case at Ipswich Assizes," Today and Tomorrow, *October 29, 1936. The American press coverage of Mrs. Wallis Simpson's divorce trial prompted this discussion of freedom and responsibility in journalism.*

In law and in custom British newspapers do not have the same privileges as ours. Here, broadly speaking, the press can print almost anything about anybody subject only to an extremely cumbersome, expensive, and embarrassing procedure for libel.

The individual who gets into court, say, in a divorce case, or is charged with a crime and brought to trial, is almost without protection against publicity. In England, on the other hand, the freedom of the individual is protected by law along with the freedom of the press. The kind of thing that happened in the Hauptmann case would in England be contempt of court; the persecution of the Lindberghs would be unlawful under the British conception of the freedom of the press. For according to British ideas the individual as well as the newspaper has rights which have to be protected jealously.

Though liberty is cherished in this country, our liberty is defective in that the rights of the individual are not sufficiently protected. Mr. Hearst, for example, is properly outraged when a Senate committee ransacks his files and publishes his communications with his editors. But Mr. Hearst will gladly publish any bit of gossip about Mrs. Simpson that he can lay his hands on. Mr. Hearst as a publisher can subject Mrs. Simpson or a college professor or anyone else to any kind of torture and indignity, and they have no recourse. They cannot answer him effectively. They cannot hold him to account. But for himself, under the principle of the freedom of the press, he claims an immunity which his papers concede to no individual who comes under the harrow.

There is something very lopsided about that situation, and American liberty is far from being as secure as it should be while that situation exists. Our laws and customs do not adequately protect the individual against the invasion of his private rights. If he is charged with a crime, he is tried not only in the courts but simultaneously and often previously in the yellow press. If he goes into court seeking a divorce or to enforce some other right which the law gives him, he must not only prove his case before the judge and jury but expose his whole private life as well. The thing has gone so far that a man who takes a woman out to dinner in a restaurant may hear a few days later over the radio that he is that way about her.

In fact, the American public has become curiously insensitive to private rights. The courts, in criminal cases, in divorce cases, in cases where the evidence is sensational, are shamefully timid in asserting their own decorum and in protecting the individual. Congress continually abuses most gravely its own prerogatives. Individuals are attacked in debates, they are charged, tried, and condemned in legislative hearings, without any of the ordinary legal protection that every man is supposed to enjoy.

Where individual rights are not jealously protected, freedom is imperfect and its foundations are precarious. For men become subservient, timid, and they lose the habits of self-reliance when they feel they are defenseless.

"Notes on the Freedom of the Press," Today and Tomorrow, *April 25, 1936.*

The First Amendment forbids Congress to make laws abridging the freedom of the press, but it does not guarantee to the press any other privilege or immunities which all other citizens do not enjoy.

The distinction is important because it discloses the principle that the freedom of the press in America is protected not merely by the First Amendment but in a much more substantial degree by all the Constitutional guaranties given to all persons.

It follows from this that the press can never defend its own liberties alone. The defense, which has to be everlastingly vigilant, must be given to the whole system of liberties—to the rights of all individuals, the limitation under the law of all organs of government, and the capacity of all men to defend their rights before independent tribunals. The freedom of the press, as we know it in America, is not something apart from this general system of liberty. It is dependent upon this general system and the press can continue to enjoy its liberties only by preserving that system.

This is not only the broadest ground upon which to defend the freedom of the press, but it is also the ground which the people as a whole will thoroughly respect. For I do not think that the people would feel easy in their minds if it were argued, for example, that the privacy of Mr. Hearst's telegrams must be held inviolate but that the privacy of the Lindbergh family need not be, that in the name of the freedom of the press Mr. Hearst may refuse to have his instructions to editors published whereas Colonel Lindbergh may not refuse to have his child's photograph published.

There is something about such a position which does not square with that sense of justice which must in the last analysis underlie any conception of liberty. It seems to me that it is an indefensible position and that it raises questions which all who control publicity are bound to examine. What are the rights of individuals as against unreasonable searches and seizures by the press in the field of their reputations and their private lives? Those rights are not clearly defined today. Yet they must exist, and in so far as they can be defined they must be acknowledged by anyone who sees the freedom of the press as part of, rather than as independent of, a free society.

The gatherings of newspapermen in Washington and in New York during the past ten days have produced also some interesting episodes involving the relation between public officials and the press. They have raised again the everlasting question of whether criticism is fair criticism, whether unfavorable news reports are impartial news reports.

It is only human for officials to feel that unfavorable news and critical comment is biased, incompetent, and misleading. There is no denying the sincerity of their complaints and there is no use pretending that any newspaperman can regularly give the whole objective truth about all complicated and controverted questions. The theory of a free press is that the truth will emerge from free reporting and free discussion, not that it will be presented perfectly and instantly in any one account.

But officials find it hard to remember that. Conscious of their own good intentions, it seems incredible to them that any honest and informed man should seriously disagree, and when they are in the heat of a political battle very few can ever believe that their opponents are as honest as their supporters. That is to be expected. But at least they might remember that their complaints against their critics on the ground of bias would carry more weight if occasionally they were heard to complain that some correspondent had praised unduly their achievements.

Much might be said about the personal relations between politicians and newspapermen. They are invariably delicate and difficult. For obviously they must be close: correspondents must see much of the men they write about. Yet if they do, they soon find themselves compelled to choose between friendship and the ties of loyalty that come from companionship on the one hand, the stern embarrassing truth on the other. This is the unpleasantest side of newspaper work and I have never heard of any way of avoiding it. When a personal friend becomes a public man, a predicament soon arrives in which friendship and professional duty are at odds.

For my own part, I have known only one high public official in my life for whom this problem did not exist. That was

Calvin Coolidge. No matter what was printed about him, it seemed to make no difference in his personal relations with editors and writers. He achieved this miracle by conveying the general impression that he had never heard of the newspaper with which his guest was connected, and had never had anything printed in it called to his attention. This was, it always seemed to me, the perfect method of dealing with the press in a democracy. But Mr. Coolidge was an imperturbable man living in an interlude of quiet times, and it was perhaps rather easier for him to be a philosopher than it has been for his successors.

4 · *Television: Whose Creature, Whose Servant?*

"The TV Problem," Today and Tomorrow, *October 27, 1959.*

Television has been caught perpetrating a fraud which is so gigantic that it calls into question the foundations of the industry.

The fraud was not the work of a few cheats who had wormed their way into the company of honest men. The fraud was too big, too extensive, too well organized to be cured or atoned for by throwing a few conspicuous individuals to the wolves, and by putting on a pious show of scrupulosity about the details of the productions.

There has been, in fact, an enormous conspiracy to deceive the public in order to sell profitable advertising to the sponsors. It involves not merely this individual or that, but the industry as a whole. . . .

The size of the fraud is a bitter reflection on the moral condition of our society. But it is also sure proof that there is something radically wrong with the fundamental national policy under which television operates. The principle of that policy is that for all practical purposes television shall be operated wholly for private profit. There is no competition in television except among competitors trying to sell the attention of their audiences for profit. As a result, while television is supposed to be "free," it has in fact become the creature, the servant, and indeed the prostitute, of merchandising.

Television is expensive and the available channels are few. These channels are possessed by a few companies who are in fierce competition among themselves. But what are they competing about? About how to capture the largest mass audience which can be made to look at and listen to the most profitable advertising.

In this competition, as in Gresham's famous law of money, the bad money drives out the good. In order to capture the largest mass audience the companies have resorted to fraud, as in the case of the quiz shows. But reprehensible as it is to play the gullible public for suckers, that is not the worst of their offending. The worst things they do are first to poison the innocent by the exhibition of violence, degeneracy, and crime, and second, to debase the public taste. . . .

What to do about it? The great offense of the television industry is that it is misusing a superb scientific achievement, that it is monopolizing the air at the expense of effective news reporting, good art, and civilized entertainment. The crux of the evil is that in seeking great mass audiences, the industry has decided from its experience that the taste of great masses is a low one, and that to succeed in the competition it must pander to this low taste.

Quite evidently, this is an evil which cannot be remedied by a regulating commission or by some form of government or self-constituted censorship. The alternative, which is practiced in one form or another in almost every other civilized country, is competition—competition not for private profit but for public service. The best line for us to take is, I am convinced, to devise a way by which one network can be run as a public service with its criterion not what will be most popular but what is good.

No doubt, this network would not attract the largest mass audience. But if it enlisted the great talents which are available in the industry, but are now throttled and frustrated, it might well attract an audience which made up in influence what it lacked in numbers. The force of a good example is a great force, and should not be underrated.

We should not, I believe, shrink from the idea that such a network would have to be subsidized and endowed. Why not?

Is there any doubt that television is a mighty instrument of education—education for good or education for evil? Why should it not be subsidized and endowed as are the universities and the public schools and the exploration of space and modern medical research, and indeed the churches—and so many other institutions which are essential to a good society, yet cannot be operated for profit?

They are unwise friends of our system of private capitalism who do not recognize the fact that the higher life of our society depends on respect for and support of non-commercial institutions. It is true that the best way for this country to produce wealth is by private enterprise for private profit. But there are a lot of other things that need to be done besides producing wealth and selling goods. One of them is to inform, instruct, and entertain the people through the media of mass communications. And among these media there must be some which aim not at popularity and profit but at excellence and the good life.

That it is possible to operate non-commercial institutions is attested by the fact that we do operate successfully schools, universities, hospitals, laboratories of research. Harvard and Yale and Princeton and Columbia and Dartmouth, and so on, are not operated for profit. Their trustees do not play politics. They are concerned with excellence and not with making money. Why should not people of this sort be able to find ways to operate a television network?

"Television and Press," Today and Tomorrow, *March 3, 1960.*

Recently, the president of CBS, Mr. Frank Stanton, made a speech arguing that in principle the government, which grants the licenses, has no right to concern itself in any way with the character of the broadcasts. He calls this "free television" and asserts that all forms of regulation and accountability are wrong. What the country must have is "a vigorous, freely competing, *unrestricted* television medium."

This is probably the first time that anyone in a responsible position in the television industry has claimed for it an *unrestricted* right to set its own standards of conduct. This is certainly not the intent of the law under which Mr. Stanton operates. The intent of the law which was passed by Congress in February, 1927, was expressed, as Mr. George Sokolsky recently noted, by ex-President Herbert Hoover, then the Secretary of Commerce. Mr. Hoover said that "the ether is a public medium, and its use must be for public benefit. The use of a radio channel is justified only if there is public benefit."

Mr. Stanton would, I suppose, say in reply that the greatest public benefit will come if we leave it to the *unrestricted* judgment of the industry itself what programs are in the public interest. To support this position Mr. Stanton argues that television stations are like newspapers, and that the government has no more right to concern itself with what is broadcast than it has the right to concern itself with what is printed.

This is a thoroughly false argument. A television station is not like a newspaper. It is like a printing press. It is a mechanical medium of communication. Now let us suppose that in a whole region around some city there were only, let us say, three printing presses. They would have to print all the newspapers, all the magazines, all the books, there being no other way to get anything printed. Does Mr. Stanton imagine that under such a condition of virtual monopoly, there would be no public regulation of the printing presses?

There is an essential and radical difference between television and printing, and Mr. Stanton should not pretend that they can be or should be treated alike. It may be true, as he says, that "most metropolitan centers in the United States have more competing television stations than competing mass circulation dailies." But Mr. Stanton has missed the point. The three or four competing television stations control virtually all that can be received over the air by ordinary television sets. But besides the mass circulation dailies, there are the weeklies, the monthlies, the out-of-town newspapers and books. If a man does not like his newspaper, he can read another from out of town, or wait for a weekly news magazine. It is not ideal. But it is infinitely better than the situation in television. There, if a man does not like what the networks offer him, all he can do is to turn them off, and listen to a phonograph.

Networks, which are very few in number, have a virtual monopoly of a whole medium of communication. The newspapers of mass circulation have no monopoly of the medium of print. The situation of freedom is bound to be different, too. Free speech is a cherished principle. But how it can be exercised depends upon where it is exercised.

"The Administration and TV," Today and Tomorrow, *January 5, 1960.*

My own view is that it is not possible to define in the laws and regulations standards of quality which can be enforced. Nor do I think it would be desirable or healthy to have the regulating commission, which is essentially a policeman, set up shop to advise and even control the quality of the programs.

What then? How about relying upon voluntary self-improvement by the networks? There appears to be some evidence that they would like to do better than they have been doing, and that they would like to recover the confidence and respect which they lost during the recent exposures and the public outcry. More power to them. But we must not forget that the economic interest of the companies, which require bigger audiences for bigger revenues, is against any serious and lasting effort to use television for its highest possibilities. The companies will do as much but not much more than the traffic will bear.

That will not be enough. This country needs *some* television at the best hours which, like schools and universities, like art galleries, like the parks, like research, is not commercial, is produced not because it yields private profits but because it moves toward truth and excellence. I say "some television." We could not and should not have the government run the whole television industry. What we need is a competitor with commercial television, a competitor who has a different motive and can have, therefore, different standards.

The non-commercial competitor would have to be some kind of public corporation or authority, chartered by law, governed like a university by trustees, and operated by professionals. How could it be financed? . . . Since the air waves are public property, the government should charge rentals for them. This is quite feasible since the profits are large. Moreover, rentals could be charged not only in money which would finance the non-commercial company but also in the form of time set aside for it on the commercial networks.

There is little doubt that some non-commercial television could be financed. It would be a very good thing if an appropriate committee of Congress would make a report on the economics and the finances of the television industry.

There will be a temptation, I realize, to treat the uproar of the autumn as one of those things which pass and are forgotten. This country cannot afford to do that. For television, which is the most powerful medium of mass communications, is of enormous importance in the life of a nation. To forget about it because it is not in the headlines would be frivolous, and indeed a sign of a serious national weakness.

5 · *The Teachers and the Taught*

"The South and the New Society," Social Forces, *VI* (1927), *1.*

If we are to live in this modern age and deal successfully with it we must commit ourselves to the belief that life is an unending inquiry and that living is an unending experiment and adventure. Because we are committed to that we must maintain at all costs the liberty to think and the liberty to experiment, must maintain it against fools, against fanatics, against every vested interest.

The war for liberty never ends. One day liberty has to be defended against the power of wealth, on another day against the intrigues of politicians, on another against the dead hand of bureaucrats, on another against the patrioteer and the militarist, on another against the profiteer, and then against the hysteria and passions of mobs, against obscurantism and stupidity, against the criminal and against the overrighteous. In this campaign every civilized man is enlisted till he dies, and he only has known the full joy of living who somewhere and at some time has struck a decisive blow for the freedom of the human spirit.

But it is not enough to maintain liberty. We have a still higher and more difficult task. It is the peculiar business of education to teach people how to use the liberty they inherit and how to pass it on to the next generation, enlarged, enriched, and made more secure. It is not enough to vindicate liberty in legislatures, in courts, in the press, in school boards, and before public opinion. There is a personal discipline necessary to the use of liberty. Without the discipline men never will love liberty and never will cherish it. They will be like a savage who by accident finds a delicate instrument and carelessly throws it away.

If people are to use liberty and not to be bewildered and overwhelmed by it they must be relieved of their fears and their anxieties. You know how often through careless and superstitious ignorance in their early training men and women are poisoned with unreasoning fears. You know how many human lives are distracted and reduced to futility by subtle and uncontrollable fears. The fear of personal inferiority, the fear of what others will say, the fear of losing the social position one has, or of not acquiring the position one would like, fears of vanity, fears about love, fears about disease, fears about death. If men are to live free lives and to use liberty, the last great tyrant from which they must emancipate themselves is their own fear. Fears are the foundation of every tyranny in the world. There never was a tyrant, there never was a despot, there never was a demagogue whose power did not rest finally on the irrational and superstititious fear of his followers. We must emancipate this generation from fear. We must track down these fears to their source in early childhood. We must bring them out into the light. We must cure them with conscious understanding. We must create a generation of men who can look upon death, disease, and misfortune without flinching, who can greet the adventure of life with a regular pulse, with a clear eye, and with serene confidence. And we must make war upon the bogies, make war upon the taboos, make war upon the sacred cows, make war upon spooks and devils, and all the private hells that human fear creates.

Then, and then only, when we shall have cleansed the passions of anxiety, will we be ready to discipline the mind for its work of understanding.

"Education vs. Western Civilization," The American Scholar, X (*1941*), *184, an address delivered under the auspices of Phi Beta Kappa at the annual meeting of the American Association for the Advancement of Science, Irvine Auditorium, University of Pennsylvania, December 29, 1940.*

It was once the custom in the great universities to propound a series of theses which, as Cotton Mather put it, the student had to "defend manfully." I should like to revive this custom by propounding a thesis about the state of education in this troubled age.

The thesis which I venture to submit to you is as follows:

That during the past forty or fifty years those who are responsible for education have progressively removed from the curriculum of studies the Western culture which produced the modern democratic state;

That the schools and colleges have, therefore, been sending out into the world men who no longer understand the creative principle of the society in which they must live;

That, deprived of their cultural tradition, the newly educated Western men no longer possess in the form and substance of their own minds and spirits, the ideas, the premises, the rationale, the logic, the method, the values, or the deposited wisdom which are the genius of the development of Western civilization;

That the prevailing education is destined, if it continues, to destroy Western civilization and is in fact destroying it;

That our civilization cannot effectively be maintained where it still flourishes, or be restored where it has been crushed, without the revival of the central, continuous, and perennial culture of the Western world;

And that, therefore, what is now required in the modern educational system is not the expansion of its facilities or the specific reform of its curriculum and administration but a thorough reconsideration of its underlying assumptions and of its purposes.

I realize quite well that this thesis constitutes a sweeping indictment of modern education. But I believe that the indictment is justified and that there is a prima facie case for entertaining this indictment.

Universal and compulsory modern education was established by the emancipated democracies during the nineteenth century. "No other sure foundation can be devised," said Thomas Jefferson, "for the preservation of freedom and happiness." Yet as a matter of fact during the twentieth century the generations trained in these schools have either abandoned their liberties or they have not known, until the last desperate moment, how to defend them. The schools were to make men free. They have been in operation for some sixty or seventy years and what was expected of them they have not done. The plain fact is that the graduates of the modern schools are the actors in the catastrophe which has befallen our civilization. Those who are responsible for modern education—for its controlling philosophy—are answerable for the results.

They have determined the formation of the mind and education of modern men. As the tragic events unfold they cannot evade their responsibility by talking about the crimes and follies of politicians, businessmen, labor leaders, lawyers, editors, and generals. They have conducted the schools and colleges and they have educated the politicians, businessmen, labor leaders, lawyers, editors, and generals. What is more, they have educated the educators.

They have had money, lots of it, fine buildings, big appropriations, great endowments, and the implicit faith of the people that the school was the foundation of democracy. If the results are bad, and indubitably they are, on what ground can any of us who are in any way responsible for education disclaim our responsibility or decline to undertake a profound searching of our own consciences and a deep re-examination of our philosophy.

The institutions of the Western world were formed by men who learned to regard themselves as inviolable persons because they were rational and free. They meant by rational that they were capable of comprehending the moral order of the universe and their place in this moral order. They meant when they regarded themselves as free that within that order they had a personal moral responsibility to perform their duties and to exercise their corresponding rights. From this conception of the unity of mankind in a rational order the Western world has derived its conception of law—which is that all men and all communities of men and all authority among men are subject to law, and that the character of all particular laws is to be judged by whether they conform to or violate, approach or depart from, the rational order of the universe and of man's nature. From this conception of law was derived the idea of constitutional government and of the consent of the governed and of civil liberty. Upon this conception of law our own institutions were founded.

This, in barest outline, is the specific outlook of Western men. This, we may say, is the structure of the Western spirit. This is the formation which distinguishes it. The studies and the disciplines which support and form this spiritual outlook and habit are the creative cultural tradition of Europe and the Americas. In this tradition our world was made. By this tradition it must live. Without this tradition our world, like a tree cut off from its roots in the soil, must die and be replaced by alien and barbarous things. . . .

The men who wrote the American Constitution and the Bill of Rights were educated in schools and colleges in which the classic works of this culture were the substance of the curriculum. In these schools the transmission of this culture was held to be the end and aim of education.

Modern education, however, is based on a denial that it is necessary or useful or desirable for the schools and colleges to continue to transmit from generation to generation the religious and classical culture of the Western world. It is, therefore, much easier to say what modern education rejects than to find out what modern education teaches. Modern education rejects and excludes from the curriculum of necessary studies the whole religious tradition of the West. It abandons and neglects as no longer necessary the study of the whole classical heritage of the great works of great men.

Thus there is an enormous vacuum where until a few decades ago there was the substance of education. And with what is that vacuum filled: it is filled with the elective, eclectic, the specialized, the accidental and incidental improvisations and spontaneous curiosities of teachers and students. There is no common faith, no common body of principle, no common body of knowledge, no common moral and intellectual discipline. Yet the graduates of these modern schools are expected to form a civilized community. They are expected to govern themselves. They are expected to have a social conscience. They are expected to arrive by discussion at common purposes. When one realizes that they have no common culture, is it astounding that they have no common purpose? That they worship false gods? That only in war do they unite? That in the fierce struggle for existence they are tearing Western society to pieces? They are the graduates of an educational system in which, though attendance is compulsory, the choice of the subject matter of education is left to the imagination of college presidents, trustees, and professors, or even to the whims of the pupils themselves. We have established a system of education in which we insist that while everyone must be educated, yet there is nothing in particular that an educated man must know.

For it is said that since the invention of the steam engine we live in a new era, an era so radically different from all preceding ages that the cultural tradition is no longer relevant, is in fact misleading. I submit to you that this is a rationalization, that this is a pretended reason for the educational void which we now call education. The real reason, I venture to suggest, is that we reject the religious and classical heritage, first, because to master it requires more effort than we are willing to compel ourselves to make, and, second, because it creates issues that are too deep and too contentious to be faced with equanimity. We have abolished the old curriculum because we are afraid of it, afraid to face any longer in a modern democratic society the severe discipline and the deep, disconcerting issues of the nature of the universe, and of man's place in it and of his destiny. . . .

Just as the personal ambition of the student rather than social tradition determines what the student shall learn, so the inquiry and the research of the scholar becomes more and more disconnected from any general and regulating body of knowledge.

It is this specialized and fundamentally disordered development of knowledge which has turned so much of man's science into the means of his own destruction. For as reason is regarded as no more than the instrument of men's desires, applied science inflates enormously the power of men's desires. Since reason is not the ruler of these desires, the power which science places in men's hands is ungoverned.

Quickly it becomes ungovernable. Science is the product of intelligence. But if the function of the intelligence is to be the instrument of the acquisitive, the possessive, and the domineering impulses, then these impulses, so strong by nature, must become infinitely stronger when they are equipped with all the resources of man's intelligence.

That is why men today are appalled by the discovery that when modern man fights he is the most destructive animal ever known on this planet; that when he is acquisitive he is the most cunning and efficient; that when he dominates the weak he has engines of oppression and of calculated cruelty and deception no antique devil could have imagined.

And, at last, education founded on the secular image of man must destroy knowledge itself. For if its purpose is to train the intelligence of specialists in order that by trial and error they may find a satisfying solution of particular difficulties, then each situation and each problem has to be examined as a novelty. This is supposed to be "scientific." But in fact it is a denial of that very principle which has made possible the growth of science.

For what enables men to know more than their ancestors is that they start with a knowledge of what their ancestors have already learned. They are able to do advanced experiments which increase knowledge because they do not have to repeat the elementary experiments. It is tradition which brings them to the point where advanced experimentation is possible. This is the meaning of tradition. This is why a society can be progressive only if it conserves its tradition.

The notion that every problem can be studied as such with an open and empty mind, without preconception, without knowing what has already been learned about it, must condemn men to a chronic childishness. For no man, and no generation of men, is capable of inventing for itself the arts and sciences of a high civilization. No one, and no one generation, is capable of rediscovering all the truths men need, of developing sufficient knowledge by applying a mere intelligence, no matter how acute, to mere observation, no matter how accurate. The men of any generation, as Bernard of Chartres put it, are like dwarfs seated on the shoulders of giants. If we are to "see more things than the ancients and things more distant" it is "due neither to the sharpness of our sight nor the greatness of our stature" but "simply because they have lent us their own."

For individuals do not have the time, the opportunity, or the energy to make all the experiments and to discern all the significance that have gone into the making of the whole heritage of civilization. In developing knowledge men must collaborate with their ancestors. Otherwise they must begin not where their ancestors arrived but where their ancestors began. If they exclude the tradition of the past from the curricula of the schools they make it necessary for each generation to repeat the errors rather than to benefit by the successes of its predecessors.

"Crisis and Reform in Education," Today and Tomorrow, *February 13, 1943.*

Nearly everyone is dissatisfied with the results of modern education, and increasingly men and women are beginning to feel that it has been teaching a little about too many things without teaching enough about anything. More specifically, the conviction is growing that the schools and colleges are very "liberal" in the sense that they offer innumerable courses on no end of subjects, but that they are failing to educate their students efficiently in those disciplines which underlie all the liberal arts —namely, in the ability to read with understanding, in the ability to write and speak so as to be understood, and in the ability to use figures.

There are many who are coming to feel that if the schools and colleges had to shorten their courses, they would be forced to improve them by concentrating on the fundamental disciplines. There would be less about the anthropology of the cavemen and the sociology of the Hottentot and the psychology of the streetcar employees in Omaha. With less subjects and more attention to the elements of education, we might not be hearing from the training schools that so many college men cannot . . . "read well enough or write well enough or handle simple mathematics well enough to make good officer material." And we should have a good deal less administrative trouble in Washington if those who write the directives had learned to say what they really mean, and if all those who read directives had learned to know what they had read.

So what we call the crisis in American education may prove to be a crisis not in the sense of a disaster but in the original sense of the Greek word from which it comes, which means "to decide." We may find ourselves perforce deciding on a reform of education.

"Academic Freedom in Wisconsin," Today and Tomorrow, *December 17, 1936.*

What is the problem of academic freedom? It is, it seems to me, the problem of who shall select the teachers, who shall promote them, who shall dismiss them, who shall determine what is to be taught, who shall determine the subjects of research, who shall criticize the results. These matters have to be decided. A university is not just a collection of buildings where anyone can appoint himself to teach anything he likes. The problems of academic freedom arise from the struggle of all sorts of people to control these decisions. At one time it may be a group of rich alumni who insist that if they pay the piper they should call the tune. At another time it may be a legislature under the influence of rabble-rousers insisting, as in Tennessee some years ago, that it shall have the right to say what shall be taught as biology. At another time, as in Chicago under Mayor Thompson, it may be a demagogic patrioteer arrogating to himself the authority to say what shall be taught as history. At another time, it may be Mr. Hearst attempting to control education by terrorizing teachers and administrators and trustees. At another time, it may be a simon-pure progressive, like Governor La Follette, seeking to use the authority of the state to make the university's progressivism more simon-pure.

In other words, the control of education is claimed at various times by the plutocracy, by the mob, and by the politicians. The fight for academic freedom is the fight against the control of education by any and all of these three elements. And that means that the ultimate control of education, when it is free, must rest finally in the community of scholars. It means that a free university is one in which the selection of teachers and of studies reflects the judgment of scholars, is determined by their standards, and is independent of money, the mob, and the political power of the state.

Though there are many concrete practical difficulties in applying the principle of academic freedom, it is the only principle on which education in a progressive civilization can be based. Thus it is obviously absurd that a rich businessman should have any say as to what shall be examined, much less as to what conclusions shall be arrived at, during the research into the unknown fields of economics. To admit that would amount to saying that the partial knowledge of one generation shall govern what shall be known in the next. It is equally absurd that a Bryan, a Thompson, a Hearst should have the presumption to impose his prejudices and his ignorance on teaching and research. It is no less absurd that governors and elected representatives and politicians, whether they be progressives, conservatives, or what not, should think that they can absentmindedly shape the culture and intelligence of a people.

Surely the only civilized rule is to have teachers selected and promoted and dismissed by the men most qualified to judge them, to have their work examined by their peers, to subject them to the discipline of the criticism of men who themselves teach and study and advance knowledge and spend their days pondering the problems of education. To be sure, a university is a great physical plant, it is an intricate human organization, it has limited resources and it must meet almost unlimited demands. For that reason it has to be administered, and the scholars ought not, even if they were competent, to spend much of their time in administration.

But in a truly free university, the administrators and the governing boards, the regents, whatever they are called, will always regard themselves as trustees for the community of scholars. They will seek always to facilitate the application of the standards which come finally from the opinion of the scholars themselves; they will always take their final judgments of educational policy from the most considered judgment they can find among the scholars and educators.

And, of course, as a direct consequence of this the administrators and trustees will look upon themselves as under obligation to be guardians of the self-government of scholars against outside intervention from any quarter. So they must find the necessary money without strings attached to it. They must hold at bay the mob, incited by demagogues and obscurantists. They must resist the encroachments of the political state.

"The Harvard Anniversary," Today and Tomorrow, *May 26, 1936.*

This is an appropriate moment in the history of the world to celebrate the idea of a university and to take the occasion to define and to reaffirm most especially the basic relation between teaching and scholarship on the one hand, the power and the policies of government on the other. The Harvard anniversary is a most suitable occasion. For Harvard stands unqualifiedly for the principle that unless they are independent of each other the relation between universities and governments will not be healthy.

There are many, not only in the European despotisms but here as well, who do not hold that view, who think, to put it bluntly, that the politicians should run the professors or that the professors should run the politicians. Thus there are those who would reduce the universities to the position of bureaus in the ministry of propaganda and there are those who would invite them to become the advisers of politicians, the directors and planners of national policy.

Against these two views, the one crudely destructive, the other subtly destructive, of the advancement of learning, the celebrations this year will affirm the principle that if the universities are to do their work they must be independent and they must be disinterested.

The meaning of this principle can perhaps be grasped most readily by saying that while popular government cannot be operated without parties, it cannot be worked by parties alone. Outside the party system there must be independent authorities in whom the people have confidence. Where popular governments have been successful, those independent, nonpartisan authorities are invariably strong and greatly respected. Thus in England there is the monarchy, there is the extraordinarily competent civil service, there are the free universities and the press, there is the independent judiciary. These institutions which are apart from, and outlast, and are not involved in the struggle of parties, keep the party struggle within reasonable bounds.

In the United States there is the Constitution interpreted by an independent judiciary, and nothing in recent events has been more significant than the demonstration of the people as a whole that they like and trust the Supreme Court, not because it gives them what they think they want, but because it provides a way of having great issues passed upon by learned and competent men who have nothing to gain or to lose by their decisions.

The role of the universities, apart from their specific task of training men and advancing knowledge, is in that respect not unlike that of the courts. They are places to which men can turn for judgments which are unbiased by partisanship and special interest. Obviously, the moment the universities fall under political control, or under the control of private interests, or the moment they themselves take a hand in politics and the leadership of government, their value as independent and disinterested sources of judgment is impaired.

That is the reason why among tax-supported universities, it is so essential to have also some which, because they are privately endowed, have no reason to fear or favor the party in power. That is the reason why it is so important to resist every attempt by legislators and self-appointed censors to encroach by investigations, special oaths, and sheer terrorism on the freedom of the universities. And that is the reason, too, why the members of the university faculties have a particular obligation not to tie themselves to, nor to involve themselves in, the ambitions and purposes of the politicians, the parties, and the movements which are contending for power.

The choice has to be made. If there are to be universities which are not controlled by the government, if there are to be universities free of the government because they are privately endowed, if in accepting these endowments the universities are to be able to insist on their freedom from the promptings of private interest, then the universities themselves must also renounce the ambition to play a part in partisan political controversy.

This does not mean that professors must not be consulted in matters where they are professionally competent. But it does mean that professors must not be office holders and political advisers to office holders. For once they engage themselves that way, they cease to be disinterested men, being committed by their ambitions and their sympathies. They cease to be scholars because they are no longer disinterested, and having lost their own independence, they impair the independence of the university to which they belong.

So it is fortunate that in celebrating the founding of higher education in the United States, the center of the celebration should be a college which is peculiarly fitted by its history to represent the ideal of independence. For that ideal is deeply challenged in the world today, and that challenge must at all costs be resisted.

"The Shortage of Education," The Atlantic Monthly, CXCIII *(May 1954)*, 35, *an address delivered at the fifth annual dinner of the National Citizens Commission for the Public Schools in San Francisco on March 19, 1954.*

If we compare our total effort—in public and private schools, and from kindergarten through college—with what it was fifty years ago, the quantitative increase is impressive. We are offering much more schooling of a more expensive kind to very many more pupils. By every statistical measure, the United States has made striking quantitative progress during the past century toward the democratic goal of universal education. The typical young American is spending more years in school than his father or grandfather; a much higher proportion of young people are going to high school and beyond; and more dollars—even discounting the depreciation of the dollar—are being spent for each person's education.

Now if it were no more difficult to live in the United States today than it was fifty years ago; that is to say, if life were as simple as it was then—if the problems of private and community life were as easily understood—if the task of governing the United States at home and of conducting its foreign relations abroad were as uncomplicated as, and no more dangerous than, it was fifty years ago—then we could celebrate, we could be happy, we could be congratulating ourselves that we are making great progress in the task of educating ourselves as a democracy.

But we cannot make that comforting comparison without deceiving ourselves seriously. We cannot measure the demands upon our people in the second half of the twentieth century—the demands in terms of trained intelligence, moral discipline, knowledge, and, not least, the wisdom of great affairs—by what was demanded of them at the beginning of the first half of this century. The burden of living in America today and of governing America today is very much heavier than it was fifty years ago, and the crucial question is whether the increase of our effort in education is keeping up with the increase in the burden.

When we use this standard of comparison, we must find, I submit, that the increase in our effort to educate ourselves is of a quite different—and of a very much smaller—order of magnitude than is the increase in what is demanded of us in this divided and dangerous world. Our educational effort and our educational needs are not now anywhere nearly in balance. The supply is not nearly keeping up with the demand. The burden of the task is very much heavier than is the strength of the effort. There is a very serious and dangerous deficit between the output of education and our private and public need to be educated.

How can we measure this discrepancy? I am sorry to say that I shall have to use a few figures, trusting that none of you will think that when I use them, I am implying that all things can be measured in dollars and cents. I am using the figures because there is no other way to illustrate concretely the difference in the two orders of magnitude—the difference between what we do to educate ourselves, on the one hand, and on the other hand, what the kind of world we live in demands of us.

What shall we use as a measure of our educational effort? For the purpose of the comparison, I think we may take the total expenditure per capita, first in 1900, and then about half a century later, in 1953, on public and private schools from kindergarten through college.

And as a measure of the burden of our task—of the responsibilities and of the commitments to which education has now to be addressed—we might take federal expenditures per capita, first in 1900, and then in our time, half a century later.

We differ among ourselves, of course, as to whether we are spending too much, too little, or the right amount on defense and on the public services. But these differences do not seriously affect the argument. For all of us, or nearly all of us, are agreed on the general size and the scope of the necessary tasks of the modern federal government, both in military defense and for civilian purposes. Between the highest and the lowest proposals of responsible and informed men, I doubt that the difference is as much as twenty per cent. That is not a great enough difference to affect the point I am making. That point is that the size of the public expenditure reflects—roughly, of course, but nevertheless fundamentally—the scale and scope of what we are impelled and compelled to do. It registers our judgment on the problems which we must cope with.

Now, in 1900, the educational effort, measured in expenditures per capita, was $3.40. The task, as measured by federal expenditure per capita, was $6.85. What we must be interested in is, I submit, the ratio between these two figures. We find, then, that in 1900 the nation put out $1 of educational effort against $2 of public task.

How is it now, half a century or so later? In 1953 the educational effort was at the rate of about $76 per capita. Federal expenditures, including defense, had risen to $467 per capita. The ratio of educational effort to public task, which in 1900 was one to two, had fallen, a half century later, to a ratio of one to six.

Perhaps I should pause at this point for a parenthesis to say, for those who may be thinking how much the value of the dollar has depreciated since 1900, that I am aware of that, but for the purposes of this comparison, it makes no difference. For while the dollar was worth probably three times as much in 1900 as in 1953, we are interested only in the relative effort in 1900 and 1953. The ratio would be the same if we divided the 1953 expenditures by three or if we multiplied the 1900 expenditures by three.

You have now heard all the statistics I shall use. The two ratios—the one at the beginning of our rise to the position of the leading great power of the world, and the other the ratio a half century later, when we carry the enormous burden abroad and at home—these two ratios show that the effort we are now making to educate ourselves has fallen in relation to our needs.

I must now remind you that this disparity between the educational effort and the public task is in fact greater than the figures suggest. For in this half century there has been a momentous change in the structure of American society, and it has added greatly to the burden upon the schools.

The responsibility of the schools for educating the new generation has become very much more comprehensive than it used to be. Ever so much more is now demanded of the schools. For they are expected to perform many of the educational functions which used to be performed by the family, the settled community, the church, the family business, the family farm, the family trade.

This is a very big subject in itself—much too big for me here—except to mention it as a reminder that the comparison between our real educational effort and our real public need is less favorable than the figures of one to two in 1900, as against one to six today. For the school today has a much larger role to play in the whole process of education than it needed to play in the older American society.

Can it be denied that the educational effort is inadequate? I think it cannot be denied. I do not mean that we are doing a little too little. I mean that we are doing much too little. We are entering upon an era which will test to the utmost the capacity of our democracy to cope with the gravest problem of modern times, and on a scale never yet attempted in all the history of the world. We are entering upon this difficult and dangerous period with what I believe we must call a growing deficit in the quantity and the quality of American education.

There is compelling proof that we are operating at an educational deficit. It is to be found in many of the controversies within the educational system. I am not myself, of course, a professional educator. But I do some reading about education, and I have been especially interested in the problem of providing education for the men and women who must perform the highest functions in our society—the elucidation and the articulation of its ideals, the advancement of knowledge, the making of high policy in the government, and the leadership of the people.

How are we discussing this problem? Are we, as we ought to be doing, studying what are the subjects and what are the disciplines which are needed for the education of the gifted children for the leadership of the nation? That is not the main thing we are discussing. We are discussing whether we can afford to educate our leaders when we have so far to go before we have done what we should do to provide equal opportunities for all people.

Most of the argument—indeed the whole issue—of whether to address the effort in education to the average of ability or to the higher capacities derives from the assumption that we have to make that choice. But why do we have to choose? Why are we not planning to educate everybody as much as everybody can be educated, some much more and some less than others?

This alleged choice is forced upon us only because our whole educational effort is too small. If we were not operating at a deficit level, our working ideal would be the fullest opportunity for all—each child according to its capacity. It is the deficit in our educational effort which compels us to deny to the children fitted for leadership of the nation the opportunity to become educated for that task.

So we have come to the point where we must lift ourselves as promptly as we can to a new and much higher level of interest, of attention, of hard work, of care, of concern, of expenditure, and of dedication to the education of the American people.

We have to do in the educational system something very like what we have done in the military establishment during the past fifteen years. We have to make a breakthrough to a radically higher and broader conception of what is needed and of what can be done. Our educational effort today, what we think we can afford, what we think we can do, how we feel entitled to treat our schools and our teachers—all of that—is still in approximately the same position as was the military effort of this country before Pearl Harbor.

In 1940 our armed forces were still at a level designed for a policy of isolation in this hemisphere and of neutrality in any war across the two oceans. Today the military establishment has been raised to a different and higher plateau, and the effort that goes into it is enormously greater than it was in 1940.

Our educational effort, on the other hand, has not yet been raised to the plateau of the age we live in. I am not saying, of course, that we should spend forty billions on education because we spend that much on defense. I am saying that we must make the same order of radical change in our attitude as we have made in our attitude toward defense. We must measure our educational effort as we do our military effort. That is to say, we must measure it not by what it would be easy and convenient to do, but by what it is necessary to do in order that the nation may survive and flourish. We have learned that we are quite rich enough to defend ourselves, whatever the cost. We must now learn that we are quite rich enough to educate ourselves as we need to be educated.

There is an enormous margin of luxury in this country against which we can draw for our vital needs. We take that for granted when we think of the national defense. From the tragedies and the bitter experience of being involved in wars for which we were inadequately prepared, we have acquired the will to defend ourselves. And, having done that, having acquired the will, we have found the way. We know how to find the dollars that are needed to defend ourselves, even if we must do without something else that is less vitally important.

In education we have not yet acquired that kind of will. But we need to acquire it, and we have no time to lose. We must acquire it in this decade. For if, in the crucial years which are coming, our people remain as unprepared as they are for their responsibilities and their mission, they may not be equal to the challenge, and if they do not succeed, they may never have a second chance to try.

6 · *Of Morals, Manners, and Beliefs*

Drift and Mastery (*1914*), *Chapter 10.*

In Queenstown harbor I once talked to an Irish boy who was about to embark for America. His home was in the west of Ireland, in a small village where his sister and he helped their father till a meager farm. They had saved enough for a passage to America, and they were abandoning their home. I asked the boy whether he knew anyone in America. He didn't, but his parish priest at home did. He was going to write to Father Riley every week. Would he ever return to Ireland? "Yes," said this boy of eighteen, "I'm going to die in Ireland." Where was he going to in America? To a place called New Haven. He was, in short, going from one epoch into another, and for guidance he had the parish priest at home and perhaps the ward boss in New Haven. His gentleness and trust in the slums of New Haven, assaulted by din and glare, hedged in by ugliness and cynical push—if there is any adventure comparable to his, I have not heard of it. At the very moment when he needed a faith, he was cutting loose from it. If he becomes brutal, greedy, vulgar, will it be so surprising? If he fails to measure up to the requirements of citizenship in a world reconstruction, is there anything strange about it?

Well, he was an immigrant in the literal sense. All of us are immigrants spiritually. We are all of us immigrants in the industrial world, and we have no authority to lean upon. We are an uprooted people, newly arrived, and *nouveau riche*. As a nation we have all the vulgarity that goes with that, all the scattering of soul. The modern man is not yet settled in his world. It is strange to him, terrifying, alluring, and incomprehensibly big. The evidence is everywhere: the amusements of the city; the jokes that pass for jokes; the blare that stands for beauty, the folksongs of Broadway, the feeble and apologetic pulpits, the cruel standards of success, raucous purity. We make love to ragtime and we die to it. We are blown hither and thither like litter before the wind. Our days are lumps of undigested experience. You have only to study what newspapers regard as news to see how we are torn and twisted by the irrelevant: in frenzy about issues that do not concern us, bored with those that do. Is it a wild mistake to say that the absence of central authority has disorganized our souls, that our souls are like Peer Gynt's onion, in that they lack a kernel?

A Preface to Morals (1929), *Chapter 5.*

As a consequence of the modern theory of religious freedom the churches find themselves in an anomalous position. Inwardly, to their communicants, they continue to assert that they possess the only complete version of the truth. But outwardly, in their civic relations with other churches and with the civil power, they preach and practice toleration. The separation of Church and State involves more than a mere logical difficulty for the churchman. It involves a deep psychological difficulty for the members of the congregation. As communicants they are expected to believe without reservation that their church is the only true means of salvation; otherwise the multitude of separate sects would be meaningless. But as citizens they are expected to maintain a neutral indifference to the claims of all the sects, and to resist encroachments by any one sect upon the religious practices of the others. This is the best compromise which human wisdom has as yet devised, but it has one inevitable consequence which the superficial advocates of toleration often overlook. It is difficult to remain warmly convinced that the authority of any one sect is divine, when as a matter of daily experience all sects have to be treated alike.

The human soul is not so divided in compartments that a man can be indifferent in one part of his soul and firmly believing in another. The existence of rival sects, the visible demonstration that none has a monopoly, the habit of neutrality cannot but dispose men against an unquestioning acceptance of the authority of one sect. So many faiths, so many loyalties are offered to the modern man that at last none seems to him wholly inevitable and fixed in the order of the universe. The existence of many churches in one community weakens the foundation of all of them. And that is why every church in the heyday of its power proclaims itself to be catholic and intolerant.

But when there are many churches in the same community, none can make wholly good the claim that it is catholic. None has that power to discipline the individual which a universal church exercises. For, as Dr. Figgis puts it, when many churches are tolerated, "excommunication has ceased to be tyrannical by becoming futile."

If the rival churches were not compelled to tolerate one another, they could not, consistently with their own teaching, accept the prevailing theory of the public school. Under that theory the schools are silent about matters of faith, and teachers are supposed to be neutral on the issues of history and science which bear upon religion. The churches permit this because they cannot agree on the dogma they would wish to have taught. The Catholics would rather have no dogma in the schools than Protestant dogma; the fundamentalists would rather have none than have modernist. This situation is held to be a good one. But that is only because all the alternatives are so much worse. No church can sincerely subscribe to the theory that questions of faith do not enter into the education of children.

Wherever churches are rich enough to establish their own schools, or powerful enough to control the public school, they make short work of the "godless" school. Either they establish religious schools of their own, as the Catholics and Lutherans have done, or they impose their views on the public schools as the fundamentalists have done wherever they have the necessary voting strength. The last fight of Mr. Bryan's life was made on behalf of the theory that if a majority of voters in Tennessee were fundamentalists, then they had the right to make public education in Tennessee fundamentalist too. One of the standing grievances of the Catholic Church in America is that Catholics are taxed to support schools to which they cannot conscientiously send their children.

As a matter of fact, non-sectarianism is a useful political phrase rather than an accurate description of what goes on in the schools. If there is teaching of science, that teaching is by implication almost always agnostic. The fundamentalists point this out, and they are quite right. The teaching of history, under a so-called non-sectarian policy, is usually, in this country, a rather diluted Protestant version of history. The Catholics are quite right when they point this out. Occasionally, it may be, a teacher of science appears who has managed to assimilate his

science to his theology; now and then a Catholic history teacher will depart from the standard textbooks to give the Catholic version of disputed events during the last few hundred years. But the chief effect of the non-sectarian policy is to weaken sectarian attachment, to wean the child from the faith of his fathers by making him feel that patriotism somehow demands that he shall not press his convictions too far, that common sense and good-fellowship mean that he must not be too absolute. The leaders of the churches are aware of this peril. Every once in a while they make an effort to combat it. Committees composed of parsons, priests, and rabbis appear before the school boards and petition that a non-sectarian God be worshiped and the non-controversial passages of the Bible be read. They always agree that the present godless system of education diminishes the sanctions of morality and the attendance at their respective churches. But they disagree when they try to agree on the nature of a neutral God, and they have been known to dispute fiercely about a non-controversial text of the Ten Command-
of the community turns in the end against the reform.
ments. So, if the sects are evenly balanced, the practical sense

"Concerning Mr. Rockefeller," Today and Tomorrow, *May 25, 1937.*

Though Mr. Rockefeller was only the most conspicuous of a group of fabulously rich men, his wealth was an historical accident. Only in America, and only in the period from the Civil War to the World War, could such a fortune have been founded. Before he started his enterprises it was not possible to make so much money; before he died, it had become the settled policy of this country that no man would be permitted to make so much money. He lived long enough to see the methods by which such a fortune can be accumulated, outlawed by public opinion, forbidden by statute, and prevented by the tax laws.

The Rockefeller family have understood this very clearly. They have not pretended that their fortune represented the normal rewards of successful enterprise, and long ago they had ceased to regard it as their personal property. They have known that this fortune did not really belong to them, and that, accidentally, they were its temporary custodians.

It has been no easy task to make tolerable in a democracy the private administration of such a monstrous aggregation of wealth and power. Somehow the Rockefellers have succeeded, and in an age when sentiment has turned wholly against the private acquisition of so much wealth, they have no bitter enemies and very generally they are deeply respected.

Perhaps one of the secrets of the family's repute today is that in their philanthropy there has been none of the odor of conscience money. They have not sought to buy the good will of the mass of the people by subsidizing obviously and easily popular schemes. On the contrary, they have devoted their endowments to supporting precisely those civilized needs which popular governments are most inclined to neglect.

Whether they were aware of it or not, they have followed the advice given many years ago by Mr. Bernard Shaw when he wrote a tract called "Socialism for Millionaires," arguing that a millionaire should never give the community anything it could possibly be induced to support voluntarily. The support which the Rockefellers have given to higher education and to research is over and above anything that the American democracy of their epoch could or would have provided.

The good repute which the family has achieved is inspired by no special sense of gratitude for their generosity. As a matter of fact, the American people do not think it generous in a billionaire to give away most of his money. They expect it of him. They think it the very least he can do. But what they do respect in the Rockefellers is the absence of all cajolery and public bribery; what they admire is the conscientious and disinterested intelligence with which they have restored to the community so considerable a part of this great accumulation.

They have done much with their wealth that needed to be done, though ordinarily it would not have been done. Mr. Rockefeller's death raises the question as to how in the future, when no man will be permitted to acquire such wealth, higher learning and research are to be supported. There are many, I know, who think that the government can subsidize these higher, these indispensable, but non-popular activities. One may wonder whether the solution is as simple as that, whether government-supported institutions can hope to enjoy the same kind of undisturbed intellectual freedom which exists by virtue of private endowments like those of the Rockefellers.

We know that it does not exist in any of the collectivist states of Europe. Does it exist here in full measure where universities depend upon the annual good will of elected legislatures?

We shall have to consider that question more and more as private fortunes like that of the Rockefellers are extinguished. I do not know the answer to it. But I do know that as the higher cultural activities of the nation come to depend more and more upon popular support, we shall have to find some effective way of making them independent of the superficial currents of public opinion.

In one way or another, perhaps by inventing some sort of public endowment based on the inheritance tax, we shall have to invest large sums in enterprises that politicians do not control, though ordinary politicians will not support them unless they do control them. Just as we have in some measure succeeded in making the administration of justice independent of political control, so we shall have soon to deal with the problem of making publicly supported cultural activities independent of political control.

"Liberty and Its Many Champions," Today and Tomorrow, *December 11, 1937.*

There has been a vast amount of oratory during the last week dealing with the subject of human liberty, but barring some notable exceptions, the orators have been taking no great risks. They have been passionately concerned with the liberties that they are passionately concerned with, and comfortably blind about those liberties which happen to be the birthright of the disagreeable people they do not like. . . .

No doubt it must seem to some a counsel of perfection to say that the test of a man's love of liberty is his concern about liberties which he hates to see exercised. Yet that is the test, and anyone can see it when he remembers how passionately Hitler, for example, can defend the rights of minorities, provided they are German minorities living in Poland or Czechoslovakia. That is the extreme case, of course. But it illustrates a general rule, which is that no one really loves liberty who wants it only for himself and his party.

Nor is that general rule a piece of abstract idealism too high and too rarefied for this rough world. On the contrary, the most effective way for anyone to do his part in protecting the liberties he cares about is to defend the liberties he does not care about.

Thus there is the Civil Liberties Union, one of the truly indispensable private organizations in America, with its long and noble record of persistent and courageous defense of forgotten individuals and of hated minorities. Yet somehow the Civil Liberties Union has neither the dignity nor the prestige nor the effectiveness which its principles deserve. And the reason, I feel sure, is that the Union almost never goes into action when the liberties of anyone on the Right are attacked, though in fairness it should be recalled that the Union did most bravely defend some American Nazis a few years ago when they were being denied their legal prerogatives. . . .

And then there is the National Association of Manufacturers, which has just been in session in New York and has listened to many excellent orations on liberalism and has made many sensible and liberal declarations of its own. How much more impressive it would all have been if someone had shown that he was indignant at the thoroughly lawless behavior of Mayor Hague just across the river in Jersey City. Some indignation on that subject would have done much to give the abstractions about liberty an air of reality, and a great many persons whose opinions count would have read the rest of what was said much more diligently.

No one, to be sure, expects the N.A.M. to go on a crusade for liberty in general. It has its own proper function, which is to promote the profitable manufacture of goods. But as a sheer matter of expediency, just, if you like, as an intelligent strategical operation, the complaints against the bureaucratic tyrannies of the Labor Relations Board would have been just about twice as effective if they had been supported by some evidence of indignation at Mayor Hague and his kind.

So what looks like a counsel of perfection is very good practical politics. Unless we are to be content to have no one listen to us who does not already agree with us, it is inadvisable to say only things that our own partisans would like to hear. That is why the Civil Liberties Union ought to defend a few economic royalists and why the National Association of Manufacturers ought to defend a few C.I.O. organizers.

That is why it would have been good strategy for a New Dealer to have cared about seeing that Mr. Mellon was not persecuted. It would have been very smart if the Liberty League lawyers had looked around and tried to find one thoroughly disreputable client. It would have been intelligent on the part of Senator La Follette if, when he investigated pinkertonism among employers, he had also looked into the thugs and racketeers in the labor unions.

It is sound policy in a democracy to be the first to see the mote in one's own eye. For men like and are impressed by sincerity, and by sincerity they mean the willingness to do those things that are not immediately agreeable and personally profitable.

"Free Time and Extra Money," Woman's Home Companion, *LVII (April 1930), 31.*

We have not, I think, gone to the heart of the matter until we have recognized that play and outside interests, hobbies and recreations, can be no more than anodynes and ways of escape unless in the intimate places of the heart there is unity and peace.

To say this is to say, I suppose, that there is no substitute by the mere arrangement of outward activities for that radical arrangement of inward activity which in its many manifestations men have called religion. Those who think otherwise, whatever creeds they may profess, are the truly irreligious. For they think they can find peace of mind at the edges and not at the center of their being. They cannot. That peace is won or lost in solitude, in those moments when there are no distractions of any kind whatever, and they can feel the throb of their own energies, then when there is unveiled to them the cold clear pattern of their destiny.

It is from this experience that most of us shrink, for it is profoundly disturbing. It does not comport well with the ordinary tenor of modern life, where it has become an established convention not to reach too high or to look too deeply into hidden regions. Yet man is not a simple three-dimensional animal who can be content to live gregariously on a plane of well-ordered social arrangements. He does not domesticate perfectly. There is a strain of wildness and of excess in him which cannot be regimented or caged, and this wildness, which may drive him to the savage or the sublime, he cannot satisfy with mediocre distractions. The ordinary routine of organized pleasure, in so far as it is a problem presenting evil consequences, is evil because it seeks by artificial distraction and escape to save its patrons from looking into the mirror of their fate and there confronting that knowledge of themselves which no human soul can avoid and be completely human.

"In Defense of the Suffragettes," The Harvard Monthly, *XLIX* (*1909*), *64*.

The true problem that the practical suffragist faces is no problem of intellectual conviction. The parlor game of proving the justice of the suffragist claim has been tried for fifty years, with the result that a Ministry which professes to believe in votes for women, supported by a Parliamentary majority sufficient to carry the reform through, refuses session after session to touch the issue. It is plain that some other motive power was needed to compel reasoned support to go over into action. As Mr. Graham Wallas says, "in order to make men think, one must begin by making them feel." That was the practical conclusion to which propaganda experience brought the women in England.

With that principle in mind the suffragettes adopted their celebrated "militant tactics." They set out deliberately to raise the suffrage question from the realm of abstract idealism to the realm of what Professor James calls "forced, living, and momentous options." It is the great work of the militant suffragettes that they have made the question of votes for women a question of practical politics, which no candidate can ignore. They have made themselves such a glorious nuisance to the government by their active interest in the by-elections, in Cabinet proceedings, and Parliamentary discussion, that it is becoming impossible for an English statesman to defer doing something by being amiable enough to approve of their demands.

It is a strange situation when statesmen agree to the justice of a claim, and yet refuse to grant it. That is the situation which the English suffragists face, and that is the situation which justifies their tactics. . . . The only method left to the suffragists is the method they adopted: to advertise themselves at every opportunity, to let no day pass without reminding the country and its politicians of their demand, to raise the issue at every public meeting so that it can never fade from the memories of the people. They have carried out their program with precision and without hysteria. Their conduct has been characterized at times by anger, but generally by a largeness of humor which has won the respect of the English people, and made ridiculous the truckling methods of the politicians.

The worst that has been said against the suffragettes is that they are unladylike. They are unladylike, just as the Boston Tea Party was ungentlemanly, and our Civil War bad form. But unfortunately, in this world, great issues are not won by good manners.

"Youth and Age," Today and Tomorrow, *February 17, 1940.*

The American Youth Congress has come and gone, and there is left behind a sour taste in the mouths of those who were most eager to patronize this organization. They felt that it heralded not only a sizable vote but also the eternal springtime in which the weary earth renews itself. But somehow the Youth Congress lacked the charm of youth. Though its adult sponsors welcomed it with paeans of rhetoric about the glory of the young and the inglorious failures of the mature, a few days of the Youth Congress in person brought them no inspiration and much dismay.

The fact of the matter is that these youths were rather shockingly ill-mannered, disrespectful, conceited, ungenerous, and spoiled. They booed the President of the United States, which is never a decent thing to do, even if booing is supposed to be an exercise of civil liberty. They were so rude to the wife of the President of the United States that she had to ask them to be good enough to let her finish what she was saying. They had the impudence to sit in the galleries and boo at the Congress of the United States. They were possessed with the notion that they were in Washington to tell the country what the country owed them but scarcely a word was uttered about what they owe to the country.

There has been much discussion about how many of them were Communists and how far they are under Communist control. They answered the question beyond any reasonable doubt. As to what communism really is, how it operates, what it leads to, the great majority were obviously almost completely ignorant. A weather vane is in the same sense ignorant of what causes the winds to blow, now from one quarter and now from another. But like a weather vane the opinions of the Youth Congress were nevertheless pointed infallibly by the winds of doctrine which blow from Moscow. As the winds from Moscow have shifted, their opinions have shifted.

It is not necessary to know how many of them are active members of Communist organizations. The fact is that they are hypnotized by Moscow. So they are for the Spanish Loyalists; Moscow supported the Loyalists. They were undoubtedly against Neville Chamberlain when he was trying to appease Hitler; Moscow was then against appeasement. Now they are so super-neutral between right and wrong, between the aggressor and his victim, that Neville Chamberlain is a warmonger and Finland is beyond the pale of their sympathies; Moscow has changed its policy. They are still, no doubt, very sympathetic with the Chinese; Moscow is still supporting the Chinese. If and when Moscow comes to terms with Tokyo, we may depend upon it that the leaders of the Youth Congress will discover that General Chiang Kai-shek is a Fascist, a warmonger, and that he is trying to draw the United States into war. In short, they are not revolutionists. They are dupes.

What is serious about this is not the nature of these opinions but what has been revealed about how, as a result of recent theories of education, this new generation, or at least an articulate part of it, has learned to form its opinions. So-called progressive education is based on the notion that if you remove authority and discipline and tradition in the upbringing of young people, the unobstructed natural goodness of their hearts and minds will by spontaneous creation bring them to good ideas.

The fact is, however, that if you remove authority and discipline and tradition, what you create is an unsatisfied need, a vacuum, which is then filled by some other tradition and by some other form of authority. Thus you emancipate the young from the alleged tyranny of their own elders, and, before you know it, they are hypnotized by an alien tyranny. You teach them to believe that their own moral and political and religious tradition is an outworn idolatrous superstition, and before you can say Jack Robinson, they are worshiping the idols set up elsewhere.

Our generation, the one to which Mrs. Roosevelt belongs, has made many mistakes. One of its very greatest mistakes has been to misunderstand and then to break down the true relationship between youth and age. The true relationship is, so to speak, vertical—father and son, teacher and pupil, thinker and disciple, master and apprentice. In this relationship, experience is transmitted to the young and vitality is renewed in the mature. We have substituted a horizontal relationship in which we segregate the young in youth movements and the aged in old-age movements, and then call it progress. As a matter of fact this segregation is most reactionary, in that it breaks the connection by which the new generation takes possession of experience and improves upon it. This segregation of the generations prevents the young from growing up, and it means that when they become old in years, they remain immature in mind and character.

In the older, and truer, relationship between the generations, there is none of this sentimental foolery about youth as youth. To be young was glorious, no doubt, but it was not a career. To be young was to prepare for the duties and responsibilities to come, and what was respected in youths was not their immaturity but the eternal fact that a boy is going to be a man and a girl is going to be a woman.

And I have a notion that self-respecting young people prefer to be dealt with on that assumption—on the level, so to speak—without being sentimentalized over by their elders or apologized for by middle-aged adolescents. And I have an even stronger suspicion that what causes modern youths to have so little respect for their elders is just this sentimentality, this being patronized, condescended to, and flattered and petted. For when they see their elders carrying on in this fashion, their elders do not seem to them properly grown up.

"Cecilia Cooney," The World, *May 8, 1924.*

For some months now we have been vastly entertained by the bobbed-haired bandit. Knowing nothing about her, we created a perfect story standardized according to the rules laid down by the movies and the short-story magazines. The story had, as the press agents say, everything. It had a flapper and a bandit who baffled the police; it had sex and money, crime and mystery. And then yesterday we read in the probation officer's report the story of Cecilia Cooney's life. It was not in the least entertaining. For there in the place of the dashing bandit was a pitiable girl; instead of an amusing tale, a dark and mean tragedy; instead of a lovely adventure, a terrible accusation.

In the twenty years she has lived in this city she has come at one time or another within reach of all the agencies of righteousness. Five years before she was born her father was summoned to court for drunkenness and neglect; the Charities Department recommended then that her older brothers and sisters be committed to an institution. That did not prevent her parents bringing, with the full consent of the law, three or four more children into the world. Cecilia herself, the youngest of eight, came at four years of age into the custody of the Children's Society. Six months later, on the recommendation of the Department of Public Charity, she was turned back to her mother, who promptly deserted her.

She was next taken to Brooklyn by her aunt and for ten years or so attended parochial school. At the age of fourteen her mother brought her back to New York, took her to a furnished room, stole her clothes, and deserted her. A year later, aged fifteen, Cecilia became a child laborer in a brush factory in Brooklyn, and was associating at night with sailors picked up on the waterfront. At sixteen Cecilia was back in New York, living with her mother, working as laundress for a few months at a stretch in various hospitals. At twenty she was married, had borne a child, had committed a series of robberies, and is condemned to spend the rest of her youth in prison.

This is what twentieth-century civilization in New York achieved in the case of Cecilia Cooney. Fully warned by the behavior of her parents long before her birth, the law allowed her parents to reproduce their kind. Fully warned when she was still an infant, society allowed her to drift out of its hands into a life of dirt, neglect, dark basements, begging, stealing, ignorance, poor little tawdry excitements, and twisted romance. The courts had their chance and they missed it. Charity had its chance and missed it. Schools had their chance and missed it. The church had its chance and missed it. The absent-minded routine of all that is well-meaning and respectable did not deflect by an inch her inexorable progress from the basement where she was born to the jail where she will expiate her crimes and ours.

For her crimes are on our heads too. No record could be clearer or more eloquent. None could leave less room for doubt that Cecilia Cooney is a product of this city, of its neglect and its carelessness, of its indifference and its undercurrents of misery. We recommend her story to the pulpits of New York, to the school men of New York, to the lawmakers of New York, to the social workers of New York, to those who are tempted to boast of its wealth, its magnificence, and its power.

"The Young Criminals," Today and Tomorrow, *September 7, 1954.*

Statistics collected by the F.B.I. confirm the impression made by the recent newspaper stories of horrifying crimes committed by very young men. The figures show not only a sudden increase in the number of these crimes but also in their viciousness. In a survey of 200 cities the F.B.I. found that last year the crime rate of adults rose by 1.9 per cent while among youths eighteen years and under it rose by 7.9 per cent. From 1952 to 1953 the number of assaults committed by youths was doubled and there was a sharp rise in murders, rapes, burglaries, auto thefts, weapons carrying, and liquor violations.

It is depressing and alarming, and a lot will have to be done about it. When we ask ourselves what can be done about it, we must not, however, look for the impossible. We must not expect a "solution" of the problem in the sense that vaccination is a solution of the problem of smallpox. The criminal tendencies will always be there, reborn in each new generation, and the question is how much these tendencies can be kept under control and how far they can be domesticated. The teen-agers of 1954 are not differently constituted from the teen-agers of the past or of the future. If there is more crime and vice among them today than there used to be, it is not because there is suddenly a more criminal and vicious generation. It must be because there is less discipline, more excitement, and more tempting opportunities for vice and crime. The tendencies which are latent in every generation are in this postwar generation less effectively restrained and more actively stimulated.

When we ask ourselves what "we" can do about the under-restraint and the over-stimulation, I am not venturing to think about advising parents with direct, immediate, and specific responsibility for growing children. I am thinking of the general public, which, of course, includes the parents as citizens but is concerned with general measures.

The problem is one for which public remedies are most likely to be found by choosing the more obvious issues, and tackling them experimentally in various communities. The commissions of study which will no doubt be set up are likely to be more productive if they can study the effects of practical experiments.

Enough is known about the problem, so it seems to me, to justify our picking three lines of action for the experiment. Not everyone will agree, I realize, with the proposals for action. But no one can deny, I think, that action of some kind is called for along these three lines.

One is to increase parental responsibility. The second is to augment the disciplinary power of the schools. The third is to intervene to protect the country, and particularly the adolescents, against the morbid stimulation they now get from comic books, and much of the movies and of television. The best we can do along these three lines will not solve the problem in the sense that it will make juvenile delinquency negligible. But along these lines a beginning can be made toward bringing the lawlessness under control.

First—The law should be amended so as to hold parents liable to punishment and fines for crimes committed by their children. This is stern doctrine. But it need not and it should not be, nor is it likely to be, administered too harshly. These children are committing adult crimes, and if they are too immature to be held responsible, then the adults who are responsible for them should be held responsible for the offenses. This liability should do something to make the wayward parents who are letting their children run wild amenable to the teaching and the preaching which they now ignore.

Second—The schools are the public institutions which have to do with the formation of character and the learning of discipline. In many American communities, owing to the weakening of the family ties and of the authority of the church and of public opinion in the social order, the public schools have had thrust upon them very nearly the whole burden of civilizing the new generation.

They are not equal to the very heavy and difficult burden of performing the function not only of a school of learning but also the older function of the closely-knit family and of the powerful church. A shortage of our public education is grave but this is too big a subject for this article. This much can, however, be said briefly. If the schools are to instill the discipline that the family and the church are not instilling, they must be given much larger disciplinary powers than they now have.

Third—There can be no real doubt, it seems to me, that the movies and television and the comic books are purveying violence and lust to a vicious and intolerable degree. There can be no real doubt that public exhibitions of sadism tend to excite sadistic desires and to teach the audience how to gratify sadistic desires. Nor can there be any real doubt that there is a close connection between the suddenness of the increase in sadistic crimes and the new vogue of sadism among the mass media of entertainment.

Censorship is no doubt a clumsy and usually a stupid and self-defeating remedy for such evils. But a continual exposure of a generation to the commercial exploitation of the enjoyment of violence and cruelty is one way to corrode the foundations of a civilized society. For my own part, believing as I do in freedom of speech and thought, I see no objection in principle to censorship of the mass entertainment of the young. Until some more refined way is worked out of controlling this evil thing, the risks to our liberties are, I believe, decidedly less than the risks of unmanageable violence.

"Why We Accept Cheating," Look, *XXIV (March 29, 1960)*, 42.

A big change has come into American life. It is not that our behavior is demonstrably worse than it used to be. It may in many respects be considerably better. I have no doubt, for example, that the wars of this generation were conducted more honestly and more efficiently than was the Civil War. The big change in our time is that while our conduct may not be any worse, we are much more lax in what we think about our conduct. We are much more ready to accept and excuse the cheating that is so widespread and so common.

The popular standards of morality today allow for much more dishonesty than they did sometime back.

There are some who would argue that this softening of our consciences is a change for the better. It does away, they point out, with much hypocrisy and self-righteousness, with much secrecy and self-deception.

I think they are right. I think that the new candor is letting light and fresh air into many dark and smelly places. It is good to be candid and compassionate, and these are the attractive virtues of our time. But it is bad to be confused. It is bad to shrug off the ideal standards by saying what is no doubt true, but only half the truth, that we are all sinners and fall far short of the ideal. This is moral confusion. This is not candor and compassion, which are virtues, but moral ignorance, which is a vice.

Why is it bad to shrug off the ideal standards of honesty in politics, business, and love? Because it defeats us and frustrates our lives. If we do not harden ourselves by stretching ourselves to reach upward to these not wholly attainable ideals, we slump down and settle into flabbiness and footlessness and boredom. When a generation becomes cynical . . . it is condemning itself to what a poet once described, if I remember his words rightly, as the everlasting pursuit of the ever-fleeting object of desire. It is a mistake to suppose that there is satisfaction and the joy of life in a self-indulgent generation, in one interested primarily in the pursuit of private wealth and private pleasure and private success.

On the contrary, a self-indulgent generation, as is this generation, in large part is an unhappy one. We are very rich, but we are not having a very good time. For our life, though it is full of things, is empty of the kind of purpose and effort that gives to life its flavor and its meaning.

The ideals of a good life are not a code of rules defined by busybodies and old gentlemen with gray beards. These ideal standards of what is good and what is honorable define the hygiene of the spirit by which the good life becomes possible.

When we ask ourselves what should be done about it all, I myself do not despair. It is clear, I think, that . . . moral indifference . . . exists among people who have no purposes beyond their private tastes and wishes and whims and ambitions. It is not surprising that they are so numerous at the present time. For they have been living in a decade which began with the disappointment and disillusionment of the Korean War, and has been followed by years in which private purposes have had the right of way over public purposes.

This will pass. The nation is growing and changing, and the problems which cannot be ignored are mounting. They will generate public purposes. And when they do generate public purposes, they will overcome the moral indifference. They will organize the spirit of those who are indifferent today because they have nothing within them that organizes their spirits.

I have no doubt that the complacency and the indifference of the fifties will be overcome in the sixties. As the private purposes are overcome by the impact and pressure of our public needs, the way will be opened to a wider examination of our moral condition. It will be open to the larger and more lasting question of the modern age. This has to do with the breakdown of purposes because there has been a failure of the capacity to believe—the capacity to believe that anything really matters very much and that anything is really better than anything else.

X

Leadership

1 · *Styles of Leadership*

A Preface to Politics (1913), *Chapter 1.*

If you stare at a checkerboard you can see it as black on red, or red on black, as series of horizontal, vertical, or diagonal steps which recede or protrude. The longer you look the more patterns you can trace, and the more certain it becomes that there is no single way of looking at the board. So with political issues. There is no obvious cleavage which everyone recognizes. Many patterns appear in the national life. The "progressives" say the issue is between "Privilege" and the "People"; the Socialists, that it is between the "working class" and the "master class." An apologist for dynamite told me once that society was divided into the weak and the strong, and there are people who draw a line between Philistia and Bohemia.

When you rise up and announce that the conflict is between this and that, you mean that this particular conflict interests you. The issue of good-and-bad-men interests this nation to the exclusion of almost all others. But experience shows, I believe, that it is a fruitless conflict and a wasting enthusiasm.

Yet some distinction must be drawn if we are to act at all in politics. With nothing we are for and nothing to oppose, we are merely neutral. This cleavage in public affairs is the most important choice we are called upon to make. In large measure it determines the rest of our thinking. Now some issues are fertile; some are not. Some lead to spacious results; others are blind alleys. With this in mind I wish to suggest that the distinction most worth emphasizing today is between those who regard government as a routine to be administered and those who regard it as a problem to be solved.

The class of routineers is larger than the conservatives. The man who will follow precedent, but never create one, is merely an obvious example of the routineer. You find him desperately numerous in the civil service, in the official bureaus. To him government is something given as unconditionally, as absolutely as ocean or hill. He goes on winding the tape that he finds. His imagination has rarely extricated itself from under the administrative machine to gain any sense of what a human, temporary contraption the whole affair is. What he thinks is the heavens above him is nothing but the roof.

He is the slave of routine. He can boast of somewhat more spiritual cousins in the men who reverence their ancestors' independence, who feel, as it were, that a disreputable great-grandfather is necessary to a family's respectability. These are the routineers gifted with historical sense. They take their forefathers with enormous solemnity. But one mistake is rarely avoided: they imitate the old-fashioned thing their grandfather did, and ignore the originality which enabled him to do it. . . .

The type of statesman we must oppose to the routineer is one who regards all social organization as an instrument. Systems, institutions, and mechanical contrivances have for him no virtue of their own; they are valuable only when they serve the purposes of men. He uses them, of course, but with a constant sense that men have made them, that new ones can be devised, that only an effort of the will can keep machinery in its place. He has no faith whatever in automatic governments. While the routineers see machinery and precedents revolving with mankind as puppets, he puts the deliberate, conscious, willing individual at the center of his philosophy. This reversal is pregnant with a new outlook for statecraft . . . it alone can keep step with life; it alone is humanly relevant; and it alone achieves valuable results.

Call this man a political creator or a political inventor. The essential quality of him is that he makes that part of existence which has experience the master of it. He serves the ideals of human feelings, not the tendencies of mechanical things.

A Preface to Morals (1929), *Chapter 13.*

The role of the leader would be easier to define if it were agreed to give separate meanings to two very common words. I mean the words "politician" and "statesman." In popular usage a vague distinction is recognized: to call a man a statesman is eulogy; to call him a politician is to be, however faintly, disparaging. The dictionary, in fact, defines a politician as one who seeks to subserve the interests of a political party *merely;* as an afterthought it defines him as one skilled in political science: a statesman. And in defining a statesman the dictionary says that he is a political leader of distinguished ability.

These definitions can, I think, be improved upon by clarifying the meanings which are vaguely intended in popular usage. When we think offhand of a politician we think of a man who works for a partial interest. At the worst it is his own pocket. At the best it may be his party, his class, or an institution with which he is identified. We never feel that he can or will take into account all the interests concerned, and because bias and partisanship are the qualities of his conduct, we feel, unless we are naïvely afflicted with the same bias, that he is not to be trusted too far. Now the word "statesman," when it is not mere pomposity, connotes a man whose mind is elevated sufficiently above the conflict of contending parties to enable him to adopt a course of action which takes into account a greater number of interests in the perspective of a longer period of time. It is some such conception as this that Edmund Burke had in mind when he wrote that the state "ought not to be considered as nothing better than a partnership in a trade of pepper and coffee, calico, or tobacco, or some other such low concern, to be taken up for a little temporary interest and to be dissolved by the fancy of the parties. . . . It is a partnership in a higher and more permanent sense—a partnership in all science; a partnership in all art; a partnership in every virtue and in all perfection. As the ends of such a partnership cannot be obtained in many generations it becomes a partnership not only between those who are living, but between those who are dead and those who are to be born."

The politician, then, is a man who seeks to attain the special objects of particular interests. If he is the leader of a political party he will try either to purchase the support of particular interests by specific pledges, or if that is impracticable, he will employ some form of deception. I include under the term "deception" the whole art of propaganda, whether it consists of half-truths, lies, ambiguities, evasions, calculated silence, red herrings, unresponsiveness, slogans, catchwords, showmanship, bathos, hokum, and buncombe. They are, one and all, methods of preventing a disinterested inquiry into the situation. I do not say that anyone can be elected to office without employing deception, though I am inclined to think that there is a new school of political reporters in the land who with a kind of beautiful cruelty are making it rather embarrassing for politicians to employ their old tricks. A man may have to be a politician to be elected when there is adult suffrage, and it may be that statesmanship, in the sense in which I am using the term, cannot occupy the whole attention of any public man. It is true at least that it never does.

The reason for this is that in order to hold office a man must array in his support a varied assortment of persons with all sorts of confused and conflicting purposes. When then, it may be asked, does he begin to be a statesman? He begins whenever he stops trying merely to satisfy or to obfuscate the momentary wishes of his constituents, and sets out to make them realize and assent to those hidden interests of theirs which are permanent because they fit the facts and can be harmonized with the interests of their neighbors. The politician says: "I will give you what you want." The statesman says: "What you think you want is this. What it is possible for you to get is that. What you really want, therefore, is the following." The politician stirs up a following; the statesman leads it. The politician, in brief, accepts unregenerate desire at its face value and either fulfills it or perpetrates a fraud; the statesman re-educates desire by confronting it with the reality, and so makes possible an enduring adjustment of interests within the community.

The chief element in the art of statesmanship under modern conditions is the ability to elucidate the confused and clamorous interests which converge upon the seat of government. It is an ability to penetrate from the naïve self-interest of each group to its permanent and real interest. It is a difficult art which requires great courage, deep sympathy, and a vast amount of information. That is why it is so rare. But when a statesman is successful in converting his constituents from a childlike pursuit of what seems interesting to a realistic view of their interests, he receives a kind of support which the ordinary glib politician can never hope for. Candor is a bitter pill when first it is tasted but it is full of health, and once a man becomes established in the public mind as a person who deals habitually and successfully with real things, he acquires an eminence of a wholly different quality from that of even the most celebrated caterer to the popular favor. His hold on the people is enduring because he promises nothing which he cannot achieve; he proposes nothing which turns out to be a fake. Sooner or later the politician, because he deals in unrealities, is found out. Then he either goes to jail, or he is tolerated cynically as a picturesque and amiable scoundrel; or he retires and ceases to meddle with the destinies of men. The words of a statesman prove to have value because they express not the desires of the moment but the conditions under which desires can actually be adjusted to reality. His projects are policies which lay down an ordered plan of action in which all the elements affected will, after they have had some experience of it, find it profitable to co-operate. His laws register what the people really desire when they have clarified their wants. His laws have force because they mobilize the energies which alone can make laws effective.

It is not necessary, nor is it probable, that a statesman-like policy will win such assent when it is first proposed. Nor is it necessary for the statesman to wait until he has won complete assent. There are many things which people cannot understand until they have lived with them for a while. Often, therefore, the great statesman is bound to act boldly in advance of his constituents. When he does this he stakes his judgment as to what the people will in the end find to be good against what the people happen ardently to desire. This capacity to act upon the hidden realities of a situation in spite of appearances is the essence of statesmanship. It consists in giving the people not what they want but what they will learn to want. It requires the courage which is possible only in a mind that is detached from the agitations of the moment. It requires the insight which comes only from an objective and discerning knowledge of the facts, and a high and imperturbable disinterestedness.

2 · *The Predicaments of Leadership*

A Preface to Politics (1913), *Chapter 3.*

I, for one, am not disposed to blame the politicians and the businessmen. They govern the nation, it is true, but they do it in a rather absent-minded fashion. Those revolutionists who see the misery of the country as a deliberate and fiendish plot overestimate the bad will, the intelligence and the singleness of purpose in the ruling classes. Business and political leaders don't mean badly; the trouble with them is that most of the time they don't mean anything. They picture themselves as very "practical," which in practice amounts to saying that nothing makes them feel so spiritually homeless as the discussion of values and an invitation to examine first principles. Ideas, most of the time, cause them genuine distress, and are as disconcerting as an idle office boy, or a squeaky telephone.

I do not underestimate the troubles of the man of affairs. I have lived with politicians—with Socialist politicians whose good will was abundant and intentions constructive. The petty vexations pile up into mountains; the distracting details scatter the attention and break up thinking, while the mere problem of exercising power crowds out speculation about what to do with it. Personal jealousies interrupt co-ordinated effort; committee sessions wear out nerves by their aimless drifting; constant speechmaking turns a man back upon a convenient little store of platitudes—misunderstanding and distortion dry up the imagination, make thought timid and expression flat, the atmosphere of publicity requires a mask which soon becomes the reality. Politicians tend to live "in character," and many a public figure has come to imitate the journalism which describes him. You cannot blame politicians if their perceptions are few and their thinking crude.

"Democracy, Foreign Policy and the Split Personality of the Modern Statesman," The Annals of the American Academy of Political and Social Science, *CII* (*1922*), *190*.

That there is a dark truth about most public men I am convinced. Nothing seems to me more certain than that most of them are leading dark, illicit, and subterranean lives of moderation and reason. They flaunt their vices to the public; they shiver and quake at the thought that some indiscreet journalist will expose them to the world as men of virtue and common sense. I can think at this moment of several leading politicians in Washington who would rather be whipped than have it known how sound are their views on the bonus, the tariff, the inter-allied debts and the League of Nations. A journalist could do them no greater injury than to repeat things which would convince the majority of their audience that these public men were worthy of the utmost confidence.

This sort of thing is world-wide, as almost anyone can testify who knows, for example, the difference between what the statesmen at Paris were accustomed to say in confidence, especially at breakfast, and what they gave forth in speeches to their constituents. . . . There is very little doubt that if you could lock all the prime ministers of Europe in a soundproof room, their real views would soon show an amount of agreement that their public utterances never reveal.

The split personality of the modern statesman is an almost daily experience in the life of a journalist. You find yourself dealing with two sets of facts and opinions: the private facts and opinions of the great man, and the public version of those facts and opinions which the great man feels called upon to maintain. And as a journalist you must help him maintain the public version on penalty of losing his confidence; that is to say, on penalty of not learning privately what he privately believes.

For example, you write an editorial urging a party leader not to deceive his constituents by telling them they are about to receive large installments of interest on the war debts. The next day his friend Jim calls you on the phone and assures you that the great man is quite sound on the debt question. Jim has talked to him and the great man is nobody's fool. Get that straight. So don't be excited about it. Keep cool. The people aren't ready for that sort of thing yet; but the great man is leading them on slowly, step by step, toward the appalling and dazzling truth. When will he tell them the truth? Ah, that depends. If things go well and if impatient journalists don't stir up the opposition prematurely, the time will come when the truth will be told. And, in the meantime, is it not better to have the great man remain where he is, with his sound views on this great question, than to let him be turned out by someone who will not only do just what he is doing, but will also believe in doing it?

When this sort of thing happens once, you are angry. When it happens under all sorts of circumstances, you realize that it is not simply a question of personal integrity. You begin to realize that you are feeling the effects of a revolutionary change in the technic of diplomacy. You are forced to acknowledge, I think, that here is an aspect of the transition from a diplomacy which was the private concern of a small class of insiders to a diplomacy which is compelled to satisfy the fluctuating politics of a legislature and the still vaguer sentiment of the country as a whole. The transition, to be sure, is not complete, and probably it will never in our time be carried to its logical conclusion.

Much, indeed, that is meant to seem like perfect obedience to popular sentiment is in reality a carefully stage-managed show. The so-called plenary sessions of the various international congresses are a prime example. These stately gatherings are a concession to the ritual of democracy, rather than decisive and executive councils. Even more than in our national party conventions, the things which are publicly decided have been privately decided beforehand.

Nevertheless, in the hotel rooms or in the nearby villa, where decisions are privately made, the negotiators are to an unprecedented degree conscious of opinion in the legislature and among the voters in the dim distance. They are continually aware of the fact that if they guess wrong about their henchmen or the rank and file, they will be broken politically.

And yet these opinions which the statesman is forever trying to estimate are rarely a clear guide to the questions before him. From the official point of view they are danger signals, telling him where he must not trespass at all, where he may venture at his peril, and where he must make a wide and troublesome detour. All democratic statesmen respect these signposts, or they are ruined. They differ in their reading of them. Some of them can tell the difference between popular taboos that are deeply founded, and taboos which are organized, publicity-man bluff. Some statesmen cannot tell the difference, and to them every stray cat, every goat and every donkey looks like a sacred cow.

Allowing for personal differences among statesmen, differences of courage and interest in truth, we must note that almost without exception, especially in the realm of foreign affairs, the modern statesman is caught in a contradiction: he must defer to the force of opinion because that is where power resides; yet he must deal with affairs in which public opinion is only a very partial, and almost always a merely negative, guide to policy. Soon he discovers that there is no pre-established harmony between government *for* the people and government *by* the people. And his indulgence in rhetoric, his evasions of the real issue, his fright at plain speech, his descent into florid abstraction, is, in a very large degree, the attempt to effect a working compromise between that which at the moment interests the people and that which he believes to be in the interest of the people. Between his guess at what the public wishes and his own best judgment of what the public needs, he generally manages to split his personality into two selves, neither of which is on friendly terms with the other.

This great democratic difficulty becomes most apparent in international relations, although samples of it are only too evident within the national boundaries. But at least in domestic affairs the parties concerned speak the same language, have common habits and more or less similar environments. The other side, and the other aspects, cannot be wholly dodged, and so they receive some consideration. But in foreign affairs the others concerned in the business are fenced off, frequently by a spike fence, each not only within its own language and tradition but within its own experience. . . .

Only on the unnecessary assumption that their presence in public office is essential to the safety of the Republic, is it necessary for public men to drift with the tides of opinion. For how can opinion ever arrive at a real view of a great international question if those on the inside, if those in the know, spend their time waiting for instructions from those of us on the outside who cannot possibly know? On questions as complex as those awaiting settlement in the world today, it is utterly impossible to rely on the mysterious wisdom of the people. And any statesman who pretends that he does rely on it, or can, is trifling with questions of life and death.

For since knowledge of these intricate and far-reaching

matters cannot be obtained by consulting your conscience or your sentiments about the bonus or the income tax, the only possible means by which democracy can act successfully in foreign affairs is access to the knowledge which the insiders possess, because the sources of information are in their hands. For the executive in any democratic country to keep his knowledge a secret, and then wait to act until public opinion approximates what he secretly believes, is absurd in theory and unworkable in practice. It ends in drift, factionalism, and the deterioration of the standards of public life.

The problems of the modern world are puzzling enough without complicating them still further by permitting our leaders to abdicate their leadership, because they might be attacked and lose votes. The best wisdom the insiders have may not be enough to save European civilization from an era of deep decay. But it would be intolerable to think that we had not prevented that decay because we declined to act according to such lights as we have. At least we might try, even at the risk of the next Congressional election, yes, even at the risk of defeating a few senators, to have our leaders speak their whole minds, and act on their own full judgment of what the situation requires.

The Good Society (*1937*), *Chapter 16.*

The hankering for schemes and systems and comprehensive organization is the wistfulness of an immature philosophy which has not come to terms with reality, no less when the conservators of vested interests would stabilize the modern economy in status quo by protective laws and monopolistic schemes than when the revolutionist makes blueprints of a world composed of planned national economies "co-ordinated" by a world-planning authority. Neither takes any more account of reality than if he were studying landscape architecture with a view to making a formal garden out of the Brazilian jungle.

For the greater the society, the higher and more variable the standards of life, the more diversified the energies of its people for invention, enterprise, and adaptation, the more certain it is that the social order cannot be planned *ex cathedra* or governed by administrative command. We live in such an immensely diversified civilization that the only intelligible criterion which political thinkers can entertain in regard to it, the only feasible goal which statesmen can set themselves in governing it, is to reconcile the conflicts which spring from this diversity. They cannot hope to comprehend it as a system. For it is not a system. They cannot hope to plan and direct it. For it is not an organization. They can hope only to dispense lawful justice among individuals and associations where their interests conflict, to mitigate the violence of conflict and competition by seeking to make lawful justice more and more equitable.

It requires much virtue to do that well. There must be a strong desire to be just. There must be a growing capacity to be just. There must be discernment and sympathy in estimating the particular claims of divergent interests. There must be moral standards which discourage the quest of privilege and the exercise of arbitrary power. There must be resolution and valor to resist oppression and tyranny. There must be patience and tolerance and kindness in hearing claims, in argument, in negotiation, and in reconciliation.

But these are human virtues; though they are high, they are within the attainable limits of human nature as we know it. They actually exist. Men do have these virtues, all but the most hopelessly degenerate, in some degree. We know that they can be increased. When we talk about them we are talking about virtues that have affected the course of actual history, about virtues that some men have practiced more than other men, and no man sufficiently, but enough men in great enough degree to have given mankind here and there and for varying periods of time the intimations of a Good Society.

But the virtues that are required for the overhead administration of a civilization are superhuman; they are attributes of Providence and not of mortal men. It is true that there have been benevolent despots and that for a little while in a particular place they have made possible a better life than their subjects were able to achieve without the rule of a firm and authoritative guardian. And no doubt it is still true that a community which does not have the essential discipline of liberty can choose only among alternative disciplines by authority. But if a community must have such a guardian, then it must resign itself to living a simple regimented existence, must entertain no hopes of the high and diversified standard of life which the division of labor and modern technology make possible. For despots cannot be found who could plan, organize, and direct a complex economy.

To do that would require a comprehensive understanding of the life and the labor and the purposes of hundreds of millions of persons, the gift of prophesying their behavior, and the omnipotence to control it. These faculties no man has ever possessed. When in theorizing we unwittingly postulate such faculties, we are resting our hopes on a conception of human nature which has no warrant whatever in any actual experience. The collectivist planners are not talking about the human race but about some other breed conceived in their dreams. They postulate qualities of intelligence and of virtue so unlike those which men possess that it would be just as intelligible to make plans for a society in which human beings were born equipped to fly like the angels, to feed on the fragrance of the summer breezes, and endowed with all possible knowledge.

Thus while the liberal philosophy is concerned with the reform of the laws in order to adapt them to the changing needs and standards of the dynamic economy, while the agenda of reform are long and varied, no one must look to liberalism for a harmonious scheme of social reconstruction. The Good Society has no architectural design. There are no blueprints. There is no mold in which human life is to be shaped. Indeed, to expect the blueprint of such a mold is a mode of thinking against which the liberal temper is a constant protest.

The Public Philosophy (1955), *Chapter 2.*

At the critical moments in this sad history, there have been men, worth listening to, who warned the people against their mistakes. Always, too, there have been men inside the governments who judged correctly, because they were permitted to know in time, the uncensored and unvarnished truth. But the climate of modern democracy does not usually inspire them to speak out. For what Churchill did in the thirties before Munich was exceptional; the general rule is that a democratic politician had better not be right too soon. Very often the penalty is political death. It is much safer to keep in step with the parade of opinion than to try to keep up with the swifter movement of events.

In government offices which are sensitive to the vehemence and passion of mass sentiment, public men have no sure tenure. They are in effect perpetual office seekers, always on trial for their political lives, always required to court their restless constituents. They are deprived of their independence. Democratic politicians rarely feel they can afford the luxury of telling the whole truth to the people. And since not telling it, though prudent, is uncomfortable, they find it easier if they themselves do not have to hear too often too much of the sour truth. The men under them who report and collect the news come to realize in their turn that it is safer to be wrong before it has become fashionable to be right.

With exceptions so rare that they are regarded as miracles and freaks of nature, successful democratic politicians are insecure and intimidated men. They advance politically only as they placate, appease, bribe, seduce, bamboozle, or otherwise manage to manipulate the demanding and threatening elements in their constituencies. The decisive consideration is not whether the proposition is good but whether it is popular—not whether it will work well and prove itself but whether the active talking constituents like it immediately. Politicians rationalize this servitude by saying that in a democracy public men are the servants of the people.

This devitalization of the governing power is the malady of democratic states. As the malady grows the executives become highly susceptible to encroachment and usurpation by elected assemblies; they are pressed and harassed by the higgling of parties, by the agents of organized interests, and by the spokesmen of sectarians and ideologues. The malady can be fatal. It can be deadly to the very survival of the state as a free society if, when the great and hard issues of war and peace, of security and solvency, of revolution and order are up for decision, the executive and judicial departments, with their civil servants and technicians, have lost their power to decide.

3 · *Leadership and Opinion*

"The False Gods," Today and Tomorrow, *May 20, 1932.*

From what source come these unmanly fears that prevail among us? These dark forebodings? This despairing impotence? What is it that has shaken the nerves of so many? It is the doubt whether there exists among the people that trust in each other which is the first condition of intelligent leadership. That is the root of the matter. The particular projects which we debate so angrily are not so important. The fate of the nation does not hang upon any of them. But upon the power of the people to remain united for purposes which they respect, upon their capacity to have faith in themselves and in their objectives, much depends. It is not the facts of the crisis which we have to fear. They can be endured and dealt with. It is demoralization alone that is dangerous.

A demoralized people is one in which the individual has become isolated and is the prey of his own suspicions. He trusts nobody and nothing, not even himself. He believes nothing, except the worst of everybody and everything. He sees only confusion in himself and conspiracies in other men. That is panic. That is disintegration. That is what comes when in some sudden emergency of their lives men find themselves unsupported by clear convictions that transcend their immediate and personal desires.

The last ten years have been a time of exceptionally drastic change in the underlying convictions of Western men. For reasons which it is not easy to state briefly or even clearly to discern, it seems as if in this decade the change in life brought about by science and machinery and the modern city, by democracy and by popular education, had struck with full impact and with cumulative force against the traditional morality, the social conventions, and the ideals of the mass of men.

That a period of profound spiritual bewilderment had to ensue was inevitable. But this bewilderment has been greatly aggravated in the United States by what I believe may truthfully be called the moral apathy of those in high places. At the beginning of the decade the national government was attacked by brutal and conspicuous corruption. No clear word about it was spoken by those in high places. On the contrary, they sat silent, hoping that the people would forget, calculating that the evil would be overlooked. Is it surprising that public spirit weakened when it was demonstrated from the highest places that the corruption of government was not something anyone ought to care deeply about?

During this decade the country has been making the experiment of outlawing an ancient and general human appetite. Those in high places have known quite well how badly the experiment was working, what stupendous lawlessness and corruption the prohibition law was producing. Yet in all this time no candid word, no straightforward utterance, no honest inquiry about this matter has come from any high place. The problem has been muffled in hypocrisy, in miserable ambiguities, and in equivocation, to a point where any open, public debate of the matter has become impossible.

During this same decade those in high places have steadfastly preached to the people that it was their destiny to have two-car garages and eight-tube radio sets. That was the ideal they held out before the people, to be acquisitive, to seek feverishly to become richer and richer, to prostrate themselves before the Golden Calf. To read today the rhapsodies which issued from the highest places during the last decade is to find the main reason why now, when the nation must call upon all its resources in integrity and magnanimity and public spirit, a clear devotion to the national interest is not surely available.

For if you teach a people for ten years that the character of its government is not greatly important, that political success is for those who equivocate and evade, and if you tell them that acquisitiveness is the ideal, that things are what matter, that Mammon is God, then you must not be astonished at the confusion in Washington, or the nonchalance of James J. Walker, or the vermin who in a hundred different ways exploited the tragedy of the Lindbergh baby. You cannot set up false gods to confuse the people and not pay the penalty.

Those in high places are more than the administrators of government bureaus. They are more than the writers of laws.

They are the custodians of a nation's ideals, of the beliefs it cherishes, of its permanent hopes, of the faith which makes a nation out of a mere aggregation of individuals. They are unfaithful to that trust when by word and example they promote a spirit that is complacent, evasive, and acquisitive.

It is not only against the material consequences of this decade of drift and hallucination, but against the essence of its spirit that the best and bravest among us are today in revolt. They are looking for new leaders, for men who are truthful and resolute and eloquent in the conviction that the American destiny is to be free and magnanimous, rather than complacent and acquisitive; they are looking for leaders who will talk to the people not about two-car garages and a bonus, but about their duty, and about the sacrifices they must make, and about the discipline they must impose upon themselves, and about their responsibility to the world and to posterity, about all those things which make a people self-respecting, serene, and confident. May they not look in vain.

"Our Leaders," Today and Tomorrow, *August 21, 1941.*

When the President quotes Lincoln's remark that the people "have got the idea into their heads that we are going to get out of this fix somehow by strategy," he ought not to forget that the ideas the people get into their heads about this fix, they get from their responsible leaders. They get them from the words and acts of the President, his spokesmen in Congress, and his appointees. They get them from the words and acts of the Republican opposition. If the people do not realize the gravity of the fix they are in, it is because the President has made them feel that he was himself trying to get out of the fix by clever strategy and brilliant tactics, and because the Republican organization in Congress has been trying by its strategy and tactics to win the next election.

In a crisis of this sort the state of mind of the people is the direct reflection of the quality of their responsible leaders. The people themselves cannot possibly lead themselves by holding mass meetings, distributing postcards, and taking Gallup polls. They must be led. They expect to be led, and if they do not find leaders who have that high seriousness which the occasion demands, they will accept leaders who pander to, and seek to profit by the universal human weakness for taking, whenever possible, the cheap and easy way.

An appallingly dangerous and demoralizing and humiliating situation has developed in Congress during the last fortnight. It is due to the fact that in default of a high seriousness in the President's leadership of the people, the Republican opposition in Congress has decided it was free to play partisan politics, even at the risk of disorganizing the Army, repudiating its commander, demoralizing the people, and shattering the influence of the United States throughout the world. The decision of the Republican organization to make a partisan issue of the Army extension bill was in the last degree reckless. But the politicians would never have dared to gamble so recklessly with the fate of the country if from the other side, from the President himself, the people had been treated as grown men and women who are faced with a tremendous ordeal in which they must rise far above their normal selves.

Mr. Roosevelt himself has not dealt with the people as Lincoln dealt with Mrs. Livermore. For a while he has repeatedly made addresses which describe truthfully, profoundly, and eloquently the gravity of our position; invariably these utterances have been punctuated and deflated by subsequent smart-aleckisms and wisecracks.

Listening to Mr. Roosevelt has been like listening to a radio station from which the announcer gives forth epoch-making news and appeals to patriotism, interspersed with advertisements for soft mattresses and efficient laxatives.

It is not necessary, or remotely desirable, that the leader of a people in a crisis like this should be always grim, solemn, and fanatic. It is a relief, when one thinks of the sulphurous gloom of Hitler, to think of a Churchill or a Roosevelt and be reminded, by their gusto and their buoyancy, of the decencies of life. But it is essential that the greatest matters, those involving the fate of the nation, should not be reduced to triviality by trivial comment, or, worse still, cheapened by wisecracks.

It is a solemn and a heavy, not a light and clever, task to summon a people from their ordinary ways of life to face one among the few very greatest moments in the history of mankind. Of course it is difficult. Of course millions will listen to and prefer to believe those who tell them they need not rouse themselves, and that all will be well if only they continue to do all the pleasant and profitable and comfortable things they would like best to do.

Of course the contest is hard and the debating is fierce, and the polls of opinion uncertain: the President must ask the people to give up comfort and ease, personal ambition and private profit, and be ready, it may be, for blood and tears; his political opponents need only tell the people to keep their comforts, to hug their private ambitions and pursue their private profit, to sit in safety and they will be forever safe.

What has the President to offer the people in return for the sacrifices they are called upon to make? Only their duty done, their country's future, the honor and the glory of being fit to stand with those who made the nation and preserved it. It is easier for a politician to tell the boys to go home, to tell their mothers their sons need never be in danger, to tell everyone that there is no need to go short of gasoline or to endure the incredible suffering of not having silk stockings and a new automobile. Of course it is harder to ask people to take the hard way than it is to tell them they can safely and profitably take the easy way.

But it has to be done. Washington had to do it, Lincoln had to do it, Churchill has had to do it, Roosevelt has to do it. The world is on fire. The alarm has to be rung and kept ringing, first and without stopping by the President, until the fire is put out. However much pleasanter it might be to do so, the American people cannot sleep through that fire, or they too will be trapped in the flames.

"The President and the People," Today and Tomorrow, *January 29, 1942.*

Mr. Churchill seems to be the only statesman in the world who really believes that the people can and should be enabled to understand the war. Certainly he is the only one who goes to them whenever events have taken a new turn and tells them even in broad outline what has happened and why it has happened. Surely the willingness to explain what he has been doing is, even more than his great gifts of speech, the secret of his leadership. Mr. Churchill does not deal with his people on the assumption that

Someone had blundered:
Theirs not to make reply,
Theirs not to reason why,
Theirs but to do and die.

For while he accepts full responsibility for the great decisions, he also holds himself fully accountable for them. Having explained the reasons which led him to make the decisions, he not only allows his people and their representatives to pass upon them. He insists that they must pass upon the decisions and take their share of the responsibility. This is how the democratic method can, when it is really used, strengthen and unify a nation. Mr. Churchill says little about democracy in the abstract. Yet he does more about it in practice than any other living man. He knows that a leader remains close with the people when he acts on the belief that they can be trusted. He has proved in this war that the people respond by feeling that they can trust a man who trusts them.

Our presidential system of government does not lend itself as readily as the parliamentary system to this reciprocity between the leader and the people. The President, unlike the Prime Minister, is irremovable; Congress, unlike the House of Commons, is not responsible for the Executive, and cannot be compelled, on pain of dissolution and an appeal to the people, to accept the responsibility of supporting the Administration or of changing the Administration.

Thus the habit of intimacy and frankness between Executive and Congress is not promoted here, and there has rarely been an American President who was on terms of trust and friendship with Congress. American Presidents, be they Roosevelt or Wilson, Hoover or Coolidge, are not in the habit of explaining themselves as Churchill explains himself. They announce, they proclaim, they declaim, they exhort, they appeal, and they argue. But they do not unbend and tell the story, and say why they did what they did, and what they think about it, and how they feel about it. Thus the general effect is secretive and stand-offish, which certainly does not warm the heart in a time of trouble.

Yet admitting all the difficulties of our political system, above all the appalling irresponsibility in speech and action which is so often displayed on the floors of Congress and in the committees, it is certainly disconcerting that the first account of the meaning of what happened at Pearl Harbor, and that the first explanation of the strategic position in the Pacific, should have come from the Prime Minister of Great Britain. That will not do. Mr. Roosevelt has a long, hard, bitter war to conduct, and he cannot conduct it successfully without explaining it continually to the people.

Programs, pronouncements, and publicity releases are no substitute for the story and the explanation from the lips of the man who is finally responsible. All the "morale-builders"—a horrid word which is enough to destroy anyone's morale—from O.C.D. to O.F.F. will be of no avail unless and until Mr. Roosevelt forms the habit of confiding in the American people as Mr. Churchill confides in the British people. The American people are not children, and they will have to be treated as adults if they are to face the grim future as men and women.

"Mirror of the Spirit," Today and Tomorrow, *February 25, 1943.*

There is no better or more practical rule in what it is now the fashion to call public relations or propaganda than a famous remark attributed to George Washington. During one of the most difficult periods of the Constitutional Convention in Philadelphia, when the whole project of a strong national government hung in the balance because of pressure from the smaller states, Washington asked the delegates to disregard what was supposed to be expedient and to "raise a standard to which the wise and the honest can repair."

Like most, I had always admired this slogan, but had regarded it as one of those noble and pious generalities which are said by the immortal great and are too rarefied for our own affairs. Then one day last autumn I happened to be talking with a friend of mine, who is the editor of a London newspaper, about how the people of London had taken the bombing raids. "Many of us," he said, "were anxious about that before the raids started in September, 1940; we did not know how the people of a modern city would stand up to it. And when the first raid came and hit the East End of London, neither the government nor the newspapers knew just what the people who had been hit were thinking and how they would take it. But that evening we decided to assume that they had acted heroically, as Englishmen should, and the next morning we printed all the stories that came in to us of their bravery, their good humor, and their uncomplaining patience. Right then and there we fixed the pattern of how people ought to behave in an air raid. Perhaps they would all have behaved that way anyway. But you know there is good and bad in all of us, and the right example at the right moment can make all the difference in the way men act."

Then I understood as never before what it means in practice to raise a standard—a standard of behavior—to which the wise and the honest can repair.

We in particular need to meditate upon the wisdom of this truth about human affairs. For the conditions under which Americans have to fight this war are morally very difficult. Our men are fighting across the seas while the nation at home is immune from the risks of battle. This separation is our chief moral problem. For the men who are abroad in dangerous places or in lonely posts, there is little chance as there is in England or in Russia or in China to come home on leave, or to be sustained by the feeling that near them and all about them there is the warmth of those they love and the reassuring familiarity of their native land. The ordeal of the American warrior is the ordeal of loneliness and of distance, and the dread that he is far away and forgotten and that his hard task is not understood.

For the people at home, who never feel the blows of the enemy, it is not easy to feel themselves close to and part of the great undertaking in which their sons and their lovers are engaged. Many, but by no means all of the people at home, are living through the ordeal of loneliness and of distance and of anxiety, and finally for some there is only their loss and their grief. For all those who have a poignant personal stake in the distant enterprise, the ordeal is harder because of the distance. They do not expect to see their men until the war is over. They wait for letters that do not come very often. And because they are so safe themselves, they feel all the more separated because they are unable to have the supreme consolation of sharing in some measure at least the tasks of their men.

The rest, and they are still the great majority, who are safe at home and have no man at the front, do not find it easy to keep themselves vividly aware of what this war demands of them. They are the ones who get themselves most involved in the trivialities of the inconveniences of wartime, who make a spectacle of themselves snatching for profits and wages, and insisting upon their prerogatives and worrying about how much they can withhold now in order to have a better start than others when the war is over.

It is to them that Washington's injunction to raise a standard is most relevant. They are the people who are not living in the history of their age, and do not imagine it, and tend, therefore, not to rise to the level of it.

The mechanics of politics and of the press tends, if it is not consciously and resolutely reversed, to depress rather than to raise their spirits. Every congressman and every newspaperman is like a doctor: he spends most of his time hearing from the people who have a pain, and if he is not on guard he is likely to think that the country consists entirely of people with a pain in the neck. He forgets how many people there are who do not have a pain in the neck, or are disposed to grin and bear it if they have. That is why objective sampling of opinion, as in the Gallup and *Fortune* polls, has so consistently shown that the American people are saner, more resolute, and more enlightened than they are supposed to be.

The tendency of the elected representative, however, is to take the quiet mass of his constituents for granted and to worry about the ones who write him the strongest letters about their pains in their necks. These are the people he tends to represent, and by representing them their attitude tends to become the standard which is raised. Hearing so much from Congress about pains in the neck, the rest begin to discover that they too have pains in the neck.

The ordinary mechanism of news reporting has a similar tendency. The 10 per cent or so of the chiselers, operators on the black market, hand-wringers and breast-beaters, precisely because they are out of the ordinary, have to be reported as news. Undoubtedly it is the business of a free press to make public what goes wrong. But somehow we have to keep in mind the fact that the behavior of the wise and the honest is not to be ignored and taken for granted, that it must be reported and celebrated, and set high and conspicuously as the standard and example. If not, we shall be getting too low an opinion of ourselves and shall be lowering our behavior to conform to our opinions.

Nor will this raising of the standard be a departure from the truth. For the truth about America today is that, with all our mistakes and shortcomings, by the manner in which the nation is responding to this difficult war the people are writing one of the great chapters in American history. No one should rob them of their right to find strength in being proud of it. No one should deny them the mirror in which they may see themselves as a grateful posterity will see them.

4 · *Some Lessons for Leaders*

"The Bogey of Public Opinion," Vanity Fair, *XXXVII (December 1931), 51.*

The calculating politician who is always waiting for a good safe majority before he moves does well enough in times when nothing much is at stake and nobody particularly cares. But in times like these a persistent effort to please the voters is an almost sure way to antagonize them. There are two reasons for this. The first is that the man in office is judged by results and not by his intentions, and in time of crisis results come quickly. Thus a statesman who is afraid to balance his budget because taxes and economy are unpopular is not forgiven if bankruptcy ensues. It does him no good to tell the voters: "I let the deficit grow, because I knew you did not want to be taxed or to have salaries reduced." The people do not want to be taxed, but still less do they want to go bankrupt. They will not reward the politician for having been so kind as to humor them. They will punish him for having failed to save them from ruin.

There is another reason why putting the pleasure of the voters first is very bad politics in a time like this. It is that when men are in trouble they want nothing so much as to feel that near them is strength and resolution. In pleasant weather the captain of a ship may make himself popular by dancing with the girls and being a regular fellow with the boys. But in dirty weather they want him on the bridge attending to the ship and not to the passengers. They do not want him to consult the passengers to find out if anyone objects to his blowing the foghorn or to changing his course.

The effort to calculate exactly what the voters want at each particular moment leaves out of account the fact that when they are troubled the thing the voters most want is to be told what to want. The private citizen knows perfectly well that he is in no position to understand the real state of affairs in a crisis of this magnitude. He knows how it has hit him, and for the rest he must rely on what he is told. Now if public men at the seats of authority sit and wait for a mass of bewildered private citizens somehow to produce "public opinion," the practical effect is simply to destroy confidence in public men. The people look elsewhere for leadership, and since they must look to people who have no responsibility in fact and perhaps even no sense of responsibility, the result is an excited milling hither and thither and the formulation of demands. For when people are not led they get to demanding, and the possibility of national effort is lost in factional outcries.

It is not only more dignified but it is also shrewder in a time like this for a public man to fix his attention upon the things that need to be done, to announce them with conviction, to fight for them without hesitation, and to trust that the common sense and the idealism of the people will support him. If the people won't have it and he is beaten, what of it? No man and no party has any messianic mission, and the chance of defeat is a normal risk of the politician's trade. As a matter of fact the risk of being straightforward is certainly no greater, and may be less, than that of waiting and calculating. For popularity arising from catering to popular whims is like walking a tightrope; it can be done for a while, but a man cannot go far that way. The enduring popularity of public men does not come from trying to guess what the people will applaud but from conveying to them the feeling that they can rely on the superior judgment of that man when they need him. It is no comfort whatever to know that he is a good judge of public opinion; they will really trust him only if they have some evidence that he is a good judge of the public interest.

"Too Much Is Too Much," Today and Tomorrow, *December 9, 1932.*

American public men in the management of their own lives are usually the most helpless creatures in the world. The demands upon them are infinite, and very few know how to preserve for themselves the time needed for study and consideration. Often it seems that more of them are ruined by an inability to brush aside interruptions than by any other course. Few of them have learned to say no to invitations, to refuse themselves to the unending stream of visitors, to shut their minds against unnecessary problems which are thrust upon them. The result is that the greater part of their time and energy goes into the least important part of their task. They spend a day and a night traveling somewhere or other to make a speech, and they have ten absent-minded minutes between useless appointments to read a report. They spend hours with bores, celebrities, and nabobs, and minutes with experts who could really advise them. Their offices are as private as the waiting room of a railroad station and their thoughts as consecutive as a radio program.

The great leader and the great executive in public affairs is never the man who tries to cook everyone's dinner and to sew the buttons on everyone's shirt. He is the man who, in the words of Mr. Justice Holmes, has an instinct for the jugular, who strikes only at the vital points, and lets others do the barbering and manicuring of public life. Simplicity and concentration produce lucidity and decision, and these in turn produce effectiveness and confidence.

The man of affairs is only a human being with limited capacity and limited time and strength. He cannot be the great White Father to all the world and an elected Providence to his nation. The temptation is to try to be. It must be sternly resisted. If he is to survive at all under the pressure of modern affairs he must make up his mind once and for all that he will prefer the most important things to the less important ones, the central to the peripheral, and that he will let somebody else besides himself play a part in running the world.

"The Pace of Things," Today and Tomorrow, *October 20, 1933.*

The novice plants the seeds and then the next morning before breakfast rushes out into the garden to see whether they have sprouted. Seeing no sign of life above ground, he digs up the seeds to have a look at them. The amateur cook would like to eat the cake when he has mixed the dough. The bad golfer looks up to see where his shot has landed before he has hit the ball. The results are invariably disappointing. In the application of measures during this crisis most of us fall into these bad habits, and raise unnecessary difficulties and disappointments. It is the part of wisdom in human affairs to have a true sense of the pace of action and the timing of events.

One of the most dangerous forms that unwisdom can take is to fix a date and say: unless this or that is achieved by that date, all is lost. In the months preceding the World Economic Conference, for example, statesmen all over the world made a point of telling their people that they must do or die at London on June twelfth. There was to be either recovery or catastrophe at a certain point in the calender. What was the result? Though there was neither catastrophe nor recovery, the unwarranted expectations brought on such corresponding disappointment, that the whole effort, necessarily complex and difficult, of international co-operation was brought to a complete standstill. The world has to forget what it expected in June before it can again begin to do what it can.

The same unfortunate habit of mind has played a part in the Disarmament Conference. Because Europe was deeply disturbed last spring, men whose ardor for peace is beyond question allowed themselves to make the mistake of proclaiming to the peoples that unless there was an immediate treaty a great disaster would ensue. Such talk merely aggravated the situation. With Europe deeply disturbed, the prospects of an immediate treaty were poorer, not better; therefore, insisting upon a treaty, when it was not possible to make one, tended to add to the disturbance rather than to allay it. In a critical situation the wise man promises only what he can surely realize; anything more than that sharpens the crisis by raising false expectations.

In our domestic affairs we have indulged heavily in calendar-worship. In Washington, for example, the administration of the N.R.A. has been beset by a kind of breathless anxiety that certain definite results had to be achieved on a particular day. There had to be x million men at work by Labor Day. There had to be x million more by the New Year. And if there were not, the whole thing was a failure. At least two different kinds of mischief have resulted from this feeling that the whole experiment was a race against the clock inexorably ticking its way to the millennium or to disaster.

It inspired the N.R.A. administrators to attempt much more than they could effectively handle. Instead of taking up the problem of making codes for industries in the order of their importance, achieving a series of definite reforms where they were most urgently needed, the N.R.A. jumped for the blanket code and got itself entangled in a maze of inconsequential matters pertaining to little industries and little shops, to industries which are relatively in good condition, and left itself all too little energy and time for considered action on the industries that most needed attention. . . .

It has also distorted the perspective of the people. All through the summer they were taught to believe that the Blue Eagle was the sole bringer of recovery, and that it was a swiftly moving bird. The expectations raised from Washington could not conceivably have been met. The result has been to distract attention from the very substantial progress that has been made and to fix attention upon the promises that have not been fulfilled. There is impatience, manifesting itself in many troublesome forms, because the N.R.A. promised too much too soon. At the same time the administrators have neglected to make the country understand the true function and the real possibilities of N.R.A.: its promise of a more orderly and stable industrial system worked out by consultation and consent. Such a system can be begun quickly; it cannot be established by Christmas. Even the dictatorships, where everything is done so lickety-split, have allowed themselves, in the case of Russia, five years; in the case of Germany, four years. The N.R.A. would have borrowed less trouble for itself if it had recognized that in a marathon race a runner does not try to sprint the first mile.

An equally mischievous form of anxiety about the clock is that now prevailing in the circles most concerned about a sound and stable currency. A phobia is rapidly being evolved which has fixed upon the assembling of Congress in January as the Day of Judgment for our monetary system. It is a dangerous phobia. If we put ourselves into the state of mind where we have to solve the monetary problem in the next sixty days, we shall only make more likely the dangers that we fear.

For it may not be possible to solve the monetary problem in sixty days, and it is the height of unwisdom to inculcate the belief that, if we do not, we shall never solve it. I am not arguing that we should drift; on the contrary, I have ventured to believe that we should have begun at least as early as July to exercise control and steady the exchange. But it is one thing to exercise control and to demonstrate your control; it is quite another to settle the question finally. It may require more than sixty days to find the level of depreciation from the old gold parity which can be made to work, and more than sixty days to work out with the British, and then with the French, practicable rates of exchange. It would be folly, therefore, to build up an expectation that would produce either a wrong decision or no decision followed by great perturbation because there was no decision.

The safe thing to do is to forget the calendar, have faith in the American people and the American Congress, and assume that they will trust the President's leadership as long as he makes it evident that he knows what he is doing. In the money question it is not the calendar but the problem itself that needs attention and discussion.

This is, I hope, no plea for complacency or inaction. It is a plea for a recognition that when you set the kettle on the stove you cannot make it boil faster by blowing on it.

"Dulles: A Tribute," Today and Tomorrow, *May 26, 1959.*

John Foster Dulles lived long enough to know before he died that among his countrymen he had no enemies and that his critics and opponents liked and admired him. This is unusual and significant. For Dulles was a highly controversial figure in a dangerous time, and when we have explained to ourselves why at the end he stands out above his battles, we shall have paid him a fitting tribute.

The explanation does not lie in this or that policy or in any moral generalization. It lies in the fact that he was in the great tradition of what is required of a man in his public and his private life. The eulogies speak of him as a dedicated man, and in the exact sense of that overused word he was dedicated to the function of a public servant.

Perhaps the highest function of a public servant in a free and democratic society is to preserve its oneness as a community while he fights the battles which divide it. John Foster Dulles never lost sight of that. He never forgot, as so many public men do, that after the issue which is up for debate is settled, those who took part in the debate must still live and work together. That is the reason why among his countrymen there is no rancor, and why the sorrow of his opponents and critics is genuine.

Like most men, he preferred praise to criticism and agreement to opposition. But he did not demand conformity. He did not regard dissent as perversity, he respected debate and the practice of free journalism.

I can speak here from the heart, having been for some thirty years his friend and on many questions of policy a critic.

Long experience has taught me how rare it is in public men to accept public criticism without private resentment, which only too often spreads to their wives and their sisters and their brothers and their aunts. To be free of that kind of resentment is the mark of a thoroughbred, and the Dulles family are thoroughbreds, born to and trained to the demands of public life. They really do their public duty as they see it, without letting their private feelings take hold of them.

"Fulbright and Kefauver," Today and Tomorrow, *March 29, 1951*

There is no mechanical gadget by which the moral level of public life can be maintained. There is no spasm of popular righteousness which will raise it much for very long. All depends on the code of conduct which is fashionable. All depends on the working rules of behavior which the leading and conspicuous men and women in a society practice because they believe them, which most of the others conform with as a matter of course, and which no one can violate with a feeling that he is doing what everyone else is doing.

In the realm of morals the example set by the prominent is decisive. It is far more important than the exposure of the wicked. In fact, the example of the prominent shows those who administer and enforce the laws what is expected of them. This will determine how faithfully and how actively the wicked are exposed.

For that reason a civilized society must demand of those who have the ambition to lead it a higher standard of disinterestedness than they would live up to if they had no public ambitions. *Noblesse oblige*. This is not, though some may think so, a highfalutin' and perfectionist view of the obligations of leadership. In the case of the captain of the ship, for example, who must save all other lives before his own, so high a standard of conduct is regarded not as fancy and foolish but as indispensable to the discipline and safety of the ship.

A Preface to Morals (1929), *Chapter 15.*

The trouble with the moralists is in the moralists themselves: they have failed to understand their times. They think they are dealing with a generation that refuses to believe in ancient authority. They are, in fact, dealing with a generation that cannot believe in it. They think they are confronted with men who have an irrational preference for immorality, whereas the men and women about them are ridden by doubts because they do not know what they prefer, nor why. The moralists fancy that they are standing upon the rock of eternal truth, surveying the chaos about them. They are greatly mistaken. Nothing in the modern world is more chaotic—not its politics, its business, or its sexual relations—than the minds of orthodox moralists who suppose that the problem of morals is somehow to find a way of reinforcing the sanctions which are dissolving. How can we, they say in effect, find formulas and rhetoric potent enough to make men behave? How can we revive in them that love and fear of God, that sense of the creature's dependence upon his creator, that obedience to the commands of a heavenly king, which once gave force and effect to the moral code?

They have misconceived the moral problem, and therefore they misconceive the function of the moralist. An authoritative code of morals has force and effect when it expresses the settled customs of a stable society; the pharisee can impose upon the minority only such conventions as the majority find appropriate and necessary. But when customs are unsettled, as they are in the modern world, by continual change in the circumstances of life, the pharisee is helpless. He cannot command with authority because his commands no longer imply the usages of the community: they express the prejudices of the moralist rather than the practices of men. When that happens, it is presumptuous to issue moral commandments, for, in fact, nobody has authority to command. It is useless to command when nobody has the disposition to obey. It is futile when nobody really knows exactly what to command. In such societies, wherever they have appeared among civilized men, the moralist has ceased to be an administrator of usages and has had to become an interpreter of human needs. For ages when custom is unsettled are necessarily ages of prophecy. The moralist cannot teach what is revealed; he must reveal what can be taught. He has to seek insight rather than to preach.

The disesteem into which moralists have fallen is due at bottom to their failure to see that in an age like this one the function of the moralist is not to exhort men to be good but to elucidate what the good is. The problem of sanctions is secondary. For sanctions cannot be artificially constructed; they are a product of agreement and usage. Where no agreement exists, where no usages are established, where ideals are not clarified and where conventions are not followed comfortably by the mass of men, there are not, and cannot be, sanctions. It is possible to command where most men are already obedient. But even the greatest general cannot discipline a whole army at once. It is only when the greater part of his army is with him that he can quell the mutiny of a faction.

The acids of modernity are dissolving the usages and the sanctions to which men once habitually conformed. It is therefore impossible for the moralist to command. He can only persuade. To persuade he must show that the course of conduct he advocates is not an arbitrary pattern to which vitality must submit, but that which vitality itself would choose if it were clearly understood. He must be able to show that goodness is victorious vitality and badness defeated vitality; that sin is the denial and virtue the fulfilment of the promise inherent in the purposes of men. The good, said the Greek moralist, is "that which all things aim at"; we may perhaps take this to mean that the good is that which men would wish to do if they knew what they were doing.

If the morality of the naïve hedonist who blindly seeks the gratification of his instincts is irrational in that he trusts immature desire, disregards intelligence, and damns the consequences, the morality of the pharisee is no less irrational. It reduces itself to the wholly arbitrary proposition that the best life for man would be some other kind of life than that which satisfies his nature. The true function of the moralist in an age when usage is unsettled is what Aristotle, who lived in such an age, described it to be: to promote good conduct by discovering and explaining the mark at which things aim. The moralist is irrelevant, if not meddlesome and dangerous, unless in his teaching he strives to give a true account, imaginatively conceived, of that which experience would show is desirable among the choices that are possible and necessary. If he is to be listened to, and if he is to deserve a hearing among his fellows, he must set himself this task which is so much humbler than to command and so much more difficult than to exhort: he must seek to anticipate and to supplement the insight of his fellow men into the problems of their adjustment to reality. He must find ways to make clear and ordered and expressive those concerns which are latent but overlaid and confused by their preoccupations and misunderstandings.

5 · *A Gallery of Leaders*

A Preface to Politics (*1913*), *Chapter 4.*

The man who comes forward to shape a country's policy has truly no end of things to consider. He must be aware of the condition of the people; no statesman must fall into the sincere but thoroughly upper-class blunder that President Taft committed when he advised a three months' vacation. Realizing how men and women feel at all levels and at different places, he must speak their discontent and project their hopes. Through this he will get power. Standing upon the prestige which that gives, he must guide and purify the social demands he finds at work. He is the translator of agitations. For this task he must be keenly sensitive to public opinion and capable of understanding the dynamics of it. Then, in order to fuse it into a civilized achievement, he will require much expert knowledge. Yet he need not be a specialist himself, if only he is expert in choosing experts. It is better indeed that the statesman should have a lay, and not a professional, view. For the bogs of technical stupidity and empty formalism are always near and always dangerous. The real political genius stands between the actual life of men, their wishes and their needs, and all the windings of official caste and professional snobbery. It is his supreme business to see that the servants of life stay in their place—that government, industry, "causes," science, all the creatures of man do not succeed in their perpetual effort to become the masters.

I have Roosevelt in mind. He haunts political thinking. And indeed, why shouldn't he? What reality could there be in comments upon American politics which ignored the colossal phenomenon of Roosevelt? If he is wholly evil, as many say he is, then the American democracy is preponderantly evil. For in the first years of the twentieth century, Roosevelt spoke for this nation, as few Presidents have spoken in our history. And that he has spoken well, who in the perspective of time will deny? Sensitive to the original forces of public opinion, no man has had the same power of rounding up the laggards. Government under him was a throbbing human purpose. He succeeded, where Taft failed, in preventing that drought of invention which officialism brings. Many people say he has tried to be all things to all men—that his speeches are an attempt to corral all sorts of votes. That is a left-handed way of stating a truth. A more generous interpretation would be to say that he had tried to be inclusive, to attach a hundred sectional agitations to a national program. Crude: of course he was crude; he had a hemisphere for his canvas. Inconsistent: yes, he tried to be the leader of factions at war with one another. A late convert: he is a statesman and not an agitator—his business was to meet demands when they had grown to national proportions. No end of possibilities have slipped through the large meshes of his net. He has said some silly things. He has not been subtle, and he has been far from perfect. But his success should by judged by the size of his task, by the fierceness of the opposition, by the intellectual qualities of the nation he represented. When we remember that he was trained in the Republican politics of Hanna and Platt, that he was the first President who shared a new social vision, then I believe we need offer no apologies for making Mr. Roosevelt stand as the working model for a possible American statesman at the beginning of the twentieth century.

Critics have often suggested that Roosevelt stole Bryan's clothes. That is perhaps true, and it suggests a comparison which illuminates both men. It would not be unfair to say that it is always the function of the Roosevelts to take from the Bryans. But it is a little silly for an agitator to cry thief when the success of his agitation has led to the adoption of his ideas. It is like the chagrin of the Socialists because the National Progressive Party had "stolen twenty-three planks," and it makes a person wonder whether some agitators haven't an overdeveloped sense of private property.

I do not see the statesman in Bryan. He has been something of a voice crying in the wilderness, but a voice that did not understand its own message. Many people talk of him as a prophet. There is a great deal of literal truth in that remark, for it has been the peculiar work of Bryan to express in politics some of that emotion which has made America the home of new religions. What we know as the scientific habit of mind is entirely lacking in his intellectual equipment. There is a vein of mysticism in American life, and Mr. Bryan is its uncritical prophet. His insights are those of the gifted evangelist, often profound and always narrow. It is absurd to debate his sincerity. Mr. Bryan talks with the intoxication of the man who has had a revelation; to skeptics that always seems theatrical. But far from being the scheming hypocrite his enemies say he is, Mr. Bryan is too simple for the task of statesmanship. No bracing critical atmosphere plays about his mind; there are no cleansing doubts and fruitful alternatives. The work of Bryan has been to express a certain feeling of unrest—to embody it in the traditional language of prophecy. But it is a shrewd turn of the American people that has kept him out of office. I say this not in disrespect of his qualities, but in definition of them. Bryan does not happen to have the naturalistic outlook, the complete humanity, or the deliberative habit which modern statecraft requires. He is the voice of a confused emotion.

Woodrow Wilson has a talent which is Bryan's chief defect—the scientific habit of holding facts in solution. His mind is lucid and flexible, and he has the faculty of taking advice quickly, of stating something he has borrowed with more ease and subtlety than the specialist from whom he got it. Woodrow Wilson's is an elegant and highly refined intellect, nicely balanced and capable of fine adjustment. An urbane civilization produced it, leisure has given it spaciousness, ease has made it generous. A mind without tension, its roots are not in the somewhat barbarous undercurrents of the nation. Woodrow Wilson understands easily, but he does not incarnate; he has never been a part of the protest he speaks. You think of him as a good counselor, as an excellent presiding officer. Whether his imagination is fibrous enough to catch the inwardness of the mutterings of our age is something experience alone can show. Wilson has class feeling in the least offensive sense of that term: he likes a world of gentlemen. Occasionally he has exhibited a rather amateurish effort to be grimy and shirt-sleeved. But without much success; his contact with American life is not direct, and so he is capable of purely theoretical affirmations. Like all essentially contemplative men, the world has to be reflected in the medium of his intellect before he can grapple with it.

Yet Wilson belongs among the statesmen, and it is fine that

he should be in public life. The weakness I have suggested is one that all statesmen share in some degree: an inability to interpret adequately the world they govern. This is a difficulty which is common to conservative and radical, and if I have used three living men to illustrate the problem it is only because they seem to illuminate it. They have faced the task and we can take their measurement. It is no part of my purpose to make any judgment as to the value of particular policies they have advocated. I am attempting to suggest some of the essentials of a statesman's equipment for the work of a humanly centered politics. Roosevelt has seemed to me the most effective, the most nearly complete; Bryan, I have ventured to class with the men who though important to politics should never hold high executive office; Wilson, less complete than Roosevelt, is worthy of our deepest interest because his judgment is subtle where Roosevelt's is crude. He is a foretaste of a more advanced statesmanship.

A Tribute to Theodore Roosevelt, *Written for The Woman's Roosevelt Memorial Association on the seventy-seventh anniversary of his birth, October 27, 1935.*

In regard to Theodore Roosevelt, it would be absurd for me to pretend that I can write objectively. As a boy nine years old I saw him, just returned from the Spanish War, on the veranda of a hotel in Saratoga; from that day until that great night in Madison Square Garden, when he spoke after he had been shot in Milwaukee, I was his unqualified hero-worshiper. He became for me the image of a great leader and the prototype of Presidents. The impression is indelible and, if I wished, I could not even now erase it. So persistent is it that in any complete confession I think I should have to say that I have been less than just to his successors because they were not like him.

To have captured the imagination of a boy is in itself no proof of greatness, and often, when I have admitted the prejudice, friends of mine have challenged me to show that Theodore Roosevelt was more than a glamorous person, and in cold truth an epoch-making figure. It can, I believe, be shown. It is today more evident than it was twenty years ago that his seven years as President were a decisive period in American history.

Theodore Roosevelt was the first President who knew that

the United States had come of age—that not only were they no longer colonies of Europe, and no longer an immature nation on the periphery of Western civilization, but that they had become a world power. He was the first to realize what that means, its responsibilities and its dangers and its implication, and the first to prepare the country spiritually and physically for this inescapable destiny. The outward symbol of that tremendous awakening is the Panama Canal, which he created because he had the historic insight to see that it was the vital link needed to complete the winning of the West. In the perspective of time this achievement will grow ever greater in its importance because it consummated the building of the nation and marked its entrance upon the stage of world affairs.

This same fundamental insight into the truth that the period of American maturity had opened made Theodore Roosevelt the first President who realized clearly that national stability and social justice had to be sought deliberately and had consciously to be maintained. There were pioneers and social reformers before him, of course, but he was the first President to grasp the fact that justice, opportunity, prosperity were not assigned to Americans in perpetuity as the free gift of Providence. He saw that once the period of settlement and easy expansion had come to an end, the promise of American life could be realized only by a national effort. He knew the history of other nations. He knew the pathology of nations—the exhaustion of natural resources, the deterioration of agriculture, the accumulation of wealth and the congestion of poverty, the concentration of power and the concentration of proletarian masses in great cities. He was the first President to awaken the American people to the knowledge that they had come into a time when, to insure a good life for their descendants, they must brace themselves to a new nationalism.

All that has happened to us since he was the dominant leader of the people has been the working out of his prophetic insight. Our mistakes—in the war, in the peace settlement, in the postwar crises—have turned upon the fact that we did not awaken soon enough or completely enough to the responsibilities of our new position at home and of our new role in the world. The mentality against which his whole career was a protest, the mentality of weak and complacent and selfish unpreparedness for responsibility, has been the radical cause of our greatest difficulties. But the historians will say, I am convinced, that Theodore Roosevelt began the work of turning the American mind in the direction which it had to go in the twentieth century.

It is not in the battles he fought, in the measures he sponsored, that his immortality resides. It is in this change of direction, it is in this new orientation of the American political tradition, it is in his insight into the imperatives of national policy. Though he did not see all that was in the world or its whole future, he was the first President to see that even for Americans the world is round and that even for them the future is not to be a repetition of the past.

He left to his countrymen, too, a testament in which are the virtues they need most for their new tasks. One was an unremitting sense that American unity is plural, that it can be preserved, therefore, only by a continuing equilibrium among its many regions, classes, interests, and faiths. The famous rhetorical device "on the one hand" and "on the other hand," which Mr. Dooley celebrated so hilariously, was the manifest sign of a profound realization that American unity can never be absolute, rigid, or simple, that it must always be a balance of many interests, each moderately and tolerantly pursued.

Another of the paramount political virtues which he left to the peoples was that means and ends must not be separated, that they must have no policy which they are not prepared to pay for. One of the cardinal vices of liberal democracies is that they are wishful in their thinking, that they demand many things for which they are unwilling to pay the bills. They are disposed to grandiose policies based on bluffing, to words that are not really meant, to clever tactics and ingenious stratagems. Theodore Roosevelt was an inveterate hater of all of this, not only because it outraged his sense of integrity but because he had the intuitions of a natural ruler of men and knew that wishful policies lead to disaster and humiliation.

If it is the intangible essence of a great man that survives the longest, like Lincoln's patient charity, it is not unlikely that in the American Olympus, Theodore Roosevelt will become the legendary patron of those who believe that a great people in its great decisions must have the integrity to say what it means and to mean what it says. It is a simple truth—continually and easily forgotten.

"A Gentleman at Des Moines," Today and Tomorrow, *August 8, 1940.*

The incident at Des Moines, when Mr. Willkie rebuked an audience which had booed Secretary Wallace, will permit many to hope that the campaign can still be conducted in a manner which suits the gravity of the times. For regardless of the outcome, the campaign will be a national disaster if the partisans treat their opponents as enemies and seek to excommunicate them from the community of honorable and patriotic citizens. Without self-restraint and a certain chivalry in public men the Democratic system of government will crack under the fierce pressure of contemporary events. Thus one of the indubitable causes of the ruin of France was the savagery with which the politicians attacked one another and intrigued against one another. Not only did the fury of their partisanship render impossible a coherent and effective policy; the manner in which public men assassinated the honor of public men bred a cynicism and contemptuous indifference which devitalized the people.

Since the early days of the Republic, there has been in this respect a sad deterioration of public morals. It is true that Washington and Hamilton, Adams and Jefferson were cruelly attacked and foully slandered by many editors and pamphleteers and agitators. But one has only to read their own speeches and letters to see how they held themselves above rancor, how consistently they maintained an elevation of feeling in their public utterances, how faithfully they preserved the courtesies of debate and that magnanimity which alone can dignify partisan conflict. They were great gentlemen who gave order and unity and faith to the feeble, discordant Colonies; and the example of their behavior was perhaps as important an element in their achievements as the wisdom and the courage with which they designed the Constitution and fixed the policies of the young Republic.

It is usually believed by amateurs in politics that a public man cannot hope to be elected unless he talks down to the people. As regards presidential candidates, at least, these amateur politicians are most certainly wrong. At bottom they are wrong because, as my old colleague F.P.A. once remarked, the average man is a good deal above the average. The people who do not vote mechanically and as a matter of blind habit, and are, therefore, open to persuasion in a campaign, are quickly aware of it when they are being talked down to. The effect is subtly irritating and repellent. They feel the condescension, they feel the implied reflection on their intelligence and on their character, and they tend to wonder whether the candidate who is addressing them in baby-talk may not be hiding from them the facts of life.

Moreover, as they have common sense, they know quite well that the great political issues are immensely difficult. When they hear the man who is a candidate for the responsibility of dealing with these issues reduce them to catch phrases and to nursery fables about the industrious little bees and the pretty little pigs, they are not impressed by what a human fellow he is; they put up with it, wondering whether he understands the issues and is equal to them. So the candidate who really wishes to impress the people will at least once on every great question speak as a statesman should, stating his position thoroughly, even technically, in a manner to disclose his command of the facts and his grasp of principles. After that he and his supporters can simplify and explain and beat the drum and do the circus. But if the candidate himself never does anything but popularize and vulgarize, the net impression he leaves will be that when he talks down, it is because he is already down there.

It is more than ever necessary in these days that a candidate for the highest office should convince the nation that they are in the presence of someone who is able to lead them, not merely to wait for the Gallup poll and follow. There is bewilderment; the people would like a President who is lucid. There is great anxiety; the people would like a President who is resolute and imperturbable. There is suspicion and division; the people would like a President who is boldly magnanimous and chivalrous. There is vast disorder in human affairs and there are tremendous tasks to be done; the people would like a President who will organize their energies and, thereby, give them that courage and confidence which can be reached these days only as men, ceasing to brood and worry impotently, are put to work doing efficiently some hard job they believe it is necessary to do.

The amateur politicians as well as the old routineers of politics misjudge wholly, I think, the mood of the people if they think the voters want to be coddled, ingratiated, and talked down to. The awakened people of this country will no more be reassured by soft, complacent talk than will a man who knows he is sick and is told by a doctor, who is obviously deceiving him, to forget it and not to worry. The remedy for the nervous anxiety which is so general today is an insistence upon the manly virtues, upon the hard, unfrightened virtues, which overcome fear by the simple and ancient remedy of ceasing to be afraid. For fear itself is much worse than the dangers it anticipates apprehensively, and against the contagion of fear in a nation the certain protection is the example of courage—high-souled, disinterested, trans-personal—in public men.

For when the leaders are frightened, soft, untruthful, so meanly ambitious that they stoop to conquer, there is no vision and the people perish.

"Al Smith," Today and Tomorrow, *October 7, 1944.*

Those who knew him best admire Al Smith the most, and all would wish, if they could, to perpetuate his fame. They cannot do this in the ordinary way by erecting a monument to some manifest public achievement with which his name will always be identified. For the greatness of Al Smith was that of the great performer—of the artist who acts his part, who plays his instrument, better than his audience have ever heard it done before. When the show is over, there is no record except in their own memories to prove his excellence, and only their personal testimony remains.

The stage on which he played his part was not the nation and not the world but the City and the State of New York. On that local stage he was, I shall always believe, the foremost master in our time of the art of popular government. He did not contend with the greatest issues of this epoch; he governed only one state of the Union during an interval in the 1920's of relative quiet and ease. But though he dealt with issues that few now remember, the way in which he dealt with them left an impress upon those who watched him and followed him that they do not forget.

When we try to define his peculiar distinction, we may say, I think, that he made good government popular in New York. That calls for rare gifts in any democracy. For the business of governing, when you really settle down to it, is over long stretches prosaic and tedious. To a degree which threatens the maintenance of democratic institutions, politicians who must appeal to masses of the voters, make their living by talking about almost everything but the business of governing. Even in war time most political oratory has about as much relation to the conduct of the war and the making of peace as the radio plugs for laxatives, deodorants, and hair tonics have to the news of the day.

The greatest menace to popular government lies in this separation between what responsible officials have to do when they administer the government and what politicians talk about when they appeal for votes. For this means that democratic institutions are not educating the people for the tasks of government. While Al Smith was Governor of New York, he bridged this chasm as no one before or since has ever bridged it. He was able to fascinate great audiences with the business of financing and administering public affairs, and to make them share his own interest in problems that the ordinary public relations expert would say were too dull and over the people's heads.

It would be easy to think that he did this because he was such an engaging and amusing human being, and such a good showman. But that would be, I think, to miss the main point, which is that Al Smith knew the city and state like the palm of his hand: he knew the City Hall and the Legislature, and all the men who had been in them, and the institutions in every part of the state, and who was the head man and who was the janitor. When he thought about the public business, he was not thinking about a mass of boring papers on his desk at Albany but about the living persons and objects that went to make up the business of government.

His mastery of the subject was his real stock in trade; no one who heard him had the least doubt that he knew what he was talking about. There lay the difference between Al Smith and others who also in their own way had popular magic and a catchy style. He stood out above all the other showmen, and grew in popular confidence while they declined, because his were the honest goods, and the people, if they are given long enough to realize it and to choose, do in fact see through the charlatans.

His career is a standing contradiction to the notion, now so current, that experts in public relations can create a synthetic public man, that professionals can be hired to write speeches which will endow him with a fictitious personality, and make him seem to be what he is not. Al Smith was his own public relations expert as every first-rate public man has to be in the field, however large or small, where he works. The notion never entered his head that someone who was not running for office, who had not been elected to office, who had never walked the floor at night worrying over its responsibilities, could be his conscience, his brain, and his voice. He would have said, I am sure, that the man who could do that for him ought to be the Governor of New York. For "public relations" is another name for political leadership, the one function of a chief executive that it is impossible to delegate.

Al Smith's speeches were prepared in conversations with his kitchen Cabinet, and by cross-examining those who had expert knowledge. But no ghost wrote his speeches. When he had got all the advice and the suggestions he wanted, he jotted down on an envelope the points he wished to cover, and then he went out before the audience and made, not read, a speech. No one can do that who is not so full of his subject that he has more to say than he has time to say, and is so sure of his knowledge that he is not afraid of making boners. But the effect was convincing in a way that no speech can be which the audience feels intuitively was written by someone who may have known more about the subject than the man who is reading it.

I do not suppose that this conveys much to those who did not know Al Smith when he was at the peak of his powers. For it is not easy to put into words a quality so indefinable, yet so overwhelmingly impressive when you meet it, as his luminous gift of mind and heart for making government altogether sincere in its contact with the people.

"The President's Task 1. The Double Mandate," Today and Tomorrow, *October 10, 1933.*

The Roosevelt Administration has, it seems to me, been singularly skillful in not making itself the prisoner of its own pronouncements. Here and there it has stumbled as, for example, in the promise that the N.R.A. would put I forget how many million men to work by Labor Day, in the threat of a boycott which the good sense of the country so sensibly rejected, in the grimaces at Henry Ford, in the pledge to the farmers not merely to help them but to give them the exact quota of prosperity which they had just before the war. These have been slips. They have been exceptions to the rule. For in the main the

President has made it his practice not to paint pictures and make promises, but to contrive expedients and decide practical issues.

In this habit of his mind he has shown himself to be an amazingly successful leader in a period of crisis. He has known better than to imagine that a great nation of free men could be indoctrinated with any consistent set of principles. So, like the wisest of the English-speaking statesmen, he has preferred to find his political and economic principles in the necessities of each particular situation, limiting his output of high-sounding generalizations to the indisputable truths of honor, courtesy, and ordinary morals. This step-by-step empiricism is utterly incomprehensible to men of certain temperaments. They think a statesman should have a complete theory about the history of the human race, a comprehensive program about its future; in brief, that he should forget he is mortal and plant himself on the Judgment Seat. The preference of the English-speaking peoples for crossing bridges when you come to them, and discovering the reason why you have come when you are halfway across, seems to them in varying degree confused, illogical, illiterate, and even hypocritical. By its enemies it is described as muddling, by its practitioners as muddling *through*. But whatever it is, the record of history goes to show that it levies a lighter tax of blood and tears, of anguish and bitterness than the more perfected, the more theoretically consistent, and more exalted systems of governing men.

"The Savannah Speech," Today and Tomorrow, *November 21, 1933.*

At Savannah the President undertook to put into words the spirit which animates his leadership. He had been accused of "great experimentation." He was proud to plead guilty to the charge. The settlement of America was a great experiment. The independence of the Colonies was a great experiment. The establishment of the American Republic was a great experiment. The objective of those experiments was to provide a broader economic opportunity for all men so that each should have a better chance to show the stuff of which he is made. That also was his objective. The principle of those experiments was that of self-government. That principle was his also.

But the problems had changed. When changes are impending, wise statesmen foresee what time is bringing and try to shape institutions and mold men's thoughts and purposes in accordance with the change that is silently coming on. The unwise are those who bring nothing constructive to the process, and who greatly imperil the future of mankind by leaving great questions to be fought out between ignorant change on the one hand and ignorant opposition to change on the other.

One could ask for no simpler and no sounder conception of the task of an American leader in times like these: that he should seek to understand the changes that are coming, and then to guide and control them so that they may be wrought out peaceably and in accordance with the American tradition. There surely is a standard to which most men can repair.

In raising this standard, in appealing to the spirit of 1776, in proclaiming the right and the need to experiment, the President is bound to recognize that the very essence of the experimenting spirit is the constant re-examination of premises and of methods. When a dictatorship imposes new institutions upon a people, and then gags the critics, it is not conducting an experiment. When a democracy enacts a new measure, and then proscribes the opposition as unpatriotic or venal, it is not conducting an experiment. Only when the statesman really desires to know every objection to his plan, and to modify his plan when the objection is convincing, can he be said to be honestly experimental. . . .

I do suggest that one of the great dangers which besets any ruler of men is the tendency to find himself surrounded entirely by men who have not the wish to disagree with him or the courage to speak their minds. The power of the chief of a state is so immense and so dazzling that for fear of incurring his disfavor, or in anticipation of favors to come, the men around him are disposed to say yes as often as possible, to say no infrequently and with insufficient emphasis. The wise ruler will always seek to protect the independence of his own colleagues; for statesmen are more often ruined by their subservient friends than by their avowed opponents.

That is why experienced political observers, when they study a political leader, look at the outset for evidence as to whether he is the kind of man who likes to be surrounded by strong men or by weak men, by colleagues or by courtiers, by advisers who merely reinforce one another or by advisers who check and balance one another. If there has been of late a growing disquietude in the country, it is not due wholly to toryism; it has deeper roots in the apprehension that the fervor of the great experimentation is producing in some quarters in Washington a headstrong temper which causes men to feel: So and so does not wholly agree with much that is being done; then off with his head; let only the initiated deal out the New Deal. . . .

And so, if the Roosevelt Administration is to follow the high American tradition, there must always be room in it for men who seek the same great ends but think differently about methods and measures. If there is no room for them, the New Deal is not an experiment; it is a dogmatic revelation.

Quite evidently it is not a revelation, or one could find somewhere its principles set down in orderly and consistent form. They are not set down anywhere. No speeches have been made by the President which expound, except in very general terms, the principles of the New Deal; and there is no book by any members of the brain trust which throws light on more than an aspect of the immense undertaking in which the President is engaged. There are indicators of direction, there are attitudes, dispositions, and ideals. But no one has yet done for the New Deal what Adam Smith and Jeremy Bentham did for English Liberalism in the nineteenth century.

One may rejoice that the doctrine has not crystallized. For there is much to be learned before our current theories can be treated as more than very tentative hypotheses. It is not probable that any set of minds has yet diagnosed finally what the President has called the chronic illness that has beset us for a dozen years. It follows that if the new measures are to be carried out as true experiments, and not as shots in the dark, it is most important that men of diverse opinion should collaborate, and that every tendency to factionalism, to dogmatism, and to the establishment of a cult be resisted.

"Zigzag Between Right and Left," Today and Tomorrow, *February 14, 1935.*

The latest bulletin from the front is that Mr. Roosevelt has taken "a turn to the right." Before long there will be another bulletin saying he has turned to the left. For I have a strong suspicion that Mr. Roosevelt will continue to use all his political gifts to continue on this zigzag course. Though it is disconcerting to those who want to nail fast the rudder and drive ahead, Mr. Roosevelt is no mean navigator and he knows that in the teeth of the wind and amidst hidden rocks the good sailor moves most safely if he can tack and turn and maneuver.

As a matter of historical experience, it is clear that a responsible and effective statesman can rarely be classified as all conservative or all radical. George Washington led an armed revolution against the established order and then helped to make a Constitution which has conserved the results of that revolution. The Tory Party in Great Britain introduced political democracy into the British constitution. Bismarck established social insurance in Germany. Theodore Roosevelt brought the railroads under regulation; and Woodrow Wilson, aided and abetted by William Jennings Bryan, presided over the making of the Federal Reserve System, which is now regarded by many conservatives as sacrosanct.

It is all very confusing to those who would like their politics neat and simple, black or white, right or left. But human affairs are more complicated than human formulas and, therefore, especially bewildering to those who are so conservative that, as someone has said, they will not look at the new moon out of respect for the old, and to those who are so radical that, as George Santayana once said, they redouble their effort when they have forgotten their aim. . . .

Another point to bear in mind amidst all the rumors about the rise and fall of radical or conservative members of the Administration is that it requires one state of mind to grow indignant and to agitate about a social evil, another state of mind to invent a legislative remedy, and still another state of mind to administer the remedy so that the reform sticks and works. A few men, but very few, can agitate, legislate, and administer; most men are good at one stage in a reform and not at another. And, therefore, a President who is interested in reforms that endure because they work is bound to use different men at different times. To the men themselves, except those who have some philosophy, this raising of officials to prominence and then reducing them to relative obscurity usually looks like ingratitude, the betrayal of the cause, surrender to the enemy, and what not.

A very good illustration is to be found in the Securities Exchange Commission under the rule of Mr. Joseph P. Kennedy. When the abuses of the security markets were being exposed, Mr. Kennedy took no part in the exposure, and presumably little would have been done about them if it had depended upon him. Nor is it likely that he would have taken a leading part in the drafting of the legislation. But once the laws had been enacted, the men who had had the courage and the ardor to write them were far from fitted to administer them. They had fought a victorious war, and, like so many warriors, they could not make peace. Then came Mr. Kennedy, as suspect by the warriors as a pacifist by triumphant generals, and in a short time, by sheer political and administrative wisdom, he made the new financial system a practicable reality and then insured its survival.

He illustrates very well the remark of F. S. Oliver that revolutions can be successful only if at just the right moment politicians take charge. For it is the politician, using the word in its favorable sense, who knows human nature as it is in normal times and is not so fanatical about principles that he cannot bend them to human nature.

"Roosevelt Is Gone," Today and Tomorrow, *April 14, 1945.*

The nation has received the news of Roosevelt's death with profound sorrow but without dismay. Surely he would have wanted it to be that way. For the final test of a leader is that he leaves behind him in other men the conviction and the will to carry on.

The man must die in his appointed time. He must carry away with him the magic of his presence and that personal mastery of affairs which no man, however gifted by nature, can acquire except in the relentless struggle with evil and blind chance.

Then comes the proof of whether his work will endure, and the test of how well he led his people: whether when he is no longer able to give voice to their hopes, they still have the same hopes, whether the course which he laid out when he was in power fixes the place where the broad highways will run over which the nation will continue to move. If not, then a man is great only in his own moment, a spectacular accident, like a comet which does not alter the course of things.

But if others can finish what he began, can decide what he had not yet decided, can plan what he did not have time to plan, can do what needs doing beyond the things he actually did, then his work is founded in reality and endures.

In the first hours after the President was dead, men took consolation in gratitude, and in their confidence that the nation itself now knows where it is going, and why, and how, felt relief from the shock and loss.

This noble mood can pass away as it did after Lincoln and Wilson were dead, and high resolve be squandered and dissipated in the quarrels of the pygmies. A wise but saddened man once said: "The tragedy of wars is that peace is made by the survivors."

No people has greater reason to know this than we have: we who know what came after Lincoln and after Wilson. Only by bearing it ever in mind can we make sure that all our highest hopes and purposes do not disintegrate under the harsh factionalism of our public life, the pitiless pressures which are the price of our freedom, and the indiscipline which accompanies our individualism. . . .

Roosevelt lived to see the nation make the crucial decisions upon which its future depends: to face evil and to rise up and destroy it, to know that America must find throughout the world allies who will be its friends, to understand that the nation is too strong, too rich in resources and in skill, ever to accept again as irremediable the wastage of men who cannot find work and of the means of wealth which lie idle and cannot be used. Under his leadership, the debate on these fundamental purposes has been concluded, and the decision has been rendered, and the argument is not over the ends to be sought but only over the ways and means by which they can be achieved.

Thus he led the nation not only out of mortal danger from abroad but out of the bewilderment over unsettled purposes which could have rent it apart from within. When he died, the issues which confront us are difficult. But they are not deep and they are not irreconcilable. Neither in our relations with other peoples nor among ourselves are there divisions within us that cannot be managed with common sense.

The genius of a good leader is to leave behind him a situation which common sense, without the grace of genius, can deal with successfully. Here lay the political genius of Franklin Roosevelt: that in his own time he knew what were the questions that had to be answered, even though he himself did not always find the full answer. It was to this that our people and the world responded, preferring him instinctively to those who did not know what the real questions were.

Here was the secret of the sympathy which never ceased to

flow back to him from the masses of mankind, and the reason why they discounted his mistakes. For they knew that he was asking the right questions, and if he did not always find the right answers, someone, who had learned what to look for, eventually would.

"The Eisenhower Mission," Today and Tomorrow, *January 5, 1954.*

Looking back over his first year and forward to his second, the President must be aware that in the great mass of our people, who wish him so well, there is a strain of doubt and disappointment. It would be an exaggeration, in fact it would be quite misleading, to say that he is in trouble with the people, or that he has lost their confidence and his popularity among them. Their willingness and their eagerness to rally around him are if anything greater than they were when he was drafted out of the Army to run for President of the United States.

It may be too bold, perhaps even presumptuous, to put into words what it is that is lacking. Yet the President will be hearing a great deal in the months to come from his partisan opponents and from his hidden enemies, and it can do no harm for one of his supporters, and an early one, to speak his piece.

What has been lacking in this first year so much too much of the time has been a clear realization by Eisenhower himself of why he was drafted for President and what the multitudes who rallied to him are looking for. But when he has been true to himself, when Eisenhower has been himself in his appointed role, the response of the people has always been quick and very great.

His appointed role, the role for which he was chosen—the role for which he is fitted—is that of the restorer of order and peace after an age of violence and faction.

Nobody who knew Dwight Eisenhower when he was a Major General, and when he was Supreme Commander, and Chief of Staff, and President of Columbia University, and the military chief of NATO would ever have picked him to be a "dynamic," "progressive," and "crusading" President of the United States. He has often talked of himself in these terms. But they are not his terms, and when he has not been himself, he has become separated from and not united with the people who wish to follow him.

To be a dynamic, progressive, and crusading President calls for a knowledge and an experience of civil affairs and of American politics which General Eisenhower did not have, and could not possibly be expected to acquire at the age of sixty. To be "dynamic" and "progressive," and to be a "crusader" in a great and complicated country calls for much more knowledge and political instinct and political know-how than are needed for not being dynamic and progressive and a crusader.

Nobody who knew him, and the American scene in which he would have to work, would have turned to Eisenhower if in 1952 the times had demanded a dynamic progressive crusade. The fact was, however, that by 1952 this country and the Western world had had all the dynamism, all the innovation, all the crusading that human nature can take.

For more than twenty years the people had had more than enough upheaval in their lives, of ups and downs, of being drafted, taxed, and moved around, of excitement, of fervor and of fear and of hope, of big words and hot feelings. They had lived through the great depression, through the innovations of the New Deal, through a double war—one in Europe and one in the Pacific—through the cold war, through the terrible and mean Korean War, through all the turmoil and effort of bolstering up the non-Communist nations, and of re-arming the United States.

By 1952 the time had come when more dynamism, more excitement and more frenzy, could lead only to catastrophe abroad and dissension at home. It had become imperative that this country collect itself, that it consolidate itself, that it restore its confidence in itself, that it find a way to quiet its frayed nerves, to allay its suspicions, and that it regain its composure and its equanimity.

That was the wellspring of the Eisenhower movement. He was the man who was above party and above faction. He was the man outside the issues that were dividing the nation. He was the protector of the things on which Americans are united. He was a strong man, invulnerable to all suspicion, and of good will. He was to fill a role which in the unfolding of history needed to be filled.

When he has acted in the role which is his destiny and is in his character, he has done well. He has done what only he in the circumstances of our time could have done. Thus he has not only ended the fighting in Korea, but he has reduced, as no one else could have done, the general danger of a spreading, indecisive, and catastrophic war in the Far East.

When, on the other hand, Eisenhower is not in his own character, when he adopts a role for which he was not cast, he is all thumbs and usually in trouble. He has not done well as a crusader, as a progressive, as a dynamic politician, as a partisan, or as a factional manipulator and appeaser. Had the country needed, had the people wanted, that kind of President, then Dwight Eisenhower ought not to be in the White House.

Nor would he be there if the mood and instinct of the people had been for that kind of President. It is not the mood of the people, and the people do not rally to his support when, attempting to live up to a false image of himself, he does not act in his true role. But, on the other hand, the experience of the first year shows that the people do immediately rally to his support whenever, abroad or at home, he appears as the restorer of order and of peace.

"For Charles DeGaulle," **Today and Tomorrow,** *June 5, 1958.*

What has happened in France illustrates a truth which I first came upon years ago in a history of the French Revolution. It is that a regime, an established order, is rarely overthrown by a revolutionary movement; usually a regime collapses of its own weakness and corruption and then a revolutionary movement enters among the ruins and takes over the powers that have become vacant.

Thus it is simply not true, as some are saying, that a democratic and free system of government has been overthrown by a conspiracy of colonels and extremists, connived at by generals and right-wing politicians, among them General DeGaulle himself. The Algerian war, which has been a military failure and in its cruelties is a disgrace to the good name of France, was presided over by a Socialist politician who owed his appointment to a Socialist Prime Minister. As respects North Africa, the authority of the French government in Paris had collapsed long before the insurrection broke out last month. As early as February, after the bombing of the Tunisian village of Sakiet-Sidi-Youssef, it was as plain as the nose on one's face that the Paris government was impotent to govern.

It is false, therefore, to look upon General DeGaulle as the man who overthrew, or connived at the overthrow of, the parliamentary government. He has come to power because that government could no longer pretend that it was able to govern.

It has been said by some that while General DeGaulle himself is not a Fascist, he is an old man, like Hindenburg in Germany, who in his senility will make way for a French Hitler. All I can say is that, having seen him recently, he did not seem in the least senile to me; he was then, as he has always been, a man of extraordinary historical insight and imagination, in this respect second only, I would say, if not equal, to Churchill. There is in DeGaulle no trace of the modern vulgar dictator, of the Hitler, Mussolini, Peron, or Nasser, and he has shown in his books that his mind is profound and that his style—since he uses no ghost writer—is a true expression of his mind.

There has never been any doubt, it has seemed to me, that he is an authentic bearer of the central traditions of the Western society. He does not use its values as stereotypes and slogans, as the battered catch phrases that political orators have made of them. His mystery, which communicates itself to the French when they are in trouble, is that, being authentic and not time-serving, he touches those chords of memory which bind a nation together.

"The Fascination of Greatness," Today and Tomorrow, *September 7, 1943.*

Mr. Churchill lunched with the Washington correspondents last week. At the end there were few among us who would not have agreed with the Lord Mayor of the English city when he said in the dark days of 1940 that a speech by the Prime Minister is like a week end in the fresh air. I do not remember a time when Washington so badly needed fresh air. In fact, it needs a gale of wind out of heaven to blow away the dust, the cobwebs, and the stinks of intrigue, vanity, jealousy, and vindictiveness.

Mr. Churchill's remarks, which were given as answers to questions from the correspondents, cannot be quoted. In fact he revealed no secrets and said nothing that is not already known to the attentive reader of the newspapers. Yet somehow he restored and refreshed the faith and confidence of a corps of men whose duty it is to report and interpret the conduct of the war.

We may well ask why and we may ask how. For Mr. Churchill is not only the Prime Minister of Great Britain. He is also the one certainly authentic example of greatness in a public man who moves among us. In these times which try men's souls, we are not equal, but we have to learn to be equal to them. We may then remember the profound saying of Whitehead that "moral education is impossible without the habitual vision of greatness." For Churchill's special gift, which enhances all the others, is his moral quality: he draws men out of their meaner selves and fascinates them with greatness.

The fascination of Churchill is not merely in his wit, or even in his humor which keeps him so near to his fellow men, or in his genius for war. We may find it is his eloquence, provided we do not, as Cardinal Newman said, "consider fine writing to be . . . a sort of ornament superinduced, or a luxury indulged in, by those who have time and inclination for such vanities." Churchill's eloquence is the man himself, and the secret of his fascination is his magnanimity.

It becomes more ample with the years. For when men age, they may grow vain, irascible, and self-centered. Or they may grow wise, benign, compassionate, and universal. Churchill has aged well. At the pinnacle of his fame, we saw him the other day treating the humblest man asking the most impertinent question with that courtesy which only those display who really respect the dignity of other men. He does not talk down to other men, nor does he talk over them. He talks to them because they have a right to know. Thus he rallies men to his standard because he engages that which is noble in them. And even in his wrath against the enemy, which is awe-inspiring, there is not the malice of the small man but the chivalry of the good warrior.

In these energies of the spirit, he radiates upon the cause in which we are engaged an habitual vision of greatness. The war as he reveals it is not only strategy and logistics and production, not a mere series of bombings, landings, ship movements, factory schedules, rationing, and taxes, but the historic drama of our century. Nations cannot wage a war of this magnitude unless they carry with them in their minds and hearts such a measure of its depth and its scope.

That is why our spirits languish when their daily food is only the military communiques, press releases, and an absolutely intolerable flood of gossip journalism, pipe-line journalism, and intrigue journalism, about who is in the doghouse now, and how the courtiers at the palace are planning to cut one another's throats, and how misunderstood and unappreciated are those who hand out the dope to those who then lick their boots.

The air is foul and stale with it all and, as we come to the climax of the war, the air must be cleared and cleansed. We have fallen into the vice which Chaucer called "the synne of accidie"—that sloth and torpor of the soul which makes us sluggish in the exercise of virtue. We spend our days pawing over the intrigues and machinations of little men. We have fallen to these depths because, though the nation is engaged greatly, it is denied the habitual vision of greatness. *"They fainted, and were scattered abroad, as sheep having no shepherd."*

The springs of greatness in a public man lie finally, as they do in Winston Churchill, in the conviction that he must serve the truth and not opinion, that he must do what is right whether or not he is sure to succeed. That was how in the darkest hours of 1940 Churchill made the choice between honor and calculation. When none could calculate the future of Britain he settled the issue on the ground of honor and of duty.

This is the way of greatness. In the supreme moments of history, terms like duty, truth, justice, and mercy—which in our torpid hours are tired words—become the measure of decision. We, unhappily, are acting as if we had forgotten them. We seem to be ashamed to utter them, in part because we tremble at the gibes of the Philistines, but in the main because they are remote from our habitual feeling.

Yet the outcome of this war will break men's hearts if we allow ourselves to sink to the meaner measure of our conduct. We are trying to be too shrewd, too clever, too calculating, when what the anxious and suffering peoples cry out to us for is that we practice the elemental virtues and adhere to the eternal verities. They alone can guide us through the complications of our days. The straight and righteous path is the shortest and the surest.

XI

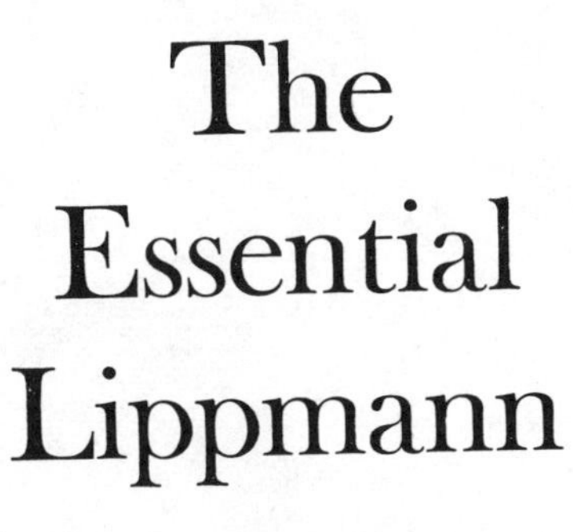

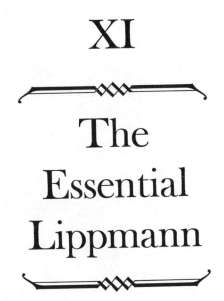

The Essential Lippmann

1 · *The Scholar in a Troubled World*

"The Scholar in a Troubled World," The Atlantic Monthly, CL (1932), 148, *an address delivered as the Phi Beta Kappa Oration at the Commencement exercises of Columbia University on May 31, 1932.*

In addition to the anxieties which he shares with all other men in days like these, there is a special uneasiness which perturbs the scholar. He feels that he ought to be doing something about the world's troubles, or at least to be saying something which will help others to do something about them. The world needs ideas; how can he sit silently in his study and with a good conscience go on with his thinking when there is so much that urgently needs to be done? And yet, at the same time, he hears the voice of another conscience, the conscience of the scholar, which tells him that as one whose business it is to examine the nature of things, to imagine how they work, and to test continually the proposals of his imagination, he must preserve a quiet indifference to the immediate and a serene attachment to the processes of inquiry and understanding.

As in Browning's Grammarian, there is in him the peculiar grace that before living he would like to learn how to live. But as a man of his time he is impelled against his instincts to enter the arena, to speak with a certainty he does not possess about measures which he knows to be a mere gamble with the unknown. When the telephone begins to ring, calling him to give out interviews, and to draft memoranda, and to attend conferences, he is afraid to say with the high assurance of the Grammarian: "Leave Now for dogs and apes! Man has Forever." He drops his studies, he entangles himself in affairs, murmuring to himself: "But time escapes: Live now or never!"

Thus his spirit is divided between the urgency of affairs and his need for detachment. If he remains cloistered and aloof, he suffers in the estimation of the public, which asks impatiently to know what all this theorizing is good for anyway if it does not show a way out of all the trouble. If he participates in affairs, he suffers no less. For it will quickly be revealed that the scholar has no magic of his own, and to the making of present decisions he may have less to contribute than many who have studied his subject far less than he. But most of all he suffers in his own estimation: he dislikes himself as he pronounces conclusions that he only half believes; he distrusts himself, and the scholarly life, because, when the practical need for knowledge is so great, all the books in all the libraries leave so much unsettled.

This conflict of the spirit is, of course, most acute among those who profess knowledge of the affairs on which nations are now divided. It cannot much concern the mathematician and the astronomer, the physicist, the chemist, or the biologist. They may be distracted by the uproar about them, but they are not invaded by demands that they provide solutions. But the conflict must greatly oppress every student of economics and of politics, of law, of education, and of morals. For in these realms there is an insistent presumption that prolonged study should have produced immediate practical wisdom, that from the professors should issue knowledge of how to decide the current controversies.

It is this presumption that I should like to examine. For from it springs the conflict between the demands of the contemplative and the active life. We assume that a profound study of politics ought to produce a statesman, a profound study of economics ought to produce a man of affairs, a profound study of the law ought to produce a legislator, a judge, or an advocate. Yet we know that it rarely happens. Nevertheless, we continue to assume and expect, and then are disappointed when the scholar is ineffective in affairs, or half-hearted and distracted in his search for truth. Yet the notion that the contemplative life is a preparation for immediate participation in the solution of current problems is by no means to be taken for granted. In fact, the traditions of human wisdom are against it. They are replete with lamentations, like those of Gregory when, having left his monastery to assume the Papacy, he cried out that he was "borne ever onward by the disturbance of those endless billows" and had almost lost sight of the port which he had left.

It is permissible, then, to question this presumption, even though such doubt is so contrary to the temper of our times. I venture to question it, not on the ground of Pope Gregory's lament, that his soul had to engage in the business of worldly men and was defiled in the dust of earthly occupations, but specifically on the ground that in the present phase of democracy there is an intrinsic reason why the theoretical study of public affairs does not, and cannot, provide the immediate practical wisdom to manage public affairs.

For, at the point where knowledge is to be applied in action, there is a highly variable and incalculable factor. That factor is the will of the people. Therefore, when the student of politics is asked to recommend a particular course of action, he must say, if he is candid, that his system of ideas rests upon a foundation of assumptions about human conduct; that these assumptions are necessarily generalized and abstract; and that, therefore, they discount the willfulness and uncertainty of the immediate situation. But practical decisions depend in large part upon appraising swiftly just this element of willfulness and uncertainty in public opinion and individual response. A knowledge of the past and reflection upon the behavior of men in analogous circumstance may illuminate and steady the appraisal, but there is as yet no science which controls it.

The art of practical decision, the art of determining which of several ends to pursue, which of many means to employ, when to strike and when to recoil, comes from intuitions that are more unconscious than the analytical judgment. In great emergencies the man of affairs feels his conclusions first, and understands them later. He proceeds by a kind of empathy, relying upon a curious capacity for self-identification with the moods of others and upon a sense of the realities which he can rarely expound. Those who have this gift must be immersed in affairs; they must absorb much more than they analyze; they must be subtly sensitive to the atmosphere about them; they must, like a cat, be able to see in the dark. They pay a price for their capacities. Only the very greatest men of affairs see beyond the moment. But at the instant of decision they can often act with an assurance and sometimes with a rightness which it is impossible to deduce from the principles of any theoretical system.

The political sciences, since they deal with conduct, must rest upon some positive conception of human motives. It is not, I think, possible to formulate principles of government or of economics on the assumption that human motives are incalculable. There are no principles that could be worked out which would be equally true for a nation of heroes and saints, a community of ascetics and of swindlers or thieves. The political thinker must make some assumptions about the character and the working motives of people. These assumptions must necessarily be simpler and more stable than those which are actually in play at any particular moment of decision. Shall he, for example, assume that each man intelligently pursues his own interest? If he adopts this abstraction, he can produce an imposing and coherent doctrine. The classical economists did that, and, granting the premise, a perfectly intelligible social policy can be deduced from it. But observation soon shows that even if it were true that men desire their own interest exclusively, they are usually too little informed and too gullible to know what it is.

But once the economist admits this, he must go further and admit that practical judgment as to the best course at any moment is dependent upon what to him is mere guesswork, upon a surmise as to what choices are open as a result of the particular mixtures of understanding and ignorance, partisanship and propaganda, national, sectional, sectarian, and class prejudice, then prevailing among the people, as well as upon the personal idiosyncrasies, and special bias, of the men temporarily in power. As an economist he has no particular aptitude for making these surmises. Thus if, for example, he attempts to estimate a nation's capacity to pay a war debt in the course of three generations, no process of economic reasoning will give him the answer. For the capacity to pay is in some important degree a function of the will to pay, and to judge that he must make a guess about the whole political future of a people. He must guess at the evolution of its prejudices.

It appears, then, that our ability to derive practical guidance from theoretical studies is fundamentally limited by the part which transient prejudice plays in human conduct. I venture to think that this is the core of the difficulty which confronts the man of affairs when he turns to the scholar for advice, and the scholar when he seeks to give advice. No theoretical system of political economy has ever been constructed by the mind of man which rests upon incalculable human conduct. Yet in our modern democracies, most particularly in the modern American democracy which is so unsettled in its life and in its convictions, the working motives of men are so highly volatile that they defy theoretical formulation and systematic analysis.

We are compelled, I think, to recognize that in no other critical period of the modern world has transient opinion played so great a role in affairs. If, with this in mind, we examine the deliberations which accompanied the establishment of the Republic, we must be impressed, it seems to me, with the greater capacity of the eighteenth-century thinkers to reach definite practical conclusions from their general principles. I, for one, never read in the *Federalist* without a feeling of envy that no one living today believes in general principles as did the authors of those essays, or is able to use his principles so confidently and effectively. These men possessed an intellectual clarity that we have wholly lost. They were the masters of their subject in a way that we are not.

I do not believe that this is wholly a matter of superior genius. I imagine it must be due, in some measure, to the fact that in their time, and well down into the nineteenth century, the mass of men were, as Gladstone put it, passive. They had prejudices, but they were stable prejudices. The patterns of popular conduct varied very little, so that political thinkers and men of affairs could reason with some confidence about their behavior.

But by the second half of the nineteenth century the passive democracy had become an active democracy. Under the impact of the Industrial Revolution and of popular education, the popular mode of life became radically unsettled, and with it the fixed prejudices, the normal expectations, the established conventions, the enduring convictions of the older world. They were replaced by new ambitions and transient opinions. An immense uncertainty entered public life, and consequently into the premises of all the sciences that deal with public affairs. The modern world became revolutionary in its essence, for no abiding tradition of any kind remained.

If this analysis is correct, then it follows that we must not expect society to be guided by its professors until, or perhaps I should say unless, the fluctuating opinions that now govern affairs are replaced by clear, by settled, moral values. Either men must have the stable prejudices of the ancestral order or they must have stable conventions they have rationally accepted; on either foundation a political science which actually controlled events might be built up. But upon a foundation of merely transient opinions derived from the impressions of the moment, undirected by any abiding conception of personal and social values, no influential political science can be constructed, and, it may be, no enduring political state.

A recognition of this underlying difficulty—that systematic principles cannot be derived from or applied to a democracy ruled by willful and uncertain opinions—would go a long way toward resolving the conflict which now unsettles the scholar's spirit. It would give him the courage to preserve that detachment which his instinct demands. It would give him the resolution to shut out the distracting demands for interviews and statements and conferences and all the other paraphernalia of active intervention in affairs. If, nevertheless, he is moved to intervene, he can do so at least knowing that in that role he is not a scholar, but merely one more amateur as to things in general, however much he may be the specialist of something in particular. He will no longer be astonished that he is puzzled by the complexity of the actual, or undervalue his own theoretical life and in the presence of the immediate let himself be overawed by the superior assurance of the man of affairs.

The more fully he understands the real reason why today theory is so divorced from practice, the more he will realize how supremely important it is that those who have the gift for theory should imperturbably cultivate it. For what is most wrong with the world is that the democracy, which at last is actually in power, is a creature of the immediate moment. With no authority above it, without religious, political, or moral convictions which control its opinions, it is without coherence and purpose. Democracy of this kind cannot last long; it must, and inevitably it will, give way to some more settled social order. But in the meanwhile the scholar will defend himself against it. He will build a wall against chaos, and behind that wall, as in other bleak ages of the history of man, he will give his true allegiance, not to the immediate world, but to the invisible empire of reason.

In that realm of being, the scholar makes his genuine contact with the affairs of men. The life of man has other dimensions besides the troubled surface and the present moment. To the controversies arising out of the play of transient prejudice upon circumstances he can perhaps contribute technical knowledge. He can contribute no particular wisdom that is peculiarly his own. His concern is with the formulation and establishment of modes of thought that underlie and might reorganize the prejudiced will, and cure it of that transiency which is the fundamental source of all our troubles. He does not manage the passing moment. He prepares the convictions and the conventions, the hypotheses and the dispositions which might control the purposes of those who will manage future events. Thus in this crisis his chief duty is to understand, so that the next one may be more intelligible. This crisis is what it is. The men who will decide the issues may change their opinions a little; it is too late for them to change their habits, and within the grooves of those habits the immediate decisions will be made.

The true scholar is always radical. He is preoccupied with presumptions, with antecedents and probabilities; he moves at a level of reality under that of the immediate moment, in a world where the choices are more numerous and the possibilities more varied than they are at the level of practical decisions. At the level of affairs the choices are narrow, because prejudice has become set. At the level of thought, in the empire of reason, the choices are wide, because there is no compulsion of events or of self-interest. The immediate has never been the realm of the scholar. His provinces are the past, from which he distills understanding, and the future, for which he prepares insight. The immediate is for his purpose a mere fragment of the past, to be observed and remembered rather than to be dealt with and managed.

This view of the scholar's life will seem to many a mere elegy to a fugitive and cloistered virtue. Yet I doubt whether the student can do a greater work for his nation in this grave moment of its history than to detach himself from its preoccupations, refusing to let himself be absorbed by distractions about which, as a scholar, he can do almost nothing. For this is not the last crisis in human affairs. The world will go on somehow, and more crises will follow. It will go on best, however, if among us there are men who have stood apart, who refused to be anxious or too much concerned, who were cool and inquiring, and had their eyes on a longer past and a longer future. By their example they can remind us that the passing moment is only a moment; by their loyalty they will have cherished those things which only the disinterested mind can use. They are the men who will forge the instruments that Shelley dreamed of:

> Those instruments with which High Spirits call
> The future from its cradle, and the past
> Out of its grave, and make the present last
> In thoughts and joys which sleep, but cannot die,
> Folded within their own eternity. . . .

2 · *The Method of Reason*

A Preface to Politics (*1913*), *Chapter 4.*

Surely the task of statesmanship is more difficult today than ever before in history. In the face of a clotted intricacy in the subject matter of politics, improvements in knowledge seem meager indeed. The distance between what we know and what we need to know appears to be greater than ever. Plato and Aristotle thought in terms of ten thousand homogeneous villagers; we have to think in terms of a hundred million people of all races and all traditions, crossbred and inbred, subject to climates they have never lived in before, plumped down on a continent in the midst of a strange civilization. We have to deal with all grades of life from the frontier to the metropolis, with men who differ in sense of fact, in ideal, in the very groundwork of morals. And we have to take into account not the simple opposition of two classes, but the hostility of many—the farmers and the factory workers and all the castes within their ranks, the small merchants, and the feudal organization of business. Ours is a problem in which deception has become organized and strong; where truth is poisoned at its source; one in which the skill of the shrewdest brains is devoted to misleading a bewildered people. Nor can we keep to the problem within our borders. Whether we wish it or not we are involved in the world's problems, and all the winds of heaven blow through our land.

It is a great question whether our intellects can grasp the subject. Are we perhaps like a child whose hand is too small to span an octave on the piano? Not only are the facts inhumanly complicated, but the natural ideals of people are so varied and contradictory that action halts in despair. We are putting a tremendous strain upon the mind, and the results are all about us; everyone has known the neutral thinkers who stand forever undecided before the complications of life, who have, as it were, caught a glimpse of the possibilities of knowledge. The sight has paralyzed them. Unless they can act with certainty, they dare not act at all.

That is merely one of the temptations of theory. In the real world, action and thought are so closely related that one cannot wait upon the other. We cannot wait in politics for any completed theoretical discussion of its method; it is a monstrous demand. There is no pausing until political psychology is more certain. We have to act on what we believe, on half-knowledge, illusion, and error. Experience itself will reveal our mistakes; research and criticism may convert them into wisdom. But act we must, and act as if we knew the nature of man and proposed to satisfy his needs.

In other words, we must put man at the center of politics, even though we are densely ignorant both of man and of politics. This has always been the method of great political thinkers from Plato to Bentham. But one difference we in this age must note: they made their political man a dogma—we must leave him an hypothesis. That is to say, that our task is to temper speculation with scientific humility.

A paradox there is here, but a paradox of language, and not of fact. Men made bridges before there was a science of bridge-building; they cured disease before they knew medicine. Art came before æsthetics, and righteousness before ethics. Conduct and theory react upon each other. Hypothesis is confirmed and modified by action, and action is guided by hypothesis. If it is a paradox to ask for a human politics before we understand humanity or politics, it is what Mr. Chesterton describes as one of those paradoxes that sit beside the wells of truth.

Public Opinion (1922), *Chapter 28.*

There is an inherent difficulty about using the method of reason to deal with an unreasoning world. Even if you assume with Plato that the true pilot knows what is best for the ship, you have to recall that he is not so easy to recognize, and that this uncertainty leaves a large part of the crew unconvinced. By definition the crew does not know what he knows, and the pilot, fascinated by the stars and winds, does not know how to make the crew realize the importance of what he knows. There is no time during mutiny at sea to make each sailor an expert judge of experts. There is no time for the pilot to consult his crew and find out whether he is really as wise as he thinks he is. For education is a matter of years, the emergency a matter of hours. It would be altogether academic, then, to tell the pilot that the true remedy is, for example, an education that will endow sailors with a better sense of evidence. You can tell that only to shipmasters on dry land. In the crisis, the only advice is to use a gun, or make a speech, utter a stirring slogan, offer a compromise, employ any quick means available to quell the mutiny, the sense of evidence being what it is. It is only on shore where men plan for many voyages, that they can afford to, and must for their own salvation, deal with those causes that take a long time to remove. They will be dealing in years and generations, not in emergencies alone. And nothing will put a greater strain upon their wisdom than the necessity of distinguishing false crises from real ones. For when there is panic in the air, with one crisis tripping over the heels of another, actual dangers mixed with imaginary scares, there is no chance at all for the constructive use of reason, and any order soon seems preferable to any disorder.

It is only on the premise of a certain stability over a long run of time that men can hope to follow the method of reason. This is not because mankind is inept, or because the appeal to reason is visionary, but because the evolution of reason on political subjects is only in its beginnings. Our rational ideas in politics are still large, thin generalities, much too abstract and unrefined for practical guidance, except where the aggregates are large enough to cancel out individual peculiarity and exhibit large uniformities. Reason in politics is especially immature in predicting the behavior of individual men, because in human conduct the smallest initial variation often works out into the most elaborate differences. That, perhaps, is why when we try to insist solely upon an appeal to reason in dealing with sudden situations, we are broken and drowned in laughter.

For the rate at which reason, as we possess it, can advance itself is slower than the rate at which action has to be taken. In the present state of political science there is, therefore, a tendency for one situation to change into another, before the first is clearly understood, and so to make much political criticism hindsight and little else. Both in the discovery of what is unknown, and in the propagation of that which has been proved, there is a time differential, which ought to, in a much greater degree than it ever has, occupy the political philosopher. We have begun, chiefly under the inspiration of Mr. Graham Wallas, to examine the effect of an invisible environment upon our opinions. We do not, as yet, understand, except a little by rule of thumb, the element of time in politics, though it bears most directly upon the practicability of any constructive proposal. We can see, for example, that somehow the relevancy of any plan depends upon the length of time the operation requires. Because on the length of time it will depend whether the data which the plan assumes as given, will in truth remain the same. There is a factor here which realistic and experienced men do take into account, and it helps to mark them off somehow from the opportunist, the visionary, the Philistine, and the pedant. But just how the calculation of time enters into politics we do not know at present in any systematic way.

Until we understand these matters more clearly, we can at least remember that there is a problem of the utmost theoretical difficulty and practical consequence. It will help us to cherish Plato's ideal, without sharing his hasty conclusion about the perversity of those who do not listen to reason. It is hard to obey reason in politics, because you are trying to make two processes march together, which have as yet a different gait and a different pace. Until reason is subtle and particular, the immediate struggle of politics will continue to require an amount of native wit, force, and unprovable faith, that reason can neither provide nor control, because the facts of life are too undifferentiated for its powers of understanding. The methods of social science are so little perfected that in many of the serious decisions and most of the casual ones, there is as yet no choice but to gamble with fate as intuition prompts.

But we can make a belief in reason one of those intuitions.

We can use our wit and our force to make footholds for reason. Behind our pictures of the world, we can try to see the vista of a longer duration of events, and wherever it is possible to escape from the urgent present, allow this longer time to control our decisions. And yet, even when there is this will to let the future count, we find again and again that we do not know for certain how to act according to the dictates of reason. The number of human problems on which reason is prepared to dictate is small.

"Thanksgiving Day," Today and Tomorrow, *November 24, 1932.*

There can be no novelty in remembering that this Thanksgiving Day differs most radically from the first one more than three centuries ago in that then the Pilgrim Fathers were thankful because they had wrung meager subsistence from the reluctant earth, whereas today their heirs are dismayed by the bounty of nature and the productivity of man. Yet that difference, obvious as it is to everyone, is the heart of the difficulty of modern man.

It has taken him these three hundred years to conquer this earth and to invent the tools which make it possible for him to obtain securely a plenty that was beyond the dream of the Pilgrim Fathers. But he has not yet learned how to enjoy that conquest, to manage those tools, and to distribute that plenty. And so, with incalculable power and inexhaustible resources at his command, multitudes are in want, and all the nations are anxious.

In few places, therefore, will this Thanksgiving Day be celebrated with complacency. Those who could be comfortable will not be very comfortable. Few, if they wished to do so, could forget the suffering about them. They cannot but remember the human disaster of their world, and to ask themselves again and again what it is that they have done and have left undone which produced the disaster and prolongs it. And if they ask for anything today, it must be for the imagination to conceive, the patience to understand, the courage to deal with the hidden and complex causes of all this vast confusion and waste.

Simple charity, they must realize, is obviously not enough. Remembrance of the forgotten men and women is not enough. Generosity in sharing is not enough. These are all indispensable. But they are not enough. The greater need is for wisdom in government and in public life, a wisdom which is attainable only by a will to listen, a will to abate prejudice, a will to find common grounds of understanding, and a continual preference for an accurate, an objective, and disinterested view of affairs. We live in a world which is suffering not from the scarcity of nature, but from our own lack of the knowledge and discipline necessary to manage it. Therefore, no charity and no benevolence is complete which is not accompanied by an unremitting effort to learn the difficult art of self-government in a world where it is now possible for all men to be secure and well provided for.

"States of Mind," **Today and Tomorrow,** *May 11, 1933.*

In the troubled periods of history many things are taken out and examined which in quieter times are left undisturbed. Great argument then ensues and, at the level of civilized discussion as distinguished from merely barbarous conflict, men tend to divide, some appealing to what they call "reason" and some to "experience." As passions rise, the cry goes up from the left that the country is in the grip of stupid and selfish men, and from the right there is heard angry complaint that crackbrained theorists are upsetting all the household gods.

For subjects which are as complicated as the government of human societies there are, unfortunately, no well-established methods of thinking out solutions. We know quite well that simple logical deductions will not yield us workable policies amidst the contrariness of human nature. We know, too, that many rules of action which have worked well for a long time will often produce disaster when they are blindly followed. Thus it comes about that in decisions which have to be reached when there is great disturbance, men cannot rely upon a "theory" or upon "experience," but must look for that mixture of reason and experience, charity, sympathy, and wit which is called wisdom.

For the changing world that confronts us is both new and old. It is never wholly what it used to be, and therefore the old rules are never wholly reliable. It is never entirely new, and therefore we are fools if we do not look for guidance in the book of experience. Yet experience is a very big book. The history of man has a stupendous range, and to find in his history the precedents from the past which really apply to the immediate moment is not so simple as many would like to believe. One can learn from history. And no man should pretend to govern men who has not steeped his mind in the human tradition. But what history teaches is above all humility, that pride of opinion and easy certainty are folly, and then that he who would search for the lessons of experience will never reach the end. Daily he must put to the test of his clearest insight into the immediate what he thinks he has gathered from the books he has read and the stories he has heard.

There is no easier way to deal with human affairs. Thus at the moment we are in the midst of great discussions about the meaning and the value and the management of money. For some obscure reason, though the fact itself is self-evident, money is a subject which excites the human mind to an extraordinary degree. It is a subject which brings forth promptly a torrent of panaceas and an opposing torrent of invincibly dogmatic assertions. I have letters in considerable quantities from sincere and able men who have worked themselves into a messianic conviction that a mere change in the gold content of the dollar will bring peace and happiness to mankind. And I have equally fervent letters from men who declare that the country is threatened with ruin at the mere suggestion that any one might consider the advisability of altering the price of gold as fixed by law on June 28, 1834.

How, amidst this clash of insistent men, are the rest of us to find a course to follow? Only, it seems to me, by rejecting all arbitrariness of mind, whether it be the expectation of instant cures or the prophecies of certain disaster, or an unwillingness to confess error, and then by remaining collected and alert, ready to change our action as we watch for and interpret the signs and the reports. That is the way armies are directed and ships at sea are steered, and that is the only way in which a human society can be governed in a time of crisis. No doubt it would be more comfortable to be able to say that the course was clear, that every action can be definitely foreseen, and that every contingency has been provided for. It would be much more comfortable. But then it would be much more comfortable if there were no crisis.

3 · *Some Bits of Self-Counsel*

"Two Revolutions in the American Press,"
The Yale Review, XX (*1931*), *433*.

Not long ago I visited a theater which specializes in the presentation of newsreels. After President Hoover had received the usual delegation on the White House lawn, after the girls had gone through setting-up exercises on the beach at Miami, and Senator Johnson had denounced foreign entanglements, the screen announced that the next picture would present the greatest living expert on love, Professor X of Berlin, who had just arrived in New York to continue his studies. When the professor's moving and talking image appeared, there was roar of ribald laughter. For the greatest living expert on love was an elderly, spectacled professor approximately the shape of a watermelon standing on end.

Reflecting on the matter I felt contrite at having expected the professor of love to look like a great lover. For, said I to myself, were he constructed on the lines of the Apollo Belvedere, endowed with the arts of Casanova and the combustibility of Mr. John Gilbert, how could he find time to be a professor or have the heart to tell the whole truth? I had fallen into the vulgar prejudice of assuming that only the performer can understand his art, whereas it is often the case that the critic understands the play better than the actor. For while the performer's own account of his art is entitled to respect and consideration, it has no intrinsic authority and it is open to heavy discount in the light of our human propensity to justify our own actions in the past and our hopes in the future.

"During the Intermission," Today and Tomorrow, *July 2, 1932.*

The author of this dispatch is no more fit at this moment to write about the struggle to nominate a President than the delegates are to make a nomination. He is, as they are, so stupefied by oratory, brass bands, bad air, perspiration, sleeplessness, and soft drinks that the fate of mankind is as nothing compared with his longing for a bath, a breakfast, and a bed. We have been given the third degree, and no man who has been through what we in Chicago have been through since about nine o'clock Wednesday evening will ever again have difficulty in realizing how a blameless man, if he were tortured enough, might be persuaded to confess that he had stolen the crown jewels and eloped with Caesar's wife.

With such shreds of mentality as remain with me, I think I can dimly remember that some time before dawn on Friday the Roosevelt managers decided to proceed with the balloting and settle the matter. I recall, too, that we were informed in the press gallery that the Roosevelt bandwagon would start at the end of the first ballot. I can also recall that when their bandwagon did not start, the Roosevelt managers wanted to adjourn in order to have time to find out what they had to offer whom, particularly what they had to offer Speaker Garner, Mr. Hearst, Governor White of Ohio and Mayor Cermak of Chicago in order to obtain the votes necessary to save mankind. It also remains in my memory that at this point in the proceedings Mayor Hague of Jersey City and the other allied generals wanted to continue balloting on the theory, it would seem, that no man can betray you when he is asleep.

However, by about nine o'clock this morning it had been amply demonstrated that unless somebody betrayed somebody else, there never would be a nomination. So as this is being written the delegates are in bed and their bosses, if they come from the Northeast, their leaders if they come from the South and West, are trying to negotiate the great betrayal which is now absolutely essential to a successful conclusion of these proceedings.

It may be that before these lines are printed, the matter will have been arranged by the bosses and the leaders, or that at any rate the convention will somehow have found a way to break out of jail. Nothing that can now be arranged or decided will please all the delegates. That alone appears at this hour to be fairly certain. All else would be vain prophecy, and prudently I refrain from guessing what tomorrow morning's newspapers will say, knowing that though the ancient oracles often pretended to be in an inspired stupor, here in Chicago everyone is really stupefied and no one is inspired.

"Total War and Coexistence, I," Today and Tomorrow, *June 18, 1951. With the following introductory note Lippmann announced to his readers that he was taking what turned out to be a six-month "sabbatical" from* Today and Tomorrow.

I do not expect to write any more for some months to come. The editor has agreed to a rather long intermission after I had reminded him that I have now been writing these articles on current events for twenty years, and that anyone who has been that long in the boiler room of the ship had better come up on deck for a breath of fresh air and a look at the horizon. I told the editor that I had come to feel that it was time for me to go back to writing a book which I began long ago. . . .

So I have gone off to the country, leaving unanswered the editor's question—which was whether, the times being so critical, it is right to turn away even for a few months from the news of the day to certain of the perennial issues of the human condition.

Untitled Column, Today and Tomorrow, *October 10, 1933.*

I have spent a nice vacation, thank you, reading industrial codes, General Johnson's speeches, statistics about banks and piggy sows, and a sufficient mixture of threats, promises, predictions, and warnings to make a man purr with contentment while his hair stands on end. Nature did her best: the sea, the sky and the woods of Maine could not have been less concerned with our fretfulness, of convincing that human destiny is not determined finally by the news of the front page. But in vain does a man imagine that a man can go anywhere these days and shut himself away from the clamor of the front page. Even when the newspaper does not come, he is trying to imagine what is in the newspaper he has not seen. There is too much at stake to put public affairs long out of mind, the security and well-being of us all, the peace of the world, the liberties of man. Thus a genuine holiday is impossible; the best one can do, I find, is to fret quietly for a few weeks instead of openly in public print.

There is, however, much to be said for a little silence now and then, especially for those who act on or write currently about public matters. For a large part of the mischief and folly of the world comes from rushing in, taking a position, and then not knowing how to retreat. There is something about making a speech or writing an article which perverts the human mind. When the utterance is published, the Rubicon has been crossed and the bridges have been burned. It seems to end the inquiry, and after that we almost cease to be interested in the truth, being so preoccupied to prove that we already possess it. What between the demand of the audience for an infallible preceptor, the vanity of the speaker, and the terrorism of those who lie in ambush ready to quote what he said last year against what he may believe this year, the impulse is almost irresistible, once a man has published his opinion, to say: That's my story and I stick to it. In private intercourse anyone who sticks to his story regardless is set down by his friends as slightly batty. In public life he passes for a very strong fellow.

"A Spell Is Broken," Today and Tomorrow, *December 4, 1934.*

It is said that one of the Czars of Russia, walking in his park, came upon a sentry standing before a small patch of weeds. The Czar asked him what he was doing there. The sentry did not know; all he could say was that he had been ordered to his post by the captain of the guard. The Czar then sent his aide to ask the captain. But the captain could only say that the regulations had always called for a sentry at that particular spot. His curiosity having been aroused, the Czar ordered an investigation. But no living man at the court could remember a time when there had not been a sentry at that post and none could say what he was guarding.

Finally, the archives were opened and after a long search the mystery was solved. The records showed that the Great Catherine had once planted a rosebush in that plot of ground and a sentry had been put there to see that no one trampled it. The rosebush died. But no one had thought to cancel the order for the sentry. And so for a hundred years the spot where the rosebush had once been was watched by men who did not know what they were watching.

It is always difficult to know that the rosebush is dead and that you are standing guard at an empty place. This is particularly true of the hopes and fears which sweep across the modern world, and for a time possess men's minds and govern their conduct.

"Intermission," Today and Tomorrow, *May 28, 1938.*

Large portions of mankind are under the spell of men who seem to go to bed with their boots on, and are magnificent and grandiloquent even in their sleep. This fact is the great fact of our time, and raises all kinds of immediate and urgent practical issues that have to be met.

But if I read history correctly, the ultimate remedy in such periods as this, when mankind becomes exalted beyond its capacity, is not any one of the logical solutions that reasonable men propose, but a gradual exhaustion of the operatic emotions, a growing indifference to the issues, and, with the coming of a new generation, a loss of interest in the subject matter of the quarrel. That is the way the religious wars of the sixteenth century really ended, in a benign lack of interest in the dispute, in a civilized unconcern with the grandiose claims of the partisans, and in the discovery that there are other and better things to attend to.

It does not seem to me likely that the great issues which now embroil mankind will be resolved either by war or by statesmanship. They are in the deepest sense insoluble in that they arise out of passionate differences about human values. In conflicts of this sort, there is never a decisive victory for the partisans of one view; the ultimate victory is to those who are interested in other human things, in things that finally displace and obscure the burning but insoluble issues. In the sixteenth century it was the view of Erasmus that finally prevailed and brought peace, not that of the irreconcilables on either side of the barricades. And perhaps in our time, if catastrophe can be postponed, it can be averted by the generation that did not start these quarrels and can have no true interest in perpetuating them.

A Preface to Morals (1929), *Chapter 15*.

The philosophy of the spirit is an almost exact reversal of the worldling's philosophy. The ordinary man believes that he will be blessed if he is virtuous, and therefore virtue seems to him a price he pays now for a blessedness he will some day enjoy. While he is waiting for his reward, therefore, virtue seems to him drab, arbitrary, and meaningless. For the reward is deferred, and there is really no instant proof that virtue really leads to the happiness he has been promised. Because the reward is deferred, it too, becomes vague and dubious, for that which we never experience, we cannot truly understand. In the realm of the spirit, blessedness is not deferred: there is no future which is more auspicious than the present; there are no compensations later for evils now. Evil is to be overcome now and happiness is to be achieved now, for the kingdom of God is within you. The life of the spirit is not a commercial transaction in which the profit has to be anticipated; it is a kind of experience which is inherently profitable.

And so the mature man would take the world as it comes, and within himself remain quite unperturbed. When he acted, he would know that he was only testing an hypothesis, and if he failed, he would know that he had made a mistake. He would be quite prepared for the discovery that he might make mistakes, for his intelligence would be disentangled from his hopes. The failure of his experiment could not, therefore, involve the failure of his life. For the aspect of life which implicated his soul would be his understanding of life, and, to the understanding, defeat is no less interesting than victory. It would be no effort, therefore, for him to be tolerant, and no annoyance to be skeptical. He would face pain with fortitude, for he would have put it away from the inner chambers of his soul. Fear would not haunt him, for he would be without compulsion to seize anything and without anxiety as to its fate. He would be strong, not with the strength of hard resolves, but because he was free of that tension which vain expectations beget. Would his life be uninteresting because he was disinterested? He would have the whole universe, rather than the prison of his own hopes and fears, for his habitation, and in imagination all possible forms of being. How could that be dull unless he brought the dullness with him? He might dwell with all beauty and all knowledge, and they are inexhaustible. Would he, then, dream idle dreams? Only if he chose to. For he might go quite simply about the business of the world, a good deal more effectively perhaps than the worldling, in that he did not place an absolute value upon it, and deceive himself. Would he be hopeful? Not if to be hopeful was to expect the world to submit rather soon to his vanity. Would he be hopeless? Hope is an expectation of favors to come, and he would take his delights here and now. Since nothing gnawed at his vitals, neither doubt nor ambition, nor frustration, nor fear, he would move easily through life. And so whether he saw the thing as comedy, or high tragedy, or plain farce, he would affirm that it is what it is, and that the wise man can enjoy it.

"Books and Things," The New Republic, *IV (August 7, 1915), 24*

The other night I sat up late reading one of those books on politics which are regarded as essential to any sort of intellectual respectability. It was a book that might be referred to in the Constitutional Convention at Albany. As I read along I was possessed with two convictions about the author. The first was that he had worn a high hat when he wrote the book; the second, that he had no teeth, which made him a little difficult to understand. And all through that hot and mosquito-ridden night the disintegration of his vocabulary went churning through my head . . . "social consciousness . . . sovereign will . . . electoral duties . . . national obligations . . . on moral, economic, political, and social grounds . . . social consciousness . . . sovereignty . . . electoral . . . social . . . sovereign . . . national . . . sovereign . . ." Each word was as smooth and hard and round as a billiard ball, and in the malice of my sleeplessness I saw the toothless but perfectly groomed man in a high hat making patterns of the balls which were handed to him by his butler.

As the night dragged along, the callowest prejudices came to the surface and all fairer and reputable judgment deserted me. I heard myself say that this ass who plagued me couldn't possibly have any ideas because he didn't have any vocabulary. How is it possible, I asked, to write or think about the modern world with a set of words which were inchoate lumps when Edmund Burke used them? Political writing is asphyxiated by the staleness of its language. We are living in a strange world, and we have to talk about it in a kind of algebra. And of course if we deal only with colorless and vacant symbols, the world we see and the world we describe soon becomes a colorless and vacant place. Nobody can write criticism of American politics if the only instruments at his command are a few polysyllables of Greek and Latin origin. You can't put Bryan and Hearst and Billy Sunday into the vocabulary of Aristotle, Bentham, or Burke. Yet if you are going to write about American politics, can you leave out Bryan and Hearst and Billy Sunday, or even Champ Clark? The author I had been reading did leave them out completely. He talked about the national will of America as if it were a single stream of pure water which ran its course through silver pipes laid down by the Constitutional Fathers.

I tried to recall any new words which had been added to the vocabulary of social science. Boss, heeler, machine, logrolling, pork-barrel—those were the words which meant something at Washington or in Tammany Hall, but my author would no more have used them than he would have eaten green peas with a knife. Anyone who did use them he would have regarded as a mere journalist, and probably a cocksure young man at that. Then I remembered that the diplomats had made current a few fresh words within the last generations—hinterland, pacific penetration, sphere of influence, sphere of legitimate aspiration; they had meaning, because nations went to war about them. But the real contributions, curiously enough, have come not from the political theorist, but from novelists, and from philosophers who might have been novelists.

H. G. Wells and William James, I said to myself, come nearer to having a vocabulary fit for political uses than any other writers of English. They write in terms which convey some of the curiosity and formlessness of modern life. Speech with them is pragmatic, and accurate in the true sense. They are exact when exactness is possible, blurred when the thought itself is blurred. They have almost completely abandoned the apparatus of polysyllables through which no direct impression can ever penetrate. They do not arrange concepts, they gather precepts, and never do you lose the sense that the author is just a man trying to find out what he thinks. But the political writer who gave me the nightmare never admitted that he was just a man. He aimed at that impersonal truth which is like the inscription on monuments.

He regarded himself as a careful person. His method was to retrieve in qualifying clause whatever he had risked in assertion. So he achieved a compendium of things-that-can't-be-done, a kind of anthology of the impossible. His notion of getting at the truth was to peel it, like Peer Gynt's onion, though Peer Gynt had the sense to be surprised that there was nothing to an onion but the layers.

My temper grew worse as I reflected on the hypnotic effect of books done in this manner, on the number of men whose original vision is muffled by verbal red tape and officialism of the spirit. The true speech of man is idiomatic, if not of the earth and sky, then at least of the saloon and the bleachers. But no smelly or vivid impression can win its way through these opaque incantations with which political science is afflicted. They forbid fresh seeing. An innocence of the eye is impossible, for there are no words to report a vision with; and visions which cannot be expressed are not cultivated. No wonder, I thought, political philosophizing means so little in human life. Its woodenness is the counterpart of a wooden politics, its inhumanity is the inhumanity of a state machine. The language is callous, unmoved, and unmoving, because it aims to reflect rather than to lead the life upon which it comments. Dead speech is good enough for thoughts that bring no news, and it is to the timidity of political thought that we must ascribe its preference for a dead language. In these tomes over which we yawn at night, there are occasionally ideas which might shake the world. But they do not shake it, for they are written for people who do not like to shake it. They are hedged with reservations, fortified with polysyllables, and covered over with the appalling conceit that here is truth—objective, impersonal, cold.

I generalized rashly: That is what kills political writing, this absurd pretense that you are delivering a great utterance. You never do. You are just a puzzled man making notes about what you think. You are not building the Pantheon, then why act like a graven image? You are drawing sketches in the sand which the sea will wash away. What more is your book but your infinitesimal scratching, and who the devil are you to be grandiloquent and impersonal? The truth is you're afraid to be wrong. And so you put on these airs and use these established phrases, knowing that they will sound familiar and will be respected. But this fear of being wrong is a disease. You cover and qualify and elucidate, you speak vaguely, you mumble because you are afraid of the sound of your own voice. And then you apologize for your timidity by frowning learnedly on anyone who honestly regards thoughts as an adventure, who strikes ahead and takes his chances. You are like a man trying to be happy, like a man trying too hard to make a good mashie shot in golf. It can't be done by trying so hard to do it. Whatever truth you contribute to the world will be one lucky shot in a thousand misses. You cannot be right by holding your breath and taking precautions.

"The Job of the Washington Correspondent," The Atlantic Monthly, *CCV (January 1960), 47. On his seventieth birthday Walter Lippmann addressed an overflow meeting of the National Press Club, and at the conclusion of his remarks he received a standing ovation.*

Last summer, while walking in the woods and on the mountains near where I live, I found myself daydreaming about how I would . . . explain and justify the business of being opinionated and of airing opinions regularly several times a week.

"Is it not absurd," I heard the critic saying, "that anyone should think he knows enough to write so much about so many things? You write about foreign policy. Do you see the cables which pour into the State Department every day from all parts of the world? Do you attend the staff meetings of the Secretary of State and his advisers? Are you a member of the National Security Council? And what about all those other countries which you write about? Do you have the run of 10 Downing Street, and how do you listen in on the deliberations of the Presidium in the Kremlin? Why don't you admit that you are an outsider and that you are, therefore, by definition, an ignoramus?

"How, then, do you presume to interpret, much less to criticize, and to disagree with, the policy of your own government or any other government?

"And, in internal affairs, are you really much better qualified to pontificate? No doubt there are fewer secrets here, and almost all politicians can be talked to. They can be asked the most embarrassing questions. And they will answer with varying degrees of candor and of guile. But if there are not so many secrets, you must admit that there are many mysteries. The greatest of all the mysteries is what the voters think, feel, and want today, what they will think and feel and want on election day, and what they can be induced to think and feel and want by argument, by exhortation, by threats and promises, and by the arts of manipulation and leadership."

Yet, formidable as it is, in my daydream I have no trouble getting the better of this criticism. "And you, my dear fellow," I tell the critic, "you be careful. If you go on, you will be showing how ridiculous it is that we live in a republic under a democratic system and that anyone should be allowed to vote. You will be denouncing the principle of democracy itself, which asserts that the outsiders shall be sovereign over the insiders. For you will be showing that the people, since they are ignoramuses, because they are outsiders, are therefore incapable of governing themselves.

"What is more, you will be proving that not even the insiders are qualified to govern them intelligently. For there are very few men—perhaps forty at a maximum—who read, or at least are eligible to read, all the cables that pour into the State Department. And then, when you think about it, how many senators, representatives, governors, and mayors—all of whom have very strong opinions about who should conduct our affairs—ever read these cables which you are talking about?

"Do you not realize that, about most of the affairs of the world, we are all outsiders and ignoramuses, even the insiders who are at the seat of government? The Secretary of State is allowed to read every American document he is interested in. But how many of them does he read? Even if he reads the American documents, he cannot read the British and the Canadian, the French and the German, the Chinese and the Russian. Yet he has to make decisions in which the stakes may well be peace or war. And about these decisions, the Congress, which reads very few documents, has to make decisions too."

Thus, in my daydream, I reduce the needler to a condition of sufficient humility about the universal ignorance of mankind. Then I turn upon him and with suitable eloquence declaim an apology for the existence of the Washington correspondent.

"If the country is to be governed with the consent of the

governed, then the governed must arrive at opinions about what their governors want them to consent to. How do they do this?

"They do it by hearing on the radio and reading in the newspapers what the corps of correspondents tell them is going on in Washington, and in the country at large, and in the world. Here, we correspondents perform an essential service. In some field of interest, we make it our business to find out what is going on under the surface and beyond the horizon, to infer, to deduce, to imagine, and to guess what is going on inside, what this meant yesterday, and what it could mean tomorrow.

"In this we do what every sovereign citizen is supposed to do but has not the time or the interest to do for himself. This is our job. It is no mean calling. We have a right to be proud of it and to be glad that it is our work."

4 · *A Declaration of Faith and Hope*

Class Dinner Speech for the Thirtieth Reunion of the Harvard Class of 1910 (*June 18, 1940*).

I think I am speaking for all of you when I say that we have come here in order that we may pause for a moment in which to fortify our faith and to renew our courage and to make strong our spirit.

We have come back to Harvard, and when we go away, we shall have realized what ordinary words can scarcely make real to us: we shall realize what it is that is threatened with destruction, what it is that we are called upon to defend. We walk again through the Yard and we shall think of the three centuries during which on this ground men have believed in the dignity of the human soul, and how, believing this, they have cherished, and labored patiently in, the great central tradition of the Western world. This memory will fortify our faith, and we shall say to ourselves that this glory which is ours, this glory which we have known since our youth, this glory which has given to each of us whatever there is in him that matters at all, we shall say that this glory shall not perish from the earth.

We have come back here, along with those we love, to see one another again. And by being together we shall remember that we are part of a great company, we shall remember that we are not mere individuals isolated in a tempest, but that we are members of a community—that what we have to do, we shall do together, with friends beside us. And their friendliness will quiet our anxieties and ours will quiet theirs. And as they live up to what we expect of them, we shall find the resolution to live up to what they expect of us. And so we shall renew our courage and we shall find the strength that we shall need.

I am speaking solemnly because in this, the most solemn hour of the history of the modern world, no one here tonight will imagine he can divert himself by forgetting it. I do not know whether we shall see again in our lives a peace that we shall believe can last. But what we can have, though the world roars and rages about us, is peace of mind, a quiet place of tranquillity and of order and of purpose within our own selves. For it is doubt and uncertainty of purpose and confusion of values which unnerves men. Peace of mind will come to men only when, having faced all the issues clearly and without flinching, they are decided and resolved.

For myself I like to think these days of the words of Washington which Gouverneur Morris reported, words spoken when the Constitutional Convention in Philadelphia seemed about to fail: Washington, said Morris, "was collected within himself. His countenance had more than usual solemnity. His eye was fixed, and seemed to look into futurity." "It is" (said he) "too probable that no plan we propose will be adopted. Perhaps another dreadful conflict is to be sustained. If to please the people, we offer what we ourselves disapprove, how can we afterwards defend our work? Let us raise a standard to which the wise and honest can repair. The event is in the hands of God."

Upon the standard to which the wise and honest will now repair it is written: "You have lived the easy way; henceforth, you will live the hard way." It is written: "You came into a great heritage made by the insight and the sweat and the blood of inspired and devoted and courageous men; thoughtlessly and in utmost self-indulgence you have all but squandered this inheritance. Now only by the heroic virtues which made this inheritance can you restore it again." It is written: "You took the good things for granted. Now you must earn them again." It is written: "For every right that you cherish, you have a duty which you must fulfill. For every hope that you entertain, you have a task that you must perform. For every good that you wish to preserve, you will have to sacrifice your comfort and your ease. There is nothing for nothing any longer."

For twenty years the free peoples of the Western world have taken the easy way, ourselves more light-heartedly than any others. That is why we are stricken. That is why the defenses of Western civilization have crumbled. That is why we find ourselves tonight knowing that we here in America may soon be the last stronghold of our civilization—the isolated and beleaguered citadel of law and of liberty, of mercy and of charity, of justice among men and of love and of good will.

We mean to defend that citadel; we mean, I believe, to make it the center of the ultimate resistance to the evil which is devastating the world, and more than that, more than the center of resistance, we mean to make it the center of the resurrection, the source of the energies by which the men who believe as we do may be liberated, and the lands that are subjugated redeemed, and the world we live in purified and pacified once more. This is the American destiny, and unless we fulfill that destiny we shall have betrayed our own past and we shall make our own future meaningless, chaotic, and low.

But we shall not resist the evil that has come into the world, nor prepare the resurrection in which we believe, if we continue to take, as we have taken so persistently, the easy way in all things. Let us remind ourselves how in these twenty years we have at the critical junctures taken always the road of the least effort and the method of the cheapest solution and of greatest self-indulgence.

We participated in a war which ended in the victory of the free peoples. It was hard to make a good and magnanimous peace. It was easier to make a bad and unworkable peace. We took the easiest way.

Having sacrified blood and treasure to win the war, having failed to establish quickly and at the first stroke a good and lasting peace, it was too hard, it was too much trouble to keep on trying. We gave up. We took the easy way, the way that required us to do nothing, and we passed resolutions and made pious declarations saying that there was not going to be any more war, that war was henceforth outlawed.

Thus we entered the postwar twenties, refusing to organize

the peace of the world because that was too much trouble, believing—because that was no trouble at all—that peace would last by declaring that it ought to last. So enchanted were we with our own noble but inexpensive sentiments that, though the world was disorganized and in anarchy, we decided to disarm ourselves and the other democracies. That was also the easy way. It saved money. It saved effort.

In this mood we faced the problems of reconstruction from the other war. It was too much trouble to make a workable settlement of reparations and of the war debts. It was easier to let them break down and wreck the finances of the world. We took the easier way. It was too much trouble to work out arrangements for the resumption of trade because it was too much trouble to deal with the vested interests and the lobbyists and the politicians. It was easier to let the trade of the world be strangled by tariffs, quotas, and exchange controls. And we took the easy way. It was easier to finance an inflationary boom by cheap money than it was to re-establish trade based upon the exchange of goods. We indulged ourselves in the inflationary boom and let it run (because it was too much trouble to check it) into a crash that threw about twenty-five millions, here and abroad, out of work, and destroyed the savings of a large part of the people of all countries.

Having got to that, it was too hard to liquidate the inflation. It was easier to cover up the inflation and pretend that it did not exist. So we took the easier way—we maintained the tariffs, we maintained the wage costs and the overhead expenditures of the boom, and thus made it impossible to recover from the crash.

The failure of the recovery produced at the foundations of Western civilization a revolutionary discontent. It was easy to be frightened by the discontent. So we were properly frightened. But it was hard to make the effort and the sacrifice to remedy the discontent. And because it was hard, we did not do it. All that we did was to accuse one another of being economic royalists on the one hand, economic lunatics on the other. It was easier to call names than it was to do anything else, and so we called names.

Then out of this discontent there was bred in the heart of Europe from the Rhine to the Urals an organized rebellion against the whole heritage of Western civilization. It was easy to disapprove, and we disapproved. But it was hard to organize and prepare the resistance: that would have required money and effort and sacrifice and discipline and courage. We watched the rebellion grow. We heard it threaten the things we believe in. We saw it commit, year after year, savage crimes. We disliked it all. But we liked better our easygoing ways, our jobs, our profits, and our pleasures, and so we said: it is bad but it won't last; it is dangerous but it can't cross the ocean; it is evil, but if we arm ourselves, and discipline ourselves, and act with other free peoples to contain it and hold it back, we shall be giving up our ease and our comfort, we shall be taking risks, and that is more trouble than we care to take.

So we are where we are today. We are where we are because whenever we had a choice to make, we have chosen the alternative that required the least effort at the moment. There is organized mechanized evil loose in the world. But what has made possible its victories is the lazy, self-indulgent materialism, the amiable, lackadaisical, footless, confused complacency of the free nations of the world. They have dissipated, like wastrels and drunkards, the inheritance of freedom and order that came to them from hard-working, thrifty, faithful, believing, and brave men. The disaster in the midst of which we are living is a disaster in the character of men. It is a catastrophe of the soul of a whole generation which had forgotten, had lost, and had renounced the imperative and indispensable virtues of laborious, heroic, and honorable men.

To these virtues we shall return in the ordeal through which we must now pass, or all that still remains will be lost and all that we attempt, in order to defend it, will be in vain. We shall turn from the soft vices in which a civilization decays, we shall return to the stern virtues by which a civilization is made, we shall do this because, at long last, we know that we must, because finally we begin to see that the hard way is the only enduring way.

You had perhaps hoped, as I did when we came together for our twenty-fifth reunion, that tonight we should have reached a point in our lives when we could look forward in a few more years to retiring from active responsibility in the heat of the day, and could look forward to withdrawing into the calm of a cooler evening. You know that that is not to be. We have not yet earned our right to rest at ease. . . .

I like to think, in fact I intend to go away from here thinking, that having remembered the past we shall not falter, having seen one another again, we shall not flinch.

Index

ABOUT THE AUTHOR

WALTER LIPPMANN was born in New York City on September 23, 1889. He was educated at Harvard University, where he took his Bachelor's Degree in 1909, and did graduate work in philosophy, particularly under George Santayana, 1909-10. An associate editor of the *New Republic*, subsequently he was the editor of the New York *World* until February, 1931; from that time until the end of 1962 he was a special writer for the New York *Herald Tribune* and other newspapers. From June to October 1917, he was the assistant to the Secretary of War; he was secretary of the organization directed by Colonel House to prepare data for the Versailles Peace Conference; he was a member of the Board of Overseers of Harvard University; a member of Phi Beta Kappa, the National Institution of Arts and Letters, and the American Academy of Arts and Letters. *The Essential Lippmann* is a selection from his writings published over more than fifty years.

CLINTON ROSSITER was John L. Senior Professor of American Institutions at Cornell University. Among his numerous works are *Conservatism in America*, *The American Presidency*, and *Seedtime of the Republic*.

JAMES LARE is Professor of Political Science at Occidental College, Los Angeles.